STATS™ 1996 BASEBALL SCOREBOARD

John Dewan, Don Zminda, and STATS, Inc.

STATS
PUBLISHING

Published by STATS Publishing

A division of Sports Team Analysis & Tracking Systems, Inc.

Dr. Richard Cramer, Chairman • John Dewan, President

Cover photo by Michael Yelman, Active Images

STATS is a registered trademark of Sports Team Analysis and Tracking Systems, Inc.

First Edition: March, 1996

ISBN 1-88406421-3

Acknowledgments

The *Baseball Scoreboard* isn't the biggest book STATS produces, but for many of us, it's our very favorite. We want to thank the people who helped put it together.

Drew Faust, Steve Moyer, Dave Mundo and Allan Spear contributed essays this year along with publications staff members Jim Henzler, Scott McDevitt and Rob Neyer. Dave and Jim were the programmers primarily responsible for producing the data. In addition, Scott and Rob were the assistant editors who helped on all aspects of the book, and Scott was responsible for working with our publications software. Awesome, baby.

Future STATS Hall of Famer Chuck Miller was our chief stat-checker, with some able assistance from Kenn Ruby. And for the seventh year in a row, John Grimwade created the illustrations which appear throughout the book. Whose pen is hottest? Why, John's, of course.

Thanks as always to the other full-time employees at STATS, starting with our managers: Art Ashley, Mike Canter and Sue Dewan (Systems); Steve Moyer (Operations); Bob Meyerhoff (Finances and Human Resources); Stephanie Seburn (Marketing Support and Administration); and Jim Capuano (Sales). Thanks also to staff members Kristen Beauregard, Ethan Cooperson, Buffy Cramer-Hammann, Ron Freer, Jim Guthrie, Ginny Hamill, Mike Hammer, Tim Harbert, Jason Kinsey, Stefan Kretschmann, Marge Morra, Betty Moy, Jim Musso, Brynne Orlando, Jim Osborne, David Pinto, Jeff Schinski, Leena Sheth, Mike Wenz and Peter Woelflein.

Thanks to Lou Gorman for contributing the Foreword, and to Bob Wirz of Wirz and Associates for his help. Thanks as always to Bill James, lifelong friend of STATS. . . and statisticians. And our biggest thanks goes to the "cheering section": Jason and Erica Dewan; Mike, Nancy and Steve Cacioppo; and Sharon Zminda.

— John Dewan and Don Zminda

This book is for every parent who strives to create a home that is a happy and safe world for their children. And also for my family, especially my wife Wendy, daughter Courtney and our little one on the way.
— Jim Capuano

Table of Contents

II. GENERAL BASEBALL QUESTIONS   87

III. QUESTIONS ON OFFENSE   108

IV. QUESTIONS ON PITCHING   148

V. QUESTIONS ON DEFENSE   186

Foreword

by Lou Gorman

There is no denying that statistics play a definite role in many of the decisions and judgments that management has to make throughout the course of the year. Naturally, statistics are not the only criteria in which management evaluates a player, but they most certainly play an important role.

Baseball is a game of numbers. It is one of the great joys of the game that a fan can find out how his or her team and certain players did just by looking at the box scores. There are others who like to read about the game from the columnists and beat writers. The *STATS Baseball Scoreboard* is a marvelous compilation of essays and articles coupled with some of the most interesting stats in all of baseball to satisfy both types of fans.

The *Scoreboard* is also an invaluable tool and source of information for anyone within professional baseball due to its practical application of the numbers. It goes beyond the vast amount of numbers to explain in essays and articles what statistics mean. The *STATS Baseball Scoreboard* also explores certain trends that develop during the season and delves into performances to create a more accurate picture of just how each player contributed to the success of his team and how his performance rated. From a management standpoint this information can be used as an integral part of contract negotiations, the salary arbitration process, signing free agents, making trades and in many other areas of player performance and evaluation.

If you are intimately involved in this game, or even if you're a fan who enjoys watching baseball at the park or on television, the *STATS 1996 Baseball Scoreboard* can increase your knowledge and insight into the finer points of the game. It will enhance your enjoyment tenfold. Once you have this book, your understanding and appreciation of the great game of baseball will never be the same again.

James "Lou" Gorman recently retired from his position as Executive Vice President of Baseball Operations for the Boston Red Sox. He continues to serve the Red Sox as a consultant.

Introduction

It's hard to believe, but this is the seventh edition of the *STATS Baseball Scoreboard*. The *Scoreboard* is a book of questions and answers about baseball, and there was a time when we thought we might run out of new questions about the fascinating game of baseball. But that hasn't happened yet, and we doubt that it ever will.

If you're unfamiliar with this book, what we do in the *Baseball Scoreboard* is use the statistics of the game to try to unlock some of its secrets. For instance, you've probably heard announcers and managers moaning that "every time we walk the leadoff man in an inning, he comes around to score." But how often does it really happen? The answer is in this year's *Scoreboard*. Or you've probably wondered who the best clutch hitters in baseball really are. That's another subject we tackle this year. Or you might be interested in whether Mo Vaughn and Barry Larkin were the correct choices for the MVP awards. We look into the qualifications of two other worthy candidates—Edgar Martinez and Greg Maddux—in our Seattle and Atlanta essays.

Many of the questions are so topical that we repeat them every year—like which late relievers get the most easy save opportunities or which hitters have the best chance to hit 500 career home runs. We're unabashed disciples of Bill James here at STATS, and if you're wondering where to find the leaders in such standard Jamesian categories as runs created, secondary average or pitchers' games scores, this is the place.

We strive to make our essays understandable and fun to read, and many include John Grimwade's entertaining and informative illustrations. All our numbers come from the incomparable STATS database, and in our effort to give you enough of them so that you can reach your own conclusions, there's an appendix with additional data for most of the essays.

We think that by the time you finish this book, you'll know a little bit more about baseball than when you started. And since learning is an interactive process, we encourage you to write us with comments and suggestions for future editions of the *Scoreboard*. See you again next year with a new batch of questions and answers.

— Don Zminda

I. TEAM QUESTIONS

Baltimore Orioles: How Amazing Is Ripken's Streak?

In a baseball season dominated by labor strife and bickering among millionaires, Cal Ripken's trot around Oriole Park at Camden Yards on the evening of September 6 couldn't have come at a better time. On that night, Ripken eclipsed Lou Gehrig as baseball's ultimate iron man, playing in his 2,131st consecutive game—completing a journey he began nearly 14 years earlier, on May 30, 1982. From Ripken's fourth-inning homer to ESPN's 23 minutes of silence (thank you, Chris Berman), it was simply a perfect night.

For the record, here's the updated list of baseball's longest consecutive-game streaks, along with each player's primary position during the streak, and their streak as a percentage of Ripken's current number.

Player	Career	Streak	Pct	Position
Cal Ripken	1981-1995	2153	--	Shortstop
Lou Gehrig	1923-1939	2130	98.9	First Base
Everett Scott	1914-1926	1307	60.7	Shortstop
Steve Garvey	1969-1987	1207	56.1	First Base
Billy Williams	1959-1976	1117	51.9	Outfield
Joe Sewell	1920-1933	1103	51.2	Shortstop
Stan Musial	1941-1963	895	41.6	Outfield
Eddie Yost	1944-1962	829	38.5	Third Base
Gus Suhr	1930-1940	822	38.2	First Base
Nellie Fox	1947-1965	798	37.1	Second Base

For many baseball fans, one of the most remarkable aspects of Ripken's streak was that he compiled it while playing shortstop. Outside of catcher, shortstop is the most demanding defensive position on the diamond. Shortstops are constantly in motion—cutting, diving, throwing, pivoting, and taking throws at second on stolen-base attempts. Yet Ripken was able to avoid the injuries associated with all of those actions, day after day, season after season.

But look at the list above, and you'll see that there is indeed precedent for a streak like Ripken's. Both Everett Scott and Hall of Famer Joe Sewell compiled streaks in excess of 1,000 games while playing the position. Here are some of their career batting and fielding numbers (at shortstop only), along with Ripken's, through the end of last season.

Player	H	BA	HR	RBI	SB	Field%	Range Factor
Cal Ripken	2371	.276	327	1267	34	.979	4.64
Everett Scott	1455	.249	20	549	69	.965	5.12
Joe Sewell	2226	.312	49	1051	74	.951	5.37

Given their offensive production, it's very easy to see how Ripken and Sewell remained in the lineup each day. But Everett Scott? Here's a player who never hit above .280 in his career, could never draw a walk (.281 lifetime on-base percentage) and had absolutely no power (.315 lifetime slugging percentage). True, Scott played most of his career in a very tough era for hitters, but 1,307 games is still a very long time, especially for a player with limited offensive skills. So why did the Red Sox, and then the Yankees, keep Scott in the lineup? As you might guess, the answer lies in his performance in the field. Look at Scott's defensive numbers during his prime seasons, and you'll see that he had few equals with the glove.

Everett Scott—1917-1924

Year	Team	Field%	League Field%	Range Factor	League Range Factor
1916	Boston	.967	.939	4.60	4.86
1917	Boston	.953	.932	5.08	4.83
1918	Boston	.976	.939	5.47	5.24
1919	Boston	.976	.942	5.07	5.04
1920	Boston	.973	.944	5.36	5.00
1921	Boston	.972	.941	5.90	5.15
1922	New York	.966	.946	5.45	5.04
1923	New York	.961	.947	4.34	4.82
1924	New York	.966	.949	5.08	4.82

In those nine seasons, Scott's fielding percentage at shortstop was always well above the league average. And his range factors were better than the league average in seven of the nine seasons. How did that performance stack up against his contemporaries? From 1916 to 1923, Scott led American League shortstops in fielding percentage *in every season*. In addition, he led the league in putouts twice, assists twice and double plays twice. Who knows? As Craig Wright has suggested, maybe Ripken actually had an *advantage* playing shortstop during his streak, in that his defense could justify his staying in the lineup, even when he was enduring horrible slumps at the plate.

Staying on our "shortstop kick" for a moment, we thought it would be interesting to see how many other shortstops have put together "perfect attendance" (playing in every game) in a single season since 1982, the year Ripken began his streak. Cal, of course, has 13 such seasons since then (he played in only 160 games out of a possible 162 in 1982), while the rest of the major leagues has seven—accomplished by three players.

Year	Player	Team	Games
1982	Alfredo Griffin	Toronto	162
1983	Alfredo Griffin	Toronto	162
1985	Tony Fernandez	Toronto	161
1985	Alfredo Griffin	Oakland	162
1986	Tony Fernandez	Toronto	163
1986	Alfredo Griffin	Oakland	162
1994	Mike Bordick	Oakland	114

Tony Fernandez has four Gold Gloves to his credit and Alfredo Griffin one, emphasizing (as with Everett Scott) that defense at shortstop can keep you in the lineup regardless of your offensive skills. Both Fernandez and Griffin have posted some outstanding range factors in their careers—well above the league average over that span. Take heart, Kevin Stocker (.218 batting average last season). Your future might be much brighter than you think.

Here at STATS, we stayed very busy in preparation for Ripken's magic night. In particular, we compiled a list of every player who had been on the disabled list since 1982, as well as the salary paid to the player during his time on the shelf. The process was mind-numbing at times, but it yielded some very interesting results and helped put Ripken's achievement in perspective. Here's some of what we discovered:

1982-1996

Total salary paid to players while on DL	$611,814,107
Trips to DL by pitchers	1,621
Trips to DL by position players	1,844
Trips to DL (total)	3,465

That dollar figure is a general manager's worst nightmare, simply money down the drain from his point of view. As you might imagine, pitchers make up a huge chunk of those heading to the DL. As the chart below shows, those trips aren't short ones, either. Take a look at the players who have been paid the most money while on the DL, as well as those spending the most days on the shelf since 1982. Pitchers are well represented.

Salary while on DL since '82		Days on DL since '82	
Teddy Higuera	$8,361,206	Danny Cox	656
Bryan Harvey	$8,343,208	Atlee Hammaker	587
Mike Witt	$6,575,688	Don Aase	570
Duane Ward	$6,391,304	Nick Esasky	529
Jose Guzman	$6,165,359	Steve Ontiveros	525
Tom Browning	$5,605,519	Mike Witt	497
Mark McGwire	$5,398,614	Teddy Higuera	494
Darryl Strawberry	$5,302,561	Mike Morgan	487
Lenny Dykstra	$5,286,356	Todd Worrell	487
Glenn Davis	$5,133,783	Rick Sutcliffe	480

Cal Ripken's totals? Zero and zero, respectively.

It's indeed true that Ripken has had some strokes of luck during his streak, but luck happens when talent meets opportunity, and Ripken has had plenty of both. Will his record ever fall? That's almost impossible to predict. A player beginning a streak on Opening Day, 1996 would have to play until late May or early June, 2009, to eclipse Cal's mark. Maybe by then, Ripken will have decided to slow down a bit.

— Scott McDevitt

A complete listing for this category can be found on page 226.

Boston Red Sox: How Many Games Will Wakefield Win?

By now, the story should be more than familiar. Call it "The Rise and Fall and Rise of Tim Wakefield, Baby-Faced Knuckleballer". . .

First, the rise. Minor league first baseman who can barely hit his weight messes around with a knuckleball during warmups. Manager suggests to organization that the kid be shifted to the mound. Within three years, kid is starring in the major leagues and wins a pair of postseason games.

Then the fall. The dancing knuckleball consistently waltzes its way out of the strike zone, and suddenly the kid can't get anybody out. After a tough season in the majors, he spends all of 1994 in the minor leagues, sports ugly numbers (5-15, 5.84) and wonders if it's all over.

And finally, redemption. In 1995, a short and successful stint in the minors with a new organization precedes an amazing two-month run as our knuckleballer wins 14 of his first 15 decisions and winds up third in American League Cy Young balloting.

If Tim Wakefield's story wasn't already familiar to you, it certainly is now. But what the story generally lacks is a little historical perspective. Most of us know that good knuckleball pitchers tend to enjoy long careers, because the pitch puts very little strain on the arm. Phil Niekro and Hoyt Wilhelm both pitched into their late forties, and a number of knuckleballers have lasted nearly that long.

	Wins at age 28	Career wins	Percentage at 28
Eddie Rommel	118	171	69.0
Dutch Leonard	18	191	9.4
Jim Tobin	36	105	34.3
Hoyt Wilhelm	15	143	10.5
Wilbur Wood	28	164	17.1
Phil Niekro	17	318	5.3
Charlie Hough	28	216	13.0
Tom Candiotti*	22	117	18.8
Totals	282	1425	19.8

*Still active.

What does that mean for Wakefield? Well, it means he shouldn't give up his hopes for a long and productive career just because he's 29 and has won only 30 major league games. We drew up a list of all relatively pure knuckleball pitchers who registered at least 100 career victories. The chart on the previous page lists all eight of them, along with the number of games they won through age 28 (seasonal age).

(By the way, Joe Niekro isn't on the list because he began his major league career with a conventional repertoire. And Eddie "Knuckles" Cicotte relied heavily on a shine ball.)

As you can see, with 30 wins "already," Wakefield has exceeded the pace of most of history's top knuckleballers. The only pitcher appreciably ahead is Eddie Rommel, the oldest hurler on the list and something of an anomaly among flutterballers in that he peaked in his twenties.

It's instructive to add up what all those guys did, and even with Rommel it's apparent that knuckleballers do the vast majority of their best work after they turn 29. Why? There are a number of reasons. For one thing, baseball people generally don't trust knuckleballers, so practitioners often have to doubly earn every chance they get. At the same time, it often takes years to develop the consistent mechanics which are absolutely necessary if one is to throw strikes with the knuckleball.

Getting back to Wakefield, what can we expect from him in the future? Well, it would be a stretch to suggest that he'll match the records of the knuckleballers in the chart. After all, we didn't include those pitchers who simply didn't last long enough to win 100 games. Nevertheless, the 100-win group won only 19.8 percent of its games before the age of 29. At that rate, Wakefield will end his career with 152 victories. And if we remove Rommel from the equation, that number shoots all the way up to 229 career victories for Wakefield. I'm sure he'd settle for something in the middle.

However many games Wakefield ends up winning, this is all good news for him and his "young" knuckleballing brethren, Milwaukee's Steve Sparks (30, nine wins) and Philadelphia's Dennis Springer (31, zero). And don't forget Tom Candiotti; at 38 (117 wins), he might just now be hitting his prime.

— Rob Neyer

California Angels: Does Their Late-Season Collapse Spell Doom?

While the Seattle Mariners deserve a lot of credit for winning the American League West last year, there's no doubt that the California Angels helped them win it by falling apart late in the season. After the games of August 15, the Halos were 64-38 and held a 10½ game lead over the second-place Texas Rangers. However, they went 14-29 the rest of the way and wound up losing the title to the Mariners—who had trailed the Angels by 12½ games on August 15—in a one-game playoff.

Will the Angels be haunted by their 1995 collapse this season? The past can often be a useful guide, so we looked at the six most famous "late-season folds" of the last 50 years, then checked to see how those clubs performed the next year. Here's how they did:

Famous Late-Season Collapses Since World War II

Team	Record			Next Season	
1951 Dodgers	97-60	2nd		96-57	1st
1962 Dodgers	102-63	2nd		99-63	1st
1964 Phillies	92-70	2nd		85-76	6th
1969 Cubs	92-70	2nd		84-78	2nd
1978 Red Sox	99-64	2nd		91-69	3rd
1987 Blue Jays	96-66	2nd		87-75	3rd

Despite some notorious collapses—like the 1964 Phillies, who blew a six-and-a-half game lead with 12 to play, or the '62 Dodgers, who couldn't hold a four-game lead with seven left—all six teams were comfortably over .500 the next year, and the two Dodger teams won pennants. However, all but one team had a lower winning percentage the next year, with the average team dropping from .595 to .565—about five fewer wins in a 162-game season. Even so, a club playing .565 ball would win about 92 games in a 162-game schedule, and that's good enough to qualify for the playoffs in many seasons.

Let's take a brief look at the makeup and subsequent history of these six teams:

1951-52 Dodgers. This is the Dodger club which blew a 13½ lead to Bobby Thomson and the Giants—one of the most heartbreaking losses in major league history. For the most part, though, the Bums seemed to shrug it off. This team had a lot of veterans on it—Duke Snider and Gil Hodges were the only members of the starting lineup younger than 29—and many of the players had been on the 1947 and 1949 teams which won the National League pennant. The Dodgers came back and won the N.L. pennant in 1952, and would win flags again in 1953, 1955 and 1956. They won the '55 World Series with a roster that included a number of players from the 1951 club.

1962-63 Dodgers. After grabbing the lead in September, this Dodger club blew a four-game lead with seven left; the Giants tied them at the wire, forcing a best-of-three playoff. Then, just like the 1951 team, they lost the pennant after taking a two-run lead into the bottom of the ninth of the final playoff game. This was a much younger team than the 1951 bunch, but they responded in very much the same way, winning both the pennant and World Series in 1963, and then winning two more pennants in 1965 and 1966. As with the '51 club, it may have helped that many of the 1962 Dodgers had been on the 1959 team which *had* prevailed in a tight pennant race.

1964-65 Phillies. After blowing a six-and-a-half game lead with 12 to play in 1964, the Phillies were in the pennant chase for much of 1965 before winding up sixth with 85 victories. They were competitive again in 1966, winding up fourth, eight games out of first, and they were over .500 again in 1967 (82-80), though well off the pace. By then they had a lot of old players on their roster, and they went into a sharp decline starting in 1968. The 1964 team had a mixture of veterans and younger players, but none of them were around by the time the Phils began winning division titles in the mid-1970s.

1969-70 Cubs. After leading the National League East for most of the way in 1969, the Cubbies fell apart in September and lost the flag to the Miracle Mets. This club, which had a lot of players in their mid-to-late twenties along with older veterans like Billy Williams and Ernie Banks, played winning ball for the next few years, but never were able to win a title. As for 1970, the Cubs were strong contenders again, ultimately finishing second, five games behind the Pirates.

1978-79 Red Sox. After blowing a double-digit lead in the second half of the 1978 A.L. East race, the Red Sox were third with 91 victories in 1979. They continued to play winning ball, but didn't win another pennant until 1986, by which time all but one of the '78 players (Bob Stanley) were gone. Their makeup was a lot like that of the '69 Cubs, with a lot of regulars in their mid-to-late 20s. In this case, having won a pennant previously—many of these Red Sox had been with the 1975 team which made it to the World Series—didn't seem to help.

1987-88 Blue Jays. The "Blow Jays" blew a three-and-a-half game lead with seven games to play, and got swept by their main rival, the Tigers, on the final weekend when one victory would have put them in a playoff game. A fairly young team, the Jays bounced back very well. In 1988, they finished only two games behind the division-winning Red Sox. In 1989, they won the division by two games before bowing in the playoffs. In 1990, they were second again by two games to the Red Sox. In 1991, they won the East again, but again lost in the playoffs. Finally, in 1992 they broke through and won the World Series, repeating again in 1993.

All these teams seemed to recover quite well from their late-season collapses. The two Dodger teams would win a pennant the very next season, and a third, the Blue Jays, remained a perennial contender and eventually became a two-time World Champion. The '64 Phillies, '69 Cubs and '78 Red Sox could never nail down that elusive flag, but they did continue to play winning ball in subsequent years.

Overall, one has to think that the Angels will recover from this. Even if they don't win a division or make the playoffs, they should be comfortably over .500 this year, with a reasonable chance to grab that elusive flag sometime over the next few seasons.

— Don Zminda

Chicago White Sox: Is Thomas Too Selective in RBI Situations?

Over the past five seasons, Frank Thomas has batted .323, the second-best average in baseball next to Tony Gwynn. His .450 on-base percentage over that period is the best in the game. His slugging average of .598 ranks second only to Barry Bonds (averages based on a minimum of 2,000 plate appearances, 1991-95). He has hit 175 home runs, tying Bonds for second place behind Albert Belle's 186. He has driven in 100 or more runs every year, and his 564 RBI are the most in baseball over the period. He has also *scored* at least 100 runs every year, and his total of 526 runs scored ranks second (by five runs) to Bonds.

That's not good enough for some people.

There's a school of thought—one often heard on Chicago sports call-in shows, in the local press, and even suggested by Bob Uecker in an NBC broadcast a couple of years ago—that Thomas is "too selective in RBI situations." The notion is that Thomas' job is to drive in runs, and that when he draws a walk with runners in scoring position, he's somehow not living up to his responsibilities.

The first question we need to answer is whether Thomas does indeed draw an abnormal number of walks when there are runners in scoring position. So we ranked major league hitters on the basis of walks per plate appearance with men in scoring position over the last three seasons. Here's the top 10 (minimum 425 PA with runners in scoring position):

Most Walks per Plate Appearance, Scoring Position—1993-95

Player	Avg	OBP	SLG	AB	H	HR	RBI	BB	BB/PA
Barry Bonds	.327	.527	.590	324	106	19	169	150	.306
Mickey Tettleton	.260	.449	.514	319	83	22	161	117	.260
Frank Thomas	.305	.465	.563	387	118	23	209	141	.250
John Olerud	.321	.475	.468	380	122	7	176	119	.231
Ken Griffey Jr	.256	.414	.534	320	82	23	138	93	.219
Dave Justice	.303	.438	.518	363	110	21	170	92	.197
Robin Ventura	.279	.413	.448	451	126	17	202	116	.196
Darren Daulton	.263	.404	.469	350	92	14	162	88	.195
Rafael Palmeiro	.287	.416	.516	376	108	19	173	94	.191
Tony Phillips	.252	.394	.390	349	88	10	129	84	.189

(minimum 425 PA with men in scoring position)

Thomas does indeed draw a high percentage of walks, ranking third behind Barry Bonds and Mickey Tettleton over the period. On the other hand, Thomas drove in 209 runs when he *did* swing the bat, the top figure on the leaders list. So he must have taken the bat off his shoulder at least a few times.

Now let's look at the players who averaged the *fewest* walks per plate appearance with runners in scoring position over the last three years:

Fewest Walks per Plate Appearance, Scoring Position—1993-95

Player	Avg	OBP	SLG	AB	H	HR	RBI	BB	BB/PA
Dante Bichette	.321	.355	.572	439	141	27	222	25	.051
Ed Sprague	.211	.288	.317	426	90	6	144	40	.081
Royce Clayton	.249	.308	.332	413	103	4	143	38	.082
Carlos Baerga	.324	.373	.501	441	143	16	220	44	.085
Andres Galarraga	.321	.385	.595	402	129	26	204	41	.087
Derek Bell	.279	.351	.413	419	117	12	168	44	.090
Terry Pendleton	.272	.338	.407	378	103	9	141	41	.095
Sammy Sosa	.282	.354	.497	443	125	24	178	49	.097
Marquis Grissom	.258	.327	.390	387	100	10	139	45	.100
Charlie Hayes	.300	.366	.489	427	128	16	194	50	.101

Dante Bichette, Carlos Baerga and Andres Galarraga are three players who would never be accused of "not swinging the bat in RBI situations." Bichette and Baerga both drove in more runs with men in scoring position over the period than Thomas did, but not appreciably more—four or five runs a year. However, Thomas had more plate appearances with men in scoring position than any of the others. Let's level the playing field and see how many runs each would drive in given 175 plate appearances with men in scoring position, roughly a season's work for a good middle-of-the order hitter. We'll throw in another hitter sometimes accused of being "too selective," Barry Bonds:

RBI with Men in Scoring Position, 1993-95

Player	RBI/PA	Per 175 AB
Bichette	.453	79
Galarraga	.433	76
Baerga	.425	74
Thomas	.371	65
Bonds	.345	60

The non-selective hitters did drive in more runs than either Thomas or Bonds did. But that 14-RBI difference between Bichette and Thomas doesn't mean that Thomas was costing his team 14 runs. Or any runs. One of the best measures of total offensive production is on-base plus slugging percentage; over the past three seasons, Thomas has an OBP+SLG of 1.028 with men in scoring position, a figure that ranks well ahead of Bichette's OBP+SLG of .927. Think of it this way: while Bichette might drive in an occasional extra run with men in scoring position, he's also using up more outs in an effort to bring those runs home. Meanwhile Thomas is getting on base. . . and increasing his club's run potential even when he doesn't drive in the run himself. The big difference between the two players shows up not in the RBI column, where Thomas is certainly competitive with anyone, but in the runs *scored* column. While Bichette has scored more than 100 runs only once in his career, Thomas has scored 100 or more in each of his five full seasons.

One could argue, in fact, that rather than being too selective in RBI situations, Thomas is *not being selective enough*. Over the last three years, Thomas has batted .331 and slugged .669 when runners were *not* in scoring position; he batted .305 and slugged .563, more than 100 points lower, with runners *in* scoring position. Pitchers clearly don't want to give Thomas much to hit with ducks on the pond, and in an effort to bring home the run, he'll sometimes swing at a bad pitch and make himself a less effective hitter. He's human.

Overall, we don't find much of anything to knock about Thomas' approach. Like Ted Williams, another hitter accused of being "too selective," Thomas both scores *and* drives in more than 100 runs a year on a regular basis. And that's a lethal combination. While he wants to drive in runs as much as any middle-of-the-order hitter, Thomas understands his "job" is not to drive in runs; it's to help his club win games. The figures show he's doing it pretty well.

Let Thomas be Thomas.

— Don Zminda

A complete listing for this category can be found on page 228.

Cleveland Indians: How Good *Was* Belle Last Year?

Albert Belle may not have won the American League's Most Valuable Player award last year, but even his detractors would have to agree that Belle had an amazing season. With 52 doubles and 50 home runs, Belle became the first player in history to top the 50 mark in both categories in the same season. With 103 extra-base hits, he was the first player to record more than 100 extra-base hits in a season since Stan Musial in 1948. . . and the first American Leaguer to reach the century mark since Hank Greenberg in 1937. There's also Belle's 121 runs scored, his 126 RBI, his .690 slugging average. . . we could go on and on. It was just a great year.

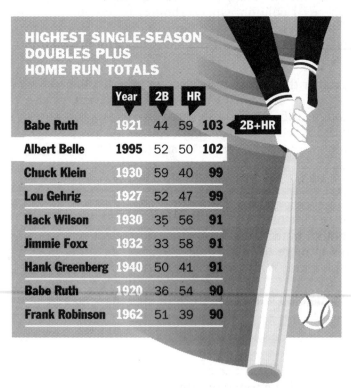

HIGHEST SINGLE-SEASON DOUBLES PLUS HOME RUN TOTALS

	Year	2B	HR	
Babe Ruth	1921	44	59	103 ◄ 2B+HR
Albert Belle	1995	52	50	102
Chuck Klein	1930	59	40	99
Lou Gehrig	1927	52	47	99
Hack Wilson	1930	35	56	91
Jimmie Foxx	1932	33	58	91
Hank Greenberg	1940	50	41	91
Babe Ruth	1920	36	54	90
Frank Robinson	1962	51	39	90

Belle got a lot of publicity for compiling more than 100 extra-base hits, so we won't bother showing you an all-time leaders list for that category. But one all-time list you probably haven't seen is the one above: the players with the biggest totals of doubles plus home runs in a season. Triples require speed as well as power, and Belle doesn't have a lot of speed, which is why he belted only one triple in 1995. But 2B+HR is more of a pure power category, and you can see just how powerful Belle was. Babe Ruth is the only other player in history to reach three figures in doubles plus homers, and the Babe's total from his great 1921 campaign—often considered the best year any hitter ever had—tops Belle by only one.

Of course, as great as Belle's numbers were, they *should* have been even greater. Due to the strike, the 1995 season was only 144 games long instead of the usual 162 (although, with all the work stoppages we've had since 1972, it's hard to tell what "usual" *is* any more). Look at how much more impressive his numbers are when projected to a 162-game schedule:

Belle Projected to 162 games

	G	AB	R	H	2B	3B	HR	TB	RBI	BB	SO	Avg	OBP	SLG
Actual	143	546	121	173	52	1	50	377	126	73	80	.317	.401	.690
Projected	161	614	136	195	59	1	56	424	142	82	90	.318	.401	.691

These numbers are even more awesome, and with them Belle would have had a much higher place on four all-time single-season leaders lists:

Belle in 144 Indian Games

Category	Total	All-Time Ranking
Doubles	52	22nd all-time, most since 1993
Homers	50	18th all-time, most since 1990
Extra Base Hits	103	4th all-time, most since 1948
Total Bases	377	50th all-time, most since 1986

Belle Projected to 162 Games

Category	Total	All-Time Ranking
Doubles	59	7th all-time, most since 1936
Homers	56	6th all-time, most since 1961
Extra Base Hits	116	3rd all-time, most since 1927
Total Bases	424	7th all-time, most since 1948

(rankings include ties)

Of course, had the scheduled games (all from April) been played, there's no certainty that Belle could have maintained the same hitting pace he set over the 143 contests he *did* play. But he certainly would have embellished some already awesome season totals.

But then, that's also true of the Indians as a team. The Tribe posted a .694 winning percentage in their 144 games last year; project that percentage to 162 contests, and you wind up with 112 wins, or one more than the American League record held by the 1954 Indians. As with Belle, we'll never know what Cleveland would have done with those extra 18 games. We *do* know what they accomplished in 144 games, and it was pretty amazing.

— Don Zminda

A complete listing for this category can be found on page 229.

Detroit Tigers: What Happens When a Veteran Manager Leaves?

The Tigers will begin a new era on Opening Day, as Buddy Bell takes over the managerial reigns from veteran skipper Sparky Anderson. Although the Tigers haven't fared well in recent years (no division championships since 1987), Bell will still have some big shoes to fill. Anderson won 1331 games in his 17 seasons in Detroit, highlighted by a World Series title back in 1984, and leaves a huge legacy—having also captured five division titles, four pennants and two world championships with Cincinnati in the 1970s. In an era where managers are "hired to be fired," Anderson and Tommy Lasorda might prove to be the last two vintage veteran skippers we see in the majors.

So what can we expect from Bell and the Tigers in their first post-Sparky season? Hoping to make a guess, we thought it would be interesting to see how teams have handled the departure of a veteran manager in the past. To do so, we compiled a list of post-war skippers (those who started managing after 1945) who had spent at least 1,000 games with the same team in a single stint. By "single stint" we mean that the manager didn't come-and-go to accumulate 1,000 games with the same team (like Bobby Cox in Atlanta). As it turns out, 29 managers fit the mold. Five of them—Anderson, Lasorda, Tom Kelly, Tony La Russa and Jim Leyland—managed in 1995, leaving 24 cases to analyze.

Here they are, along with the seasons of their "stint," their record during that period, and the team's record—in both the manager's final season, and the season after his departure. For managers that resigned or were fired in midseason, we've held them accountable for the season they started, be the results good or bad.

Manager, Team	Years	Final Season			Next Season		
			W	L		W	L
Leo Durocher, Giants	1948-55	1955	80	74	1956	67	87
Casey Stengel, Yankees	1949-60	1960	97	57	1961	109	53
Paul Richards Orioles	1955-61	1961	95	67	1962	77	85
Danny Murtaugh, Pirates	1957-64	1964	80	82	1965	90	72
Al Lopez, White Sox	1957-65	1965	95	67	1966	83	79
Gene Mauch, Phillies	1960-68	1968	76	86	1969	63	99
Bill Rigney, Angels	1961-69	1969	71	91	1970	86	76
Leo Durocher, Cubs	1966-72	1972	85	70	1973	77	84
Ralph Houk, Yankees	1966-73	1973	80	82	1974	89	73

Manager, Team	Years	Final Season			Next Season		
			W	L		W	L
Gene Mauch, Expos	1969-75	1975	75	87	1976	55	107
Walter Alston, Dodgers	1954-76	1976	92	70	1977	98	64
Red Schoendienst, Cardinals	1965-76	1976	72	90	1977	83	79
Sparky Anderson, Reds	1970-78	1978	92	69	1979	90	71
Danny Ozark, Phillies	1973-79	1979	84	78	1980	91	71
Earl Weaver, Orioles	1968-82	1982	94	68	1983	98	64
Bill Virdon, Astros	1975-82	1982	77	85	1983	85	77
Chuck Tanner, Pirates	1977-85	1985	57	104	1986	64	98
Tony La Russa, White Sox	1979-86	1986	72	90	1987	77	85
Whitey Herzog, Cardinals	1980-90	1990	70	92	1991	84	78
Davey Johnson, Mets	1984-90	1990	91	71	1991	77	84
Buck Rodgers, Expos	1985-91	1991	71	90	1992	87	75
Roger Craig, Giants	1985-92	1992	72	90	1993	103	59
Bobby Valentine, Rangers	1985-92	1992	77	85	1993	86	76
Total			1855	1845		1919	1796
Winning Percentage			.501			.517	

Overall, the teams in the study did a little bit better in the season after the veteran manager departed—about two more wins the following year on average. The Tigers are certainly hoping for more improvement than that in 1996, and history does give Detroit a sliver of hope. The 1993 Giants made by far the biggest improvement in this group, winning a whopping 31 more games under Dusty Baker than in Roger Craig's final season. It's true that the acquisition of Barry Bonds had a lot to do with that, but even Bonds isn't worth 31 wins. Six other teams improved by at least 10 games: the 1992 Expos (16), 1970 Angels (15), 1991 Cardinals (14), 1961 Yankees (12), 1977 Cardinals (11) and 1965 Pirates (10). We'll put an asterisk by the '61 Yankees, the team with Maris and Mantle that clubbed 240 home runs. With all respect to Ralph Houk (Casey Stengel's successor), your average circus chimp could have managed that club to the pennant.

Whatever expectations there are for Bell, they certainly couldn't match those of John McNamara, who took over from Sparky as the Cincinnati skipper in 1979—one year after the Reds won 92 games, but finished second in the N.L. West behind the Dodgers for the second straight season.

That '79 Cincinnati team featured Ken Griffey, George Foster, Johnny Bench and Joe Morgan. Bell's first team certainly can't match *that* talent.

Along with Anderson, three other skippers qualify as "veterans" with two clubs. Leo Durocher enjoyed successful stints with both the Giants and Cubs. Gene Mauch, who never again got the Phillies closer than fourth place after their famous 1964 collapse, also served as the first manager of the Montreal Expos. And Tony La Russa was at the helm for more than 1,000 games with both the White Sox and Athletics. He's since moved on to St. Louis, with Art Howe taking over in Oakland.

In addition to the '61 Yankees, four other teams made it to postseason with their new manager—the '77 Dodgers, '79 Reds, '80 Phillies and '83 Orioles. Sorry, Detroit fans, but that isn't any reason for celebration. All five of the new managers inherited very talented clubs. We've already touched on the '61 Yankees and '79 Reds, but the other three teams also had a history of recent success before their new skipper arrived. The '77 Dodgers still had the nucleus of their '74 N.L. championship team (Steve Garvey, Davey Lopes, Ron Cey, Steve Yeager, Tommy John, Don Sutton and Doug Rau), and won 92 gamesin 1976. The '80 Phillies were loaded, having already won division titles in '76, '77 and '78. That squad featured Pete Rose, Mike Schmidt, Greg Luzinski and Steve Carlton. And the '83 Orioles? Baltimore fans might remember the agony of losing the '82 division title to Milwaukee on the final day of the season, giving Earl Weaver a less-than-uplifting sendoff. Both the '82 and '83 teams featured Eddie Murray, Cal Ripken, Ken Singleton, Jim Palmer, Mike Flanagan, Scott McGregor and Dennis Martinez. Joe Altobelli inherited a fine club.

With the Yankees and Orioles both acquiring big-dollar talent in the offseason, the Tigers will need more than managerial magic to turn around a 60-84 record. Detroit fans should note that Bell comes to the Tigers from Cleveland—an organization that has become the perfect blueprint for turning around a franchise. The Indians made a commitment to their young talent in the early 1990s, and the results have been spectacular. It will be interesting to see if Bell attempts to rebuild the Tigers in the same fashion.

— Scott McDevitt

Kansas City Royals: Does the "New" Kauffman Stadium Favor Hitters or Pitchers?

In 1993, Royals Stadium was renamed "Kauffman Stadium" in honor of team founder Ewing Kauffman. In 1995, the stadium perhaps should have been renamed again, because a number of changes were made that practically made it a new ballpark.

From the day it opened in 1973, Royals/Kauffman Stadium meant two things: artificial turf, distant fences, and spacious gaps in the outfield. The result was few home runs, but plenty of drives to the wall resulting in doubles and triples. In the 20 seasons prior to 1995, the Royals led the American League in doubles and/or triples 10 times. In that same span, 13 doubles and triples titles were captured by Royal players (mostly Willie Wilson and George Brett). On the other hand, the club has *never* led the A.L. in home runs, nor has any individual Royal.

But in 1995, the Royals tore out the ersatz grass and altered the dimensions. Beautiful *real* grass was planted—actually, it was trucked in—and the fences were brought in *and* down. The power alleys went from 385 feet to 375, straightaway center from 410 to 400, and the height of the wall was dropped from 12 feet to nine.

What happened? About what you'd expect: considering both the Royals and their opponents, doubles and triples were way down, homers were way up:

Kauffman Stadium—Before & After

	Avg	2B/G	3B/G	HR/G	Runs/G
1993-94	.272	4.27	0.61	1.34	9.54
1995	.264	3.26	0.49	1.63	8.76
Pct. Change	-3.0	-23.7	-19.7	+21.6	-8.2

With doubles and triples demonstrably down, the number of runs scored would obviously have dropped precipitously if the fences hadn't been moved. But moving the wall in 10 feet most of the way around certainly didn't turn Kauffman Stadium into a home-run haven. In 1993-94, the Royals played in the toughest home-run park in the American League. In 1995, even with homers up almost 22 percent, it was still the third toughest homer park.

The scarcity of home runs in Kansas City has long led commentators to describe Kauffman as a pitcher's park, but that wasn't really the case. All those other extra-base hits, plus a relative lack of foul territory, left the park generally neutral in regard to scoring runs. And in 1993 and '94 it was a very *good* hitter's park.

So they used to call Kauffman a good pitcher's park, even though it really wasn't. And you know what? Even though the broadcasters will now suggest that Kauffman is a good hitter's park because the fences are closer, it really isn't. At least in its first season, Kauffman was a *pitcher's* park, cutting run production eight percent from the average A.L. ballpark. The added home runs simply didn't make up for the drastic decreases in doubles and triples.

Kansas City's switch to grass has to be welcomed, as does the lowering of the fence, which should result in some of those thrilling homer-saving catches. On the other hand, the American League lost one of its more extreme ballparks, and that makes things a little less interesting from our perspective.

— Rob Neyer

Milwaukee Brewers: Who Were the Best Replacement Players?

Among other things, 1995 will be remembered in baseball as the "Year of the Replacement Player." In case you've forgotten, these were the players rounded up by major league teams last spring to fill in until the big boys came back from the strike. . . which they finally did at the last minute, thanks to a court injunction. However, some of the replacements eventually saw action during the season, and it wouldn't be stretching it to say that, for the most part, their life was hell. But in some places the replacement players won a surprising amount of acceptance, and that's where the Milwaukee Brewers enter the picture.

Before we get into the Milwaukee situation, let's look at the replacement players as a group. According to *Baseball America,* a total of 19 spring replacement players were recalled by major league teams at some point during the season. One of them, infielder Joel Chimelis of the Giants, was greeted with such hostility by his teammates that the Giants sent him back to the minors before he even got into a game. Here is a list of the 19 players, along with their ages and major league records in 1995:

1995 Replacement Players

Team	Hitter	Pos	Age	G	AB	H	HR	RBI	Avg
WSox	Doug Brady	2B	25	12	21	4	0	3	.190
LA	Mike Busch	3B	26	13	17	4	3	6	.235
KC	Edgar Caceres	2B	31	55	117	28	1	17	.239
SF	Joel Chimelis	3B	27	–	–	–	–	–	–
KC	Jeff Grotewold	DH-C	29	15	36	10	1	6	.278
Hou	Dave Hajek	2B	27	5	2	0	0	0	.000
Bos	Ron Mahay	OF	24	5	20	4	1	3	.200
Min	Dan Masteller	1B	27	71	198	47	3	21	.237
KC	Jose Mota	2B	30	2	2	0	0	0	.000

Team	Pitcher	Age	G	GS	IP	H	W	L	S	ERA
KC	Scott Anderson	32	6	4	25.1	29	1	0	0	5.33
Det	Mike Christopher	31	36	0	61.1	71	4	0	1	3.82
Mil	Brian Givens	29	19	19	107.1	116	5	7	0	4.95
Mil	Jamie McAndrew	27	10	4	36.1	37	2	3	0	4.71
Hou	Craig McMurtry	35	11	0	10.1	15	0	1	0	7.84
Yanks	Dave Pavlas	32	4	0	5.2	8	0	0	0	3.18
Cin	Rick Reed	30	4	3	17.0	18	0	0	0	5.82
Mil	Ron Rightnowar	30	34	0	36.2	35	2	1	1	5.40
Mil	Joe Slusarski	28	12	0	15.0	21	1	1	0	5.40
Tex	Scott Taylor	28	3	3	15.1	25	1	2	0	9.39

Most of these players were veteran minor leaguers in their late 20s or older. It's interesting that two of them, Jose Mota and Jamie McAndrew, were the sons of former major leaguers (and union members). Some of the replacements had seen major league action in the past; in most cases the action was brief, but one of them, Craig McMurtry, had pitched in over 200 major league games, and another, Rick Reed, had made a total of 39 starts over seven seasons. A few of them had been considered decent prospects at one time in their careers. But by the spring of 1995, all 19 were fringe players who felt that if they didn't seize the opportunity to play in the spring, they might never get another chance to make a major league club.

As you can see from the 1995 stats, most of the replacement players made little of what was usually a brief major league trial. But there were exceptions, and that's where the Brewers come to the fore. The Brewers used four pitchers—McAndrew, Brian Givens, Ron Rightnowar and Joe Slusarski—extensively by replacement-player standards, and McAndrew would undoubtedly have seen a lot more action if he hadn't gotten hurt. The Twins used first baseman Dan Masteller in nearly half their games, and the Royals gave second baseman Edgar Caceres more than 100 at-bats. The most successful replacement player was probably pitcher Mike Christopher of the Tigers, a well-traveled reliever who got into 36 games and proved to be one of the Tigers' most reliable pitchers.

If you wanted to call somebody the "Babe Ruth of the Replacements," I guess it would be Mike Busch of the Dodgers, who hit three home runs in 17 late-season at-bats. Busch, you might remember, was greeted with intense hostility by his Dodger teammates, with veteran outfielder (and labor leader) Brett Butler leading the opposition. The Dodgers eventually reached an uneasy truce with Busch, but not before a national television audience witnessed him sitting alone on the Dodger bench during his first game, with his teammates treating him like he had leprosy or something. Despite that, Busch made an important contribution to the Dodgers' drive to the N.L. West title, winning the last game of the regular season with a three-run homer.

The way Busch was treated was fairly typical, which is why the Brewers, Royals, Twins and Tigers were the only teams which dared give the replacements more than minimal action. The Brewers were far out ahead in using their replacements, and to the surprise of many, there was little or no commotion over it. What was the difference between Milwaukee and the other places? There were a couple of factors at work. One is that Brewer owner Bud Selig is also the acting commissioner, and the Brewers had little choice but to accept the presence of these players. However, some sort of protest—silent or otherwise—might have been expected, and you have to credit manager Phil Garner for avoiding that. Garner, more than any other major league manager, seemed able to articulate what a lot of people felt: that these players weren't bad guys at all, but people who responded in a very human way when put in a difficult situation. Garner might also have pointed out something else: that a lot of the other Brewers had been fringe players themselves, but ones who had been a little luckier than their replacement brethren.

Certainly you have a lot more sympathy with the Brewer replacements than you would, say, with Craig McMurtry, a guy who'd already made a good major league living, and who'd benefitted considerably from the efforts of his union. Whatever. . . we're not going to get into extensive ethical discussions over this. But one thing stands out from this whole sorry affair: Phil Garner was able to get his players to put aside their differences and work together under very difficult circumstances. You'd have to consider that a sign of a pretty good skipper.

— Don Zminda

Minnesota Twins: Is It Tougher to "Zone In" in a Domed Stadium?

The idea for this article was suggested by a number of our friends, including Strat-O-Matic's Hal Richman and our own Craig Wright. It was also raised not by a Twins fan, but by a fellow from Seattle who roots for the Mariners. However, the question asked by Dan Tomlinson—"Are outfielders' zone ratings inherently lower in domed stadiums?" applies to the Twins as well it does to the Mariners. Dan commented that "you always hear announcers babbling about how tough it is to play the outfield in domed stadiums because a player can't take his eyes off the ball for even a second." He also noted that a number of outfielders with big defensive reputations, but who play in domes, had below-par zone ratings. Among those he mentioned were the Twins' Kirby Puckett and Ken Griffey Jr. of his own favorite club, the Mariners.

Dan's arguments seemed to make sense; after all, zone ratings measure a player's skill at tracking down balls in his fielding area, or "zone." And if he has trouble picking up the ball, it's going to be difficult to do that. We decided to look at the data. Here's an overall look at outfielders' zone ratings over the last three years, dome vs. outdoors:

OF Zone Rtg Indoors/Dome—1993-95

Stadium Type	Zone Rtg
Domes	.803
Outdoors	.823

The zone ratings *were* lower in domed stadiums. However, the difference wasn't as big as we thought it might be. Are zone ratings significantly lower in some domed stadiums than in others? They are. Here's a breakdown of outfielders' zone ratings in the majors' five domed stadiums for the last three seasons; ratings at SkyDome are only for games in which the dome was closed for the entire contest:

OF Zone Rtg, Domed Stadiums—1993-95

Stadium	Zone Rtg
Olympic Stadium	.850
SkyDome	.821
Astrodome	.806
Metrodome	.791
Kingdome	.763

Wow. . . what a difference. Zone ratings at Montreal's Olympic Stadium were actually *higher* than in games played outdoors, and the indoor games at SkyDome showed no real difference. But the ratings are much lower in games at the Metrodome—where the light-colored roof seems to play havoc with an outfielder's ability to catch the ball—and lower still at the Kingdome.

As you'd expect, some Minnesota players are affected by the Metrodome much more than others. Here's an individual breakdown for all Twins outfielders who had at least 100 chances in domed stadiums over the last three years:

Twins' Zone Ratings Outdoors vs. Dome—1993-95

Player	Minn	Domes	Outdoors	Diff
Alex Cole	.797	.801	.789	.012
Pedro Munoz	.769	.767	.777	-.010
Marty Cordova	.834	.848	.867	-.018
Kirby Puckett	.780	.774	.793	-.019
Shane Mack	.829	.826	.856	-.030
Rich Becker	.795	.808	.848	-.041

(minimum 100 chances in domes)

Alex Cole is not considered a great outfielder, but his zone rating was actually higher in games at the Metrodome than it was in outdoor contests. On the other hand, Rich Becker, who was considered an excellent defensive player during his minor league career, has performed very well on the road but has had all kinds of problems in domes, and especially at the Metrodome. As for Kirby Puckett, he *is* hampered by the Metrodome, but since he's also below average outdoors, you can't say that his low zone ratings are purely a product of playing in the Metrodome.

"But what about Griffey and the Kingdome?" you might be asking. If you've studied outfielder zone ratings in the past—and if you've read past editions of this book—you're probably aware that perennial Gold Glover Ken Griffey Jr. has always had surprisingly low zone ratings. We even presented a detailed study of the subject in the *Scoreboard* last year, and the numbers strongly indicated that the low rating was legitimate, and that Griffey simply wasn't able to get to as many balls as other center fielders might have. But was the problem not Griffey, but the Kingdome? Using the same three-year data, we compared Griffey's zone ratings—both at at home and on the road—with other center fielders who played against Seattle. Here are the figures:

Ken Griffey Zone Ratings—1993-95
At Kingdome

	Griffey	All Other CF
Chances	479	825
Outs	364	644
Zone Rating	.760	.781

Seattle Road Games

	Griffey	All Other CF
Chances	441	823
Outs	347	691
Zone Rating	.787	.840

Griffey did have a higher rating in Seattle road games than when he was playing at the Kingdome. However, center fielders from the *road* team actually had higher zone ratings at the Kingdome than Griffey did—something you wouldn't expect, since Griffey has the advantage of familiarity after playing so many games there. And Griffey's zone ratings were well below those of his center-field opponents in Seattle *road* games. So Gold Glove or not, we're sticking with the same conclusion we reached in years past: while he's obviously an athletic player with some defensive skills, Griffey simply doesn't get to as many balls as he should.

That aside, the problems at the Metrodome and Kingdome do bear some watching. If the figures continue to show the same effect in future years, we might want to consider making home/road adjustments to outfielders' zone ratings.

— Don Zminda

A complete listing for this category can be found on page 230.

New York Yankees: Is Mattingly a Hall of Famer?

In 1995, Yankee captain Don Mattingly finally led his Yankee club to the postseason, only to lose a dramatic five-game series to the Seattle Mariners. Yes, this was *his* Yankee club. In Steinbrenner's era of quick fixes through high-priced free agent signings, Mattingly remained a constant for the Bronx Bombers, adding his name to a long list of Yankee greats.

Will Mattingly also add his name to the list of baseball's greats in Cooperstown? That's a tough call. Fortunately for us, Bill James wrote a book on the Hall of Fame, *The Politics of Glory*, in which he presents many enlightening methods for determining a player's Hall-of-Fame chances. We'll start by applying some of those methods to Mattingly.

An obvious argument for any Hall of Fame candidate is that if player A is similar to player B, and player B is in the Hall of Fame, then player A should be, too. Bill's method for evaluating this argument is Similarity Scores. He starts with the premise that if two players had identical career totals, and played the same defensive position, their similarity score would be 1,000. For each difference between them, something is subtracted (see the glossary for a complete definition). Let's look at the five most-similar players to Don Mattingly whose careers are now over:

	G	AB	R	H	2B	3B	HR	RBI	BB	Avg	OBP	Slg	SS
Don Mattingly	1785	7003	1007	2153	442	20	222	1099	588	.307	.358	.471	--
Cecil Cooper	1896	7349	1012	2192	415	47	241	1125	448	.298	.337	.466	943
Hal McRae	2084	7218	940	2091	484	66	191	1097	648	.290	.351	.454	887
Tony Oliva	1676	6301	870	1917	329	48	220	947	448	.304	.353	.476	861
Carl Furillo	1806	6378	895	1910	324	56	192	1058	514	.299	.355	.458	855
Jim Bottomley	1991	7471	1177	2313	465	151	219	1422	664	.310	.369	.500	853

How "similar" are these players to Mattingly? To quote Bill (from his *1986 Baseball Abstract*):

> Similarity scores around 800 indicate players who. . . have very prominent, obvious similarities, but some easily identifiable distinctions.

> Similarity scores above 850 indicate players who. . . can usually be described as substantially similar.

> Similarity scores above 900 indicate very similar players.

> Similarity scores above 950 are rare, and usually indicate that the

true similarities of the two players. . . have been emphasized by chance patterns.

Cecil Cooper was a very similar player to Don Mattingly, and briefly a contemporary of Mattingly, playing from 1971 to 1987 for Boston and Milwaukee.

Cooper led the league in doubles twice; Mattingly did it three times. Cooper led the league in RBI twice; Mattingly did it once. Cooper played in five All-Star games; Mattingly played in six. But there are some things Mattingly accomplished that Cooper did not. Mattingly captured the MVP award in 1985, and finished in the top 10 three other times. Cooper never captured an MVP award; his best finishes were fifth in 1980, 1982 and 1983. While Cooper won the Gold Glove twice and led the league in fielding once, Mattingly captured nine Gold Gloves and led the league in fielding seven times. Mattingly also led the league in hits twice, won a batting title, and led the league in slugging once. Mattingly has the higher career marks for batting average, on-base percentage and slugging.

As for the other players on the list, none is as similar to Mattingly as Cooper. Hal McRae played a few years longer than Mattingly. He hit for a lower average, though he did even that out with a higher walk rate. McRae was also used largely as a DH. The system does not differentiate much between first basemen and designated hitters, though Mattingly was one of the best ever at fielding first base. Tony Oliva is a viable Hall of Fame candidate—Bill James lists him as the best right-field candidate *not* enshrined at Cooperstown. Carl Furillo is another right fielder who is a candidate for the Hall of Fame, though his numbers are not quite as good as Mattingly's or Oliva's. None of these players is currently in the Hall. The next most-similar player to Mattingly, Jim Bottomley with a score of 853, *is* in the Hall. Elected in 1974, Bottomley is a marginal Hall of Famer who benefited from favoritism evident on the Veterans Committee in the '70s.

James has also developed a Hall of Fame Career Monitor to help predict whether a player will go into the Hall of Fame. The Monitor awards points for a player's accomplishments. If the player scores a total of 100 or more points, the system predicts that he will go into the Hall of Fame. Let's walk through this for Don Mattingly.

1. For batting average, award 2 1/2 points for each season of hitting .300 (in a hundred or more games), 5 points for hitting .350, 15 points for hitting .400. Seasons are never double-counted: a .350 season is not also counted as a .300 season. Mattingly hit .350 once, and .300 on five other occasions. He scores 17.5 points.

2. Award the player 5 points for each season of 200 hits, and 3 points for each season of 100 runs or RBI. Mattingly had 200 hits three times, two seasons with 100 runs scored, and five seasons with 100 RBI. He scores 36 points, 53.5 so far.

3. Award the player 10 points for hitting 50 HRs in a season, 4 points for hitting 40 HRs, and 2 points for hitting 30 HRs. Mattingly hit 30 HRs three times for six points. He has 59.5 so far.

4. Award the player 2 points for hitting 45 doubles in a season, one point for hitting 35. Mattingly hit 45 doubles twice and 35 in six other seasons. He scores 10 points, 69.5 so far.

5. Award the player 8 points for each MVP award, 3 points for playing in an All-Star game, 2 points for winning a Gold Glove as acatcher, shortstop or second baseman, one point for a Gold Glove at another position, and one point for either of the recognized Rookie of the Year Awards. Mattingly won the MVP in 1985, played in the All-Star game six times, and won the Gold Glove in nine seasons for a total of 35 points. He has 104.5 so far.

6, 7, 8. All these award points for playing on World, league or division championship teams. Zero points for Mattingly.

9. Award additional points for leading the league in batting average (6 points), home runs (4), RBI (4), runs scored (4), hits or stolen bases (2), doubles or triples (1). Mattingly led the league in average once, in RBI once, in hits twice, and in doubles three times for 17 more points. He now has 121.5 points.

10. For career totals, give the player 50 points for 3,500 career hits, 40 points for 3,000, 15 points for 2,500, and 4 points for 2,000. Mattingly scores four points; he now has 125.5.

11. Award the player 30 points for 600 career HRs, 20 points for 500 HRs, 10 points for 400 HRs, 3 points for 300 HRs. Mattinglydoes not score.

12. Give the player 24 points for a lifetime average of .330, 16 points for .315, and eight points for .300. Mattingly earns eight points with a .307 average. He now has 133.5 points.

The rest of the system awards points for playing tougher defensive positions, and Mattingly does not earn any further points. According to Bill, 130 points is the level of an almost-certain Hall of Famer.

For comparison's sake, Cecil Cooper scores a 95.5, falling short of the

100-mark for Hall of Famers. The reason? His best years weren't as great as Mattingly's. In his 1985 MVP season, Mattingly drove in an eye-popping 145 runs, thanks to Rickey Henderson, who led the league with 146 runs scored. Cecil Cooper, who did enjoy several fine seasons, never had a really big MVP-type season.

Well, I'll say it. Don Mattingly *will* get into the Hall ofFame. Not only is he a viable candidate, he has many other biases working in his favor. He hit for a high average, though his on-base percentage is not particularly impressive. A high average impresses the voters. He was an RBI guy, not a run scorer. This also impresses the voters. And his nickname is Donnie Baseball. He's well liked in the baseball community, from top to bottom. And he's *the* Yankee candidate of the '80s. This will work in his favor as well.

— Drew Faust

[I like Don Mattingly, also—in fact, he and I share the same birthday, April 20, though in different years—but I think he'll have a very tough time making the Hall of Fame. The problem is all those mediocre years at the end of his career; those are the ones that the voters will remember first. Still, his total on Bill's Hall of Fame point system is much higher than I had imagined, and you have to give him a chance. — Don Zminda]

A complete listing of this category can be found on page 231.

Oakland Athletics: Did McGwire Have the Best Home-Run Season Ever?

If only Mark McGwire could stay healthy. . .

Last year, for the third season in a row, McGwire did *not* stay healthy, as back and foot problems limited him to 104 of the Athletics' 144 games. Yet looking at his power numbers, you'd hardly know McGwire missed any time at all. Despite all that time on the shelf, he hit 39 homers—fifth most in baseball (tied)—and drove in 90 runs. McGwire drove in those 90 runs despite the fact that he had only 87 hits, thus becoming one of only two players in major league history to have more RBI than hits in a season (minimum 300 AB). His other figures were impressive as well: 88 walks, a .441 on-base percentage, a .685 slugging average.

How good was McGwire's home-run ratio of 39 homers in only 317 at-bats? The best ever among players with 300 or more at-bats. His season stands atop an awesome group of sluggers led by Babe Ruth. Here's the top 10:

Best At-Bat to HR Ratios—Season

Player, Team	Year	AB	HR	AB/HR
Mark McGwire, Oak	1995	317	39	8.13
Babe Ruth, Yanks	1920	458	54	8.48
Babe Ruth, Yanks	1927	540	60	9.00
Babe Ruth, Yanks	1921	540	59	9.15
Mickey Mantle, Yanks	1961	514	54	9.52
Hank Greenberg, Det	1938	556	58	9.59
Roger Maris, Yanks	1961	590	61	9.67
Hank Aaron, Atl	1973	392	40	9.80
Babe Ruth, Yanks	1928	536	54	9.93
Jimmie Foxx, A's	1932	585	58	10.09

(Minimum 300 AB)

McGwire, as you can see, has the best ratio—and by a good margin. Unfortunately, he also has the fewest at-bats of any player on the list, so we'd have to rate Ruth's 1920, 1927 and 1921 seasons as a little more impressive. But McGwire continues to post some amazing numbers whenever he's in the lineup, which is all too seldom. Over the last three years, he's totaled only 178 games and 536 at-bats, or approximately one full season's worth of action. In those 536 AB, he's produced 57 homers and 139 RBI, while drawing 146 walks. If only he could stay healthy. . . but he can't.

For a better understanding of that, let's compare McGwire's lifetime stats with Fred McGriff, another slugging first sacker who reached the majors at almost exactly the same time—both broke in with a handful of at-bats in 1986. Here's how they stack up:

Player	Gm	AB	H	HR	RBI	Avg	OBP	SLG
McGriff	1291	4512	1284	289	803	.285	.386	.535
McGwire	1094	3659	921	277	747	.252	.369	.523

In 1986-87, McGriff got into only 110 games, while McGwire played in 169. Yet McGriff, who's stayed healthy, has now played in nearly 200 more games than McGwire, and recorded close to 900 more at-bats. What have all those missed at-bats meant to McGwire? Well, if he'd been able to bat 4,512 times like McGriff has while maintaining his current ratio of one homer every 13.2 at-bats, he'd now have 342 homers instead of only 277, and 500-plus career home runs would be well within his sights. He still might make it, but oh, what he might have done. . .

While researching the material for this essay, we uncovered a couple of statistical tidbits that show exactly what big-hitting seasons the 1994 and 1995 campaigns have been. The first is that if you enlarge the at-bat-per-home-run chart at the beginning of this article, you find that seven of the top 27 ratios—more than one-fourth—came from either 1994 or 1995. Along with McGwire's top figure, there's six guys from 1994: Jeff Bagwell (13th, 10.3), Kevin Mitchell (14th, 10.3), Matt Williams (15th, 10.3), Frank Thomas (17th, 10.5), Barry Bonds (21st, 10.6) and Ken Griffey Jr. (27th, 10.8). Pretty amazing.

Then there's the RBI-to-hit ratio we mentioned about McGwire. Until 1995, no hitter had ever averaged more than one RBI per hit in a season of 300 or more at-bats. In 1995, both McGwire and Paul Sorrento did it, and Jay Buhner just missed. The chart on the next page lists the all-time top five:

Highest RBI-to-Hit Ratios, Season

Player, Team	Year	RBI	Hits	Ratio
Paul Sorrento, Cle	1995	79	76	1.04
Mark McGwire, Oak	1995	90	87	1.03
Jay Buhner, Sea	1995	121	123	0.98
Jim Gentile, Bal	1961	141	147	0.96
Oyster Burns, Bro	1890	128	134	0.96

(Minimum 300 AB)

These are truly slugging seasons we're living through.

— Don Zminda

A complete listing for this category can be found on page 232.

Seattle Mariners: Should Edgar Have Been the MVP?

When it was announced that the Baseball Writers Association of America (BBWAA) had selected Boston's Mo Vaughn as the 1995 American League MVP, most of the uproar came from the supporters of Cleveland's Albert Belle. But lost in the discussion was the season of Seattle's Edgar Martinez, who led the league in batting average and on-base percentage, while finishing second in slugging percentage. I like to call these three statistics "the *real* Triple Crown"—for a couple of reasons. First, a player's home-run total depends greatly on his home ballpark. And second, a player's RBI total is heavily influenced by where he hits in the batting order, as well as plain old dumb luck. On-base percentage and slugging percentage are much more representative of a player's offensive ability. Here are how the three players in question stacked up in 1995, with a top-10 finish in the A.L. indicated in parentheses:

	BA	OBP	SLG	MVP votes
Mo Vaughn	.300	.388	.575 (6)	**308**
Albert Belle	.317 (8)	.401	.690 (1)	**300**
Edgar Martinez	.356 (1)	.479 (1)	.628 (2)	**244**

Leaving Belle out of the argument for a moment, it's hard to see how Vaughn finished ahead of Martinez in the MVP voting. Martinez outhit Vaughn by a whopping 56 points, outslugged him by 53 and drew 48 more walks. In addition, Martinez helped keep the Mariners in the A.L. West pennant race while Ken Griffey was out for several months with a broken wrist; if Vaughn was vital to his team winning a division title, Edgar was just as vital to the Mariners. Even giving Vaughn every possible intangible—baserunning, defense, leadership, etc—it's still hard to accept that Vaughn was more worthy than Martinez.

So *should* Martinez have been the MVP? We thought it might be interesting to see how the BBWAA has treated those with Martinez-like seasons since they first began giving out the MVP Awards in 1931. We dug up those seasons in which a player finished in the top two in his league in batting average, on-base percentage and slugging percentage—a feat matched by Martinez in 1995. Since 1931, there have been 52 such seasons. We won't list them all, but here are the players who have accomplished the feat more than once:

Top Two In BA, OB% and SLG%—Two or More Times

Player		Seasons
Stan Musial	9	1943, 1944, 1946, 1948, 1949, 1950 ,1951, 1952, 1957
Ted Williams	8	1941, 1942, 1946, 1947, 1948, 1949, 1956, 1957
Jimmie Foxx	4	1932, 1933, 1938, 1939
Carl Yastrzemski	3	1965, 1967, 1970
Mickey Mantle	3	1956, 1957, 1962
George Brett	2	1980, 1985
Frank Robinson	2	1962, 1966
Johnny Mize	2	1937, 1939

(Since 1931)

Musial and Williams are obviously heads above the rest of the group, but it's also interesting to see who's *not* on the list. Hank Aaron (1959) and Willie Mays (1957) accomplished the feat only once. That should show you how difficult a trick it is.

A few notes about Ted Williams. In five of the eight seasons listed for the Thumper, he not only finished in the top two in all three categories, but finished *first in all three*. Unbelievably, he didn't win the MVP Award in *any* of those five seasons, including two campaigns (1942 and 1947) in which he won the "conventional" Triple Crown. There's been much written about those two MVP votes (Joe Gordon won in 1942, Joe DiMaggio in 1947), so I won't dive into it here. But can you now understand why Williams was never too friendly with the media?

Okay, back to Martinez. Edgar didn't match Williams' "triple feat," but he did finish first in two of the three categories and second in the other. Consequently, we thought it would be more fair to concentrate on just those seasons—ones in which a player led the league in only two of the categories (not all three), while finishing second in the other. There are 26 such seasons since 1931, accomplished by 17 players.

Player		Hall of Fame?
Stan Musial	5	Yes
Jimmie Foxx	3	Yes
Ted Williams	2	Yes
Carl Yastrzemski	2	Yes
Mickey Mantle	2	Yes
Edgar Martinez	**1**	**??**
Pedro Guerrero	1	No
Fred Lynn	1	No
Dave Parker	1	No
Rod Carew	1	Yes
Billy Williams	1	Yes
Frank Robinson	1	Yes
Norm Cash	1	No
Hank Aaron	1	Yes
Chick Hafey	1	Yes
Johnny Mize	1	Yes
Babe Ruth	1	Yes

That's some unbelievable company Martinez has joined. Twelve of the 17 are enshrined in Cooperstown, and even the non-Hall of Famers—Guerrero, Lynn, Parker and Cash—had outstanding careers. Guerrero was perhaps the most underrated offensive performer of the 1980s, spending the prime of his career in Dodger Stadium, where hitters go to die. Lynn was the A.L. MVP in his rookie season of 1975, and might have gone to Cooperstown had it not been for years of injuries. Parker, with an MVP to his credit, still might find his way to Cooperstown. And although Cash never matched the awesome 1961 numbers he posted early in his career, he still finished with 377 lifetime home runs. Good company indeed.

But what about the MVP? Here is the breakdown of the MVP voting for the 26 seasons comparable to Martinez' listed above.

Finish	Number
Finished 1st	9
Finished 2nd	5
Finished 3rd	3
Finished 4th	5
Finished 5th	3
Other	1

Even with a season like Martinez', you're hardly a lock for the MVP Award. Should Martinez have been the MVP in 1995? Probably. Was his third-place finish inconsistent with what the BBWAA has done in the past? Not really. Martinez' 1995 season was the 17th in which a player led the league in two of the three categories while finishing second in the third, yet didn't win the MVP Award.

So who was the "Other" listed above? That belongs to Carl Yastrzemski in 1965, when he led the A.L. in on-base percentage and slugging percentage, yet finished *10th* in the MVP voting. That's right, 10th! Minnesota short-stop Zoilo Versalles won the award that season for the pennant-winning Twins, batting .273 with 19 homers and 77 RBI, while committing 39 errors. You figure it out.

—Scott McDevitt

A complete listing of this category can be found on page 233.

Texas Rangers: Did Rodriguez Deserve the Gold Glove?

The Gold Gloves for catchers last year went to Ivan Rodriguez in the American League and Charles Johnson in the National. Not coincidentally, those two were the most successful major league backstops when it came to throwing out prospective basestealers. But the position is "catcher," not "thrower," and there's a lot more to the job than gunning down baserunners. Rodriguez' 1995 Gold Glove was his fourth straight, but did he deserve it? Let's compare Rodriguez to Seattle's Dan Wilson. Wilson has a good defensive reputation, and he finished second to Rodriguez in innings caught in the A.L.

First let's look at the throwing stats. Here are the top five American League catchers when it came to throwing out runners last season:

Catcher	SBA	CS	Pct.	AL Rank
Ivan Rodriguez	71	31	43.7	1
Jorge Fabregas	55	20	36.4	2
Terry Steinbach	93	33	35.5	3
Dan Wilson	97	30	30.9	4
Ron Karkovice	97	30	30.9	4

Wilson wasn't all that far behind Rodriguez in throwing out runners, but Ivan clearly had the advantage. And notice that far fewer runners *tried* to steal against Rodriguez, which is yet another way that he limited the opposition running game. Advantage, and a big one: Rodriguez.

But as we noted, catchers have numerous duties unrelated to the running game; they also field. That includes receiving the ball cleanly from the pitcher, making the occasional throw to the bases, holding on to throws from the outfield, etc. We can crudely sum up all those skills by adding together errors, passed balls and wild pitches; the fewer the better. Both catchers recorded eight passed balls, so we can toss that from the equation. That leaves errors and wild pitches, and Wilson comes out on top. Wilson made five errors, Rodriguez eight. And where Wilson saw 36 wild pitches whiz by, Rodriguez allowed 49! Yes, some catchers are severely disadvantaged by forkballers and knuckleballers, but Rodriguez can't really claim either excuse. Some critics have noted that Rodriguez doesn't show great mobility behind the plate, and those 49 wild pitches support that notion. Advantage: Wilson.

What about pickoffs? Rodriguez picked off six baserunners last season, Wilson zero. But two of Rodriguez' errors came on pickoff attempts, so overall his pickoff efforts were basically a wash. Advantage: None.

I can just hear the statistics-haters now: "All your fancy numbers are nice, but a catcher's most important job is calling the pitches, and that doesn't show up in the numbers." Wanna bet? We track something called "Catcher ERA," which is simply the ERA recorded when a particular catcher is behind the plate. Here are Rodriguez and Wilson in 1995, compared to the other catchers on their teams:

Catchers	Innings	CERA
Rodriguez	1065.0	4.76
Other Tex C	220.0	4.17
Wilson	1017.0	4.36
Other Sea C	272.1	4.99

Rodriguez doesn't fare particularly well in this area when compared to the other catchers on his team. On the other hand, it's only one season; in 1994, Rodriguez was *better* than Junior Ortiz, the only other Ranger backstop. But look at Dan Wilson. He coaxed substantially better performances from his pitchers than did his backups. And that should count for quite a bit. Advantage: Wilson.

Let's review. . . Rodriguez threw out daring baserunners at a substantially better rate than did Wilson. On the other hand, Wilson was apparently better at blocking pitches in the dirt, and he made three fewer errors despite making many more throws on steal attempts. In fact, aside from Rodriguez' throwing arm, most of the evidence suggests that Wilson was a better defender in 1995. Rodriguez is a fine catcher, but our vote for the Gold Glove would have gone to Dan Wilson.

— Rob Neyer

Toronto Blue Jays: Did Nixon Make the "Presidential All-Star" Team?

There's a lot of stuff about Blue Jay players in this book, and frankly most of it is pretty depressing; for the Jays, the last two years have been difficult ones. So we thought we'd devote this essay to a subject near and dear to all Canadians: the American presidency.

If you're wondering where *that* came from, it all started when the Blue Jays signed Otis Nixon. Jim Capuano, our Director of National Sales (a note from Jim: "Buy *several* copies of this book!"), pointed out that the Jays already had Joe Carter. And a quick look at the record books revealed that players named Adams (Glenn), Johnson (Cliff), Jefferson (Jesse), Jackson (Roy Lee) and Wilson (Mookie) had all worn Toronto blue at some point in their careers. All names of American presidents! That set Jim to wondering what a "presidential all-star team" would look like. This being a presidential election year, it seemed like a perfect subject.

We started out by trying to familiarize ourselves with all the major league players, past and present, who shared presidents' last names. There were a lot of them, but most had the common presidential last names like Johnson, Jackson or Wilson. But did you know that there has been only one Lincoln in major league history? It was the immortal Ezra Lincoln, who went 3-14 with a 5.28 ERA in his only major league season, 1890. . . after which he was shot by a crazed fan named John Wilkes Booth. (Just a little "American presidential history" there, Toronto fans. . .) And did you know that there have been no players at all named Polk, Fillmore, Arthur, McKinley, Roosevelt, Taft, Coolidge, Truman or Eisenhower? Since one of our rules in picking the team was that we'd choose only one player per presidential last name, this makes our task none too easy.

Before we get to the team, we thought we'd do a little "presidential roll-call," baseball style. All the names listed here, including nicknames, were those of authentic major league players. . .except for one case, in which we chose an umpire. In the cases of the presidents who had no players with the same last name, we used a little poetic license and worked in a player's name in a different way. So ladies and gentlemen, here's your 42 baseball presidents:

A Presidential Roll Call

1. George "Claudell" Washington
2. John "Ace" Adams
3. Thomas "Reggie" Jefferson
4. James "Scotti" Madison
5. James "Zach" Monroe
6. John Quincy "Sparky" Adams
7. Andrew "Shoeless Joe" Jackson
8. Martin "Deacon" Van Buren
9. William Henry "Chuck" Harrison
10. John "Lefty" Tyler
11. "Dion" James Knox Polk
12. Zachary "Dummy" Taylor
13. "Frank" Millard Fillmore
14. Franklin "Billy" Pierce
15. James "Jim" Buchanan
16. Abraham "Ezra" Lincoln
17. Andrew "The Big Train" Johnson
18. U.S. "Mudcat" Grant
19. Rutherford B. "Blimp" Hayes
20. James "Bill" Garfield
21. Chester A. Arthur "Fletcher"
22. Grover "Reggie" Cleveland
23. Benjamin "Ben" Harrison
24. Grover "Elmer" Cleveland
25. William "Bill" McKinley (umpire)
26. "Stork" Theodore Roosevelt
27. William Howard Taft "Wright"
28. Woodrow "Mookie" Wilson
29. Warren G. "Charlie" Harding
30. Calvin Coolidge "Julius Caesar Tuskahoma McLish"
31. Herbert "Buster" Hoover
32. Franklin "Stubbs" Roosevelt
33. Harry Truman "Clevenger"
34. Dwight "Bernard" Eisenhower

35. John "Brickyard" Kennedy
36. Lyndon "The Big Unit" Johnson
37. Richard "Otis" Nixon
38. Gerald "Whitey" Ford
39. Jimmy "Joe" Carter
40. Ronald "Rip" Reagan
41. George "Bullet Joe" Bush
42. Bill "Big Jim" Clinton

What an impressive list. We found ourselves wondering how different American history might have been if these really *had* been the presidents' names. Don't you think "Mookie" Wilson would have excited the electorate a little more than "Woodrow" did? Wouldn't every American fondly remember the administration of good old Rutherford "Blimp" Hayes? And wouldn't the Adamses have been more than dull, boring one-term presidents had their names been "Ace" and "Sparky"? On the other hand, Zachary "Dummy" Taylor and Franklin "Stubbs" Roosevelt (he *hated* that name!) might never have been elected at all. . .

On to the All-Star team. Remember our rule: only one player per presidential last name. Here are our picks, including a four-man pitching staff:

Presidential All-Stars

Pos	Player	Yrs	Avg	HR	RBI
C	Gary Carter	19	.262	324	1225
1B	Von Hayes	12	.267	143	696
2B	Tony Taylor	19	.261	75	598
3B	Sparky Adams	13	.286	9	394
SS	Donie Bush	16	.250	9	436
OF	Joe Jackson	13	.356	54	785
OF	Hack Wilson	12	.307	244	1062
OF	Claudell Washington	17	.278	164	824

Pos	Pitcher	Yrs	W	L	ERA
P	Walter Johnson	21	417	279	2.16
P	Whitey Ford	16	236	106	2.74
P	Billy Pierce	18	211	169	3.27
P	Babe Adams	19	194	140	2.75

Not the greatest team we've ever seen, but not bad, either. And we guarantee that this club would have destroyed any "Royal Family All-Star Team". . . even if John Tudor were pitching. The Presidential pitching staff is particularly strong, led by Hall-of-Famers Walter Johnson and Whitey Ford. The infield is a little underpowered, but you've got to like the power trio of Jackson, Wilson and Carter. Three hard-hitting Democrats. The hardest choice in picking the team, incidentally, was over which Jackson to put in the outfield: Shoeless Joe or Reggie? Since the presidency is hardly immune to scandals, Shoeless Joe seemed like a good pick to us.

And what of this year's presidential race—any hot prospects? Well, like everybody else, we thought the race lost a little bit of luster after Colin "Boog" Powell dropped out. There's still Bob "Lester" Dole, who went 2-for-4 in his only game back in 1875. But for a "presidential baseball fan," only one choice quickens the blood: who else but Lamar "Grover Cleveland" Alexander?

Be sure to register.

— Don Zminda

Atlanta Braves: Did Maddux Deserve the MVP Award?

No one would dispute that Greg Maddux had an extraordinary season in 1995. With a 19-2 record, a 1.63 ERA and league leadership in six different pitching categories (ERA, wins, winning percentage, innings pitched, complete games and shutouts), Maddux was a unanimous choice for his fourth straight National League Cy Young Award.

But did Maddux deserve the N.L. Most Valuable Player Award as well? Many people in baseball feel that a pitcher—at least a starting pitcher—should not be eligible for the MVP award. "They have their own award [the Cy Young Award]," one common argument goes. But as long as the rules state that pitchers are eligible for the MVP award—and they do—that particular argument has no relevance. Another argument, one you hear all the time, goes, "A pitcher who works every five days *can't* be as valuable as a guy who's in the lineup every day. Therefore a starting pitcher shouldn't be considered for the MVP." As if to underscore this point, one voter relegated Maddux to 10th place on his MVP ballot (was this the same guy who had Charlie Hayes seventh?). Let's begin a Q&A on the Maddux-for-MVP issue with that very question; our system of analysis, we'll say up front, is modeled after the arguments made by Bill James in the 1979 and 1987 *Bill James Baseball Abstracts* in discussing two classic pitcher-vs.-hitter MVP debates: Ron Guidry/Jim Rice in 1978, and Roger Clemens/Don Mattingly in 1986.

Can a pitcher who works every five days be as valuable as someone who's in the lineup every day?

Yes, of course he can. I know it, you know it, and even the people who make this stupid argument know it. They prove it time after time by their own actions.

If you don't believe this, let's create a hypothetical situation. Let's say the Atlanta Braves traded Maddux, the third-most valuable player in the National League last year according to the voters, for Dante Bichette, the man who finished second. Would people in Atlanta be saying, "Wow, what a great trade! Sure, we hate to lose Maddux, but he only works once every five days, and we got *an everyday player* for him! A guy who's more valuable!" Would anybody in Atlanta make that argument? Would anybody *anywhere* be congratulating the Braves for getting Bichette in exchange for Maddux? Of course not; everybody would be saying that the Braves ought to have their heads examined. And for a good reason: because Maddux is *a more valuable player* than Bichette. It's a no-brainer.

Even if the Braves traded Maddux for Barry Larkin, the league's MVP last year, would people think the Reds got robbed simply because Maddux isn't an everyday player? No; they'd look at this as one great player—one extremely *valuable* player—being dealt for another, and then debate all winter about which one was greater.

It's an idiot's argument.

OK, then HOW can a pitcher who works every five days be as valuable as someone who plays every day?

Simply because when he *is* on the field, he has a far greater effect on his team's chance of winning or losing the game than anybody else in the lineup. The pitcher's effect is so great that it makes up for those four days he's off.

As Bill put it in the 1987 *Abstract*, one simple way of grasping this is to compare a starting pitcher's batters faced over the season with the number of plate appearances a full-time hitter logs. Last year, for instance, Maddux faced 785 batters; Larkin came to the plate 567 times. Granted Larkin also played in the field, ran the bases, etc., but that only helps even things out. As James put it in 1987,

> In order to believe that the pitcher, working one day in five, is more valuable than the hitter working every day, all you have to accept is that a pitcher has five times as much impact on the games in which he appears. That seems, to put it mildly, most reasonable. I mean, I ain't never seen a form chart give the starting first basemen.

So how can we weigh the relative impacts of a very good pitcher with those of a very good position player?

By weighing their relative ability to produce, or prevent, runs.

We'll begin as Bill did, comparing a hitter's runs created with a pitcher's runs allowed. Let's compare Maddux with Barry Larkin, the MVP winner last year. According to Bill's formulas, Larkin created 108 runs last year. The next step would be to ask how many runs created the Reds would have received if they'd had a "replacement-level" player at shortstop, rather than Larkin. This is defined as a player who creates one run less per 27 outs than the league average for that position. A replacement-level shortstop in the National League would have contributed 3.21 runs per 27 outs last year. Larkin made 356 outs in 1995, so the replacement would have created about 42 runs. The Cincinnati park has very slightly favored the pitcher over the last few years, so let's make that 41 runs. Larkin, with his

108 runs created, contributed 67 extra runs to the Cincinnati offense.

OK, but what about his defensive contributions?

This is the hardest area to judge. Larkin won the National League Gold Glove at shortstop last year, but it's hard to measure his value from his defensive stats, which frankly aren't very impressive. So we're going to give him the benefit of the doubt and say he saved his team 20 runs in 1995. This is very generous. Our colleagues Pete Palmer and John Thorn, in *Total Baseball*, use a complicated formula to derive a figure known as "fielding runs," which is their estimate of the number of runs an individual player saved his club compared to an average player at each position. In most years the *best* player in the league, regardless of position, will be credited with saving his team around 25 runs. Larkin's stats from 1995 don't put him anywhere near that level, but let's say the stats underestimate his value and give Larkin credit for saving 20 runs compared to a replacement-level shortstop. So in total we credit him with being about 87 runs better than the replacement level. What does that mean in terms of wins? Most statisticians figure that a contribution of 10 runs equals one win, so our estimate is that Larkin's play meant nearly nine extra wins for the Reds. That's a pretty valuable player.

So Larkin was 87 runs better than a replacement-level position player. How many runs better was Maddux than a replacement-level starting pitcher?

Maddux permitted 39 runs last year in 209.2 innings; only one of those runs was unearned, so we'll just stick with the 39. The average National League pitcher permitted 4.65 runs per nine innings, and we'll again figure that a replacement-level pitcher would be one run worse, permitting 5.65 runs per nine. We don't need to make a park adjustment to this figure, since the Atlanta stadium has been absolutely neutral over the last three seasons. A pitcher permitting 5.65 runs per nine innings would allow 132 runs in the same 209.2 innings that Maddux pitched. Thus Maddux was 93 runs better than a replacement-level pitcher.

But what about the Atlanta defense? Didn't they save Maddux some of those runs?

Yes, the Braves do play good team defense, and it undoubtedly helped save Maddux some runs. However, the Braves were last in the league in double plays, and none of the Braves' starting infielders has ever won a Gold Glove, so let's not overestimate how much they helped Maddux, an extreme groundball pitcher. (Actually, one of the fielders who helps Maddux the most is Maddux himself, a six-time Gold Glove winner. However, his own contributions with the glove would already show up in his runs-per-nine-innings figure.) Let's say a replacement-level pitcher working for the Braves would have allowed 5.4 runs per nine innings rather than 5.65, which seems reasonable. Over Maddux' 209.2 innings, that makes the replacement-level pitchers six runs better, cutting his advantage to 87 runs rather than 93.

How above Maddux' contributions on offense? He's a pretty good hitter for a pitcher.

Yes, but he didn't contribute much in 1995, batting .153 with no RBI and six sacrifice hits. For the season he created exactly 2.9 runs on offense. Even that makes him a little better than average hitter for a pitcher, but probably not enough to give him credit for even one extra run.

Let's summarize what we've done so far:

Larkin vs. Maddux—MVP Race

Category	Larkin	Maddux
Runs	108	39
Replacement Runs	41	132
Advantage	+67	-93
Defense	+20	-6
Total	+87	+87

That's a flat-out tie. But what about other factors—clutch performance, for example?

Well, Larkin was terrific in the late innings of close games, hitting .397 with great peripheral stats. And he batted .349 with runners in scoring position. On the other hand, Maddux held *his* opponents to a .187 average in the late innings of close games, and a .157 mark with men in scoring position. And after all, the man's record was 19-2. Hard to find any advantage for Larkin there.

How did their clubs do without each of them in the lineup?

With Larkin in the lineup last year, the Reds went .595 (78-53). Without him, they were 7-6 (.538). However, four of those losses came in the second half of September when they were coasting home with the N.L. Central crown in tow; prior to September 17, they'd gone 6-2 without Larkin. When Larkin sat out back-to-back series on the road against two good teams, the Astros and Rockies, in June, the Reds won four of the six games. Without Maddux, the Braves were a .586 club (68-48), 20 games over .500. But in the 28 games Maddux started, they were 22-6 (.786), an additional 16 games over the break-even point in a little under one-fifth of their schedule. Can anyone who reads over those figures conclude that *Larkin* was the one who was more valuable?

One last question before we leave the subject. Would one of the other position players who finished high in the MVP voting—say Bichette or Mike Piazza—have fared better in a comparison with Maddux?

Not really. Bichette created 121 runs last year, but remember that he was playing in one of the best hitter's parks ever created. After adjusting for the park we found him to be only 26 runs better than a replacement-level left fielder. His defense wouldn't add much to that. Piazza created 103 runs in a tough park to hit, and after adjusting for the park he was 67 runs better than a replacement-level catcher. Piazza also plays an important defensive position, but by all accounts he doesn't play it very well. Even if we gave him a few runs for defense, he wouldn't be close to Maddux.

So who should it be?

The numbers indicate that it's dead-even between Larkin and Maddux, but remember that we gave Larkin the extreme benefit of the doubt in an area—defense—that the raw figures don't really support. And Maddux has several other factors in his favor. He was on the winningest team in the league; he was, by any objective measure, the most valuable player on that team; his team posted a winning percentage 200 points higher when he was in the lineup than it did when he wasn't. And of course, you can't forget that it was Maddux, not Larkin, whose 1995 season is being compared with the best ever.

Look, we've got two very fine players here. One of them, the position player, posted the kind of numbers that were excellent, but which—if you saw them while flipping through a record book—would never jump out at you and say "MVP." It was the sort of season that only wins an MVP award when there are no other standout candidates. Except that in this case there was: the brilliant pitcher who posted some of the greatest numbers any pitcher has recorded since the Dead Ball Era. . . while leading his club to the best record in the league.

We don't know about you, but given that choice, we know who *we'd* have voted for. Greg Maddux should have been the National League MVP last year. . . even though he "wasn't an everyday player."

— Don Zminda

Chicago Cubs: Will Ryno Be Able to Come Back?

It's the age of the comeback. First Michael Jordan, then Magic Johnson, and now Ryne Sandberg. Here in the Chicago area, we can't help but wonder if Dick Butkus and Bobby Hull won't be putting on the pads again this fall.

But the real question in Chicago, or at least on the North Side—home of Harry Caray, Wrigley Field and the Cubs—is how well Ryno will play after taking a season-and-a-half vacation from baseball. To answer that question, we made a list of all the players since 1941 who missed a full season, then came back at age 34 or older and returned to full-time major league duty (100-plus games). From that group, we considered only the players with, at least arguably, Hall of Fame ability. Sandberg, 36 this spring and already with decent Cooperstown credentials, meets all of these qualifications.

Anyway, here's the list, a fairly short one:

Superstars Return After Missing 1+ Years

Player	Age	Year	Games	Hits	AB	Avg	HR	RBI
Hank Greenberg	29	1940	148	195	573	.340	41	150
	35	1946	142	145	523	.277	44	127
Billy Herman	33	1943	153	193	585	.330	2	100
	36	1946	122	130	436	.298	3	50
Luke Appling	36	1943	155	192	585	.328	3	80
	39	1946	149	180	582	.309	1	55
Ted Williams	32	1951	148	169	531	.318	30	126
	35	1954	117	133	386	.345	29	89
Jackie Jensen	32	1959	148	148	535	.277	28	112
	34	1961	137	131	498	.263	13	66
Dave Winfield	36	1988	149	180	559	.322	25	107
	38	1990	132	127	475	.267	21	78

By the way, we only considered seasons in which the player saw action in at least 100 games. Ted Williams, for example, played a few games in both 1952 and '53, but we only looked at 1951 and 1954.

The first four players on the list are in the Hall of Fame, and the last, Dave Winfield, certainly will be someday. The only non-Hall of Famer is Jackie

Jensen, whose fear of flying caused him to skip the 1960 season after leading the American League with 112 RBI in 1959.

What will Sandberg do in 1996? First let's look at the average numbers posted by the six players above:

Player	Age	Games	Hits	AB	Avg	HR	RBI
Averages	33	150	180	561	.321	22	113
	36	133	141	483	.292	19	78

The average "early retiree" played his last full season at age 33, then came back at 36. . . just like Sandberg. And if we assume that Sandberg will experience the same dropoff as his predecessors, we can arrive at some projected numbers for 1996, presented in the following chart:

		Ryne Sandberg						
	Age	Year	Games	Hits	AB	Avg	HR	RBI
Last Full Yr	33	1993	117	141	456	.309	9	45
Projected	36	1996	104	110	393	.281	8	31

Well, it's not perfect, largely because Ryno missed a bunch of games in 1993. We think he'll almost certainly play more than 104 games in 1996, which of course would mean his other raw stats will go up as well. However, that .281 batting average looks like a realistic figure.

One cautionary note: Of the six players we studied, five were rather forcibly removed from the game. Greenberg, Herman, Appling and Williams all went to war, while Winfield underwent serious back surgery. Jackie Jensen, on the other hand, "voluntarily" retired. . . like Sandberg. And of the six, Jensen suffered the most serious dropoff, and his comeback season was also his last. Might it be that voluntary retirement is indicative of a loss of desire that can't be regained?

Michael Jordan would argue otherwise, and so would we. Hall of Famers are Hall of Famers, and they don't lose their amazing abilities even after a long vacation. Sandberg might not be an All-Star this year—the National League boasts a number of quality second basemen—but he should be a solid performer.

— Rob Neyer

Cincinnati Reds: Will the Reds Keep Winning Under Knight?

The Cincinnati Reds, who played .590 ball and won the National League Central Division title last year, will have a new skipper in 1996. Davey Johnson is gone; his replacement will be Ray Knight, a rookie skipper who served on Johnson's coaching staff the last two years. Now Knight, who was slated to take Johnson's job even *before* Johnson brought home a winner (Knight's title in 1995 was "assistant manager"), will be expected to keep on winning.

How easy will it be for Knight to get the Reds into the playoffs again? The same question applies to Joe Torre, who's taking over a Yankee club which made the playoffs last year under Buck Showalter. We decided to go back to 1960 and look for situations where a club qualified for postseason play under one manager, then began the next season with a new skipper in command. Before looking at the data, our assumption was that this was something which hardly ever happened—maybe a couple of times with the Yankees under George Steinbrenner, but seldom if ever otherwise. To our surprise, we discovered 12 instances where a team which qualified for postseason play changed skippers prior to the start of the next season. Here's the list:

Replacing a Championship Manager—1960-94

Team	Year	Old Mgr	W	L	Pct	Year	NewMgr	W	L	Pct
Yanks	1960	Stengel*	97	57	.630	1961	Houk*	109	53	.673
Yanks	1963	Houk*	104	57	.646	1964	Berra*	99	63	.611
Yanks	1964	Berra*	99	63	.611	1965	Keane	77	85	.475
Cardinals	1964	Keane*	93	69	.574	1965	Schoendienst	80	81	.497
Twins	1969	Martin*	97	65	.599	1970	Rigney*	98	64	.605
Pirates	1971	Murtaugh*	97	65	.599	1972	Virdon*	96	59	.619
Athletics	1973	Williams*	94	68	.580	1974	Dark*	90	72	.556
Athletics	1975	Dark*	98	64	.605	1976	Tanner	87	74	.540
Yanks	1980	Howser*	103	59	.636	1981	Michael-Lemon*	59	48	.551
Phillies	1981	Green*	59	48	.551	1982	Corrales	89	73	.549
Angels	1982	Mauch*	93	69	.574	1983	McNamara	70	92	.432
Blue Jays	1985	Cox*	99	62	.615	1986	Williams	86	76	.531
Total			**1133**	**746**	**.603**			**1040**	**840**	**.553**

* Finished in 1st place

There are a couple of teams on the list in unique situations due to the 1981 players' strike. The 1981 Phillies won a playoff spot by winning the first half of that year's split season. They then switched managers from Dallas Green to Pat Corrales prior to the 1982 campaign. Similarly, the Yankees won the 1980 A.L. East title under Dick Howser, then made the playoffs for winning the 1981 first half under Gene Michael. . . though by the time the playoffs rolled around, Bob Lemon was running the club. Since both teams had qualified for the playoffs in Year 1, we counted them as part of the study.

The most fascinating discovery from this study was that though the Yankees made this sort of switch more than anybody (four times), all but one of the switches took place in the years *before* Steinbrenner got control of the club. The first time was when the Yanks moved Casey Stengel out of the manager's job following their loss to the Pirates in the 1960 World Series. The new skipper, Ralph Houk, was an immediate success, winning 109 games and the World Series in 1961. Houk won the American League pennant the next two years as well, but the Yanks switched managers again after the 1963 campaign, moving Yogi Berra into the skipper's spot as Houk became the club's general manager. Like Houk, Yogi won a pennant in his first year, 1964, but the Yankees nonetheless bounced Yogi after the club's seven-game loss to the Cardinals in the World Series. His replacement, oddly enough, was the manager who'd beaten the Yanks in the Series, Johnny Keane. Keane himself had nearly been fired during that year's National League pennant race, with Leo Durocher apparently all set to take over the club before the Cards put on a late rush and caught the Phillies at the wire. Feeling that the Cardinals had shown a lack of faith in him during the pennant race, Keane quit almost as soon as the Series was over. Obviously, George Steinbrenner and Marge Schott don't have a patent on front-office turmoil!

Several other managers were able to win a flag the year after inheriting a champion. In 1969, the Minnesota Twins won the A.L. West title under Billy Martin, but Twins owner Calvin Griffith replaced Martin with Bill Rigney after the Twins got swept by the Orioles in the playoffs. Rigney produced another West crown for the Twins in 1970, but like Martin, lost three straight to the Orioles in the ALCS.

In 1971, the Pittsburgh Pirates won the World Series under veteran manager Danny Murtaugh, but when the Series was over, Murtaugh decided to retire. The Bucs replaced him with coach Bill Virdon, and Virdon was able to lead Pittsburgh to the N.L. East title in 1972. However, the Pirates lost the NLCS in five games to the Reds that fall. When the Bucs played poorly through most of '73, they bounced Virdon late in the year and brought back Murtaugh.

The next club to replace a winning manager was the Oakland Athletics during the wild reign of owner Charles O. Finley. The A's won the World Series in both 1972 and 1973 under Dick Williams, but Williams got into a contract dispute with Finley after the '73 Series, and when the next season began, Alvin Dark was the skipper. Dark won the World Series in his first year with the A's and then took the A.L. West crown the year after that, 1975. The A's lost in the playoffs that year, however, and when 1976 arrived, Chuck Tanner was managing the team. Tanner *didn't* win a pennant, though he did finish second.

There was one other case where a club replaced a manager who'd won a title, then won again the next year with a new man. This time it *was* with Steinbrenner pulling the strings. He did it in his own imitable way. In 1980, the Yanks won 103 games and the A.L. East title under rookie skipper Dick Howser. But the Yanks got swept by the Royals in the playoffs, and in 1981 Gene Michael took over the team. Michael lasted until September, when Steinbrenner bounced him and brought in Bob Lemon. Under the split-season format, the Yanks qualified for the playoffs for having won the first half under Michael. Lemon led the club to the World Series, but the Yanks lost to the Dodgers in six games.

Overall, championship clubs which changed managers prior to the start of the next season saw their winning percentage drop on average from .603 to .553—about eight fewer wins over a 162-game schedule. But it's normal for a team with a high winning percentage to win fewer games the next year. . . and given that six of the 12 teams in the study finished first again the next season, there's no reason to think that Knight can't bring home another flag for the Reds. Ditto for Joe Torre in New York. And if they don't, the Reds and Yankees can always change skippers *again*.

— Don Zminda

Colorado Rockies: How Much Did Coors Help the Hitters?

Despite what your favorite veteran broadcaster might tell you about how a home run in one park is just as good as a home run in any other park, the fact is that the Colorado Rockies hitters were helped more than plenty by their cozy new park.

We took the Rockies' 1995 road batting numbers, doubled them and compared them to every other team's total numbers. Shockingly, the team that compared most closely to the Coors-less Rockies was the punchless St. Louis Cardinals.

1995 Rockies Road Hitting (times two) vs. 1995 Cardinals Overall

Team	2B	3B	HR	RBI	BB	SO	AVG	OBP	SLG
Rockies	238	24	132	558	454	1042	.247	.315	.384
Cardinals	238	24	107	533	436	920	.247	.314	.374

We also took the best Rockies hitter, MVP candidate Dante Bichette, and did the same with him, doubling his 1995 road numbers and comparing them to all other 1995 hitters' totals. Coincidentally, the best match was a St. Louis Cardinal, right fielder Brian Jordan.

1995 Bichette Road (times two) vs. Brian Jordan Overall

Player	AB	H	2B	3B	HR	RBI	BB	SO	AVG	OBP
Bichette	554	166	38	2	18	90	22	118	.300	.329
Jordan	490	145	20	4	22	81	22	79	.296	.339

The similarities extend beyond the numbers. Both are big, strong, athletic "tools" players known for their exceptional throwing arms. The point is not that Dante Bichette is a worthless player outside of Coors Field. However, no one was campaigning for Brian Jordan as MVP last year.

To Bichette's credit, he was smart enough to re-sign with Colorado for three years, greatly enhancing the chance for the Bichette mystique to continue. What would really be interesting to see is what a righty banger who's *not* helped by his home park, like Albert Belle, Frank Thomas or Mark McGwire, could do in a full, healthy season at Coors. The numbers could be Ruthian.

Of course, there is a flip side to this. The Rockies' batting stats are of course helped tremendously by Coors Field, but how much are their pitching stats hurt? This time, we took the Rockies' road pitching stats, doubled them and compared them to every other team's totals. Would you believe the Rockies pitching staff compared best to the Los Angeles Dodgers?

Rockies 1995 Road Pitching (times two) vs. 1995 Dodgers Overall

Team	ERA	H	HR	AVG	OBP	SLG
Rockies	3.70	1200	106	.254	.330	.375
Dodgers	3.66	1188	125	.243	.311	.372

So naturally, let's do the same for the Rockies' best 1995 starter, Kevin Ritz. (It was amazing in itself to realize how good—and unnoticed—a season Ritz had in 1995. I guess all the stories about how he is a new pitcher are true.) Ritz' Coors-less twin was the Cubs' Jamie Navarro, whose comeback was much more publicized, probably in great part due to his 14-6 record, which far bettered Ritz' 11-11.

Kevin Ritz 1995 Road (times two) vs. Jaime Navarro Overall

Pitcher	ERA	IP	H	HR	AVG	OBP	SLG
Ritz	3.25	194.0	176	8	.247	.311	.329
Navarro	3.28	200.1	194	19	.251	.303	.362

Despite the fact that the Rockies have been a highly successful team thus far, they might suffer from the "reverse park curse" for as long as they call Coors Field home. In brief, Rockies management will always tend to think that the team needs better pitching while the hitting is fine, when in fact the opposite is true. . . but disguised by home-park illusions. In many cases like these (the Astros always think they need power hitters, the Cubs always are worried about pitching), the team never quite gets over the hump.

Colorado did lead the league in hitting and trail in pitching in 1995. However, with the previously unheard of hitter-friendly effect of Coors Field, you probably won't see any National League pennants hanging there until their road-hitting numbers improve.

— Steve Moyer

Florida Marlins: What Kind of Career Will Sheffield Have?

Gary Sheffield is a terrific young player. He's also a player with an injury history. . . which is one reason you might not have noticed how good he's been. Over the last two years, various ailments—along with the two work stoppages—have limited Sheffield to 150 games and 535 at-bats. That's approximately one full season of work for a full-time player. If we combine those two seasons, here's what Sheffield's numbers look like:

Gary Sheffield—Last 2 Seasons Combined

G	AB	R	H	2B	3B	HR	RBI	BB	SO	SB	CS	Avg	OBP	SLG
150	535	107	158	24	1	43	124	106	95	31	10	.295	.416	.585

That's one terrific "season"; only trouble is, it took Sheffield two years to do it. Since he came up to the majors to stay in 1989, Sheffield has never played 150 games in a season, and he's played at least 140 only twice, in 1992 and '93. In his healthiest season, 1992, Sheffield hit 33 homers, drove in 100 runs and led the N.L. in hitting with a .330 average. So all those injuries have to be maddening. Like Mark McGwire, who we discussed in the Oakland essay, a consideration of Sheffield's career inevitably raises the question of what might have been.

Sheffield will be 27 this year, the age at which many players have their greatest season, and if he can avoid injuries it's entirely possible that he could hit .330 with 40-plus homers. But what of the longer term? What does Sheffield's past tell us about his future?

We can't answer a question like that with certainty, of course, but we *do* have a tool that can help us make some intelligent speculation: Bill James' similarity scores. The system is discussed at some length in the New York Yankees essay on Don Mattingly, and you can turn to that essay if you want to know more about it. Briefly, similarity scores compare players' statistical lines and look for similarities among them. The higher the score, the more similar the players' numbers are.

In the Yankee essay we looked at similarity scores for players' entire careers—for instance, the player whose career was most like Don Mattingly's is Cecil Cooper. Sheffield's career has a long way to go, so what we'll do in this essay is look at players who had the most similar career totals through the age of 26, Sheffield's 1995 age. Here are the 10 players whose numbers were most similar to Sheffield's at that point of their careers; all of them have similarity scores of 950 or higher, which is a very strong correlation:

10 Most Similar Careers to Gary Sheffield (through Age 26)

Player	AB	R	H	2B	3B	HR	RBI	BB	SO	SB	Avg	OBP	SLG
Andre Dawson	2829	414	795	140	40	110	387	175	468	145	.281	.327	.475
Reggie Smith	2890	438	810	156	27	107	393	289	386	66	.280	.346	.464
Vic Wertz	2392	390	693	128	27	87	461	344	313	4	.290	.381	.475
Bobby Murcer	2365	378	659	103	22	108	359	300	347	49	.279	.359	.478
Bobby Bonds	2837	537	779	132	30	126	385	318	734	179	.275	.350	.476
Ellis Valentine	2520	312	711	144	12	100	379	155	368	56	.282	.322	.468
Billy Williams	2484	360	725	117	29	107	379	248	323	32	.292	.357	.492
Harold Baines	3184	420	908	153	36	119	501	225	450	27	.285	.330	.468
Kent Hrbek	2816	405	815	156	15	117	474	319	415	11	.289	.362	.480
Dave Winfield	2842	413	796	127	23	100	421	299	431	95	.280	.347	.447
Gary Sheffield	2696	399	774	139	12	117	430	298	295	96	.287	.361	.478

Like Sheffield, all these players posted impressive numbers through the age of 26. There is one Hall of Famer in Billy Williams, along with two others who are good bets to make the Hall: Dave Winfield and Andre Dawson. Of course, there are also players whose careers were curtailed by injuries, and a lot of other players who were very good but not great.

There is one striking difference between Sheffield and the Cooperstown-caliber trio of Williams, Winfield and Dawson: all of *them* displayed much more durability in their early years than Sheffield has. Through 26, Williams and Dawson had played 150 games in a season three times; Winfield twice. Sheffield has never had a 150-game season (and wouldn't have had one even without the two strikes). Frankly, Sheffield looks a lot more like Ellis Valentine, who played 150 games only once in his career and who was out of baseball by the time he reached his early 30s. That's not a very comforting thought to Marlin and Sheffield fans.

Of course, those are the extremes; the list of similar players also includes lots of guys with excellent—but less than immortal—careers like Reggie Smith and Harold Baines and Bobby Bonds. All in all, there seems to be a good chance that Sheffield will post some impressive career numbers before he's through. But the chances that he'll get it together, stay healthy and have a truly great career would appear pretty slim.

— Don Zminda

A complete listing for this category can be found on page 234.

Houston Astros: Should a Fast Catcher Be Shifted to a New Position?

Astros second baseman Craig Biggio has succeeded in pulling off one of the most unusual position switches in major league history. Biggio began his career as a catcher, and while he wasn't the worst receiver in the world, he wasn't the best, either. What Biggio did have going for him was something few catchers either possess or need: speed. From 1989 to 1991, his first three full seasons in the majors, Biggio swiped a total of 65 bases—a remarkably high total for a catcher. So figuring that his speed was wasted behind the plate, the Astros took a big gamble and shifted Biggio to second base in 1992.

The switch couldn't have turned out better. Biggio took a little while to adapt to his new position, but he eventually mastered it well enough to win Gold Gloves in 1994 and 1995. And freed of the burdens of catching, he became a much better hitter. He became a better basestealer, too: along with batting over .300 in each of the last two years, Biggio has stolen a total of 72 bases in 84 attempts. He even led the National League in steals in 1994—something that probably would have been impossible if he were still squatting behind the plate for 1,000 innings a year.

The success of the Biggio switch made us wonder if other fast young catchers might have been better off at another position. We went through the record books and looked for catchers who shared two traits: they were all 27 years old or younger, and they each had at least one season with 15 or more stolen bases (minimum 60 games caught). Here is the complete list of catchers who met those requirements since 1920:

Young Catchers with 15+ Steals in a Season (Since 1920)

Catcher, Team	Year	Games	SB	Age
Fran Healy, KC	1974	138	16	27
John Stearns, Mets	1978	141	25	26
John Stearns, Mets	1979	121	15	27
Benito Santiago, SD	1987	146	21	22
Benito Santiago, SD	1988	136	15	23
B.J. Surhoff, Mil	1988	106	21	23
Craig Biggio, Hou	1989	125	21	23
Craig Biggio, Hou	1990	113	25	24
B.J. Surhoff, Mil	1990	125	18	25
Craig Biggio, Hou	1991	139	19	25
Brad Ausmus, SD	1995	100	16	26

(Age 27 or younger; minimum 60 games caught)

As you can see, this is a fairly short list, and one entirely composed of players from the 1970s on. There were a good number of basestealing catchers in the early days of the game, but between 1917 and 1974, no young catcher could steal as many as 15 bases in a season. Since then, there have been a bunch of them, starting with Fran Healy in 1974.

Probably the closest match to Biggio was B.J. Surhoff, the former Brewer who signed with the Orioles prior to the 1996 season. Surhoff was both a catcher and a shortstop during his amateur days, but the Brewers kept him behind the plate for most of his first six seasons with the club. Like Biggio, Surhoff showed potential as a basestealer, swiping 53 bases in the three seasons from 1988 to 1990. But after that his numbers declined, and by the time the Brewers finally moved him to third base in 1993, he was no longer the basestealing threat who had gone 21-for-27 on the basepaths in 1988. While Surhoff probably never could have become as good a basestealer as Biggio, it's very likely that all those years of catching cost him a chance to be a consistent 25-steal man. Like Biggio, Surhoff was never that great a catcher, and you have to think he would have had a better career had he been shifted to another position a little earlier in his career, as Biggio was.

Another interesting case was John Stearns, the Mets' catcher in the late-1970s-early 1980s. Stearns stole 91 bases in his career, including 25 in 1978. Even as late as 1982, when he was 31, Stearns was fast enough to steal 17 bases in 24 attempts. But then he tore up his elbow, and that pretty much ended his career. Like Biggio and Surhoff, Stearns wasn't considered an outstanding catcher. Had he moved to another position, he probably would have contributed more offensively and might have been able to steal 30-plus bases in a year. We'll never know.

Stearns, Biggio and Surhoff were all catchers who had good speed, but who also left something to be desired behind the plate. In their cases, a position switch was definitely a good idea, and the sooner the better. But Benito Santiago and Brad Ausmus *are* considered good catchers, so their clubs have wisely kept them where they were. The tradeoff is that the longer you stay behind the plate, the more you seem to lose in speed. Santiago is a good example. After stealing 21 bases as a rookie in 1987 and 15 more in 1988, his effectiveness on the bases began to decline. In the last six seasons, Santiago has never stolen more than 10 in a year (and that just once). But since he can catch, no one has second-guessed the move.

A couple of other basestealing catchers should probably be mentioned while we're on the subject. John Wathan, the Royals' catcher of 10-15 years ago, had some great years on the basepaths, going 36-for-45 in 1982, when he was 32, and then was 28-for-35 a year later. This seems to contradict the notion that catchers lose their speed as they grow older. However, Wathan played other positions during most of his career, and in fact caught more than 100 games only once. That surely saved some wear and tear on his legs. Another intriguing case is future Hall of Famer Carlton Fisk, who stole 128 bases in his career, including 17 at the age of 37 in 1985. But Fisk aged about as well as any player in baseball history, and we think he's the exception rather than the rule.

As for Biggio, no one has questioned that shift to second base, at least not lately. It's a move that's helped him have a lot better career than he might have otherwise. . . and one which has helped the Astros as well.

— Don Zminda

A complete listing for this category can be found on page 235.

Los Angeles Dodgers: Did Teams Catch Up with Nomo the Second Time Around?

After three consecutive rough outings in August, people started saying that the National League was finally catching up to Dodgers hurler Hideo Nomo. But was that the truth or just a misguided perception?

In fairness to "The Japanese Tornado," a slump was almost inevitable at some point during the season. After all, Nomo completely dominated hitters in June and July, going 8-1 with a 1.36 ERA over that span. Included was a stretch of six games in which he struck out 10 or more batters five times—starting with a 16-strikeout performance on June 14 in Pittsburgh. Fans certainly couldn't expect him to pitch that well forever. Here is Nomo's month-by-month pitching breakdown for 1995:

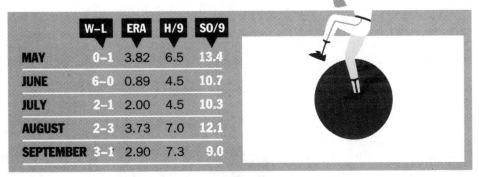

	W–L	ERA	H/9	SO/9
MAY	0–1	3.82	6.5	13.4
JUNE	6–0	0.89	4.5	10.7
JULY	2–1	2.00	4.5	10.3
AUGUST	2–3	3.73	7.0	12.1
SEPTEMBER	3–1	2.90	7.3	9.0

But did teams *really* catch up to Nomo during the season? In order to answer that question, we took a look at the opponents Nomo faced more than once last year, comparing his pitching performance during the first round of games to the subsequent rounds. Nomo faced 10 teams more than one time: the Cubs, Rockies, Marlins, Expos, Mets, Phillies, Pirates, Cardinals, Padres and Giants. Here are his totals from his first games against each of the 10 teams:

Nomo vs N.L.—First Games

GS	IP	H	W	L	ERA
10	56.2	47	3	2	4.13

Not totally impressive, now is it? But take a look at Nomo's totals for the subsequent games against each team—*after* he had seen the team a first time (and vice versa).

Nomo vs N.L.—Subsequent Games

GS	IP	H	W	L	ERA
15	115.2	66	9	3	1.79

The critics had it backwards. Hitters weren't catching up to Nomo the more they faced him—Nomo was catching up to *them*. As the data shows, a "first look" at Nomo didn't help N.L. hitters a bit last season. Take a look at the numbers in the chart to the right that hitters posted against Nomo in both sets of games.

Why aren't Nomo's August pitching numbers consistent with the rest of the data? Because two of the three "rough outings" we mentioned earlier were Nomo's first game against each team—August 15 against the Cubs and August 25 against the Phillies. He faced both clubs again in September and tore them up—allowing just two earned runs in 13.0 innings, while striking out 15.

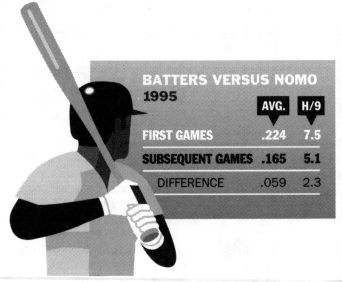

BATTERS VERSUS NOMO 1995

	AVG.	H/9
FIRST GAMES	.224	7.5
SUBSEQUENT GAMES	.165	5.1
DIFFERENCE	.059	2.3

So did *anybody* catch up to Nomo the second, third or fourth time around? Not really. In fact, Nomo's *highest* ERA in a set of "subsequent games" was 2.42 against the Mets. Might the learning curve in the majors be shorter for pitchers than for hitters? It certainly is if you're Hideo Nomo.

—Scott McDevitt

A complete listing for this category can be found on page 236.

Montreal Expos: Has Alou Changed His Style?

Expos manager Felipe Alou, in case you hadn't noticed, has had an unusual way of operating his pitching staff. . . and in particular his bullpen. Bill James identified the following Alou traits, which he described as "extremely unusual" in the 1995 *Bill James Player Ratings Book*. Those traits:

1. Alou removes his starters at the earliest sign of trouble. We keep track of what we call "quick hooks," which means removing a starter before he has pitched six innings *and* before he's given up three runs. In Alou's first two full seasons as the Montreal manager, 1993 and 1994, the Expos led the majors in quick hooks in '94 and were second in '93, just one behind the leader.

2. Alou's bullpens tend to pile up very high save totals: Montreal led the majors in saves in both 1993 and 1994.

3. Unlike many managers who save their closer for the ninth inning, Alou is not hesitant to bring in his closer earlier than that. In both 1993 and 1994, the Expos led the majors in games in which a pitcher who recorded a save worked more than one inning.

4. Alou's bullpens were predominantly right-handed, and when he brought in a relief pitcher, he didn't seem overly concerned about whether the reliever had the platoon advantage. We don't have the figures for 1993, but in 1994, Expo relievers had a platoon advantage (that is, lefty vs. lefty or righty vs. righty) against the first hitter only 45.9 percent of the time, the lowest percentage in the majors.

In 1995, there was a big change in the Montreal bullpen: ace closer John Wetteland was dealt to the Yankees prior to the season, with set-up man Mel Rojas becoming the primary finisher. With Wetteland gone and the Montreal pen not as deep as it was before, we wondered whether Alou altered his style of managing. Let's look at some figures. First, the quick hooks. Here's a list of the major league managers who had the most quick hooks during each of the last three seasons:

Quick Hooks—1993-95
1993   MIke Hargrove 35, Felipe Alou 34, Tony La Russa 31
1994   Felipe Alou 22, Jim Fregosi 17, Don Baylor 16, Tony La Russa 16
1995   Don Baylor 32, Sparky Anderson 31, Rene Lachemann 26

Here's a change right off. After finishing first or second in the majors in quick hooks in 1993 and 1994, Alou had only 20 in 1995, the 10th-highest total in the majors. Clearly Alou was more hesitant to remove a starter who was still pitching fairly well. The reason? His bullpen wasn't as deep as it was when he had Wetteland.

Now let's look at the club's save totals:

Most Saves, 1993-95

1993	Felipe Alou 61, Jim Lefebvre 56, Joe Torre 54
1994	Felipe Alou 46, Hal McRae 38, Johnny Oates 37
1995	Mike Hargrove 50, Jim Riggleman 45, Don Baylor 43

Even without Wetteland, the Expos still compiled a fairly high number of saves last year. While their save total dropped from first to a tie for fourth with 42, the Expos actually recorded a save in a slightly higher percentage of their victories (42 of 66, 64 percent) in 1995 than they did in 1994 (46 of 74, 62 percent). So there was no startling change here.

How about those saves of more than one inning? Here's the managerial top three for each of the last three years:

Saves, More Than 1 IP—1993-95

1993	Felipe Alou 30, Buck Rodgers 24, Hal McRae 20
1994	Felipe Alou 26, Dusty Baker 12, Davey Johnson 12, Hal McRae 12
1995	Lou Piniella 20, Felipe Alou 18, Davey Johnson 16

In both 1993 and 1994, Alou's Expos had far more one-plus inning saves than any other manager. The Expos were second in 1995, but considering how far ahead of the pack they were in '94, the drop was considerable. The difference? In 1993 and '94, Alou had *two* pitchers he felt could close games in Wetteland and Rojas (and indeed, both reached double figures in saves each year from 1992-94). With only Rojas around in 1995, Felipe had to hold back a little more, though he still brought in his closer earlier than most managers did.

The final category has to do with all those righties in the bullpen in 1994, which led to the Expos not getting the platoon advantage over the first hitter very often. Here's what happened in '95:

Lowest 1st-Batter Platoon Advantage for Relievers, 1994-95
1994   Felipe Alou 45.9%, Dallas Green 50.8%, Joe Torre 53.9%
1995   Cito Gaston 49.8%, Felipe Alou 53.8%, Davey Johnson 55.3%

In 1995, Alou did have some lefties in his bullpen, as Bryan Eversgerd, Gabe White and Dave Leiper were all members of the Montreal relief corps at one point or another in the season. Nonetheless, he had the second-lowest platoon advantage in the majors. His philosophy still seems to be, "I want a guy who can get people out. . . whatever hand he throws with."

Like any good manager, Alou will change his strategy to suit his personnel, and the loss of Wetteland is evident in the figures cited here. But he remains different than most managers in a couple of fundamental ways:

1. He'll still bring in his closer in the eighth much more than most managers.

2. Lefty-vs.-lefty/righty-vs.-righty doesn't matter to him when he brings in a reliever as much as his feelings about the overall ability of the pitcher.

We don't expect those traits to change much in 1996. But it might be nice if Alou, who's established himself as one of the sharpest skippers in the game, had a little better personnel to maneuver with than he did in 1995.

— Don Zminda

New York Mets: How Do Their Hurlers Compare With '69?

In the final hours before last season's July 31 trade deadline, the New York Mets dealt veteran pitcher Bret Saberhagen to Colorado, ending weeks of speculation that Saberhagen would be sent to a playoff contender. The Mets drove a hard bargain, insisting that they receive rookie righthander Juan Acevedo as compensation. Though Acevedo was hit hard in his tenure with the Rockies in 1995, some considered him the best pitcher in the Eastern League in 1994. That's quite a statement when you consider that two of the Mets' own top prospects, Jason Isringhausen and Bill Pulsipher, pitched in that league.

With the addition of Acevedo (26), the Mets now have five starting pitchers in the organization that will be between 22 and 26 years old during the 1996 season (age as of July 1). Bobby Jones (26) is the "veteran" of the quintet, having pitched two full seasons in the bigs. Bill Pulsipher (22) and Jason Isringhausen (23) were both highly-touted prospects that made their big-league debuts in 1995. And Paul Wilson (23) is a grade-A prospect who should make the jump from Triple-A in 1996.

All of this quality young pitching reminded us of another Mets club loaded with young pitching: the Amazin' Mets of 1969. Heading into the 1969 season, those Mets also had five starters between 22 and 26 years old in the organization. You may remember these guys: Tom Seaver (24 in 1969), Jerry Koosman (26), Nolan Ryan (22), Gary Gentry (22), and Jim McAndrew (25). The 1969 club did get 21 starts from then 33-year-old Don Cardwell, much as the '96 Mets should get some starts from Pete Harnisch, but we thought it would be fun to concentrate on the young pitchers.

What had the five youngsters on the '69 staff accomplished heading into that season? For a detailed look at their careers through 1969, you can consult the appendix, but only Seaver and Koosman had established themselves as major league stars by that point in their careers. The Sporting News' *Official Baseball Guide for 1970* didn't seem to think much of Gentry, McAndrew and Ryan; it described the 1969 Mets as a bunch of unknown kids: "Outside of maybe Tom Seaver and Jerry Koosman and perhaps Cleon Jones, there wasn't a regular on the club that any other team coveted." In 1968, Seaver and Koosman were a combined 35-24 for a ninth-place club that finished 73-89. They accounted for almost half of the Mets' victories, and a little math tells us that the club's winning percentage without them was just .369. Seaver and Koosman had both enjoyed success at the major league level heading into the '69 season, and built on that success. Koosman went 17-9 with a 2.28 ERA in 1969 while Seaver won the Cy Young award behind a 25-7 mark and 2.21 ERA.

Nolan Ryan and Jim McAndrew had both seen major league action prior to the 1969 season, though neither had spent a full season in the bigs. Gary Gentry had not seen any big-league action prior to 1969, but he was just 22 years old and had posted impressive minor league numbers.

So how do the 1996 hurlers compare? Again, their full records are in the Appendix, but of today's Mets pitchers, Bobby Jones is the only one with a full season of major league service under his belt. Jones actually has two full seasons behind him, having posted a 12-7 record and a 3.15 ERA in 1994 before slipping to 10-10 with a 4.19 ERA last season. Jones has not posted numbers as impressive as Seaver and Koosman had heading into the '69 season, but has been a constant in the Met rotation for the past two years, missing just one start last season.

Bill Pulsipher and Jason Isringhausen debuted in the majors last year, and both could move ahead of Jones in the 1996 rotation. Each of their minor league records are impressive. In 1995, Pulsipher joined the Mets staff in June, while Isringhausen made the jump to the bigs in July after starting in Double-A Binghamton. Along the way, Isringhausen stopped in Triple-A Norfolk long enough to collect International League Pitcher of the Year and Rookie of the Year honors. We should note that Pulsipher went down on September 11 with a strained elbow ligament, having pitched 200-plus innings for the second consecutive year.

Juan Acevedo struggled in 1995, but as we said before, some considered him the class of the Eastern League in 1994, where both Pulsipher and Isringhausen pitched.

Paul Wilson has struck out a batter an inning at every stop he's made. On top of that, he's got tremendous control. All in all, he's probably the top pitching prospect in baseball, and has more potential than anyone else on the staff. However, Wilson was 22 years old in 1995; at the same age Seaver was winning 16 games for a bad Mets club. Here's a comparison of the first two professional seasons for each pitcher:

Tom Seaver, B:R T:R, BORN: 11/17/44 (22 in 1967)

YR	TEAM	LG	W	L	G	IP	H	R	ER	TBB	SO	ERA
1966	Jacksonville	AAA	12	12	34	210.0	184	87	73	66	188	3.13
1967	Mets	MLB	16	13	35	251.0	224	85	77	78	170	2.76

Paul Wilson, B:R T:R, BORN: 03/28/1973 (22 in 1995)

YR	TEAM	LG	W	L	G	IP	H	R	ER	TBB	SO	ERA
1994	Mets	R	0	2	3	12.0	8	4	4	4	13	3.00
	St. Lucie	A	0	5	8	37.1	32	23	21	17	37	5.06
1995	Binghamton	AA	6	3	16	120.1	89	34	29	24	127	2.17
	Norfolk	AAA	5	3	10	66.1	59	25	21	20	67	2.85

On the other hand, Jason Isringhausen, probably the club's second-best pitching prospect, was much further along at the age of 22 in 1995 than Jerry Koosman was at the same age:

Jerry Koosman, B:R T:L, BORN: 12/23/1942 (22 in 1965)

YR	TEAM	LG	W	L	G	IP	H	R	ER	TBB	SO	ERA
1965	Greenville	A	5	11	27	107.0	101	70	56	56	128	4.71
	Williamsport	AA	0	2	2	12.0	11	7	5	11	11	3.75

Jason Isringhausen, B:R T:R, BORN: 09/07/1972 (22 in 1995)

YR	TEAM	LG	W	L	G	IP	H	R	ER	TBB	SO	ERA
1992	Mets	R	2	4	6	29.0	26	19	14	17	25	4.34
	Kingsport	R	4	1	7	36.0	32	22	13	12	24	3.25
1993	Pittsfield	A	7	4	15	90.1	68	45	33	28	104	3.29
1994	St. Lucie	A	6	4	14	101.0	76	31	25	27	59	2.23
	Binghamton	AA	5	4	14	92.1	78	35	31	23	69	3.02
1995	Binghamton	AA	2	1	6	41.0	26	15	13	12	59	2.85
	Norfolk	AAA	9	1	12	87.0	64	17	15	24	75	1.55
	Mets	MLB	9	2	14	93.0	88	29	29	31	55	2.81

Koosman, though, would develop rapidly. By 1968 he was in the majors for good, breaking in by going 19-12 with a 2.08 ERA. Isringhausen will have to hustle to match those numbers by 1997.

The current Mets don't yet have a Tom Seaver or a Jerry Koosman as they head to the 1996 season. None of the current crop has been dominant over the course of a full big-league season, the way Tom Seaver was as a rookie in 1967 and Koosman a year later. Those are tough acts to follow. But the current Mets do have a very talented group of starting pitchers, collectively the best young staff in baseball. Pitchers are really hard to project, especially with all the injury problems that can beset them. We can't tell if any of the Mets' current young guns will have careers as fine as Seaver's or Ryan's or Koosman's, but this staff could vault the Mets into the playoffs as early as this season. Then again, they may be a few years away. But we doubt David Lettermen will be having nearly as much fun at their expense next year.

—Drew Faust

A complete listing for this category can be found on page 237.

Philadelphia Phillies: What Happened After June 25?

Last June 25, the Philadelphia Phillies completed a successful road trip to New York and St. Louis with a 5-3 victory over the Cardinals. The win—their eighth in nine games (6-1 on the trip)—left the Phils with a record of 37-18 (the best in the National League), and a five-game lead over the second-place Atlanta Braves in the National League East race. The only club in all of baseball with a better record than the Phillies was the Cleveland Indians, and that was by a margin of just six percentage points (.679 to .673). The Phils were Phlying. . . er, flying.

Not for long. The Phils opened a seven-game home stand with a 12-3 loss to the Reds on June 27, and proceeded to drop all three games of the Cincinnati series. After breaking the losing streak with a 3-1 win over the Braves on June 30, they lost five more in a row. Then, after another victory, they lost another four straight, giving them 12 losses in 14 games. Before long the Phils were a .500 club, and then not even that. In fact, from June 26 until the end of the season, their 32-57 record was the *worst* in baseball.

What happened to the Phillies after June 25? We thought it would be helpful to look at some before-and-after figures. First, here's an overall look:

Phillies Before and After June 25

	W-L	Avg	HR/G	R/G	Opp R/G	ERA
Through 6/25	37-18	.274	0.62	4.65	3.76	3.49
6/26 to end of season	32-57	.254	0.67	4.03	5.07	4.65

You could call this "a real team effort": the dropoff affected both the offense and the pitching staff. The bigger falloff was from the mound corps, however, so let's look at the pitchers first. Here are before-and-after stats for all Phillie hurlers who worked in at least 10 games both before and after June 25:

Pitcher	Through 6/25					6/26-end				
	Gm	W	L	S	ERA	Gm	W	L	S	ERA
Toby Borland	16	0	0	1	6.86	34	1	3	5	2.55
Ricky Bottalico	22	3	1	1	1.23	40	2	2	0	3.09
Tyler Green	12	7	4	0	2.90	14	1	5	0	8.55
Michael Mimbs	10	6	1	0	3.03	25	3	6	1	5.09
Paul Quantrill	12	7	2	0	4.01	21	4	10	0	5.13
Heathcliff Slocumb	27	1	0	19	0.98	34	4	6	13	4.30
Mike Williams	10	0	1	0	3.94	23	3	2	0	2.95

Not everyone pitched worse, as both Toby Borland and Mike Williams had lower ERAs after June 25. And while Ricky Bottalico saw his ERA climb, it remained quite respectable. But the other pitchers performed much worse. Was this to be expected? Well, neither Tyler Green, Michael Mimbs, Paul Quantrill nor Heathcliff Slocumb had experienced much major league success prior to 1995, so dropoff—and probably a big one—was to be expected. While Phillie manager Jim Fregosi and pitching coach Johnny Podres are considered wizards at working with pitchers, even they have their limits. The amazing thing is probably that these guys pitched so well for as long as they did.

Now let's look at the hitters who had 100 or more at-bats both before and after June 25:

Player	Through 6/25				6/26-end			
	AB	HR	RBI	Avg	AB	HR	RBI	Avg
Darren Daulton	171	6	31	.246	171	3	24	.251
Lenny Dykstra	136	0	9	.257	118	2	9	.271
Jim Eisenreich	151	3	23	.377	226	7	32	.274
Charlie Hayes	196	6	44	.316	333	5	41	.252
Gregg Jefferies	168	4	16	.262	312	7	40	.330
Mickey Morandini	187	3	22	.289	307	3	27	.280
Kevin Stocker	155	0	18	.219	257	1	14	.218

The results here are a lot more mixed. Gregg Jefferies actually hit much better *after* June 25, and Darren Daulton, Lenny Dykstra, Mickey Morandini and Kevin Stocker didn't perform much differently after the collapse began than they did when the club was winning. Jim Eisenreich and Charlie Hayes did drop off significantly, but like most of the pitching staff, they were playing over their heads early in the season. Along with the falloff from Eisenreich and Hayes, the Phils were hampered by injuries to Daulton and Dykstra. In addition, several players who were productive prior to June 25—Mariano Duncan, Dave Gallagher and Dave Hollins—were dealt away in midseason.

Face it, the Philadelphia offense was never that great even when the Phils were winning. If their key players return to health this year, the club ought to score about as many runs as it did prior to the big slump last year. The pitching staff is a much bigger concern, unless Fregosi and Podres can pull a few more rabbits out of the hat. And that won't be easy. The *real* answer to the question of what happened after June 25 is this: the Phillies started playing down to their true level of talent.

— Don Zminda

A complete listing for this category can be found on page 239.

Pittsburgh Pirates: Is a Four-Man Rotation the Right One?

Back in the "good old days," to hear some baseball people tell it, every team in baseball had a four-man pitching rotation. In reality things were never quite that neat, but one thing *is* true: in the past 10 years or so, few clubs have attempted to use a four-man rotation.

Last year, however, two teams made a major effort to buck the trend: the Kansas City Royals and the Pittsburgh Pirates. Kansas City's experiment with a four-man rotation received a lot of attention—probably because they started the season with it, and partly because Kevin Appier was the hottest pitcher in baseball early in the year. But then Appier came down with a tender arm, the Royal staff began to struggle, and K.C. eventually ended the experiment. The Royals wound up giving their pitchers 40 starts on three days rest or less, and the numbers suggests that they would have been better off with a conventional five-man rotation:

Royals 1995 Starters by Days of Rest

Days Rest	ERA	W	L	GS	IP/S	H/9	BB/9	K/9
0-3 Days	4.55	16	15	40	6.3	9.3	3.5	6.1
4 Days	4.16	24	27	74	6.3	8.8	3.3	4.8
5+ Days	5.33	8	13	30	4.8	9.7	3.9	4.4

The Pirates' use of a four-man rotation received a lot less notice, but then who notices a club with a roster full of no-names and a 58-86 record? Maybe people *should* have paid attention to Pittsburgh's four-man experiment, however, because Jim Leyland's staff fared a whole lot better working on short rest than the Royals did. In fact, the Bucs' experience was exactly the opposite of Kansas City's; their pitchers performed *better* on three days rest or less. Much better, in fact:

Pirates 1995 Starters by Days of Rest

Days Rest	ERA	W	L	GS	IP/S	H/9	BB/9	K/9
0-3 Days	3.95	15	17	38	6.1	9.5	2.6	6.4
4 Days	5.02	14	25	71	5.9	10.3	3.0	5.3
5+ Days	5.39	10	15	35	5.2	10.4	3.6	6.7

All but one of the Pirates' short-rest starts were made by a group of six pitchers: Denny Neagle (eight starts), Esteban Loaiza (eight), Paul Wagner (seven), John Ericks (six), Jon Lieber (five) and Steve Parris (three). And as the chart shows, all but one of the pitchers, Lieber, had a lower ERA working on zero-to-three days rest than four or more.

LESS REST, MORE WINS?

	0–3 DAYS REST			4 DAYS REST			5+ DAYS REST		
	GS	W–L	ERA	GS	W–L	ERA	GS	W–L	ERA
John Ericks	6	2–3	3.35	8	0–3	5.44	4	1–3	5.32
Esteban Loaiza	8	5–1	4.74	17	2–6	4.75	6	1–2	8.37
Jon Lieber	5	2–3	9.26	3	1–1	4.86	4	0–3	6.97
Denny Neagle	8	4–2	2.10	17	6–4	4.09	6	3–2	3.40
Steve Parris	3	1–1	2.84	7	3–4	6.05	5	2–1	6.33
Paul Wagner	7	1–6	3.61	12	2–4	5.35	6	1–4	5.29
TEAM	38	15–17	3.95	71	14–25	5.02	35	10–15	5.39

Jim Leyland's first experiment with a four-man rotation came at the start of the year, and it was pretty much a complete failure. Lieber, Wagner, Neagle and Loaiza started the season's first four games; then on May 1, Wagner became the first Pirate starter to work on three days rest. He lost, 4-0. The next day Leyland gave Neagle a shot on short rest, and Neagle got knocked out after four innings (though the Pirates came back to win, 7-6). Loaiza was next, and he too got shelled, giving up 11 hits and eight runs in three and a third innings.

Leyland wasn't ready to give up, however. He waited a few days, then gave Lieber a start on three days rest on May 9. Once again, the results were terrible: five innings, six earned runs, as the Bucs got rolled by the Astros, 13-6. So Leyland put the idea on hold again. Wagner, the next pitcher to start on three days rest, also pitched poorly—five innings, four runs at Los Angeles on May 15. However, Leyland came right back and gave Neagle a short-rest start the next night, and finally it worked: Neagle was brilliant, working seven shutout innings in what was perhaps the best-pitched game the Bucs had gotten all year up to that point. However, Leyland didn't seem to like the way pitching on short rest was working for his staff as a whole, so he ended the four-man experiment. . . temporarily.

Leyland gave the four-man rotation another chance in early June, and this time it worked. He began by giving Lieber a start on three days rest at Colorado on June 3. Once again the results were terrible: four innings, nine hits, five runs. But he came back with Wagner on short rest the next night, and though the Bucs lost, Wagner pitched pretty well—six innings, three runs, which is fine work at Coors Field. Then the Pirates went to Cincinnati, and Neagle, working on three days rest for the first time since that brilliant start at Dodger Stadium, was sharp again—seven innings and two earned runs. The next night Loaiza, also on three days rest, pitched seven one-hit innings (though the Bucs eventually lost this one as well, 2-1), and a day later Lieber went seven solid innings on short rest as the Pirates won, 7-3, to break a five-game losing streak. The four-man was working at last.

Leyland continued to use his pitchers frequently on three days rest for most of June, and he made sure to give plenty of opportunities to Neagle. On June 19, 23 and 27, Neagle made consecutive starts on three days rest, and won all three games. He permitted only three earned runs in 24 innings in those starts, including a two-hit shutout against the Expos in the middle game. Overall, Neagle made five starts on three days rest in June, going 3-2 (the two losses were by scores of 3-2 and 5-4) with a 2.15 ERA.

But strangely enough, Leyland gave Neagle only one more short-rest start the rest of the season, on July 29 against the Mets at Shea. Neagle was once again outstanding, working seven shutout innings. But except for a short flurry of short-rest starts in early August—by pitchers *other* than Neagle this time—Leyland didn't give his pitchers more than a very occasional start on three days rest over the rest of the season.

Why did Leyland *not* use a four-man rotation more often, given the success he seemed to be having with the system? The main reason was that he decided to drop Wagner and Lieber from the rotation and replace them with John Ericks and Steve Parris, two rookies whom he didn't want to overwork. Both pitchers had a history of arm troubles.

Given the success of the tactic, it seems likely that the Bucs will use it again this season, at least temporarily. While it might be risky to stick with a four-man rotation for an entire year, judicious use—for a total of about 40 starts or so over the course of the season, but never for more than two or three weeks at a time—would help minimize the risk of overworking the staff, and might help improve the staff's overall effectiveness.

— Don Zminda

A complete listing of this category can be found on page 240.

St. Louis Cardinals: How Will La Russa Fare in the N.L.?

A year ago in this book, we detailed the Cardinals' recent struggles, and concluded that the club is in the middle of its worst decade (so far) since the 1910s. Their 62-81 finish in 1995 only made things worse, as the club finished last in the major leagues—by a wide margin—with 563 runs scored.

But there is hope in St. Louis for 1996. A number of solid free agents were signed, including Ron Gant and Gary Gaetti. And perhaps even better, the Cardinals signed Tony La Russa to guide the club through its turnaround efforts. If history is any guide, they could hardly have found a better man for the job. La Russa has taken over two teams in the middle of a season, and in both cases the results were immediately positive. The chart below lists the team's record the season before he arrived (Year 0), along with their record in La Russa's first season with the new club, both before and after he got there, along with his overall record with that team.

Team	Years	Year 0	Year 1 Before	Year 1 After	Totals w/Team
White Sox	1979-1986	71-90	46-60	27-27	522-510
Athletics	1986-1995	77-85	31-52	45-34	798-673

With both the White Sox and the Athletics, La Russa joined franchises in the doldrums, immediately turned the club around, and wound up posting winning records over a number of seasons. Of course, this bodes well for Cardinal fans.

But maybe La Russa is in for a different experience in the National League. Ask any N.L. partisan, and he'll tell you: "It's a lot tougher to manage in the National League than the American." The lack of a designated hitter means double-switches and pinch hitting and all that. Shoot, when Whitey Herzog was running the Cards, he even played his pitchers in the outfield.

We're not sure we buy it, but it did get us to wondering, especially in regard to Tony La Russa: Might an American League manager switching to the National face at least a temporary disadvantage? To answer that question, we first identified all the managers who served in the American League, then switched to the National anytime after 1973. Why 1973? That was the first year of the designated hitter.

In the chart below, "Year 0" refers to the team's record in the season before the new manager arrived, "Year 1" is his first season, and "Year 2" is his second. The averages at the bottom of the chart reflect a typical winning percentage for a full 162-game season.

Manager	Year 0	Year 1	Year 2
George Bamberger	41-62	65-97	16-30
Steve Boros	83-79	74-88	--
Pat Corrales	59-48	89-73	43-42
Jim Fregosi	77-85	74-75	70-92
Jim Frey	71-91	96-65	77-84
Whitey Herzog	86-76	97-78	92-70
Jim LeFebvre	77-83	78-84	84-78
Jack McKeon	65-97	67-48	89-73
Gene Michael	77-84	46-56	68-68
Lou Piniella	75-87	91-71	74-88
Frank Robinson	75-86	56-55	87-75
Buck Rodgers	78-83	84-77	78-83
Jeff Torborg	77-84	72-90	13-25
Tom Trebelhorn	84-78	49-64	--
Averages	77-85	82-80	80-82

We should first note the two major success stories of these league-switching skippers. In 1982, Herzog won a World Series with the Cardinals (here, we combined his 1980 and '81 partial seasons for our Year 1). And in 1990, then-Reds manager Lou Piniella duplicated Herzog's feat. Those successes are balanced by a pair of failures, as neither Steve Boros nor Tom Trebelhorn were asked back for a second season.

Overall, the average team went 77-85 the season before the ex-A.L. manager arrived, then improved five games in his first season. Neither figure is really a surprise. The clubs changed managers after subpar seasons, then improved slightly the next season. All teams tend to rebound from poor seasons with better ones, and vice versa.

So the numbers suggest that managers moving from the American League to the National improve by five games, which isn't too bad. But we really can't draw any conclusions from this without some context. Perhaps the average new manager improves his team by *nine* games rather than five. To provide that context, we identified all new N.L. managers since 1973 (who lasted at least half of Year 1), not including those already considered. That's our control group, and it's a big one: 50 managers, and 67 seasons (some managers took over N.L. teams more than once). Let's compare the averages of the league-switching managers with the control group:

Managers	Year 0	Year 1	Year 2
A.L. to N.L.	77-85	82-80	80-82
Control Group	75-87	77-85	80-82

That five-game improvement looks a bit more impressive now, as the control group improved by only two games in the first year of the new manager. On the other hand, by Year 2 they were even, record-wise, with the control group actually improving by two more games overall.

Conclusion? There doesn't seem to be any learning curve for managers switching from the American League to the National, designated hitter or not. This is suggested further by the Year 2 results. If there *was* a learning curve, you would expect the ex-A.L. managers to improve the team some in Year 1, then more so in Year 2 after they figured out the different strategies. But that's not what has happened. Instead, the league switchers have actually *declined* by two games in their second season, while the control group improved by three.

What does all this mean for La Russa? It would be a bit silly to say he'll improve the St. Louis record by five games. (Cardinal fans are hoping for a lot more, and given the club's offseason moves that seems fairly likely.) It does suggest that La Russa should have little trouble adjusting to the National League. He's a pretty smart guy, and frankly, baseball strategy isn't as complicated as they'd sometimes have you believe. In either league.

— Rob Neyer

San Diego Padres: Can Gwynn Keep Winning Batting Crowns?

The Padres have had their ups and downs, but the club has one constant: Tony Gwynn. Last year, at the age of 35, Gwynn won his sixth N.L. batting title with a .368 average. Only Ty Cobb (12), Honus Wagner (8), Rogers Hornsby, Stan Musial and Rod Carew (7 each) have won more batting championships than Gwynn. The obvious question is this: can Gwynn win another title or two before he's through. . . like in 1996, maybe?

At first glance, the odds would appear to be against it. Gwynn will turn 36 in May, and only five players have won batting titles at age 36 or older— including Ted Williams, who did it twice. Here's the list:

Batting Championships at Age 36 and Older

Year	League	Player	Avg	Age
1958	American	Ted Williams	.328	39
1957	American	Ted Williams	.388	38
1911	National	Honus Wagner	.334	37
1990	American	George Brett	.329	37
1957	National	Stan Musial	.351	36
1943	American	Luke Appling	.328	36

It's a select group, but there's no reason to think that Gwynn, one of the top hitters for average in major league history, couldn't accomplish what Williams, Wagner and Brett did. Then there's Gwynn's recent performance. Over the last three years he's batted .358, .394 and .368, for an incredible three-year average of .372. Here are the highest combined averages in the 33-to-35 group:

Highest 3-Year Batting Averages, Age 33-35

Player	Years	Avg
Sam Thompson	1893-95	.388
Ty Cobb	1920-22	.377
Tris Speaker	1921-23	.373
Tony Gwynn	**1993-95**	**.372**
Bill Terry	1930-32	.367
Lefty O'Doul	1930-32	.363
Ed Delahanty	1901-03	.360
Rogers Hornsby	1929-31	.357
Honus Wagner	1907-09	.348
Jack Fournier	1923-25	.345
Eddie Collins	1920-22	.345

(Minimum 1,200 PA)

Big Sam Thompson, who leads the group, saw his average drop to .298 in 1896, when he was 36. However, Ty Cobb and Tris Speaker, the only other players to post a higher average than Gwynn from age 33 to 35, batted .340 and .344, respectively, when they were 36. Gwynn seems capable of hitting at least that high in 1996, and if he does, another batting crown would be a strong possibility.

One more list offers hope that Gwynn can notch another batting title this year. We found a total of 12 players who hit .340 or better at the age of 36. Here's the list:

.340+ Avg at Age 36

Player	Year	Avg
Zack Wheat	1924	.375
Babe Ruth	1931	.373
Eddie Collins	1923	.360
Ted Williams	1955	.356
Stan Musial	1957	.351
Dan Brouthers	1894	.347
Tris Speaker	1924	.344
Cap Anson	1888	.344
Wade Boggs	1994	.342
Lave Cross	1902	.342
Roberto Clemente	1971	.341
Ty Cobb	1923	.340

(Minimum 400 PA)

No reason why Gwynn can't join this group. And since only three National Leaguers hit .340 or better last year—Gwynn, Mike Piazza and Dante Bichette—you'd have to give him one heck of chance to notch that seventh batting title in 1996.

— Don Zminda

A complete listing for this category can be found on page 241.

San Francisco Giants: Is Bonds the Best Clutch Hitter?

Who's the best clutch hitter in baseball? It depends on your definition of "clutch," of course. But two situations are usually considered sound measurements of clutch-hitting ability: hitting in the late innings of close games, and hitting with runners in scoring position. You should also consider pennant-race and postseason performance, and we'll get into that in due course. But let's begin by looking at our two regular-season categories.

We begin by examining what we call "Late & Close" situations. They occur when (1) the game is in the seventh inning or later, and (2) the batting team is either leading by one run, tied, or is trailing with the potential tying run on base. It's very similar to a save situation for a relief pitcher. Using on-base plus slugging percentage (OBP+SLG)—a simple but extremely effective measure of a player's offensive contributions—as our benchmark, here is a list of the top 10 hitters over the last five seasons (1991-1995) in Late & Close situations:

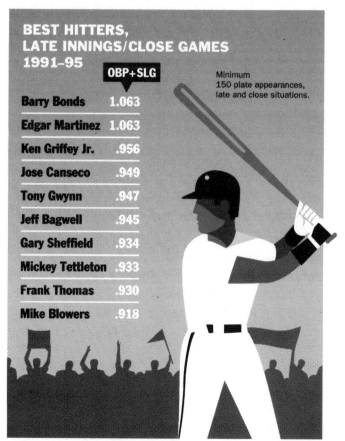

BEST HITTERS, LATE INNINGS/CLOSE GAMES 1991-95

Minimum 150 plate appearances, late and close situations.

	OBP+SLG
Barry Bonds	1.063
Edgar Martinez	1.063
Ken Griffey Jr.	.956
Jose Canseco	.949
Tony Gwynn	.947
Jeff Bagwell	.945
Gary Sheffield	.934
Mickey Tettleton	.933
Frank Thomas	.930
Mike Blowers	.918

Remarkably, there was a tie for the top spot between two of the best hitters in baseball today: Edgar Martinez of the Mariners and Barry Bonds of the Giants. But should one of the two be given the edge? Here's a detailed breakdown of how they performed late & close:

Bonds vs. Martinez, Late Innings/Close Games, 1991-95

Player	AB	H	2B	3B	HR	RBI	BB	SO	Avg	OBP	SLG
Bonds	402	126	30	2	29	92	102	68	.313	.449	.614
Martinez	284	105	26	1	9	61	73	39	.370	.500	.563

Two pretty incredible performances here. Over the last five years Martinez has recorded an amazing .370 batting average under late-inning pressure, and reached base in fully half of his plate appearances. Bonds has a big edge in power, however, and he recorded his figures over a much larger number of plate appearances. So Bonds gets the nod in our estimation.

Many of the best hitters in baseball made the leaders list in this category: guys like Ken Griffey Jr., Tony Gwynn, Jeff Bagwell, Gary Sheffield, Frank Thomas. The two surprises are Mickey Tettleton—a low-average hitter, but a very dangerous one—and Mike Blowers, who was one of the surprise stars of 1995.

Gwynn, incidentally, has batted a remarkable .377 in late & close situations over the last five years, the top average in that category. Looking at Late & Close performance over the last five years strictly in terms of batting average, the top five are Gwynn (.377), Edgar Martinez (.370), Mark Grace (.342), Shawon Dunston (.338) and Kirby Puckett (.337). Why do we rate the hitters on the basis of on-base plus slugging rather than batting average? For a good reason: it correlates better with winning.

Now let's look at the top 10 hitters with runners in scoring position—again over the last five years, with the players again ranked by on-base plus slugging percentage:

Top Hitters, Runners in Scoring Position, 1991-95

Player	OBP+SLG
Barry Bonds	1.129
Frank Thomas	1.006
Mo Vaughn	1.005
Mike Piazza	.992
Gary Sheffield	.989
Mark McGwire	.976

Player	OBP+SLG
Edgar Martinez	.971
Fred McGriff	.970
Albert Belle	.970
Tim Salmon	.969

That man Bonds again, and this time there's no doubt that he's *numero uno*. Here's his batting line with men in scoring position over the last five years:

Bonds with Runners in Scoring Position, 1991-95

	AB	H	2B	3B	HR	RBI	BB	SO	AVG	OBP	SLG
Bonds	590	194	35	8	40	327	248	86	.329	.510	.619

Wow. Opposing teams will let Bonds take a walk whenever they can get away with it, but they can't walk him ALL the time. Too bad for them.

Bonds' .329 batting average with men in scoring position over the last five years, incidentally, was the fifth best overall. The top four: Tony Gwynn .356, Paul Molitor .350, Mike Piazza .340, B.J. Surhoff .330. Obviously, if you just need a hit—any kind of hit, at any time—Tony Gwynn is your man.

So who's the best clutch hitter overall? Bonds obviously has the edge in the two categories we looked at, but remember that we also wanted to consider performance under pennant-race and postseason pressure. That's where Bonds runs into problems. Without a doubt, he's been a dud in three league championship Series (.191 average, three RBI in 68 at-bats). So let's just make him a finalist for now, along with these players:

Edgar Martinez. Martinez made the top 10 in both clutch categories. He offered still more evidence of his clutch ability with his performances in last year's A.L. West pennant race, and then with an awesome performance in Seattle's Division Series victory over the Yankees. Martinez did have a horrid LCS against the Indians (2-for-23, no RBI), but things like that can —and often do—happen in a short series.

Fred McGriff. When he was with the Blue Jays a few years ago, McGriff was considered a suspect clutch hitter. No more. He made the top 15 in both our clutch categories, and embellished his reputation as a clutch performer with a solid performance in the Braves' drive to the world championship last year (.333 postseason average, four home runs).

Frank Thomas. One of the great offensive forces in the game, Thomas made the top 10 in both clutch categories. He also hit .353 in his only postseason series in 1993. Some people say he's "too selective" in RBI situations, but if that's true, how come he drives in so many runs?

Tony Gwynn. Baseball's ultimate hit machine, and a strong performer in our clutch categories. Gwynn has had only one taste of postseason action, way back in 1984, with mixed results—great LCS (.368), so-so World Series (.263, no RBI or extra-base hits). Let's hope he gets at least one more chance before his great career is over.

Ken Griffey Jr. Strong in our two clutch categories, and a great performer in his first taste of postseason action last fall (.364-6-9). And he's staying in Seattle. What's not to like?

Gary Sheffield. A dark-horse candidate. Sheffield gets hurt a lot, and spending his career playing for lousy teams, he hasn't been in the spotlight much. But he's a fabulous hitter whenever he's in the lineup, and he ranked in the top seven in both our clutch categories. One of these years it figures to all come together for him.

Paul Molitor. Didn't make either one of our leaders lists, but he performed respectably in both. Mostly however, he deserves consideration as a great clutch hitter because of a fantastic postseason record which includes a .418 average in two World Series.

All these players are worthy candidates, but for us it came down to five: Bonds, Griffey, Martinez, Molitor and Thomas. Any one of them would have been a worthy choice as the man you'd most like to have at bat with a game on the line. But despite his postseason struggles, we felt Bonds' performance over the long haul was simply too impressive to ignore. And anyway, how do you think those Pirate clubs of his *reached* the postseason?

— Don Zminda

A complete listing for this category can be found on page 242.

II. GENERAL BASEBALL QUESTIONS

Which Managers Use the Hit-and-Run Most Effectively?

A manager wears many hats: press liaison, team psychologist, part-time hitting coach, lineup deviser. . . but by far, the most visible of all the manager's chores relate to in-game strategy: pitching changes, stolen bases, bunts, hit-and-runs, etc. The successful hit-and-run, in particular, is beloved by baseball broadcasters everywhere. But when was the last time you saw actual stats on the hit-and-run? Well, here they are. . .

First, let's look at the managers who enjoyed the best success rates when calling for the hit-and-run. For our purposes, a success is when a hit-and-run play results in the baserunner advancement with no double play.

Manager	Team	Attempts	Success%
Bruce Bochy	Padres	108	52.8
Bobby Cox	Braves	64	50.0
Buck Showalter	Yankees	47	46.8
Dallas Green	Mets	83	43.4
Tom Kelly	Twins	109	43.1
Mike Jorgensen	Cardinals	47	42.6
Terry Collins	Astros	130	40.8
Phil Garner	Brewers	67	40.3
Kevin Kennedy	Red Sox	57	38.6
Phil Regan	Orioles	70	38.6

Most of the names at the top of the list are probably no surprise; Cox, Showalter, Green and Kelly are all considered among baseball's best managers. But Padre skipper Bruce Bochy? Though he's a fairly well-kept secret, Bochy is also one of the more intelligent men in the game.

Who called the most hit-and-run plays last season? Houston's Terry Collins, who called for 130 hit-and-runs and succeeded at a solid 40.8 percent rate. Who signaled for the fewest? In the entire season, Blue Jay skipper Cito Gaston called for 20 hit-and-runs (and was successful on only five of them). Gaston's minimalist style was okay when the club was winning, but now that they're losing, he might need to take a more active role.

In addition to how often they call for the hit-and-run, we might also look at *when* managers call the hit-and-run. The chart below shows the most popular hit-and-run counts, based on popularity:

Favorite Hit-and-Run Counts

Count	Managers' Favorite
2-1	16
1-1	5
2-2	4
1-0	3
0-0	1
0-1	1

Obviously, 2-1 was the favorite hit-and-run count. The reasoning, I guess, is that the pitcher has to throw a strike on that count or risk going 3-1. Why not hit-and-run with a 3-1 count (or 3-0 or 2-0), when the pitcher knows he *really* has to throw a strike? Because at 3-1, you're better off looking for a walk than risking a baserunner. Which two managers seriously flouted convention, frequently calling for the hit-and-run on zero-ball counts? Colorado's Don Baylor favored the first-pitch strategy, while White Sox skipper Gene Lamont's favorite hit-and-run count was 0-1. Gee, and we thought he was fired because of that pitching staff. . .

— Rob Neyer

A complete listing for this category can be found on page 243.

Which Umps *Already* Speed Up the Game?

With attendance slumping and television ratings dropping in recent years, baseball's been criticized for being too "slow and boring" to appeal to today's revved-up sports fans. We don't necessarily agree with that criticism; I mean, did you ever notice how long the Super Bowl lasts? However, nobody asked us, and at the All-Star break last year, the major leagues instituted a few changes designed to hurry up the pace of the games. Though early reports indicated the changes had little or no effect, game times *did* decline in 1995. The average time of a nine-inning American League game dropped from 2:59 in 1994 to 2:56 in 1995, and from 2:48 to 2:45 in the N.L.

In 1996 further speed-up measures are being considered, and perhaps game times will continue to decline. But there's one man on the field in every game who *already* has a big effect on the pace of the game: the home-plate umpire. We thought it might be fun to return to a subject we discussed a couple of years ago, which is how game times vary according to the plate umpire.

Let's look at the American League first. Over the last five seasons, here are the fastest and slowest average game times for plate umpires (minimum 100 games umpired):

Average Game Times, AL Umps—1991-95

Fastest		Slowest	
Tim Welke	2:49	Rick Reed	2:59
Ken Kaiser	2:50	Jim Evans	2:58
Dale Ford	2:51	Larry Young	2:58
10 at	2:52	Rocky Roe	2:58

(Minimum 100 games as plate umpire)

A.L. game times tend to be significantly slower than N.L. games—about 10 minutes per game in recent years. The biggest reason for that is higher scoring due to the DH, but if you regularly watched games from both leagues, as we do, you'd probably agree there's more to it than that. American League games seem more *leisurely*, somehow. . . maybe it's the influence of guys like Pudge Fisk and Mike "The Human Rain Delay" Hargrove. But as you can see from the chart, there's a big difference between a game that Tim (the Swift) Welke umpires and one featuring Rick "Pokey" Reed behind the plate. An umpire *can* push the pace if he sets his mind to it, even in the A.L. One factor is the size of the ump's strike zone:

the guys with the slower game times are often umpires whose small strike zones result in a lot of walks.

Here's a chart showing the fastest and slowest N.L. umps over the last five seasons:

Game Times, NL Umps—1991-95

Fastest		Slowest	
Frank Pulli	2:41	Jerry Crawford	2:50
Mark Hirschbeck	2:42	Gerry Davis	2:49
Eric Gregg	2:43	Charlie Reliford	2:49
Joe West	2:44	John McSherry	2:48
Bob Davidson	2:44	Bruce Froemming	2:48

A game umpired by Frank Pulli moves along at a pace that seems out of the 1970s; he's a good nine minutes faster than the slowest N.L. ump, Jerry Crawford, and nearly *20* minutes faster than the slowest A.L umpires.

Chances are that if Pulli umpired an American League game, his average game times would slow down considerably. Even so, he might be able to push the pace of the game better than most A.L. umpires do. We may well find out over the next few years, if the proposed inter-league play comes in. Chances are that, at first, games in American League parks will feature both the DH *and* an A.L. ump behind the plate. But if that changes, it'll be fascinating to see what happens to those game times. Fast or slow, though, we can promise you that *we'll* be watching.

— Don Zminda

A complete listing for this category can be found on page 244.

Who Had the Best Months of the Year?

A month can seem like a year when a player is especially hot—or cold. Either you don't want it to end, or you can't *wait* for it to end. Baseball—and life—can be like that.

Our annual survey of the best monthly performances of 1995 begins with the hitters who posted the highest batting average in each month (we won't count April or October, since only a couple of games were played in each month):

Best Averages by Month—1995

Player, Team	Month	AVG	OBP	SLG	AB	R	H	HR	RBI
Jim Eisenreich, Phi	May	.406	.475	.580	69	11	28	1	14
Ryan Klesko, Atl	June	.435	.481	.841	69	12	30	7	22
Garret Anderson, Cal	July	.410	.422	.686	105	22	43	7	31
Brad Ausmus, SD	Aug	.424	.514	.627	59	13	25	2	15
Tony Gwynn, SD	Sept	.407	.442	.513	113	19	46	1	15

(Minimum 75 plate appearances)

No player could hit .400 for the year, but 11 players *did* hit .400 for a month, including this quintet. Ryan Klesko's June looks like the month of the year from this list. But it wasn't. More on *that* subject later.

Now for the pitchers (starters only) who had the lowest ERAs in each month:

Best ERAs by Month—1995

Pitcher, Team	Month	ERA	W	L	IP	H	BB	K
Kenny Rogers, Tex	May	0.65	5	1	41.1	32	15	32
Hideo Nomo, LA	June	0.89	6	0	50.1	25	16	60
Greg Maddux, Atl	July	1.27	4	0	49.2	33	5	49
Mike Mussina, Bal	Aug	1.15	3	2	47.0	36	10	35
Greg Maddux, Atl	Sept	0.29	4	0	31.0	21	3	29

(Minimum 25 innings)

Some truly awesome performances here, headed by Kenny Rogers' May, Hideo Nomo's June and Greg Maddux' September (he wasn't too shabby in July, either). We'll get into more detail on that trio later.

Batting average and ERA aren't the only categories that define a good month, of course. We thought we'd show you the leaders in each significant hitting category, so we can better decide who *really* had the best months of the year.

On-Base Average. Edgar Martinez, August, .560; Edgar Martinez, June, .537; Frank Thomas, May, .529; Jim Thome, August, .523; Brad Ausmus, August, .514. Edgar Martinez, we say in the Seattle essay, was arguably the best player in the American League last year—Albert Belle and Mo Vaughn notwithstanding. You can get an idea of what we're talking about when you look at his awesome OBPs in June and August. In August, when Seattle was starting to climb back into the A.L. West race—with minimal help from Ken Griffey, Jr.—Edgar batted .398, slugged .786, hit nine homers, drove in 33 runs, and drew 31 walks. So was *that* the best month of the year? We'll see.

Slugging Average. Albert Belle, Sept., .938; Albert Belle, August, .847; Mark McGwire, September, .845; Ryan Klesko, June, .841; Matt Williams, May, .811. Like Babe Ruth, who hit 17 homers in September of 1927 to reach 60 for the year, Albert Belle hit 17 homers in September of 1995 to push him to 50 for the season. He also slugged an amazing .938 that month. The best month? Well, overall Belle was probably even better in August, when he had a .381 average, a .456 OBP, 14 homers and 30 RBI along with that .847 slugging average.

Hits. Lance Johnson, July, 47; Tony Gwynn, September, 46; Mike Piazza, August, 46; Bernie Williams, August, 46; 4 with 45. Some great months here, though no candidates for the best overall. Lance Johnson's July was the start of an amazing second half.

Doubles. Mark Grace, June, 19; Jose Canseco, August, 14; Albert Belle, August, 13; Ray Lankford, May, 13; 5 with 12. At midseason, it seemed possible that Mark Grace of the Cubs might actually break one of baseball's most imposing records, Earl Webb's 67 doubles in 1931. He didn't make it, but he did lead the National League with 51.

Triples. Lance Johnson, September, 6; Kenny Lofton, August, 5; Roberto Alomar, June, 5; 8 with 4. Johnson made a great late bid to lead the A.L. in triples for a record-shattering fifth straight year. He fell short on the last day when Kenny Lofton of the Indians hit a three-bagger to top him by one.

Homers. Albert Belle, September, 17; Albert Belle, August, 14; Jay Buhner, September, 13; 4 with 12. Dueling Belles, but as we've said, August was really a better month for him, as he hit "only" .309 in September.

Wonder how many times we'll get updates this year on how many homers Albert has hit since August 1, 1995?

RBI. Dante Bichette, July, 35; Jim Edmonds, July, 34; Sammy Sosa, August, 33; Edgar Martinez, August, 33; Mike Blowers, August, 33. Altitude or not, Dante Bichette had a great month of July. So did Jim Edmonds of the Angels, who put California in charge of the A.L. West race—for a while—with his big month.

Stolen Bases. Kenny Lofton, September, 20-for-24; Otis Nixon, September, 16-for-21; Delino DeShields, September, 14-for-16; 5 with 13. A stolen-base salary drive? Kenny Lofton and Otis Nixon battled down the stretch with Tom Goodwin of the Royals for the A.L. stolen-base crown. Lofton's big finish gave him the title by four.

Wins. Hideo Nomo, June, 6-0; Tim Wakefield, July, 6-0; 5 with 5-0. Nomo-mania was at its apex in June, when the Dodger rookie went 6-0 with an 0.89 ERA. The *pitching* month of the year? Well. . .

Strikeouts. Randy Johnson, May, 62; Randy Johnson, June, 61; Hideo Nomo, June, 60; Hideo Nomo; August, 55; 2 with 54. Johnson and Nomo had this category pretty much all to themselves. But that was the case all year long, as they ranked one-two in the majors in Ks.

Enough teasing. We picked three candidates for the best month of the 1995 season by a hitter:

Best-Hitting Months of the Year

Hitter	Month	AVG	OBP	SLG	AB	R	H	2B	3B	HR	RBI	BB
Matt Williams	May	.405	.451	.811	111	23	45	7	1	12	31	10
Albert Belle	Aug	.381	.456	.847	118	28	45	13	0	14	30	16
Edgar Martinez	Aug	.398	.560	.786	98	31	39	11	0	9	33	31

Hard not to pick Belle, but Martinez had a higher average, more RBI *and* that amazing on-base average in the very same month. Edgar gets the nod.

The pitching candidates:

Best-Pitching Months of the Year

Pitcher	Month	ERA	W	L	G	GS	CG	ShO	IP	H	HR	BB	SO
Kenny Rogers	May	0.65	5	1	6	6	1	1	41.1	32	1	15	32
Hideo Nomo	June	0.89	6	0	6	6	2	2	50.1	25	2	16	60
Greg Maddux	Sept	0.29	4	0	5	5	1	1	31.0	21	0	3	29

Kenny Rogers had a fabulous month of May, finishing with a streak of 33 straight scoreless innings, but our choice came down to Nomo and Maddux. Nomo began the month of June by allowing one run on two hits in eight innings against the Mets. After three more wins in which he permitted only four earned runs and 15 hits in 24.1 innings, fanned 16 Pirates in eight innings in one of the outings and went eight or more innings each time out, he finished the month with back-to-back shutouts—a two-hitter and a six-hitter with 13 strikeouts in each game. The only pitcher who could challenge a month like that was—of course—Maddux, who permitted only one run in 31 September innings. Hard to pick against that, but Nomo gets the nod because of his heavier workload and all-around brilliance.

And now, the booby prize—the *worst* performances in each month of 1995:

Worst Months of 1995

Month	Hitter, Team	AVG	HR	RBI	Pitcher, Team	W	L	ERA
May	J.R. Phillips, SF	.105	3	7	Danny Darwin, Tor	1	4	9.47
June	Chris Hoiles, Bal	.134	3	6	Roger Pavlik, Tex	1	2	9.72
July	Kevin Bass, Bal	.147	0	1	Mark Portugal, Cin-SF	0	5	8.77
Aug	Tony Tarasco, Mon	.151	1	3	Mike Moore, Det	0	5	9.00
Sept	Chris Gomez, Det	.161	1	9	Tavo Alvarez	1	3	8.42

Mike Moore didn't even make it to the end of the year after that horrible August, and Danny Darwin didn't fare much better. And J.R. Phillips basically played himself out of a job he'd had handed to him with his dismal May performance. To these players—and their teams—a month really *did* seem like a year.

— Don Zminda

A complete listing for this category can be found on page 245.

How Often Does a Leadoff Walk Really Score?

The home pitcher walks the first batter of the inning. Inevitably, the home-town broadcaster lets out a loud sigh and proceeds to tell the audience at home that these leadoff walks almost always score (veteran fans will remember pitcher-turned-announcer Waite Hoyt moaning, "Oh, those bases on balls!" during Cincinnati Reds broadcasts). But how often *does* a leadoff walk actually result in a run scoring? And is a leadoff walk any more likely to result in a run than if the leadoff man reached base by some other means?

To find the answer, we took all leadoff walk occurrences from 1995 and found out exactly how many times they scored for each pitcher in the majors. We then looked at how often a leadoff man scored if he reached first base by another means. Here are the figures:

Leadoff Man Reaches 1st Base, 1995

	Times	Scored	Percent
Leadoff Walk	2,851	1,099	38.5
Leadoff Other OB	6,918	2,685	38.8

A leadoff walk scored close to 40 percent of the time, which is pretty damaging. But the pitcher was in trouble *any* time the leadoff man got on; the figures show that a leadoff walk is no more damaging than a leadoff single, hit by pitch, error, etc.

Here's a list of the pitchers who allowed the most leadoff walks in 1995, along with how often they scored:

Most Walks to Lead Off an Inning, 1995

Pitcher, Team	BB	Scored	Pct
Al Leiter, Tor	31	6	19.4
Wilson Alvarez, WSox	27	8	29.6
Tim Wakefield, Bos	25	10	40.0
Jason Bere, WSox	24	15	62.5
Jack McDowell, Yanks	23	6	26.1
Darryl Kyle, Hou	22	11	50.0
John Smoltz, Atl	22	8	36.4
Pedro Martinez, Mon	22	6	27.3
Sterling Hitchcock, Yanks	20	7	35.0
Pat Rapp, Fla	19	7	36.8
Kevin Gross, Tex	19	7	36.8

No pitcher gave up more leadoff walks last year than lefthander Al Leiter, at the time a member of the Blue Jays but now a Florida Marlin. It would figure that Leiter would have problems with leadoff walks, since he led the majors in overall walks allowed with 108. But Leiter wasn't hurt all that much by the walks, as only six of them scored. That's one reason why Leiter had a quality season overall, ranking eighth in the American League with a 3.64 ERA. By contrast, Jason Bere of the White Sox gave up 24 leadoff walks last year, and 15 of them scored (62.5 percent); that's a big reason why Bere had a totally *miserable* campaign (8-15, 7.19).

As the Leiter/Bere comparison indicates, leadoff walks seem to bother some pitchers a lot more than others. For instance, Reds pitcher Kevin Jarvis allowed 11 leadoff walks last year, nine of which scored. The Cubs' Jim Bullinger allowed an identical 11 leadoff walks, but only one scored.

The always amazing Greg Maddux allowed but four leadoff walks in his National League-leading 209.2 innings pitched last year. How many of them scored? Why, none, of course. But then Maddux is sort of in a world by himself. The leadoff man reached first 44 times against Maddux last year, including those four walks. Only nine of those men eventually came around to score—a 20.5 percent scoring rate that was about half the major league average.

— Don Zminda

A complete listing for this category can be found on page 246.

What Were the Longest "Foul-Ball Wars" of 1995?

For this essay, we decided to take a look at the one question every baseball fan has been asking all winter long: which batter and pitcher produced the most consecutive foul balls in a single at-bat last year? We wrote a program that went through every pitch in the majors last year (the program ran for just over 47 hours. . . seriously) and compiled a list of every instance where a batter fouled off five or more straight pitches.

What did we find? Well, the most was nine (!), by Mark Carreon off Kevin Tapani on August 7. In the sixth inning that day, Carreon came to bat with Barry Bonds at first and no one out. After fouling off the first pitch, Carreon looked at a pitchout and then fouled off the next offering before watching Bonds get thrown out trying to steal second on ball two. The Giant first baseman then proceeded to foul off the next nine pitches before (long drum roll, please). . . grounding out to second. (You were expecting a 650-foot homer?) And thus ended the longest string of fouls in 1995. The leaders from last year:

Most Consecutive Foul Balls in an At-Bat—1995

Fouls	Date	Pitcher	Batter	Inn
9	Aug 7	Kevin Tapani, LA	Mark Carreon, SF	6th
8	Jun 18	Kent Mercker, Atl	Dante Bichette, Col	1st
8	Jun 27	Bob MacDonald, NYA	Franklin Stubbs, Det	4th
8	Jul 23	Xavier Hernandez, Cin	Brian McRae, ChN	10th
8	Aug 5	Atlee Hammaker, WSox	Carlos Baerga, Cle	6th
8	Aug 14	Mike Christopher, Det	Jeff Cirillo, Mil	7th
7	12 occasions			

Overall, there were 222 different five-or-more foul sequences. In addition to the chart above, there were 43 six-foul sequences and 161 five-foul instances. The 222 matchups were composed of 164 different batters and 161 pitchers. Doug Drabek, Mike Hampton, Bobby Jones, Omar Olivares and Bill Swift all made the cut as batters (but not as pitchers), while Scott Sanders was involved as both a batter *and* a pitcher. (Just imagine what would happen if he batted against himself!)

Bobby Witt was the only pitcher with four separate foul-ball streaks, while Joe Carter, Greg Colbrunn, Curtis Goodwin and Raul Mondesi each had four different foul-ball strings.

On July 13 in Baltimore, the Royals and Orioles produced the only game with three different foul-ball streaks, with Doug Jones & Gary Gaetti, Billy Brewer & Brady Anderson, and Jeff Montgomery & Rafael Palmeiro producing the fouls. All three came in the eighth or ninth inning.

Special mention should go out to Tony Fernandez and Kevin Tapani (again). On September 12 in Cleveland, Fernandez fouled off six straight in the second inning against Ken Hill, and then fouled off six straight again in the eighth against Alan Embree! As for Tapani, not only did he set the standard against Carreon in the August 7 game mentioned above, but in the same game he warmed up with a five-fouler to Robby Thompson in the first inning!

So what's this all mean? In the overall scheme of things, probably not a whole lot. I could probably spend a few paragraphs over-analyzing the data, trying to come up with some reason why Joe Carter shows up on this list but John Olerud doesn't, or why foul-ball streaks happen the most in the first, third and eighth innings, but are rare in the second inning (this sounds like a promising thesis for you Ph.D candidates out there. . .). But I really don't see that happening. I hope you take this data as I have—a thin but interesting slice of baseball trivia.

— Allan Spear

Who Were the Best Bargains—and Worst Buys—of '95?

Big salaries are now an accepted part of baseball, and so is the endless debate over which players are earning that money, and which ones aren't. "So-and-so is an overpaid bum," a typical caller to a sports radio station will say, "and so are all the rest of those ballplayers!" Not to disappoint anybody, but we won't be taking *that* path in this article. What we hope to do is look at the subject of salary-vs.-performance in a rational way, and try to learn something.

To compare salary with performance, we first need a measuring system which creates a scale differentiating between the 1995 performance of say, Albert Belle (.317-50-126), Roberto Alomar (.300-13-66, plus a Gold Glove), Tim Raines (.285-12-67) and David Hulse (.251-3-47). . . not to mention measuring the comparable worth of pitchers in all their various roles. Fortunately, STATS has a measuring system already in place: the point system with which we rate major leaguers for our *Bill James Fantasy Baseball* game. It rates hitters and pitchers in an intelligent and complex way, even awarding points for turning double plays or making the All-Star team. If you want to know more details about the game, we suggest you turn to the ad pages at the back of the book, where you'll find info on *BJFB*. (Who knows, you might just end up in a league. . . and win.)

To get a feel for the point system, we'll tell you that Edgar Martinez earned 714.5 *BJFB* points last year, second-most in baseball behind Albert Belle (725.5). Greg Maddux was third with 676.5 points. Of the other players we discussed at the beginning of this paragraph, Alomar earned around 500 points, Raines around 400, Hulse around 200. Some players even wound up with *negative* points, like the Tigers' Mike Moore, who was awarded -48.0 points for going 5-15 with 7.53 ERA. (Does this mean that he had to give money *to* the team? Well. . .) The system probably isn't perfect, but it's good enough for what we're using it: to get a general idea of how much the player contributed in 1995.

What we did was simply divide each player's salary by the number of points he earned last year. For instance, Mark Wohlers of the Braves was paid a salary of $202,500 last year, while earning a total of 418 points; it cost the Braves $484.45 for each point that he earned, which makes him a real bargain. On the other hand, Pete Harnisch of the Mets was paid $3,000,000 while earning just 159 points; it cost the Mets $18,867.93 per point earned, and that's *no* bargain.

We could simply rate all the players according to their cost per point, but it would be pretty dull because all the players at the top of the list would be the productive rookies and second-year men like Marty Cordova or Jim Edmonds. Anyone who's been around for a few years will automatically make much more money than that, but that doesn't mean that they're not a good "buy" among their particular salary group. . . as long as they're producing. So what we've done is divide players into five different salary groups, then identify the most productive players within each group. Let's start with the lowest-salaried players, the ones who earned less than $200,000 last year:

Less Than $200,000

Player, Team	Salary	Points	Cost/Pt
Hideo Nomo, LA	109,000	505.0	215.84
Marty Cordova, Min	109,000	454.0	240.09
Quilvio Veras, Fla	109,000	428.5	254.38
Chipper Jones, Atl	114,000	427.5	266.67
Troy Percival, Cal	109,000	401.0	271.82

Hideo Nomo and Marty Cordova each earned the rookie minimum of $109,000 last year, and wound up as their respective league's Rookie of the Year. It's not surprising, then, that they were the two biggest bargains in baseball last year. Quilvio Veras, Chipper Jones and Troy Percival, three other very productive rookies, fill out the top five.

$200,000-$499,999

Player, Team	Salary	Points	Cost/Pt
J.T. Snow, Cal	200,000	468.5	426.89
Mark Wohlers, Atl	202,500	418.0	484.45
Geronimo Berroa, Oak	235,000	459.0	511.98
Vinny Castilla, Col	265,000	498.0	532.13
Heathcliff Slocumb, Phi	200,000	373.5	535.48

The second salary level we looked at was the $200,000-$499,999 group. Generally these are players who (a) have been around for a couple of years or so, (b) are still well short of being eligible for free agency and (c) haven't accomplished much yet in their careers. If they *had* accomplished something, they wouldn't be making this little money. Among this group, we found the best bargains to be J.T. Snow, Mark Wohlers, Geronimo Berroa, Vinny Castilla and Heathcliff Slocumb. All of them provided excellent production for their salary, which is still at the lower end of the spectrum. This year—with that first solid season behind them and another year of seniority to take along with it to the bargaining table—they'll be earning a whole lot more. In fact, they'll probably move into our next group. . .

$500,000-$999,000

Player, Team	Salary	Points	Cost/Pt
John Valentin, Bos	612,500	642.5	953.31
Tim Salmon, Cal	900,000	652.0	1,380.37
Mike Piazza, LA	900,000	583.0	1,543.74
Randy Velarde, Yanks	500,000	314.5	1,589.83
Jim Thome, Cle	825,000	517.0	1,595.74

The third group of players earned from $500,000 to $999,999 last year. Generally these are accomplished young players who have been around just long enough to qualify for salary arbitration, but not quite long enough to enter the free-agent market. John Valentin of the Red Sox, who produced a superb season on a relatively low salary of $612,500, was easily the biggest bargain in the group. Tim Salmon, Mike Piazza and Jim Thome match the "accomplished young player" profile; the oddball of the group was Randy Velarde, an eight-year veteran who came through with some solid numbers on a bargain salary of $500,000. Unlike the others, Velarde *was* eligible for free agency, and he cashed in big when the year ended, signing with the Angels for a much higher salary.

$1,000,000-$2,999,999

Player, Team	Salary	Points	Cost/Pt
Tino Martinez, Sea	1,025,000	537.5	1,906.98
Mickey Tettleton, Tex	1,000,000	445.5	2,244.67
Mickey Morandini, Phi	1,025,000	399.0	2,568.92
Jose Mesa, Cle	1,397,223	534.0	2,616.52
Reggie Sanders, Cin	1,984,444	567.0	3,499.90

To make a million dollars a year, a player needs to have been around a little while. All these players were either in their free-agent years, or close to it, and it's that bargaining difference—if you don't sign me for a good amount of money, I'm going to find someone else who will—that drives their salaries upward as much as their accomplishments. If not more so. How else could Jose Mesa, who entered 1995 with a career record of 34-45, a 4.89 ERA and two major league saves in six years, have been earning more than a million dollars *before* his breakthrough season? The threat of going somewhere else doesn't work for everybody, of course. For instance, Jody Reed, an accomplished veteran second baseman, didn't make a million bucks in 1994-95 combined after badly misreading the marketplace. Reed, though, turned down more than $3 million a year from his 1993 club, the Dodgers after the '93 season, so he would have to be considered an exceptional case. (As in exceptionally stupid.) As for Mesa, he *did* earn his bucks in 1995, and he'll cash in on that great year very soon. So will the other guys, if they haven't done so already.

$3,000,000 and Up

Player, Team	Salary	Points	Cost/Pt
Edgar Martinez, Sea	3,591,667	714.5	5,026.82
Dante Bichette, Col	3,375,000	657.0	5,136.99
Albert Belle, Cle	4,375,000	725.5	6,030.32
Carlos Baerga, Cle	3,650,000	533.0	6,848.03
Brady Anderson, Bal	3,333,333	484.5	6,879.94

If you've been around long enough and have had some great seasons, you're going to be making a lot of money. . . that's the economics of the game. All these players fall into that group; they were making a lot of money when the 1995 season began, and they proceeded to have the kind of season that will help them earn even more. As long as they keep performing like they did in 1995, no one will call them overpaid.

The thing is, though, that a lot get into that big-money category and then *don't* earn it. Often the reason is injuries; among the players who made millions while accomplishing little or nothing last year were Danny Jackson ($2.1 million, -1 point for the year), Bryan Harvey ($4.875 million, -9 points), Duane Ward ($4.75 million, -27.5 points) and Jimmy Key ($4.8737 million, 20 points), all of whom spent much if not most of last season on the disabled list. Sometimes, though, a player will avoid injury but *still* not accomplish much. All the players on the following list made at least $2 million and managed to stay healthy last year. The problem is that they couldn't produce anywhere near enough to justify their hefty salaries:

Player, Team	Salary	Points	Cost/Pt
Greg Swindell, Hou	4,450,000	212.0	20,990.57
Ken Hill, StL-Cle	4,525,000	214.0	21,144.86
Cecil Fielder, Det	9,237,500	414.0	22,312.80
Bill Wegman, Mil	2,375,000	105.0	22,619.05
Kevin Gross, Tex	2,889,000	125.0	23,112.00

Cecil Fielder, the best-known player on the list, did hit 31 homers and drive in 82 runs last year. But when you earn more than nine million dollars a year, that isn't quite good enough. Little wonder that the Tigers were rumored to be shopping Fielder over the winter, and not finding much interest.

— Don Zminda

A complete listing for this category can be found on page 247.

Who Were the Top Two-Sport Stars?

Today, Deion Sanders is the only athlete playing two professional sports (pending his decision on the 1996 baseball season). Deion—among others—got us to wondering, "Who are the top two-sport stars in history?" We limited our candidates to those athletes who played more than one sport simultaneously. That excludes people like Brian Jordan, who played in the defensive backfield with the Atlanta Falcons from 1989 through 1991, then concentrated full time on baseball before making it to the major leagues with the Cardinals in 1992.

A number of Football Hall of Famers played major league baseball, though none particularly well: Jim Thorpe, George Halas, Greasy Neale, Paddy Driscoll, Ernie Nevers, Ace Parker, and Red Badgro. On the other hand, not a single baseball Hall of Famer saw action in either the NBA, NFL or NHL. Christy Mathewson did play a little pro football, and Waite Hoyt, Hank Greenberg and Lou Boudreau all dabbled in pre-NBA pro hoops.

Enough background; here are the candidates for best two-sport athlete in modern pro sports history. . .

Jim Thorpe

In terms of the best *athlete*, you'd probably have to give the nod to Jim Thorpe, who won the Olympic decathlon, was for a time considered the best football player in the land, and played major league baseball. But as a pro athlete, he wasn't great. Thorpe played sparingly as a New York Giant under John McGraw, and he also saw brief duty as a Cincinnati Red. Though he's in the Pro Football Hall of Fame, Thorpe was pretty far over the hill by the time the NFL formed in 1920.

NFL	9 Yrs	465 Yds	6 TDs	
MLB	6 Yrs	.252 Avg	7 HR	82 RBI

Those early NFL stats aren't quite complete, because there wasn't a great record-keeping system in those days. But they're complete enough to tell us that Thorpe was past his prime. And he never achieved more than utility status as a National Leaguer.

Ron Reed

Ron Reed played power forward with Detroit for two seasons in the mid-1960s. One of his teammates was Dave DeBusschere, who compiled a solid 2.91 ERA in two seasons with the White Sox. But where Reed gave up basketball and enjoyed a long career in the major leagues, DeBusschere quit baseball and wound up in the Basketball Hall of Fame.

NBA	2 Yrs	8.0 Pts/Gm	6.4 Reb/Gm
MLB	19 Yrs	146-140	3.46 ERA

Reed undoubtedly could have been very good in both sports, but his limited basketball action hurts him in comparison with others we'll discuss.

Gene Conley

Conley is the only man with a World Series *and* an NBA Championship ring. Conley went 9-9 for the Series-winning Milwaukee Braves in 1957, and he also pitched in three All-Star Games. Conley played in 1952-53 with the Celtics, then took five seasons off. The layoff didn't seem to hurt his game, as he came back in 1958 and played for Boston's first three NBA championship clubs.

MLB	11 Yrs	91-96	3.82 ERA
NBA	6 Yrs	5.9 Pts/Gm	6.3 Reb/Gm

These are mighty impressive numbers. Significant action in two sports, and a total of four championships. True, Conley didn't post huge stats with the Celtics, but he was playing behind some great players.

Deion Sanders

After playing in five Pro Bowls, being named the NFL's Defensive Player of the Year in 1994, and playing a key role on each of the last two Super Bowl champions, Sanders has to be considered a Hall of Fame candidate in football. Unfortunately, his baseball achievements haven't come close to his gridiron feats. He's played parts of seven major league seasons, with a .264 lifetime batting average. Sanders' best campaign was 1992, when he hit .304 and led the majors with 14 triples despite playing only 97 games. Here are his stats through the 1995 football season:

NFL	7 Yrs	32 Int's	13 TD,	
MLB	7 Yrs	.264 Avg	33 HR	141 RBI

Not bad, but the fact remains that Deion has never played long enough or well enough to be considered anywhere near baseball's elite.

Bo Jackson

Bo Jackson is the only professional athlete selected to play in all-star games in two major sports. In 1989, he led off baseball's All-Star Game with a home run, and was named MVP. And he was named to the AFC's Pro Bowl squad in 1990, but didn't play because of injury. Jackson never gained a thousand yards in one season as a running back, but that was only because he never donned the pads until October. Consider this: had he rushed 175 more times at the same pace before getting hurt, this is how the all-time NFL leaders would look in average yards per rush:

Rank	Player	Yards/Rush
1	Marion Motley	5.70
2	Bo Jackson	5.40
3	Jim Brown	5.22

Like Deion Sanders, Jackson's baseball accomplishments were a bit more modest. He never learned the strike zone, and he never put his speed to much use. On the other hand, in addition to playing in the All-Star game in 1989, that same season Jackson hit 32 homers and knocked in 105 runs. He finished his career with a solid .474 slugging percentage. Here are his primary numbers in both sports:

MLB	8 Yrs	.250 Avg	141 HR	415 RBI
NFL	4 Yrs	515 Carries	2782 Yds	18 TD

Despite his relatively short football career, our vote for best two-sport star goes to Bo Jackson. He is the only one of these athletes who was considered a true star in two pro leagues at the same time. Given a healthy hip, he almost certainly would have finished with a Hall of Fame football career, not to mention some impressive power numbers in baseball. Bo knew football, and Bo knew baseball.

The striking thing about the history of two-sport athletes is that though there are relatively few in this era, they are generally much more successful than their counterparts of the 1920s and '30s. Why? Until relatively recently, players actually needed an offseason job to make ends meet. If that job happened to be playing another sport, all the better. Now, a player only bothers with another sport if he might have star ability. This rule does not apply to Michael Jordan.

— Rob Neyer

III. QUESTIONS ON OFFENSE

Who Hits Who?

Clutch hitting is an attribute that is constantly talked about but rarely well-defined. By what measure does one identify a true clutch hitter? Batting with runners in scoring position? Late and close hitting? Game-winning RBI? We respect and use all those measuring sticks, but in this essay we decided to try something different. We took all hitters with at least 446 plate appearances in 1995 and all pitchers who faced at least 100 batters. Then we categorized the hitters according to how well they hit against three classes of pitchers: Good (ranked in the upper third of their league in batting average allowed), Average (middle third), and Poor (bottom third). We began looking for clutch hitters, and ended up with lots more.

Let's start with the original purpose of this study. We'll call these guys "Clutch."

Top Hitters vs. Good Pitchers—1995

Batter, Team	Overall	vs. Good	Difference
Wil Cordero, Mon	.286	.341	+ .055
Sammy Sosa, Cubs	.268	.306	+ .038
Darryl Hamilton, Mil	.271	.305	+ .034
Kevin Stocker, Phi	.218	.252	+ .034
Ron Gant, Cin	.276	.295	+ .019

The name that really stands out, especially to those who live in the Chicago area, is Sammy Sosa. Sosa is constantly derided in the media for being anything but a clutch hitter. A Chicago sports-talk radio listener might think Sosa hits all his homers when it's 10-0 in the ninth inning and that all his cutoff throws go over the backstop. If stepping it up a notch against top competition is any measure of clutch ability, Sosa surely stands tall in 1995. For the record, the Good pitcher batting champs were (surprise, surprise) Tony Gwynn in the N.L. at .372 and Will Clark in the A.L. at .318.

The next group are the guys on the other end of this spectrum. We'll call them "Overmatched."

Worst Hitters vs. Good Pitchers—1995

Batter, Team	Overall	vs. Good	Difference
Jeff Conine, Fla	.302	.191	- .111
Kurt Abbott, Fla	.255	.152	- .103
Rusty Greer, Tex	.271	.172	- .099
Bret Boone, Cin	.267	.175	- .092
Chris Gomez, Det	.223	.132	- .091
Mickey Morandini, Phi	.283	.192	- .091

The Fish obviously have some problems with good pitching as the top two guys on the list are two of the Marlins' better hitters. The Good pitcher batting chumps both appear above: Kurt Abbott was the worst in the N.L. at .152 and Chris Gomez "led" the A.L. at .132.

Now let's look at the other side of the coin. Who were the best and worst hitters against the Poor pitchers? Again, we'll start with the positive side. Call these guys "Opportunists."

Top Hitters Against Poor Pitchers—1995

Batter, Team	Overall	vs. Poor	Difference
Joey Cora, Sea	.297	.429	+ .132
Jeff Kent, Mets	.278	.396	+ .118
Vince Coleman, KC/Sea	.288	.398	+ .110
Harold Baines, Bal	.299	.404	+ .105
Greg Gagne, KC	.256	.360	+ .104

Joey Cora is not exactly the most intimidating hitter in the world, but he hit like Ty Cobb against lousy pitchers. Cora is also the American League Poor pitcher batting champ for 1995 at .429. The N.L. champ, Mike Piazza, at a monstrous .446, barely missed the above chart due to his .346 overall average. Other .400 hitters against batting-practice pitchers were Kenny Lofton at .412, Dante Bichette at .410 (his legend continues as now we know he makes his living on bad pitchers at Coors Field. . . kind of like Barry Sanders on turf against seventh-graders), and Jim Thome at .403.

And finally, the last group that we'll call "Underachievers":

Worst Hitters Against Poor Pitchers—1995

Batter, Team	Overall	vs. Poor	Difference
Chili Davis, Cal	.318	.273	- .045
Cecil Fielder, Det	.243	.208	- .035
Darryl Hamilton, Mil	.271	.240	- .031
Kevin Stocker, Phi	.218	.189	- .029
Derek Bell, Hou	.334	.307	- .027

Our first repeaters appear on this chart, in the persons of Darryl Hamilton and Kevin Stocker, who apparently feel bad about their hits unless they *earn* them. That pair is surrounded by, interestingly enough, three noted "RBI men." In the "man's man" world of the RBI men, it must be tough getting up for wimpy pitchers. Like with the Good pitcher batting chumps, both appear above. Stocker trailed the N.L. at .189 and Fielder the A.L. at .208.

In conclusion, this study turned out to be quite interesting and the appendix numbers would probably be fun to type into a spreadsheet and sort all kinds of different ways. Surely the data will be even more interesting if we decide to keep running the study for a few years to see if the tendencies of one season are real tendencies or just flukes. Who knows? Maybe someday we'll see platoons depending on the quality of pitcher on the mound.

— Steve Moyer

A complete listing for this category can be found on page 248.

Which Young Hitters Will Finish with "Immortal" Numbers?

The so-called "Favorite Toy" is a mathematical formula designed by Bill James to project various career hitting totals. In a nutshell, the formula uses a player's age and recent performance to estimate his chances of reaching a particular goal. Using Bill's method, here are all the current major leaguers under 30 who have established at least a 10-percent chance of reaching 3,000 hits:

Player	Age	Current Hits	Proj. Hits	Chance
Roberto Alomar	28	1329	2574	25%
Carlos Baerga	27	971	2457	23%
Chuck Knoblauch	27	822	2245	15%
Travis Fryman	27	848	2211	13%
Gregg Jefferies	28	1106	2289	12%
Frank Thomas	27	893	2208	12%
Ivan Rodriguez	24	569	2033	10%

One thing you might notice immediately: the top three players on this list play the same position. Are we currently in a Golden Age of Second Basemen? Perhaps. That trio of keystoners is followed by Travis Fryman and Gregg Jefferies, neither of whom has displayed the consistency one expects from a future Hall of Famer.

Frank Thomas, regarded in statistical circles as a right-handed version of Ted Williams, doesn't do as well as one might expect. But remember, Williams himself didn't reach the 3,000-hit plateau, in part because—like Thomas—he drew a ton of walks. Then there's Pudge Rodriguez, the youngest player on the list. However, the Favorite Toy does not account for defensive position, and as a catcher Rodriguez' chance for 3,000 hits is almost certainly much lower than 10 percent. Among players who spent most of their career behind the plate, Ted Simmons leads the way with 2,472 hits, and that's quite a ways from three thousand.

The Favorite Toy can also tell us which players have established a decent chance for 500 home runs, another milestone which virtually guarantees a spot in the Hall of Fame. Here are the under-30 players who have established at least a 10-percent shot at 500 homers:

	AGE	CHANCE	HOME RUNS
Frank Thomas	27	58.0%	182
Albert Belle	29	55.0%	194
Ken Griffey Jr.	26	44.0%	189
Juan Gonzalez	26	27.0%	167
Sammy Sosa	27	27.0%	131
Mo Vaughn	28	20.0%	111
Mike Piazza	27	14.0%	92
Tim Salmon	27	14.0%	90
Jeff Bagwell	27	13.0%	113

The Big Hurt might not have a great shot at 3,000 hits, but he leads the list of under-30 players with a chance at 500 homers. By the way, Thomas also has established a 26-percent chance at breaking Babe Ruth's all-time record of 2,056 walks. And speaking of home-run kings, Thomas also has established a 10-percent chance at hitting 756 home runs, which would of course top Henry Aaron's mark.

Two years ago, Juan Gonzalez and Ken Griffey were on incredible home-run paces, but injuries since then have dropped both sluggers' chances at homer immortality. On the other hand, Sammy Sosa has sort of come out of nowhere in the last two years to take his place among the game's top sluggers.

— Rob Neyer

A complete listing for this category can be found on page 250.

Who Are the "Perfect Offensive Players"?

One of the biggest misconceptions in all of baseball is that a player must show "all-around" ability in order to contribute to his team's success. How many times have you heard critics argue against Reggie Jackson's greatness, citing that Jackson batted .300 only once? Apparently, Jackson's 563 career home runs and participation on 11 division championship teams doesn't seem to count for much. Turn on almost any baseball telecast, and you'll hear a reference to how slow Frank Thomas is on the bases or how Albert Belle grounds into too many double plays.

But baseball is not about stealing bases, or bunting, or executing the perfect hit-and-run or anything else. It's about producing runs—period. And the great run-producers in baseball history have always been able to do three things at the plate: hit for average, hit for power, and draw walks. In the end, very little else really matters.

A couple of Cleveland Indians fans, Richard Freedman and Neil Brown, have dubbed a player capable of performing all three run-producing skills a POP—Perfect Offensive Player. Actually, this is the same stat that John Dewan came up with around a decade ago, back in the days of the old *Chicago Baseball Report*. John dubbed any player who met the qualifying standards a member of the "3-4-5 Club," for a logical reason: in order to qualify, a player must attain a .300 batting average, .400 on-base percentage and .500 slugging percentage. As you might guess, there are very few career POPs, or 3-4-5s, in baseball history. Here they are, sorted by their number of "POP Points"—batting average plus on-base percentage plus slugging percentage:

Perfect Offensive Players—Career

Player	BA	OB%	SLG%	Points
Babe Ruth	.342	.474	.690	1506
Ted Williams	.344	.482	.634	1460
Lou Gehrig	.340	.447	.632	1419
Rogers Hornsby	.358	.434	.577	1369
Frank Thomas	.323	.450	.593	1366
Jimmie Foxx	.325	.428	.609	1362
Hank Greenberg	.313	.412	.605	1330
Ty Cobb	.366	.433	.512	1311
Stan Musial	.331	.417	.559	1307
Joe Jackson	.356	.423	.518	1297
Lefty O'Doul	.349	.413	.532	1294
Dan Brouthers	.342	.423	.519	1284

Tris Speaker	.345	.428	.500	1273
Harry Heilmann	.342	.410	.520	1272
Ed Delahanty	.346	.412	.505	1263
Mel Ott	.304	.414	.533	1251

(minimum 2,500 plate appearances)

The right two names show up at the top. It's widely accepted that Babe Ruth and Ted Williams are the two most productive offensive forces in baseball history, and the POP or 3-4-5 system certainly backs up that claim. You'll also note that Ruth, Williams and three other players—Lou Gehrig, Jimmie Foxx and Hank Greenberg—posting career slugging averages over .600, making them the only career "3-4-6 Hitters." That's even more POP.

So were there any 3-4-5s in the majors last season? You bet. In fact, eight players met the POP standards in 1995, with Frank Thomas, fifth on the career 3-4-5 list above (and the only active player on the list), ranking third last season (minimum 400 plate appearances).

POP Qualifiers—1995

Player, Team	BA	OB%	SLG%	Points
Edgar Martinez, Sea	.356	.479	.628	1463
Albert Belle, Cle	.317	.401	.690	1408
Frank Thomas, WSox	.308	.454	.606	1368
Tim Salmon, Cal	.330	.429	.594	1353
Mike Piazza, LA	.346	.400	.606	1352
Jim Thome, Cle	.314	.438	.558	1310
Manny Ramirez, Cle	.308	.402	.558	1268
Chili Davis, Cal	.318	.429	.514	1261

No wonder Freedman and Brown were so interested in this stat. The Cleveland Indians are well represented on the POP list, with Albert Belle, Jim Thome and Manny Ramirez all meeting the standard. Despite calling Dodger Stadium home, Mike Piazza was the *only* National League player to make the list (and just barely at that, with an on-base percentage right at .400). With a slugging percentage of .606, Piazza also qualified for the elite "3-4-6 Club," along with Belle, Frank Thomas and Edgar Martinez.

For Piazza, Tim Salmon, Thome and Ramirez, this is the first time on the POP list. But it's becoming ho-hum territory for Frank Thomas. Last season was the Big Hurt's *fifth* POP campaign in six major league seasons. Here are the active players who have made the POP list more than once:

Most POP Seasons—Active Players

Player	Number	POP Seasons
Frank Thomas	5	1991, 1992, 1993, 1994, 1995
Barry Bonds	4	1990, 1992, 1993, 1994
Paul Molitor	3	1987, 1993, 1994
Albert Belle	2	1994, 1995
Chili Davis	2	1994, 1995
Edgar Martinez	2	1992, 1995
Will Clark	2	1989, 1994
Ken Griffey Jr	2	1993, 1994
Tony Gwynn	2	1987, 1994
Rickey Henderson	2	1985, 1990
Eddie Murray	2	1984, 1990

We'd be neglecting our duty if we didn't put in a special word here for Pedro Guerrero. Pete, a 3-4-5 hitter in 1985 and 1987 with the Dodgers, spent last season riding the bus in Double-A. And in case you're wondering, he didn't make the minor league POP list: he did hit one of the three qualifiers with a .302 batting average (in 252 at-bats) for Midland in the Texas League, but his .376 on-base average and .437 slugging average both fell short of the POP standards.

Like Ruth and Williams on the all-time list, Thomas and Bonds are simply head and shoulders above the rest of the competition for offensive production in the 1990s. Bonds just missed making the 3-4-5 list in both 1991 (.292 batting average) and 1995 (.294), and Thomas certainly would have made it in 1990 (.330/.454/.529) with enough plate appearances. Molitor had two great seasons after heading to Toronto, but many fans forget his amazing 1987 campaign, which included a 39-game hitting streak. Another thing that jumps out on this list is Rickey Henderson, who put together two POP seasons while hitting leadoff. Those weren't flukes, folks. In the prime of his career, Rickey could have hit third in almost anyone's lineup.

The POP data again confirms that we're living in an incredible offensive era. The eight 3-4-5 hitters of 1995 certainly couldn't stack up to the unbelievable 14 of 1994, but it's still head and shoulders above 1991. Here are the number of POPs for the previous five seasons:

POPs per Season—1991-1995

Year	POPs
1995	8
1994	14
1993	7
1992	3
1991	1

For those of you who follow baseball history, you can probably guess that the decade best represented by POPs is the 1930s. Without question, you'd be right. For those of you who think the ball is juiced in *today's* game, take a look at baseball's golden offensive era.

POPs per Season—1930-1939

Year	POPs
1930	29
1931	11
1932	8
1933	5
1934	10
1935	8
1936	15
1937	11
1938	9
1939	14

Unless the major leagues go to aluminum bats, we're not likely to see anything like 1930 ever again. Hit .300? Heck, the *entire National League* hit over .300 (.303) that season. Philadelphia's Chuck Klein hit .386 in 1930, with 40 home runs and 170 RBI—and didn't win *any* leg of the Triple Crown. You get the point.

Has there ever been a season with no 3-4-5 hitters? In fact, there have been seven this century, with all of them coming after 1959. The seasons are: 1960, 1963, 1965, 1968 (no surprise), 1982, 1983 and 1986. Having been spoiled by the big-hitting seasons of the 1990s, we'd have to say that a season with no POP wouldn't be nearly as much fun.

— Scott McDevitt

A complete listing for this category can be found on page 251.

Who Soared to the Skies—and Who Crashed and Burned—in '95?

Maybe this article should be subtitled "How the Chicago White Sox Found *Another* Right Fielder."

The Sox' "right-field saga" began in the winter of 1992-93, when they took a chance on Ellis Burks, a veteran outfielder who was coming off an injury-riddled, eight-homer, 30-RBI season with the Red Sox. When his socks changed from red to white, Burks got his career back on track again. He more than doubled his power output to 17 homers and 74 RBI, and while he didn't make our annual list of players whose batting averages had risen the most, he did lift his average by a healthy 20 points (from .255 to .275). A lot of clubs would have responded by giving Burks a multi-year contract, but the Sox didn't seem convinced that Burks could stay either healthy or productive. As it turned out, they were right. Since signing a free-agent contract with the Colorado Rockies, Burks has totaled fewer at-bats in two injury-plagued years (427) than he had with the Sox in 1993 alone (499).

To replace Burks in 1994, the Sox picked a player who was even more of a long shot than Ellis had been a year earlier: Darrin Jackson, who had batted a career-low .209 for the Blue Jays and Mets in 1993. Once again they struck it rich: Jackson raised his average by a whopping 103 points—the biggest increase in the majors from '93 to '94—and like Burks, nearly doubled his power production (from 6 homers and 26 RBI to 10 homers and 51 RBI). But as with Burks, the Sox seemed skeptical that Jackson could repeat his '94 performance, and decided not to break the bank to re-sign him. Jackson wound up in Japan.

Did the White Sox worry? Nah. For the third year in a row, they brought in a long-shot candidate to play right field: Mike Devereaux, who'd batted all of .203 for the Orioles in '94. And as the chart shows, they rolled a seven for the third year in a row. Like Jackson a year earlier, Devereaux posted the biggest one-year increase in batting average for any major league regular, raising his average 96 points from .203 to .299. This time, the Sox didn't wait for the season to end to let their right fielder leave town. They shipped Devereaux to Atlanta late in the year, and Devereaux wound up making a contribution to the Braves' drive to the World Championship. The Braves didn't keep him around either, and Devereux will be back with another of his old clubs, the Orioles, in 1996.

Now, you don't have to be a White Sox right fielder to make a big jump in batting average from one year to the next. . . though it seems to help. Looking at the list, you *do* seem to need to be a talented player who under-achieved in one season, often because of injury, then probably *over-achieved* at least a little the next year. Good as Edgar Martinez is, he's probably not going to hit .356 again, and John Jaha will have a tough time repeating that .313 average. And you'll have to convince us that Scott Servais, who entered 1995 with a .222 career average, is really a .265 hitter. The best bets to remain at their 1995 levels are probably Jose Offerman, a talented offensive player who gets a fresh start with a new team in a new league, and Javy Lopez, a great young talent. As for Devereaux, who topped his .251 career average entering the 1995 season by a whopping 48 points, we think the White Sox—and the Braves—made the right move in letting him move on to another team.

BIGGEST BATTING AVERAGE CHANGES 1994–95

UP	1994	1995	CHANGE
Mike Devereaux	.203	.299	+96
Jose Offerman	.210	.287	+77
John Jaha	.241	.313	+72
Edgar Martinez	.285	.356	+71
Scott Servais	.195	.265	+70
Javy Lopez	.245	.315	+70
DOWN			
Mike Kingery	.349	.269	–80
Jeff Bagwell	.368	.290	–78
Paul Molitor	.341	.270	–71
Moises Alou	.339	.273	–66
Ken Griffey Jr.	.323	.258	–65

Minimum 250 plate appearances each year.

Year after year, the "Down" list will contain a number of talented players whose averages dropped due to injury. Given a return to full health, Jeff Bagwell, Paul Molitor, Moises Alou and Ken Griffey Jr. are likely to come back strong in 1996. . . but it won't be easy for any of them to hit as high as they did in 1994. In baseball, a player proves his worth over the course of several years, and when he performs either unusually well or unusually poorly in a particular season, you can expect his numbers to return to a more normal level a year later. The White Sox seem to understand this, which is why they didn't keep Burks, Jackson or Devereaux, and perhaps why they signed Danny Tartabull after a subpar 1995. But isn't it amazing how many clubs still let one good—or bad—year cloud their thinking about a player's worth, then wind up regretting it?

— Don Zminda

A complete listing for this category can be found on page 252.

He Can Slug, So Why Can't He Walk?

Most of the great home-run hitters of all time combined two important of-fensive skills. Not only did they possess the raw power necessary to launch their rocket shots, but they had the plate discipline required to coax a lot of walks. The two skills would seem to be complementary, since sound strike-zone judgment generally improves the chances for sluggers to force opposing hurlers to offer "fat" pitches.

In fact, of the 14 hitters in baseball history with at least 500 round-trippers, most walked at a clip that was more than twice their home-run rate. The only exceptions were Hank Aaron and Ernie Banks, both of whom drew their fair share of free passes:

Lifetime BB/HR Ratios—500+ Career Home Runs

Player	BB	HR	Ratio
Hank Aaron	1402	755	1.86
Babe Ruth	2056	714	2.88
Willie Mays	1463	660	2.22
Frank Robinson	1420	586	2.42
Harmon Killebrew	1559	573	2.72
Reggie Jackson	1375	563	2.44
Mike Schmidt	1507	548	2.75
Mickey Mantle	1733	536	3.23
Jimmie Foxx	1452	534	2.72
Willie McCovey	1345	521	2.58
Ted Williams	2019	521	3.88
Ernie Banks	763	512	1.49
Eddie Mathews	1444	512	2.82
Mel Ott	1708	511	3.34

Likewise, among the hitters who produced the 10 highest single-season home-run totals, only Roger Maris, in his historic 61-homer 1961 cam-paign, failed to walk at least 100 times. Maris did draw 94 bases on balls that year, and probably would have walked much more often had the hitter in the Yankee on-deck circle not been Mickey Mantle. Next to Maris, the fewest walks in a season by a player on the top-10 single-season list is 105 by Hack Wilson in 1930.

So walking and slugging seem to go hand-in-hand. Which brings us to Dante Bichette and his implausible 1995 campaign. In the past, Bichette's intelligence has been questioned by his own manager. He's been known to demonstrate some reluctance in backing up his fellow Rockie outfielders. And he has an annoying habit of striking an irritating crouch-type pose when he connects solidly at the plate.

Still, Bichette's impressive triple-crown numbers attracted a lot of attention last year, and he finished second in the National League's MVP voting. Bichette's home/road discrepancies have been chronicled elsewhere in this book, so we won't get into that here. But perhaps even more remarkably, Bichette was able to slug his 40 homers last year (31 at home) while walking just 22 times. His walk-to-homer ratio of .550 ranks as the all-time smallest among hitters with at least 20 dingers in a season:

	Year	BB	HR	Ratio
Dante Bichette	1995	22	40	0.55
Andres Galarraga	1994	19	31	0.61
Fred Whitfield	1965	16	26	0.62
Juan Gonzalez	1995	17	27	0.63
Abner Dalrymple	1884	14	22	0.64
Andre Dawson	1987	32	49	0.65
Bob Horner	1979	22	33	0.67
Cory Snyder	1986	16	24	0.67
Walker Cooper	1947	24	35	0.69
Dante Bichette	1994	19	27	0.70

Minimum 20 home runs.

As you can see, last season was no fluke for Bichette. The year before, Dante managed just 19 walks while crashing 27 homers, so he now has two of the 10 worst single-season walk-to-homer ratios of all time. Not surprisingly, his career ratio ranks very low as well. Among all the hitters in baseball history who have hit at least 30 homers in a season at least once, only Juan Gonzalez' walk-to-homer ratio is smaller than Bichette's. Gonzalez has totaled 169 walks and 167 homers in his career, for a ratio of 1.01; Bichette is just a shade behind with 129 walks and 126 homers for a ratio of 1.02.

While Bichette's career walk-to-homer ratio ranks second-worst all time among players with at least 30 homers in a season, his Colorado teammate Vinny Castilla ranks fifth. And if we extend the list further, Rockie first baseman Andres Galarraga would rank 22nd. What a peculiar lineup the Rockies have.

Imagine how imposing Colorado's offense would be if the Rockies' sluggers drew their fair share of free passes, thus allowing the ensuing homers to produce even *more* damage. It's scary to think what the Colorado offense would produce if their heavy-hitters got on base as often via the walk as typical sluggers do.

— Jim Henzler

A complete listing for this category can be found on page 253.

Which Teams Have the Most "Heart"?

The "heart of the order" consists of the number-three, four and five spots in the batting order—the key power slots. Last year the average major league team got 23 homers and 95 RBI from its number-three hitters, 28 and 101 from the cleanup hitters, and 21 and 87 from its number-five men. And remember, that's just the average; the top teams performed a whole lot better than that. Overall, more than 43 percent of all runs driven in last year came from the 3-4-5 spots. If the heart of your order wasn't producing, chances are your team had a lot of trouble winning.

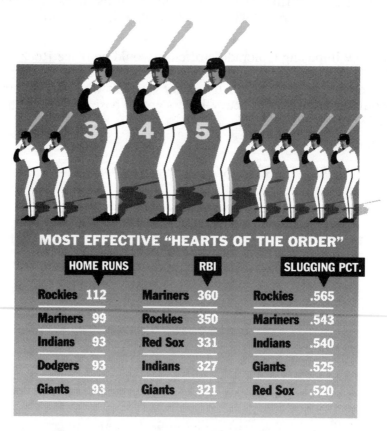

MOST EFFECTIVE "HEARTS OF THE ORDER"

HOME RUNS		RBI		SLUGGING PCT.	
Rockies	112	Mariners	360	Rockies	.565
Mariners	99	Rockies	350	Mariners	.543
Indians	93	Red Sox	331	Indians	.540
Dodgers	93	Indians	327	Giants	.525
Giants	93	Giants	321	Red Sox	.520

The chart shows the top 1995 "hearts of the order" in three categories: homers, RBI and slugging percentage. Some quick mathematics reveals that the hitters in the middle of the Seattle Mariner lineup averaged 33 homers and 120 RBI apiece, and that the 3-4-5 men from the the Colorado Rockies averaged 37 homers and 117 RBI. Fast company, indeed. Here's how we'd rank the top 1995 "hearts of the order":

1. Mariners. The M's had more RBI than anyone from their 3-4-5 hitters, and ranked second only to the altitude-aided Rockies in homers and slugging percentage. So Seattle gets our vote as the club with the most "heart," which is remarkable considering that Ken Griffey, Jr., the club's main power threat, missed more than half his team's games. Edgar Martinez, Jay Buhner and Tino Martinez usually occupied the 3-4-5 slots while Junior was out, and they did a great job of picking up the slack.

2. Indians. The Tribe boasted the highest-scoring offense in the majors, and their 3-4-5 hitters were a big reason. The Indians usually had Carlos Baerga, Albert Belle and Eddie Murray in the heart of their order, and the trio terrorized the opposition. Thanks to Belle, Cleveland cleanup hitters topped the American League in batting average (.317), doubles (53), homers (50) and slugging (.686), and finished second in RBI (127).

3. Giants. Giant 3-4-5 hitters didn't have the raw numbers to match some of the other clubs. But the Giants got great production even though they were playing in a tough park. Like the Mariners, the Jints had a great heart of the order despite being without one of the top sluggers in the majors, Matt Williams, for much of the year. Barry Bonds did more than his share to make up for the loss of Williams, with Mark Carreon and Glenallen Hill usually taking the other power spots when Williams was out.

4. Red Sox. With Mo Vaughn occupying the key number-three spot, the Bosox ranked near the top in all the important heart-of-the-order categories. Jose Canseco was an excellent cleanup hitter when healthy, and Mike Greenwell made some contributions from the five-hole.

5. Rockies. Yes, the raw numbers were there. . . but as the Colorado essay shows, the Rockies' offense wasn't nearly as potent away from Coors Field. Still, Dante Bichette, Larry Walker and Andres Galarraga—the club's normal 3-4-5 hitters—were a solid (though overrated) trio.

The *worst* heart of the order? None other than the once-mighty Toronto Blue Jays. With Paul Molitor bothered by injuries, Joe Carter showing his age, and John Olerud and Ed Sprague not providing the power that middle-of-the-order hitters need to, the Jays' heart of the order ranked last in home runs, last in RBI and last in slugging percentage.

— Don Zminda

A complete listing for this category can be found on page 254.

Which Baserunners Generate the Most Pickoff Attempts?

Which baserunners make pitchers nervous enough to keep throwing over to first? Theoretically, you'd think it would be the top basestealers—the more bases you steal, the more pitchers should be throwing over. But is that really the case?

To make this fair, we just wanted to look at situations where a pickoff was clearly an attempt to dissuade stealing. So we isolated all the situations where there was a runner on first but nobody on second.

What did we find? Well, as expected, really fast guys were near the top. Otis Nixon, Vince Coleman, Brady Anderson, Marquis Grissom, Quilvio Veras, Kenny Lofton and Chad Curtis were the top seven. But surprisingly, the top basestealers were not always among the top guys in pickoff throws. For instance, Barry Larkin, who was third in the majors with 51 steals, ranked 32nd in pickoff attempts. Lance Johnson, who was eighth with 40 steals, ranked 30th in pickoff attempts. Brian McRae finished the season with 27 swipes (tying him for 23rd), yet ranked ninth in pickoffs.

So that got us thinking. Who do pitchers get overly concerned about, and conversely, who *should* pitchers be more concerned with? So we went back to the data and, still using the runner-on-first-no-one-on-second series of events, calculated the ratio of pickoff attempts to actual steals. The top 10 who drew a minimum of 40 pickoff throws:

Most Pickoff Throws per Stolen Base—1995

Player, Team	Pickoffs	Steals	Ratio
Tim Naehring, Bos	61	0	--
Jay Bell, Pit	73	1	73.0
Jim Edmonds, Cal	67	1	67.0
Carl Everett, Mets	65	1	65.0
Jose Offerman, LA	124	2	62.0
Brent Gates, Oak	113	2	56.5
Joe Orsulak, Mets	54	1	54.0
Jeff Reboulet, Min	51	1	51.0
Shawn Green, Tor	48	1	48.0
Jon Nunnally, KC	48	1	48.0
Terry Pendleton, Fla	48	1	48.0

(minimum 40 pickoff throws)

The most overrated steal threat had to be Boston's Tim Naehring, who was the recipient of 61 pickoff throws, but didn't steal a single base!

Who are the most *underrated* basestealers? Using a minimum of 10 steals as a cutoff, Rex Hudler, is the clear winner. The Wonder Dog stole 10 bases while causing just 24 pickoffs. The bottom 10:

Fewest Pickoff Throws per Steal—1995

Player, Team	Pickoffs	Steals	Ratio
Rex Hudler, Cal	24	10	2.4
Joe Carter, Tor	39	11	3.6
Mike Lansing, Mon	66	18	3.7
Barry Larkin, Cin	127	34	3.7
Glenallen Hill, SF	86	22	3.9
Jose Valentin, Mil	57	14	4.1
Greg Colbrunn, Fla	42	10	4.2
David Hulse, Mil	59	14	4.2
Stan Javier, Oak	106	25	4.2
Mo Vaughn, Bos	47	11	4.3

(Minimum 10 steals)

A special note should go out to Mike Benjamin of 14-hits-in-three-games fame. He stole nine bases on 20 pickoffs for a 2.22 ratio, but just missed the minimum.

The main question we came away with after doing this study was this: how do you overlook Barry Larkin? All he did was finish second in the N.L. in steals and ended up winning a Gold Glove, Silver Slugger and MVP awards. Just because he hits doesn't mean he can't run, too.

— Allan Spear

A complete listing for this category can be found on page 255.

Who Gets the "Slidin' Billy Trophy"?

Slidin' Billy Hamilton was a 19th-century superstar and one of the dominant players of his era. If you wanted to pick the perfect leadoff hitter, you couldn't do much better than Slidin' Billy. He not only got on base with great regularity (his lifetime on-base percentage was .455), but could motor around the sacks once he got there (912 career steals, though the rules were a little different back then). So our annual report on the best leadoff men of the year is fittingly called the "Slidin' Billy Trophy."

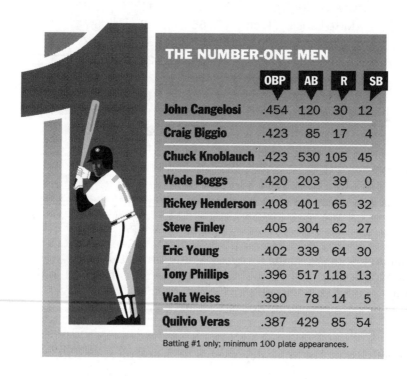

THE NUMBER-ONE MEN

	OBP	AB	R	SB
John Cangelosi	.454	120	30	12
Craig Biggio	.423	85	17	4
Chuck Knoblauch	.423	530	105	45
Wade Boggs	.420	203	39	0
Rickey Henderson	.408	401	65	32
Steve Finley	.405	304	62	27
Eric Young	.402	339	64	30
Tony Phillips	.396	517	118	13
Walt Weiss	.390	78	14	5
Quilvio Veras	.387	429	85	54

Batting #1 only; minimum 100 plate appearances.

Our feeling has always been that a leadoff man's first and foremost job is to get on base, so the chart on this page lists the players with the best OBPs last year when they were performing in the number-one spot in the batting order. It's topped by two Houston Astros, John Cangelosi and Craig Biggio. We all know Biggio as one of the top players in baseball, but Cangelosi, a journeyman who's drifted from team to team and spent considerable time in the minors? Yes, Cangelosi. With his speed and ability to get on base, he was simply outstanding when used in the number-one slot last year.

If you don't think Cangelosi was an effective leadoff man last year, we'll refer you to a little exercise that Steve Moyer, our Director of Operations, performed last year. Steve compared Cangelosi's leadoff stats with those of Vince Coleman, who supposedly turned the Mariners' season around after they obtained him and put him in the leadoff slot:

Cangelosi vs. Coleman Batting #1, 1995

	OBP	PA	Runs	PA/Run
Cangelosi	.454	152	30	5.1
Coleman	.343	493	64	7.0

Coleman averaged a run every seven trips to the plate last year. Cangelosi, though, scored a run about once every *five* plate appearances. The difference? Cangelosi's superior ability to get on base.

Still, Cangelosi was only a part-time leadoff man last year, and good as he was, so was Biggio. Our feeling is that only full-time leadoff men should be considered for the Slidin' Billy trophy, and here are our six finalists:

Steve Finley. Traded to San Diego in the mega-deal with the Astros, Finley responded with a career year. His .405 OBP as a leadoff man ranked among the leaders, and he also supplied both speed (27 steals out of the number-one spot) and power (.490 slugging average).

Rickey Henderson. Often described as the best leadoff man of all time, and with good reason; Rickey's not only baseball's all-time stolen base king, but a player who has consistently reached base over 40 percent of the time. Though obviously past his prime now, he's still one of the best.

Chuck Knoblauch. He just keeps getting better. Knoblauch tied Biggio for the second-best leadoff OBP last year, and he was first among players with at least 300 plate appearances in the number-one slot. He also ranked second among number-one hitters in runs scored (105) and walks (77), fourth in stolen bases (45) and first in hits (175). An outstanding candidate.

Kenny Lofton. The 1994 Slidin' Billy winner had another excellent season, leading the American League in stolen bases for the fourth straight year. But Lofton wasn't nearly as good last year as he'd been in 1993 and

'94. His OBP dropped 50 points to .363, and that's not quite good enough in this elite company.

Tony Phillips. Now nearly 37, Phillips shows few signs of slowing down. His .396 OBP as a number-one hitter was one of the best, and he ranked first in runs scored (119), walks (111) and home runs (26). His only negatives were a poor basestealing record (13-for-22 when batting first) and his high strikeout total. Phillips fanned 131 times as a number-one; no other leadoff man had more than 97 Ks.

Quilvio Veras. The best National League rookie this side of Hideo Nomo and Chipper Jones. Veras reached base frequently (.387 OBP from the number-one spot), then got around them in a hurry, ranking first among number-one hitters with 54 steals. And he's probably going to get even better.

All six players are strong candidates, but in our eyes it came down to Knoblauch and Phillips. Either would be a good choice, but our vote goes to Knoblauch because of his speed and superior on-base average. The 1995 Slidin' Billy Hamilton Trophy goes to Chuck Knoblauch of the Minnesota Twins. Hail to the King!

No trophy goes to the 1995 *trailers* in leadoff OBP—or to the managers who unwisely put them at the top of their batting orders. Maybe we should call this the "Ralph Houk Trophy," for the ex-Yankee, Tiger and Red Sox manager whose rule seemed to be, "I don't care if he can't get on base, I'm leading off with my second baseman!"

1995 Trailers—OBP as #1 Hitters

Player, Team	OBP	AB	R	SB
Wayne Kirby, Cle	.202	107	11	3
Pat Listach, Mil	.270	183	20	5
Curtis Goodwin, Bal	.281	131	16	6
Fernando Vina, Mil	.295	155	27	2
Marquis Grissom, Atl	.299	509	73	26
Troy O'Leary, Bos	.300	95	17	4
Darren Lewis, SF-Cin	.305	371	50	23
James Mouton, Hou	.315	116	18	15
Willie McGee, Bos	.316	149	27	3
Luis Polonia, Yanks-Atl	.319	250	36	10

When Kenny Lofton got hurt last summer, the Indians entrusted the lead-off role to substitute outfielder Wayne Kirby. They might as well have picked Clay Kirby, George Kirby, Durward Kirby or Marion Kirby, given Wayne's anemic .202 OBP out of the number-one spot. Good thing they had a 50-game lead at the time.

If you're one of those people who believed the announcers who kept telling you all October that "Marquis Grissom is the catalyst of the Braves' attack," shame on you. Grissom did have a good postseason, but for most of the year he was *hurting* the Atlanta offense, not helping it, due to his inability to get on base. And the truth is, Grissom's never been a great lead-off man, not with a .329 lifetime OBP. Give us Chuck Knoblauch or Tony Phillips any day.

— Don Zminda

A complete listing for this category can be found on page 257.

Who Puts Their Team Ahead?

There are many measures of clutch hitting, but one of the better ones is the "go-ahead RBI." Any time a player drives in a run which gives his club the lead, he's giving it a great chance to win the game—whatever inning the RBI takes place in. And that's clutch hitting by any definition.

Here are the 1995 leaders in go-ahead RBI—or "GARBI," if you prefer (alas, both Barbaro Garbey and Steve Garvey were out of baseball before we started compiling this stat):

1995 Leaders—Go-Ahead RBI	
Player, Team	RBI
Barry Bonds, SF	38
Dante Bichette, Col	37
Frank Thomas, WSox	31
Bobby Bonilla, Mets-Bal	30
Chipper Jones, Atl	29
Sammy Sosa, Cubs	29
Mark Grace, Cubs	28
Will Clark, Tex	28
Kirby Puckett, Min	28
Mo Vaughn, Bos	25
Rafael Palmeiro, Bal	25
Jeff Conine, Fla	25

In the San Francisco essay, we asserted that Barry Bonds is the best clutch hitter in the game. Here's more evidence: Bonds drove in a total of 38 runs that put the Giants ahead last year. Dante Bichette of the Rockies was a close second with 37 GARBIs. Though he had the advantage of playing in Coors Field, Bichette obviously did a fine job in the clutch last year.

The other names are all familiar, as this is clearly a list of some of the top hitters in the game. Two players deserve special mention. Chipper Jones, a rookie last year, performed like a veteran in most pressure situations. . . including this one. And Sammy Sosa of the Cubs, a player singled out by some in the Chicago media as someone who gets a lot of "meaningless RBI" (see the Cub essay), had at least 29 *meaningful* ribbies last year.

But while we like the go-ahead RBI by itself, some players will inevitably get more chances to put their team ahead than others do. So we also rank the go-ahead leaders on a percentage basis, with a player's "go-ahead opportunities" being defined as his total of number of GARBIs, plus the number of times he stranded a potential go-ahead run in scoring position. Here are the 1995 leaders in GARBI percentage:

1995 Leaders—Go-Ahead RBI Percentage

Player, Team	Opp	RBI	Pct
Barry Bonds, SF	105	38	36.2
Mark McGwire, Oak	59	20	33.9
Dave Justice, Atl	71	24	33.8
Chipper Jones, Atl	90	29	32.2
Dante Bichette, Col	118	37	31.4
Matt Williams, SF	55	17	30.9
Todd Hundley, NYN	40	12	30.0
Frank Thomas, WSox	105	31	29.5
Mark Grace, Cubs	95	28	29.5
Will Clark, Tex	96	28	29.2
Jose Canseco, Bos	55	16	29.1

(Minimum 50 total RBI)

Bonds retains his position as the number-one man. Bichette drops down a bit, but not much. As it turned out, several players had even more GARBI opportunities last year than Bichette—Kirby Puckett 126, Bobby Bonilla 123, Joe Carter 121—and Dante's success rate was impressive.

Here are the players with the *lowest* GARBI percentages last year:

1995 Trailers—Go-Ahead RBI Percentage

Player, Team	Opp	RBI	Pct
Ray Durham, WSox	76	5	6.6
Stan Javier, Oak	87	7	8.0
Brent Gates, Oak	85	7	8.2
Jay Bell, Pit	91	8	8.8
Royce Clayton, SF	78	7	9.0

None of these players are middle-of-the-order RBI types, so their clubs probably aren't too concerned about the weak percentages. However, that excuse won't cut it for Gregg Jefferies (only 11 GARBIs in 87 opportunities last year for a percentage of 12.6), Joe Carter (18 for 121, 14.9 percent), Greg Vaughn (10 for 63, 15.9 percent) and Cecil Fielder (15 for 91, 16.5 percent), among others. Unlike Sammy Sosa, we'd have to say that these guys truly *did* get a lot of RBI that weren't all that meaningful.

— Don Zminda

A complete listing for this category can be found on page 258.

Who's the Best Bunter?

Veteran managers, coaches and fans often grump that "these modern players don't know the fundamentals any more." Critics often focus on bunting, which does seem to be a bit of a lost art these days. But as this annual article shows, there are still a number of good bunters around.

There are two kinds of bunts, of course: bunting to lay down a sacrifice and bunting for a hit. Sometimes a hitter will get credit for a sacrifice when he's really trying to get a hit, and the opposite will happen as well. Usually the situation is pretty clear, however. Let's begin with sacrifices. The following players had the best success rates when attempting a sacrifice bunt last year (minimum 10 attempts):

Top Sacrifice Bunters—1995

Player, Team	SH	Att	Pct
Joey Cora, Sea	13	13	1.000
Joe Girardi, Col	12	12	1.000
Craig Biggio, Hou	11	11	1.000
Omar Vizquel, Cle	10	10	1.000
Pat Kelly, Yanks	10	10	1.000
Shane Reynolds, Hou	10	10	1.000
Mark McLemore, Tex	10	10	1.000
Andy Ashby, SD	16	17	.941
Jose Vizcaino, Mets	13	14	.929
Darren Lewis, SF-Cin	12	13	.923
Dave Mlicki, Mets	12	13	.923

(Minimum 10 sacrifice attempts)

No shortage of good bunters here, as seven players had perfect records, and the others failed on only one sacrifice attempt all year. A few pitchers make this list every year, and three did so in 1995: Shane Reynolds of the Astros, Andy Ashby of the Padres and Dave Mlicki of the Mets. Ashby also made the leaders list in 1994, as did Joey Cora and Omar Vizquel.

The chart on the next page lists the 1995 leaders in most bunt hits, and two old masters lead the way. Both Otis Nixon and Brett Butler still possess excellent speed even in their late 30s, and each remains among the slickest bunters around. Butler's 1995 performance represents a bit of a comeback, as he was a subpar 10-for-27 in strike-marred 1994.

But who gets the coveted STATS FlatBat as the best bunter overall? We picked three candidates, listed below the chart. . .

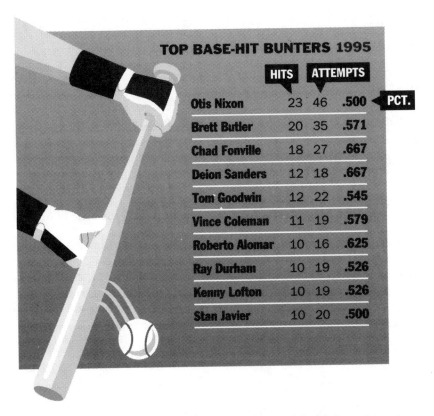

TOP BASE-HIT BUNTERS 1995

	HITS	ATTEMPTS	PCT.
Otis Nixon	23	46	.500
Brett Butler	20	35	.571
Chad Fonville	18	27	.667
Deion Sanders	12	18	.667
Tom Goodwin	12	22	.545
Vince Coleman	11	19	.579
Roberto Alomar	10	16	.625
Ray Durham	10	19	.526
Kenny Lofton	10	19	.526
Stan Javier	10	20	.500

Otis Nixon. Not only did Nixon lead the majors with 23 bunt hits, he was a perfect 6-for-6 in sacrifice attempts. Can't get much better than that.

Brett Butler. He had three fewer bunt hits than Nixon, and he did fail on one of his 11 sacrifice tries. But Butler had a higher success rate on bunt-hit attempts than Nixon, and was one of two players to reach double figures in both sacrifices and bunt hits (the other was Royal Tom Goodwin).

Omar Vizquel. A perfect 10-for-10 in sacrifice attempts, plus a superior success rate when bunting for a hit (9-for-13, 69 percent). The 1993 FlatBat winner is obviously still one of the best in the business.

It comes down to Butler and Nixon, and this one's a toss-up. Butler won the FlatBat in 1992, when he had an amazing 42 bunt hits, but Nixon, who's been one of the best for years, has never garnered the trophy. Your time has come, Otis: the STATS FlatBat for 1995 goes to Otis Nixon.

— Don Zminda

A complete listing for this category can be found on page 260.

Who's First in the Secondary?

It's probably too late, but maybe we—or Bill James, the man who invented the stat—should have renamed secondary average when we had the chance. Based on its importance in the offensive scheme of things, perhaps "primary average" would have been more appropriate.

But we're getting ahead of ourselves. For you first-time readers, secondary average is a way of measuring a hitter's contributions *aside* from batting average. Here's the formula:

$$\text{Secondary Average} = (\text{Extra Bases} + \text{BB} + \text{SB} - \text{CS}) / \text{AB}$$

The lion's share of secondary average results from the two most important offensive skills: hitting for power and getting on base. Who does those things best these days? There are a lot of fantastic hitters in the game—Edgar Martinez, Matt Williams, Ken Griffey, Albert Belle—but for the second year in a row, the kings of secondary average are Frank Thomas and Barry Bonds:

1995 Leaders—Secondary Average

Player	Team	Avg
Frank Thomas	WSox	.576
Barry Bonds	Giants	.561
Mickey Tettleton	Rangers	.522
Albert Belle	Indians	.513
Edgar Martinez	Mariners	.501
Ron Gant	Reds	.495
Reggie Sanders	Reds	.465
Jim Thome	Indians	.460
Tim Salmon	Angels	.434
Jay Buhner	Mariners	.430

After leading the majors from 1991 through 1993, Bonds has finished behind Thomas in each of the last two years, certainly no embarrassment. Bonds' reputation seems to have dropped off in the last few years, but his Hall of Fame talents remain among the best in baseball.

1995 Trailers—Secondary Average

Player	Team	Avg
Rey Sanchez	Cubs	.119
Darren Lewis	Giants-Reds	.148
Roberto Kelly	Expos-Dodgers	.157
Jose Vizcaino	Mets	.157
Joe Girardi	Rockies	.160
Kevin Stocker	Phillies	.172
Ivan Rodriguez	Rangers	.175
Brent Gates	Athletics	.177
Benji Gil	Rangers	.186
Joey Cora	Mariners	.187
Mike Bordick	Athletics	.187

He doesn't show up on the list, because he barely missed the 446 plate-appearance minimum, but Ozzie Guillen was even worse than his crosstown keystone counterpart, Rey Sanchez. Guillen bottomed out with a .099 secondary average, easily the worst among hitters with at least 250 plate appearances. Throw in Darren Lewis, who joins Guillen on the White Sox this year, and the Pale Hose certainly won't threaten the single-season American League walks record, even with patient hitters like Thomas, Ventura, Phillips, etc.

One more note on the trailers: the worst six are all National Leaguers, which might suggest that N.L. managers are more defense-oriented than their A.L. brethren. Or, more likely, it's a one-year fluke.

— Rob Neyer

A complete listing of this category can be found on page 261.

Did The Moon-Shot Boom Continue Last Season?

In last year's *Scoreboard*, we marveled over the gaudy power numbers posted by the league's sluggers during the strike-shortened 1994 campaign. Not only were players hitting *more* home runs in 1994, but they were hitting them *farther* as well—an amazing 45 homers of 450 or more feet, despite the short season. The projected total of 64 "moon shots," if 1994 had been a full 162-game season, was by far the most since we started keeping such data in 1987.

In 1995, sluggers were at it again. No, they didn't break 1994's projected moon-shot total (that mark could stand for quite a while). But they did hit a whopping 42 moon shots, which projects to 47 for a full season. In addition, 1995's sluggers nearly matched their 1994 marks in batting average, runs and homers. Take a look at the chart below, and you'll see that we're living in a great home-run era—not only because of the number of homers being hit, but because of the distances they're traveling as well.

Year	Avg	R/G	HR/G	450-ft HRs
1987	.263	9.5	2.1	32
1988	.254	8.3	1.5	32
1989	.254	8.3	1.5	19
1990	.258	8.5	1.6	32
1991	.256	8.6	1.6	19
1992	.256	8.2	1.4	16
1993	.265	9.2	1.8	47
1994	.270	9.8	2.1	64 *
1995	.267	9.7	2.0	47 *

(* Projected to full season)

One year of performance can often be discounted as a fluke. But *three* years? If the strike had never happened (and the projections held), fans would have seen an amazing 158 moon shots over the past three seasons. When you consider that there were only 150 moon shots in the *six* seasons proceeding 1993, then you begin to realize what an incredible era it is for big swingers.

Why the big jump starting in 1993? It's not a total coincidence that the moon-shot boom began when the Colorado Rockies joined the National League that season. Last season, there were six 450-plus foot homers at Coors Field—more than at any other park in the league. In fact, only two parks—Yankee Stadium and the Oakland Coliseum—saw more than three moon shots. Appropriately, the longest home run of 1995 came at Coors Field, with Raul Mondesi of the Dodgers doing the honors against Omar Olivares on May 5. The illustration shows the top five moon shots of 1995.

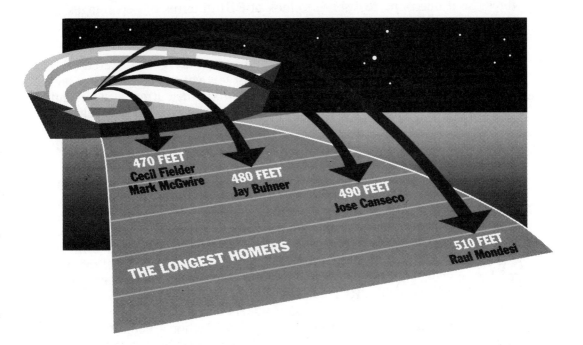

470 FEET
Cecil Fielder
Mark McGwire

480 FEET
Jay Buhner

490 FEET
Jose Canseco

THE LONGEST HOMERS

510 FEET
Raul Mondesi

None of the names above are a big surprise, especially McGwire, who hit a league-leading five moon shots last season—despite missing 40 games. Where's Albert Belle, you ask? Despite leading the majors with 50 dingers last season, Belle hit just two moon shots, both coming on the road. Surprisingly, Belle's home park, Jacobs Field, didn't see *even one* moon shot last season. Just goes to show you that it's the number of homers—not the length—that truly matters.

So will 1996 be another season full of moon shots? You would think so, with a seemingly endless array of young sluggers thriving in each league, and pitcher-friendly parks becoming tougher to find each year. Bleacher fans, bring your gloves! More than likely, there's a moon shot coming your way.

—Scott McDevitt

A complete listing for this category can be found on page 262.

Who Are the Real RBI Kings?

Many of the most popular baseball stats are expressed in terms of percentages—batting average, on-base percentage, slugging percentage, to name three. So it makes perfect sense to look at RBI in terms of percentages as well; after all, it's inevitable that some players will get more chances to drive in runs over the course of a season than others will.

The only question is, what formula should we use? We've tinkered with several RBI percentage formulas over the last few years, and each year one or two readers will write, point out a flaw or two in the current system, and suggest a refinement. Almost all the letters have merit, and last year we even ran *two* different RBI percentage formulas. We may continue to tinker with the formulas in future years, but this year we'd like to stick with the one suggested a year ago by one of our readers, Bill Penn.

The formula begins with the assumption that every trip to the plate—even one with the bases empty—is an "RBI opportunity." That's because the hitter always has a chance to drive himself in with a home run. We compute a percentage based on the hitter's actual RBI total divided by the number of RBI available to him during his plate appearances. We make one adjustment to the "RBI available" total: any runners on base if the hitter drew a walk, got hit by a pitch or reached base on catcher's interference are excluded from the "RBI available" total, except runners who were forced across the plate. Why exclude runners if the batter drew a walk? Because the hitter is performing a positive action—adding another baserunner—without costing his team either an out or a baserunner.

At any rate, here are the 1995 leaders in RBI per opportunity:

Most RBI per Opportunity—1995

Player, Team	RBI Available	RBI	Pct
Mark McGwire, Oak	549	90	16.4
Jay Buhner, Sea	854	121	14.2
Matt Williams, SF	462	65	14.1
Albert Belle, Cle	916	126	13.8
Mo Vaughn, Bos	918	126	13.7
Edgar Martinez, Sea	839	113	13.5
Juan Gonzalez, Tex	612	82	13.4
Paul Sorrento, Cle	591	79	13.4
Dante Bichette, Col	960	128	13.3
Ron Gant, Cin	668	88	13.2

(Minimum 350 Opp)

Didn't we just mention Mark McGwire's "awesome power performance"? The amazing McGwire, who hit 39 homers and drove in 90 runs in only 317 at-bats last year, is the number-one man on the list—by a pretty good margin. No big surprise there, when you think about it. The number-two man was Jay Buhner of the Mariners. Buhner finished fourth in the majors with 121 RBI, but he had fewer RBI available to him than did Albert Belle, Mo Vaughn or the major league RBI leader, Dante Bichette. Sandwiched between Buhner and Belle was Matt Williams, who—like McGwire—was injured for a good part of last year, but extremely productive when he was in the lineup.

The only real surprise on the top 10 list was Paul Sorrento, but even his name isn't all that shocking: Sorrento had 25 homers and 79 RBI in only 323 at-bats last year, which is awfully good production. But which players were the leading "RBI underachievers" of 1995? We selected an "(Un-) Magnificent Seven." All of these players had at least 800 "available RBI" last year, and generally hit in one of the power spots in the batting order (3-4-5-6). Given that, you'd expect at least 85 RBI, and probably more. Instead, all of them not only produced far fewer RBI than that, but drove in runs at a rate well below the 1995 major league average rate of 8.6 RBI per available runner:

RBI "Underachievers"—1995

Player, Team	RBI Available	RBI	Pct
Don Mattingly, Yanks	817	49	6.0
John Olerud, Tor	821	54	6.6
Roberto Kelly, Mon-LA	816	57	7.0
Ivan Rodriguez, Tex	859	67	7.8
Joe Carter, Tor	947	76	8.0
Jeff Kent, Mets	805	65	8.1
Ed Sprague, Tor	901	74	8.2

The Toronto Blue Jays' "Heart of the Order" problems (see essay on page 124) are vividly highlighted here. Remember all those years when Joe Carter was an automatic 100-RBI-a-year man? As recently as strike-shortened 1994, Carter drove in 103 runs despite having only 769 RBI available to him. Last year Big Joe had *more* chances to drive in runs—in fact only five players had more available RBI—but he produced less. Much less.

— Don Zminda

A complete listing for this category can be found on page 263.

Who Are the Human Air Conditioners?

Just call it the "Cecil & Sammy Show."

We're not talking about slugging the ball, though Cecil Fielder and Sammy Sosa are pretty darned good at that. We're talking about slugging the air. . . you know, swinging and missing. And Cecil and Sammy are *really* good at *that*. You want to know who the first two members of the Swing & Miss Hall of Fame will be? Well, consider this: we've been recording swing-and-miss totals for seven years, and Cecil (four times) and Sammy (twice) have led the majors in all but one of them. The only time they missed—well, actually, they missed thousands of times, but you know what we mean—was in 1989, when the legendary Bo Jackson topped the list. Ah, Bo. . . what a master of S&M *he* was, before he hurt that hip.

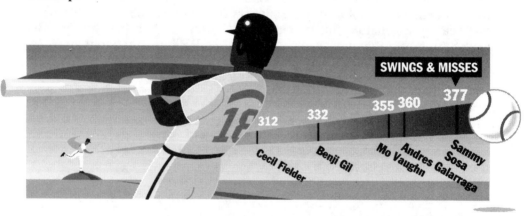

SWINGS & MISSES

312 Cecil Fielder
332 Benji Gil
355 Mo Vaughn
360 Andres Galarraga
377 Sammy Sosa

The chart shows the 1995 leaders in most swings-and-misses, and as usual, there are some pretty good players on the list—not only Fielder and Sosa, but American League MVP Mo Vaughn and one of the better players in the National League, Andres Galarraga. The only non-star is Ranger shortstop Benji Gil. The rest of the top 10 contains more quality players: Raul Mondesi (304 swings and misses), Reggie Sanders (294), Marty Cordova (291), Gary Gaetti (291) and Dante Bichette (278).

So there's nothing wrong with swinging and missing. . . as long as you produce when you *do* happen to hit the ball. Which is why Benji Gil will be hearing all winter about how he "needs to make more contact," while Sammy Sosa and Mo Vaughn *won't* hear that sort of talk. . . or at least not very much of it. But as we've pointed out in the past, the top home-run hitters aren't always guys who bat the breeze a lot. For instance, the top four players on the swing-and-miss list all swung and missed more times than Albert Belle (188) and Frank Thomas (148) *combined*. Rafael Palmeiro, another pretty fair home-run hitter, swung and missed the same number of times as Thomas, 148. And the great Barry Bonds missed on only 141 swings all year.

We also like to look at the swing-and-miss on a percentage basis, based on a player's total number of swings. *This* list contains a lot fewer quality players:

Highest % of Swings that Missed, 1995

Batter, Team	Swings	Missed	Pct
Billy Ashley, LA	462	176	38.1
Benji Gil, Tex	905	332	36.7
Steve Scarsone, SF	501	183	36.5
Melvin Nieves, SD	497	179	36.0
Craig Paquette, Oak	585	209	35.7
Ryan Thompson, Mets	556	197	35.4
Kelly Stinnett, Mets	401	139	34.7
Danny Tartabull, Yanks-Oak	578	190	32.9
Jose Oliva, Atl-StL	379	123	32.5
J.R. Phillips, SF	519	168	32.4

(Minimum 350 swings)

Most of these guys just didn't produce enough to make up for all the times they failed to make contact—beginning with the Dodgers' Billy Ashley, who produced only eight homers and a .237 average in 215 at-bats. That's not going to cut it.

Here are the players who swung and missed the *lowest* percentage of the time in 1995:

Lowest % of Swings that Missed, 1995

Batter, Team	Swings	Missed	Pct
Gregg Jefferies, Phi	779	40	5.1
Wade Boggs, Yanks	798	42	5.3
Brett Butler, Mets-LA	942	52	5.5
Tony Gwynn, SD	837	50	6.0
Joey Cora, Sea	786	51	6.5
Jody Reed, SD	706	48	6.8
Luis Sojo, Sea	569	41	7.2

Batter, Team	Swings	Missed	Pct
Darren Lewis, SF-Cin	775	58	7.5
Lance Johnson, WSox	945	77	8.1
Fernando Vina, Mil	461	39	8.5

(Minimum 350 swings)

Singles and doubles hitters abound here; the most home runs for anyone on the list were Gregg Jefferies' 11. As always, it includes the two players with the highest lifetime averages among modern players, Tony Gwynn (.336) and Wade Boggs (.334). And how consistently do *they* make contact? Well, in the seven years we've been keeping this stat, Gwynn has swung the bat 5,838 times. . . and failed to make contact on only 382 of those swings (6.5 percent)—exactly five more swings-and-misses than Sammy Sosa had in 1995 alone. Boggs' numbers are even more remarkable: 6,369 swings, only 355 misses (5.6 percent). Amazing.

— Don Zminda

A complete listing for this category can be found on page 265.

Sure Belle Was Great, But Did He Create the Most Runs?

You could argue for hours about whether or not he deserved the American League MVP award, but there's no denying that Albert Belle posted some truly awesome numbers in 1995. With 52 doubles and 50 homers—both league-leading figures—he became the first player to top the 50 mark in both categories in the same season. Belle's total of 103 extra-base hits made him the first player in 47 years to top the century mark, and the first American Leaguer in triple figures since way back in 1937. And remember that Belle posted those figures in a schedule shortened by 18 games. Had he been able to play the usual 162-game schedule, or even the pre-expansion total of 154, he probably would have had more than 110 extra-base hits; his figures project to 110 XBH in a 154-game sked, and 116 XBH over 162 contests. How good is that? Well, only two players in major league history have totaled more than 110 extra-base hits—Babe Ruth in 1921 (119 XBH) and Lou Gehrig in 1927 (117). Wow.

Along with his amazing extra-base hit total, Belle led the American League in runs scored (121, tied with Edgar Martinez), runs batted in (126, tied with Mo Vaughn) and slugging percentage (.690). But as great as his numbers were, extra-base hits make up only a part of a player's total offensive contribution, and runs scored and RBI depend to a large degree on how good an offense a player's club has. There are a number of other ways to help a club win: hitting singles, drawing walks, stealing bases, moving runners along with a sacrifice. And of course a player can *cost* his club runs by making outs. So to measure a batter's total contribution, Bill James came up with a stat called "runs created" well over a decade ago. The stat has proven its worth over the course of time, and many if not most of you are probably familiar with it. If you're not, the definition is listed in the Glossary; when you look at it you'll quickly see that runs created covers just about everything, even including penalties for getting caught stealing or hitting into double plays.

The chart on the following page shows the 1995 leaders in runs created, and as you can see, Belle did *not* lead the major leagues in this category last year—he was a surprisingly distant second to Edgar Martinez of the Mariners. Frank Thomas of the White Sox created the same number of runs as Belle—actually a fraction more, if you want to be technical; Thomas' numbers compute to 144.45 runs created, Belle's to 144.05. We've already discussed Martinez' MVP credentials in the Seattle essay, but the main reason both he and Thomas matched up so well against Belle in runs created is that they reached base much more often than Albert did. Martinez led the majors with a .479 on-base percentage, while Thomas was second with a .454 mark. Belle's OBP, while excellent at .401, ranked well behind Thomas and Martinez; in fact, he didn't even make the American League top 10. And OBP is an extremely important stat; while slugging is undeniably important, study after study has shown that the single most important thing a player can do to help his club win is get on base.

THE RUN MAKERS

Runs created

Edgar Martinez	161
Frank Thomas	144
Albert Belle	144
Tim Salmon	142
Barry Bonds	134
Rafael Palmeiro	124
Dante Bichette	121
Craig Biggio	121
Mo Vaughn	121
John Valentin	119

Tim Salmon of the Angels also had an excellent OBP last year (.429, tied for fourth best in the A.L.). That, along with his outstanding slugging totals, helped Salmon create 142 runs, only two fewer than Belle. The National League leader in runs created was the great Barry Bonds, a perennial leader in this category. Like Martinez, Thomas and Salmon, Bonds is a great slugger and a guy who's constantly on base—he's led the National League in OBP four of the last five years, including 1995.

Runs created is the basis for another Bill James stat called "offensive winning percentage"; the definition is in the Glossary. It estimates the winning percentage of nine Albert Belles (or whoever) in the context of his league in a particular season. Players who create a lot of runs in a lower-scoring league like the N.L. get more credit, and since it's a percentage, those with fewer plate appearances aren't at a disadvantage. Here are the 1995 leaders in offensive winning percentage among players who qualified for the batting title:

1995 Leaders—Offensive Winning Percentage

Player, Team	OW%
Edgar Martinez, Sea	.860
Frank Thomas, WSox	.813
Barry Bonds, SF	.806
Mike Piazza, LA	.806
Tim Salmon, Cal	.801
Jim Thome, Cle	.790
Albert Belle, Cle	.784
Ryan Klesko, Atl	.780
Reggie Sanders, Cin	.775
Larry Walker, Col	.770

(Minimum 3.1 plate appearances per scheduled game)

Martinez and Thomas are still one-two, while Bonds moves up to third, in a tie with the Dodgers' Mike Piazza, who didn't rank among the runs created leaders because he missed considerable time with injuries. Belle, interestingly, drops all the way down to seventh, behind teammate Jim Thome. So while Belle had an awesome season, it's obvious that several players did as much or more to help their clubs when they were in the lineup last year.

Speaking of contributing "when they were in the lineup," one player had a higher offensive winning percentage than even Edgar Martinez did last year. The player—surprise!—was Gary Sheffield of the Marlins, whose superb numbers added up to an .863 offensive winning percentage. Unfortunately, injuries limited Sheffield to 63 games last year. If we reduced the qualifier for offensive winning percentage to 250 plate appearances, the top five would have consisted of Sheffield, Martinez, Mark McGwire (.831), Matt Williams (.816) and Thomas. Here's hoping Sheffield, McGwire and Williams can stay healthy in 1996.

— Don Zminda

A complete listing for this category can be found on page 267.

IV. QUESTIONS ON PITCHING

Who Gets the Easy Saves?

Save percentage is a very useful stat, and one of the better ones to enter the game in recent years. However, you don't know from looking at a save percentage whether the reliever got most of his opportunities in low-pressure situations—like coming in to start the ninth with a three-run lead—or whether he was often asked to come in with the tying or winning runs on base.

That's why we like to divide save opportunities into three different categories. Here are the definitions:

Easy Save: First batter faced is not the tying run *and* the reliever pitches one inning or less. Example: Jose Mesa comes in with a 4-2 lead and no one on base to start the ninth. We call this an Easy Save Opportunity.

Tough Save: Reliever comes in with the tying run anywhere on base. Example: Mark Wohlers enters with the Braves leading 5-3, runners on first and third, and one out in the ninth. This is a Tough Save Opportunity.

Regular Save: All save opportunities that fall into neither the Easy or Tough categories are classified as Regular.

There is an enormous difference in the way major league relievers perform when trying to convert a Tough opportunity vs. one which is Regular or Easy. Here are the overall figures from 1995:

	Easy			Regular			Tough		
League	Sv	Op	%	Sv	Op	%	Sv	Op	%
A.L.	231	253	91	211	333	63	51	154	33
N.L.	217	246	88	240	351	68	56	146	38
MLB Totals	448	499	90	451	684	66	107	300	36

That's some difference—a conversion rate of about 90 percent for the easy opportunities, vs. less than 40 percent for the tough ones.

How do the opportunities break down for individual closers? Here's a breakdown for all major league relievers who saved at least 25 games last year:

Save Conversions—Major League Save Leaders, 1995

Pitcher, Team	Easy			Regular			Tough			Total		
	Sv	Op	%	Sv	Op	%	Sv	Op	%	Sv	Op	%
Jose Mesa, Cle	33	33	100	12	14	86	1	1	100	46	48	96
Randy Myers, Cubs	25	26	96	10	13	77	3	5	60	38	44	86
Lee Smith, Cal	23	24	96	14	16	87	0	1	0	37	41	90
Tom Henke, StL	19	19	100	12	14	86	5	5	100	36	38	95
Rod Beck, SF	17	18	94	13	18	72	3	7	43	33	43	77
Rick Aguilera, Min-Bos	17	17	100	12	13	92	3	6	50	32	36	89
Todd Worrell, LA	15	16	94	12	15	80	5	5	100	32	36	89
Heathcliff Slocumb, Phi	18	19	95	12	17	71	2	2	100	32	38	84
Roberto Hernandez, WSox	17	17	100	13	19	68	2	6	33	32	42	76
Trevor Hoffman, SD	20	23	87	10	13	77	1	2	50	31	38	82
John Wetteland, Yanks	22	23	96	6	11	55	3	3	100	31	37	84
Jeff Montgomery, KC	12	12	100	16	22	73	3	4	75	31	38	82
Mel Rojas, Mon	7	8	87	22	28	79	1	3	33	30	39	77
John Franco, Mets	17	17	100	11	17	65	1	2	50	29	36	81
Dennis Eckersley, Oak	20	21	95	7	14	50	2	3	67	29	38	76
Jeff Brantley, Cin	10	10	100	17	19	89	1	3	33	28	32	88
Mike Henneman, Det-Hou	14	14	100	10	12	83	2	3	67	26	29	90
Mark Wohlers, Atl	9	9	100	13	15	87	3	5	60	25	29	86

Jose Mesa of the Indians had a terrific season in 1995, posting a 1.13 ERA and converting 46 of his 48 save opportunities. However, Tribe manager Mike Hargrove did his best to make sure that Mesa was under as little pressure as possible. Of Mesa's 48 opportunities, only one came in the Tough category. Meanwhile, he had 33 Easy Save opportunities. As we said, Mesa had a terrific season, but a look at the numbers shows that he pitched under far less pressure than did, say, Rod Beck, Rick Aguilera or Tom Henke. All of *them* had at least five Tough opportunities during the year. And you could certainly argue that Henke, who was a perfect 5-for-5 in Tough opportunities and 36-for-38 overall, had as impressive a year as Mesa did.

One thing that's clear from studying these numbers over the course of several years is that managers are doing more and more to avoid Tough save opportunities for their closers. Look at the drop in Tough save opportunities per 100 games played over the last four years, plus the individual leader in Tough Save opportunities:

Tough Save Opportunities, 1992-95

Year	Games	TS Opp	Opp/100 Gm	TS Opp Leader
1992	2106	431	20.5	Jeff Russell, 16
1993	2269	421	18.6	John Wetteland, 10
1994	1600	274	17.1	Steve Reed, 8
1995	2017	300	14.9	3 with 7

While the last two years were strike-shortened, it's almost certain that we'll never see a pitcher get 16 Tough Save opportunities in a year, the way Jeff Russell did in 1992. Seasons like Mesa's—only one Tough Save chance all year—are apt to become more and more commonplace. That's something to remember when you're studying those save percentages.

— Don Zminda

A complete listing for this category can be found on page 269.

Who Pitched Better Last Year: Martinez or Candiotti?

One of my favorite pitcher seasons of all time is Nolan Ryan, 1987. He paced the National League with 270 strikeouts, a 2.76 ERA. . . *and* 16 losses, against only eight victories. What happened to Ryan in 1987? His fellow Astros in the lineup simply didn't score many runs when Ryan was on the mound. And that's the subject of this essay: run support for pitchers.

Ramon Martinez was excellent in 1995. The Dodger righthander won 17 and lost only seven, his best record since 1990. Meanwhile, knuckleballing teammate Tom Candiotti won only seven games while losing 14. But was Martinez really a better pitcher than Candiotti?

Let's compare Candiotti and Martinez in some important categories other than won-lost record:

Pitcher	GS	IP	H	BB	SO	ERA
Candiotti	30	190.1	187	58	141	3.50
Martinez	30	206.1	176	81	138	3.66

In about the same number of innings, the two pitchers struck out around the same number of hitters. Candiotti allowed more hits, but Martinez issued an N.L.-high 81 walks. Their ERAs were similar, with Candiotti slightly better. The big difference between them? The Dodgers scored 5.32 runs per nine innings behind Martinez, while Candiotti "enjoyed" only 3.45 runs of support per nine innings, the lowest figure in the major leagues.

This is nothing new for Candiotti, who has to be the hardest-luck pitcher of recent times. In the last seven seasons, Candiotti has ranked among the four least-supported pitchers in his league *five* times:

Season	Support	Lg Rnk	ERA	Record
1989	3.54	2nd Worst	3.10	13-10
1991	3.52	4th Worst	2.65	13-13
1992	3.23	2nd Worst	3.00	11-15
1993	2.53	1st Worst	3.12	8-10
1995	3.45	1st Worst	3.50	7-14

That Martinez/Candiotti pair is not particularly unique, by the way. Every season, there are a number of pairs of pitchers with similar records *except* for run support, and the resulting won-lost record.

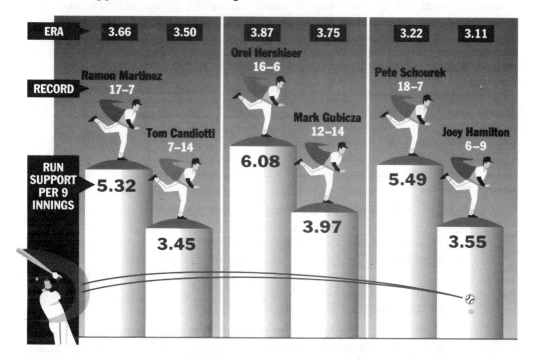

| ERA | 3.66 | 3.50 | | 3.87 | 3.75 | | 3.22 | 3.11 |

Orel Hershiser
16–6

Ramon Martinez
17–7

Pete Schourek
18–7

RECORD

Mark Gubicza
12–14

Tom Candiotti
7–14

Joey Hamilton
6–9

RUN SUPPORT PER 9 INNINGS

5.32 3.45 6.08 3.97 5.49 3.55

For example, Orel Hershiser last year started 26 games and posted a 3.87 ERA. Mark Gubicza started 33 games with a 3.75 ERA. Who was the better pitcher? Most would say Hershiser, because he went 16-6 while Gubicza was just 12-14. But the only real difference between them was run support. The amazing Indians scored 6.1 runs in support of the Bulldog, while the punchless Royals scored only 4.0 runs behind Goobie. By the way, Cleveland's Charles Nagy led the majors with 8.1 runs of support per nine innings, and he matched Hershiser's 16-6 record despite a 4.55 ERA.

Run support tends to even out over a number of seasons (though sometimes it might take a while; just ask Candiotti). If you're looking for possible surprises in 1996, you might want to start with the hard-luck pitchers of 1995, especially Joey Hamilton and Tom Candiotti.

— Rob Neyer

A complete listing of this category can be found on page 270.

Is Greg Maddux the Best. . . Ever?

"Greg Maddux is the best pitcher in the major leagues today." That's not exactly what you'd call a controversial statement, given that Maddux has captured an unprecedented four straight National League Cy Young Awards. But how about this one: "Over the last four seasons, Greg Maddux has been the best pitcher *ever*." Is that possible? Could Maddux really have been better than all those immortals with plaques in Cooperstown?

First let's look at the standard yardsticks for starting pitchers: wins and ERA. Thanks to both the modern five-man rotation and a pair of shortened seasons, Maddux has won "only" 75 games over the last four seasons. That's the best in the majors over that span, but pales compared to the four-year runs of old-timers like Walter Johnson (124) and Pete Alexander (121), and even relative newcomers like Jim Palmer (86) and Tom Seaver (84).

What about ERA? Maddux's ERA over the last four seasons is a quite amazing 1.98. Amazing for this offensive-minded era, yes. Historically amazing? Not really. Maddux's four-year ERA ranks 54th among pitchers who qualified for the ERA title in each of four straight seasons. But here's the kicker: of all the pitchers who rank ahead of Maddux, the most recent was Sandy Koufax, 1963-66 (1.86). Before *him*, you have to go all the way back to Walter Johnson, 1916 through 1919 (1.73).

Of course, there's a simple reason for that: conditions change. Pitching with a lively ball in the relatively cozy ballparks of 1995 is vastly different than pitching in the big yards of the Dead Ball Era. How to adjust? It's pretty elementary, really. We just look at ERA relative to league, which is simply the pitcher's ERA divided by the league ERA in a particular season or number of seasons. The lower, the better. In 1995, for example, Maddux posted a 1.63 ERA and the National League a 4.18 ERA, which yields a 0.390 ratio. That happens to be the fifth-best figure in major league history. The second best? Gee, you have to go all the way back to 1994, when Maddux posted an even more amazing 0.370 mark. A year ago, we slightly discounted those numbers because the season was so short. But they were obviously no fluke.

But lots of pitchers have been brilliant for a season or two, and many of them couldn't sustain that level. For example, the best single-season ratio belongs to non-Hall of Famer Dutch Leonard, who compiled a .366 mark in 1914. Four seasons, on the other hand, seems like a pretty good test. The chart below lists the top 10 four-season ratios of all time.

Pitcher	4 Years	ERA	Lg ERA	Rel ERA
Walter Johnson	1910-13	1.43	3.03	0.472
Walter Johnson	1912-15	1.45	2.98	0.487
Walter Johnson	1911-14	1.53	3.08	0.497
Greg Maddux	1992-95	1.98	3.98	0.497
Mordecai Brown	1906-09	1.31	2.51	0.522
Sandy Koufax	1963-66	1.86	3.49	0.533
Walter Johnson	1913-16	1.58	2.85	0.554
Sandy Koufax	1962-65	2.02	3.58	0.564
Christy Mathewson	1908-11	1.62	2.84	0.570
Mordecai Brown	1905-08	1.50	2.61	0.575

As if there was any question, this list strongly suggests that Maddux will wind up in Cooperstown. If we extended this to the top 50 four-season performances, you'd see 20 different pitchers. Of those 20, only Maddux and Roger Clemens (neither eligible) and Doc White are not in the Hall of Fame.

But there's another striking thing about the pitchers above: Maddux stands out because he alone doesn't possess a single overpowering pitch. Johnson had the awesome fastball, Brown had his famous three-fingered curve, Mathewson had a great fastball and of course the fadeaway. . . What does Maddux have? His best pitch is a circle change-up, hardly an offering which puts fear in the heart of enemy batters. He also throws a fine slider, an average fastball and an occasional curve.

Is Maddux the best ever over a four-year span? I'd have to say no. I'd rank him number two, right behind the incomparable Walter Johnson, who threw 464-odd more innings and won 44 more games over his best four-year span than did Maddux. And notice that the Big Train basically continued that performance for seven seasons. On the other hand, given what he has to work with, I would allow that Maddux deserves his own lofty title: "Smartest Ever."

— Rob Neyer

A complete listing for this category can be found on page 271.

Who's Better, Power or Finesse Pitchers?

One of those on-going arguments in baseball is who's better: a flame-throwing power pitcher, or a thinking finesse pitcher? Who would you rather have in Game 7: a Randy Johnson, who could throw his heater by everyone in the lineup, or a Greg Maddux, who can change speeds in order to frustrate hitters? We thought we'd investigate the two groups' differences and then try to answer that question once and for all.

Before analyzing statistics, we must decide what distinguishes a power pitcher from a finesse pitcher. We used a two-step process in deciding this. First, if a hurler could throw a 93-plus MPH fastball, he was considered a power pitcher, no questions asked. These were guys like Johnson, Kevin Appier, John Smoltz, and Pedro Martinez. On the other hand, if the gun maxed out at 85 or lower, you have a finesse pitcher. Jason Jacome, Scott Sanderson, Fernando Valenzuela, and Denny Neagle all fit that description. Then, what to do with those guys in the middle who throw *between* 85 and 93? We simply used BB+K per nine innings to classify the rest. Hurlers that fan and walk a lot of batters (i.e. Darren Oliver and Al Leiter) generally do so because they throw hard. On the flip side, control freaks that rely on batters to *hit* into outs (Bob Tewksbury) tend to have a low (BB+K)/9 ratio.

Using every pitcher that started at least five games in '95 gives us these results:

League	Type	No.	BB/9	K/9	K/BB	H/9	HR/9	ERA	W	L	Pct.
AL	Power	44	4.19	7.02	1.68	9.12	1.05	4.77	301	315	.489
AL	Finesse	60	3.11	4.86	1.56	9.74	1.10	4.71	424	400	.515
NL	Power	44	3.57	7.28	2.04	8.81	0.95	4.25	320	325	.496
NL	Finesse	56	2.67	5.52	2.07	9.43	0.97	4.13	402	386	.510

Both leagues have nearly the same percentage of power pitchers (42.3 percent for the A.L., 44.0 for the N.L.). In each league, both the walk and strikeout ratios were higher for power pitchers than they were for finesse pitchers. This jives with our definition of power/finesse pitchers. Also in both leagues, finesse pitchers give up more hits. This makes sense because as mentioned earlier, finesse pitchers rely more on their defense than do power pitchers. Hence, more ground balls may squirt through the infield for hits. Both groups also allow about the same number of home runs, and also permit a practically equal number of earned runs. Power pitchers tend to win just under 50 percent of the time, while finessers are victorious just *over* 50 percent of the time.

Why would finesse pitchers win more than their hard-throwing brothers? We suspect it's because power pitchers tend to get more chances than finesse pitchers. That means that a lot of young hard throwers get thrown into the fray before they're really ready to pitch in the majors. Conversely, finesse pitchers have to earn every chance they get, so when they finally make it to the bigs, they're ready.

Due to free agency and frequent team-jumping by players, it may be naive to think there is a big difference in players between leagues. In this example, power pitchers and finesse pitchers tend to perform similarly in each league. Also, there doesn't seem to be a major advantage for either type of pitcher. It's possible that 30 years ago the A.L. boasted more fireballers or, for example, finesse pitchers comprised most of the National League. In the '90s however, this is one difference that just doesn't seem to exist.

— Dave Mundo

Who Are Baseball's Best-Hitting Pitchers?

Although many baseball fans are welcoming the idea of inter-league play, you can bet that American League batting coaches are less than thrilled. Why? Well, it's more than likely that A.L. pitchers will be required to hit in the National League parks during inter-league games (just like in the World Series), and those batting coaches will be responsible for teaching the Mike Mussinas and Jack McDowells of the world how to swing the stick. In fact, it's very likely that pitchers in *both* leagues will spend more time working on their hitting than ever before. That additional effort could yield some interesting results in the N.L., where pitchers have already shown considerable improvement in their hitting over the last few seasons.

No, there isn't a Don Drysdale (29 career homers) or Bob Gibson (24) swinging the lumber in today's game, but in 1995, pitchers at least kept heading in the right direction—swatting a respectable 19 home runs, while keeping their batting average well above the level of three years ago.

National League Pitchers' Hitting

Year	Avg	HR
1989	.139	18
1990	.138	14
1991	.138	12
1992	.137	12
1993	.151	17
1994	.154	7
1995	.148	19

Why the big jump in home runs? Did one pitcher make a difference? Not really. Of the 19 home runs hit last season, only three pitchers—Steve Avery, John Smiley and Fernando Valenzuela—hit more than one, indicating that the improvement was indeed league-wide. And while it's true that the batting average for N.L. pitchers fell by six points, the batting average for *all* N.L. players fell by four (.267 to .263). Relatively speaking, N.L. pitchers held their own at the plate in 1995.

So who are the league's best-hitting pitchers? The illustration shows the active pitchers with the best career batting averages (minimum 150 career plate appearances).

PITCHERS WHO CAN HIT

	HR	AVG.
Omar Olivares	4	.229
Tommy Greene	4	.219
Chris Hammond	4	.215
Bill Swift	1	.211
Fernando Valenzuela	10	.204

Active pitchers with a minimum of 150 plate appearances lifetime.

St. Louis' Allen Watson took top honors in 1995, batting a remarkable .417 (15-for-36) with five RBI. Watson has proven to be anything but an easy out in his career, fanning just 13 times in 100 career at-bats. Billy Ashley, take note. Watson could also give a few lessons to the pitchers listed below, those with the five *worst* lifetime batting averages (minimum 150 plate appearances).

Worst-Hitting Pitchers—Active Career Leaders

Pitcher	Avg	AB	H	HR	RBI
Jeff Fassero	.070	143	10	0	1
John Burkett	.076	367	28	0	13
Terry Mulholland	.081	405	33	1	9
Bruce Ruffin	.082	294	24	0	7
Jim Deshaies	.088	373	33	0	12

(Minimum 150 plate appearances)

About all Fassero has going for him at the plate is consistency—he hit .063 in 1993, .068 in 1994 and .070 last season. OK, *technically* he's improving, but at that rate he'll hit the Mendoza line about the middle of the next century.

—Scott McDevitt

A complete listing for this category can be found on page 272.

How Dominant Was Percival?

Here at our STATS offices in suburban Chicago, we're still buzzing over the unbelievable season of the Northwestern University football team. Not only did the Wildcats make it all the way to the Rose Bowl, but they did it after coming from *nowhere*. You could probably put the same label on California reliever Troy Percival—baseball's equivalent of the Wildcats.

Prior to 1995, Percival had spent two seasons at Triple-A Vancouver, posting ERAs of 6.27 and 4.13 in a park generally considered pretty good to pitch in. He'd also surrendered 87 hits in 79.2 innings. But given a chance by the Angels in '95, Percival delivered in a *huge* way, posting a sparkling 1.95 ERA in 62 appearances as Lee Smith's set-up man. Word of his high-90s fastball spread in a hurry, but nothing seemed to phase Percival. Batters hit an anemic .147 against him last season—the lowest figure against any pitcher in the major leagues. He allowed just 37 hits in 74.0 innings, or 4.50 per nine innings. Let's see Darnell Autry do that.

As it turns out, Percival's 4.50 hits per nine innings wasn't just the best in 1995, but the best mark *ever* among pitchers with at least 50 innings. Take a look.

Lowest Hit/IP—Season					
Player	Team	Year	H	IP	H/9 IP
Troy Percival	California	1995	37	74.0	4.50
Mike Naymick	Cleveland	1943	32	63.0	4.57
Rob Murphy	Cincinnati	1986	26	50.1	4.65
Vicente Romo	Los Angeles/Cleveland	1968	44	84.0	4.71
Jim Brewer	Los Angeles	1972	41	78.0	4.73
Ryne Duren	New York (AL)	1958	40	76.0	4.74
Andy Messersmith	California	1968	44	81.0	4.89
Steve Mingori	Cleveland	1971	31	57.0	4.89
Dennis Eckersley	Oakland	1989	32	57.2	4.99
Toad Ramsey	Louisville (AA)	1885	44	79.0	5.01
(minimum 50 innings pitched)					

Appropriately, the list has a strong California flavor to it, especially considering that Ryne Duren, dark glasses and all, spent a couple of seasons with the Angels. Andy Messersmith is one of the more interesting names here. Like Percival, he made the list for accomplishments during his rookie season, making five starts and 23 relief appearances for the Angels in

1968. But he's better known for his fine seasons later with the Dodgers, as well as his contribution toward making free agency a reality for major leaguers. And guess what? Vicente Romo, Rob Murphy and Toad Ramsey also made the list in *their* first-full seasons, while Steve Mingori made it in his second-full season. Why did these pitchers do so well at such young ages? There are a few possible reasons, the most obvious being that batters simply weren't familiar with their stuff. Another is that younger pitchers, of course, usually have stronger arms and a little more pop on the fastball. Not everybody on the list had a blazing fastball, however; for instance, Jim Brewer's best pitch was a baffling screwball.

So where are the big names, you ask? Apart from Dennis Eckersley, they're a little farther down on the list. As you might imagine, it's much more difficult to post a low H/9 IP figure when throwing a high number of innings. Nolan Ryan's best season (1972) is just 20th all-time, but it's not too shabby considering that he threw 284 innings. For the record, Ryan allowed just 166 hits that season, or 5.26 per nine innings. And of course, he did it as a member of the Angels.

Percival will be just 26 on Opening Day, so the sky's the limit in terms of his future. But no matter what role the Angels have in mind for him—set-up man or closer—he'll be hard-pressed to match what he did last season.

— Scott McDevitt

A complete listing for this category can be found on page 273.

Which Pitchers Get The Fans Home Early?

In June of 1993, I set out on my first "real" vacation since college—a 10-day baseball smorgasbord that took me from my home in Indianapolis to St. Louis, Kansas City, Minneapolis, Milwaukee, Chicago, Detroit, Cleveland, Cincinnati and back home. I put 3,000 miles on my car during that little adventure, returning home more exhausted than when I left. But I simply didn't care—I had *lived* baseball for those 10 days. For me, nothing compared to being at the ballpark.

Ever since that experience, I've been troubled by the cries of those seemingly obsessed with speeding up the game. Baseball is not a feature film—something to be cut and edited and configured into a tidy little two-hour package. Yes, the Scott Sandersons of the world test my patience on occasion, but the idea of a "pitch clock" should be enough to terrorize any fan. What's next? A red, white and blue baseball? A three-point line?

So in the spirit of those fans who stay until the ushers whisk them away, we present 1995's highest individual pitch outings. Long games? You bet. But they also include some great performances.

Most Pitches in a Game—1995

Pitcher, Team	Date	Opp	Fin	W/L	IP	H	ER	BB	K	Pit
Randy Johnson, Sea	7/07	Cle	5-3	W	9.0	8	2	0	13	161
David Wells, Det	6/12	NY	6-1	W	8.2	4	1	5	7	158
Todd Van Poppel, Oak	8/17	Sea	3-2	ND	7.0	6	2	3	5	153
John Burkett, Fla	7/03	SD	5-2	W	9.0	7	1	3	7	148
Dave Stewart, Oak	5/18	Chi	2-4	L	7.0	9	4	3	6	148
Kenny Rogers, Tex	9/22	Cal	8-3	W	9.0	7	3	5	3	148
Chuck Finley, Cal	5/23	NY	10-0	W	9.0	2	0	2	15	147
Kenny Rogers, Tex	8/04	Cal	6-4	W	7.2	7	4	3	8	147
Andy Benes, Sea	8/24	NY	9-7	ND	7.0	8	7	6	5	147
Kenny Rogers, Tex	5/21	Mil	6-0	W	9.0	5	0	3	5	146
Steve Sparks, Mil	7/07	Cal	9-3	W	9.0	4	2	7	3	146

A couple of things stand out here, most notably the physique of the three hurlers owning 150-pitch outings. Johnson stands 6'10" and weighs 225. Wells is 6'4", 225. And Van Poppel is 6'5", 210. No matter how good his stuff is, you'll rarely find a small pitcher like Dennis Martinez (6'1", 180) with pitch counts that high. They simply don't have the stamina. The other thing that stands out is that Kenny Rogers appears three times on this list, while no other pitcher—even Johnson—appears more than once. If the

Yankees wanted a workhorse, they appear to have invested in the right guy.

Now for the other extreme. In last year's *Scoreboard*, we noted that Atlanta's Greg Maddux had two of the top 10 low-pitch games of 1994. Last season, Maddux did even better. Not only did he have three of the top 10 games, but he had *the* top three—all 88-pitch outings.

Fewest Pitches in a Nine-Inning Complete Game—1995

Pitcher, Team	Date	Opp	Fin	W/L	IP	H	ER	BB	K	Pit
Greg Maddux, Atl	06/15	Mon	2-0	W	9.0	7	0	0	3	88
Greg Maddux, Atl	08/20	StL	1-0	W	9.0	2	0	0	9	88
Greg Maddux, Atl	08/31	Hou	5-2	W	9.0	6	2	1	4	88
Mark Gubicza, KC	08/06	Min	11-1	W	9.0	4	1	0	1	89
Scott Erickson, Bal	09/27	Tor	7-0	W	9.0	3	0	0	5	91
Joey Hamilton, SD	06/14	StL	3-0	W	9.0	2	0	2	3	92
Bret Saberhagen, Mets	06/23	Atl	9-3	W	9.0	6	3	0	3	93
Kirk Rueter, Mon	08/27	SF	1-0	W	9.0	1	0	1	7	94
Bobby Jones, Mets	09/08	Mon	5-0	W	9.0	3	0	2	6	95
Bob Tewksbury, Tex	07/07	NY	10-0	W	9.0	6	0	0	5	96
Paul Wagner, Pit	09/19	StL	12-1	W	9.0	7	1	2	4	96

You'll obviously always find some control artists on a list like this—Maddux, Saberhagen, Tewksbury—but you'll encounter a few surprises as well, like Erickson and Wagner. Both of those hurlers saved their best for last, as Erickson shut down the Blue Jays in his final start of the season, and Wagner had only two more outings after his gem against St. Louis.

So you want to catch a major league game *and* your late local news? In that case, Maddux is clearly your man. Just like last season, Maddux's nine-inning games were, on average, the speediest in the majors, at 2:29. In fact, Maddux's 88-pitch gem against St. Louis was the fastest game of the year, lasting just 1:50. Mike Morgan (2:30), Tim Wakefield (2:33), Steve Avery (2:36), John Burkett (2:37) and Paul Wagner (2:38) followed the Mad Dog in average game time, with Shawn Boskie bringing up the rear. His average nine-inning game? An ugly 3:09. We tip our hats to those die-hard Angels fans, who endured both Boskie *and* Scott Sanderson in the same season.

— Scott McDevitt

A complete listing for this category can be found on page 274.

Which Relievers *Really* Put Out the Fires?

Although the role of relief pitcher has evolved dramatically over the past 30 years (Ted Abernathy unoficially led the majors in saves with just 31 saves in 1965), the statistics used for measuring relief performance haven't really kept pace. The save has obviously endured, but not without great skepticism. How about wins for relief pitchers? Do they mean anything? Not really, except that relievers get lucky from time to time, entering the game at *just* the right moment. Pittsburgh's Roy Face is probably the best example of that well-timed luck, going 18-1 in relief in 1959. How about ERA? Well, although it's the best benchmark for measuring the quality of *starting* pitchers, it's not nearly as insightful when it comes to relievers. Why? Because the runners a relief pitcher inherits don't belong to him.

So what *is* the best way to measure relief performance? One answer might be Inherited-Runner Percentage—that is, the percentage of inherited runners a relief pitcher allows to score after entering the game. Although Detroit reliever Mike Christopher didn't post intimidating numbers in 1995 —a 3.82 ERA and 71 hits allowed in 61.1 innings—the data below shows

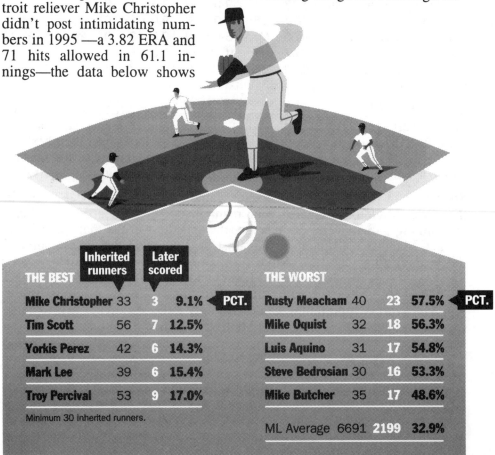

THE BEST	Inherited runners	Later scored	PCT.
Mike Christopher	33	3	9.1%
Tim Scott	56	7	12.5%
Yorkis Perez	42	6	14.3%
Mark Lee	39	6	15.4%
Troy Percival	53	9	17.0%

Minimum 30 inherited runners.

THE WORST			PCT.
Rusty Meacham	40	23	57.5%
Mike Oquist	32	18	56.3%
Luis Aquino	31	17	54.8%
Steve Bedrosian	30	16	53.3%
Mike Butcher	35	17	48.6%
ML Average	6691	2199	32.9%

that he came through when it counted most, allowing just three of 33 inherited runners to cross the plate.

Since Steve Bedrosian chalked up 184 lifetime saves and a Cy Young Award to his credit before retiring in midseason last year, you've likely heard of him. But the rest of the pitchers spend most of their time toiling in middle relief, and that's where this statistic provides the most insight. The Jose Mesas of the world simply don't inherit many runners. In fact, Mesa inherited only 12 runners (three of them scored) in 62 appearances last year. Who inherited the most runners in 1995? Three pitchers tied for the honor with 66, with nearly identical results—Roger McDowell (15 runners scored), Bob Patterson (14) and Jesse Orosco (15).

Mesa's bullpen mates—most notably Paul Assenmacher, Eric Plunk and Julian Tavarez—didn't see a terribly high number of inherited runners in 1995. But when they did, they shut the door in a hurry. Here are how the teams stacked up in inherited-runner percentage last season:

1995 Team Inherited-Runners Percentages

AL Team	Inherited	Scored	Pct	NL Team	Inherited	Scored	Pct
Indians	186	33	17.7	Rockies	260	73	28.1
White Sox	287	81	28.2	Cubs	316	93	29.4
Angels	301	91	30.2	Expos	275	83	30.2
Orioles	308	99	32.1	Braves	171	52	30.4
Rangers	321	104	32.4	Pirates	236	72	30.5
Yankees	210	70	33.3	Cardinals	186	58	31.2
Athletics	263	88	33.5	Phillies	182	57	31.3
Red Sox	253	86	34.0	Mets	148	50	33.8
Twins	272	95	34.9	Astros	267	91	34.1
Tigers	303	106	35.0	Marlins	234	81	34.6
Brewers	234	86	36.8	Reds	141	49	34.8
Mariners	248	92	37.1	Giants	269	94	34.9
Royals	222	87	39.2	Padres	219	79	36.1
Blue Jays	178	75	42.1	Dodgers	201	74	36.8

Although the two league leaders both made the playoffs, five other playoff teams—the Red Sox, Yankees, Mariners, Reds and Dodgers—finished below the major league average, indicating that maybe teams with "middle relief problems" aren't necessarily doomed.

—Scott McDevitt

A complete listing for this category can be found on page 275.

Who Holds the Fort?

Middle relievers rarely stay around long enough to pick up more than the occasional save, and they typically gain credit for a victory only when their team mounts an improbable comeback. So aside from ERA, how does one judge the effectiveness of a middle reliever? We like the "hold," a stat co-invented by our own John Dewan more than a decade ago.

What's a hold? When a reliever enters a game in a save situation and retires at least one batter, then passes the save situation to another reliever, we credit him with a hold.

Last year we wrote an entire essay on the validity of the hold, so we won't say a lot about that. Suffice to say that like the save, the hold isn't perfect, and pitchers do occasionally earn holds despite pitching poorly. But in general, the hold is a solid indicator of effective work.

Pitcher	Holds
Troy Percival	29
Bob Wickman	21
Ricky Bottalico	20
Greg McMichael	20
Julian Tavarez	19
Tim Scott	19
Dave Veres	19
Curtis Leskanic	19
Tony Fossas	19
Stan Belinda	17

The illustration lists the 1995 major league leaders in holds. At the top of the list, by a wide margin, is Angels reliever Troy Percival, about whom you can read more elsewhere in this book. Percival was simply brilliant in his set-up role, passing 29 save chances to other relievers.

Interestingly, all 10 pitchers on the list are newcomers; the 1994 top 10 was shut out in '95. On the other hand, hold success can mean a promotion is in the offing. The top two "holders" in 1994, Mel Rojas and Heathcliff Slocumb, both graduated to closer duties in 1995.

Here's how the major league clubs fared in terms of holds last year:

American League		National League	
Team	**Holds**	**Team**	**Holds**
Angels	61	Rockies	75
Red Sox	58	Cardinals	61
Indians	51	Phillies	55
White Sox	50	Marlins	51
Brewers	44	Cubs	48
Mariners	44	Astros	48
Athletics	40	Expos	45
Twins	38	Pirates	45
Rangers	35	Braves	44
Yankees	35	Dodgers	40
Tigers	35	Padres	39
Orioles	35	Giants	39
Royals	31	Reds	32
Blue Jays	21	Mets	22

Obviously, team holds depend a lot on the way a manager uses his bullpen. Faced with a ballpark that often forced the early exit of his starters, Rockies manager Don Baylor regularly signaled for a reliever to quell enemy rallies, and the Rockies paced the majors in holds by a healthy margin.

But you can't make too many generalizations about holds. Yes, the Blue Jays were terrible last year and they also finished with the fewest holds in the majors (21). But the Royals were next fewest in the American League despite a fine pitching staff. In fact, the hold numbers might best be used to evaluate managers rather than teams.

— Rob Neyer

A complete listing for this category can be found on page 276.

Which Relievers Have the Best Conversion Rates?

When a relief pitcher enters a game with a lead in the middle or late innings, he's got one of two jobs. He's expected to either (a) hold the lead until he gives way to another reliever, or (b) finish the game with the lead intact. If he does job (a), we credit him with a hold. If he does job (b), we credit him with a save. However, if he fails in *either* role, he's charged with a blown save; that's because every "hold opportunity" is technically also a save opportunity.

As we point out every year, save percentages—saves divided by save opportunities—tend to make middle relievers look bad, for a simple reason: middle men get charged with a blown save every time they lose a lead, but they seldom get a chance to record the save itself. So a few years ago we came up with the "hold-plus-save percentage," a stat which includes holds in the percentages by giving relievers an "opportunity" every time they get either a save, a blown save *or* a hold. This stat has helped show that the top middle relievers convert a very high percentage of their opportunities, just as the top closers do. The only thing we *didn't* like about the stat is that cumbersome name, "hold-plus-save percentage." So let's call it "relief conversion percentage" from now on.

Here are the 1995 leaders in relief conversion percentage (minimum 20 opportunities):

1995 Leaders—Relief Conversion Percentage

Pitcher	Holds	Saves	Opp	Pct
Jose Mesa, Cle	0	46	48	95.8
Tom Henke, StL	0	36	38	94.7
Norm Charlton, Phi-Sea	12	14	28	92.9
Greg McMichael, Atl	20	2	24	91.7
Troy Percival, Cal	29	3	35	91.4
Dave Veres, Hou	19	1	22	90.9
Lee Smith, Cal	0	37	41	90.2
Mike Henneman, Det-Hou	1	26	30	90.0
Todd Worrell, LA	1	32	37	89.2
Rick Aguilera, Min-Bos	0	32	36	88.9

(Minimum 20 opportunities)

Middle relievers have often taken the top spot in the years we've been keeping this stat, but Jose Mesa's 1995 season—48 opportunities, 46 saves—was so outstanding that no other reliever could match him. Closers took the top three spots, in fact, with Tom Henke and Norm Charlton ranking second and third. But then come three of the top middle men in the game: Greg McMichael, Troy Percival and Dave Veres. Like the top closers, each converted more than 90 percent of his opportunities in 1995, and that's simply outstanding.

These pitchers had the *worst* conversion percentages last year:

1995 Trailers—Relief Conversion Percentage

Pitcher	Holds	Saves	Opp	Pct
Rene Arocha, StL	14	0	21	66.7
Tony Castillo, Tor	5	13	26	69.2
Bill Risley, Sea	13	1	20	70.0
Bob Wickman, NYA	21	1	31	71.0
Bobby Ayala, Sea	2	19	29	72.4
Roberto Hernandez, ChA	0	32	42	76.2
Dennis Eckersley, Oak	0	29	38	76.3
Rod Beck, SF	0	33	43	76.7
Mel Rojas, Mon	3	30	39	78.6
Robb Nen, Fla	0	23	29	79.3
Danny Miceli, Pit	2	21	29	79.3

There are some high-profile names on this list, like Roberto Hernandez, Mel Rojas, Dennis Eckersley and Rod Beck. While they each recorded a high number of saves, they simply blew too many opportunities to be considered very reliable. The same goes for middle men like Rene Arocha, Bill Risley and Bob Wickman. While each of *them* recorded a respectable number of holds, they also blew a lot of chances.

The Cleveland Indians, as you might expect, had the best relief conversion percentage in baseball last year. Tribe relievers recorded 51 holds and 50 saves while blowing only 10 chances all year, for an outstanding conversion rate of 91.0 percent. Next came the Cardinals with 61 holds and 38 saves in 112 chances, for a conversion percentage of 88.4 percent, followed by the Angels (61 holds, 42 saves in 118 opportunities, 87.3 percent). The majors' shakiest bullpen belonged to the Toronto Blue Jays, who converted only 43 of their 61 opportunities (21 holds, 22 saves, 18 blown saves) last year, for a conversion percentage of 70.5 percent. How the mighty have fallen!

— Don Zminda

A complete listing for this category can be found on page 277.

Whose Heater is Hottest?

The title of this article, we point out every year, is a little misleading. The subject is the pitchers who averaged the most—and fewest—strikeouts per nine innings, and you can certainly record a high strikeout total without having a 95 MPH heater. But a blazing fastball sure doesn't hurt.

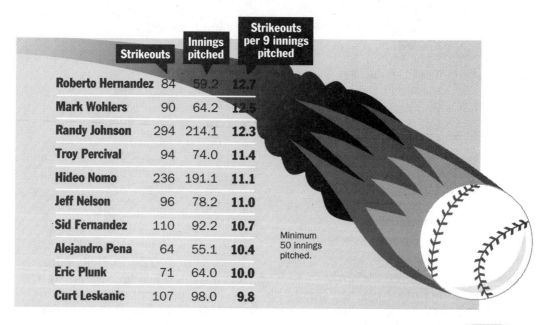

	Strikeouts	Innings pitched	Strikeouts per 9 innings pitched
Roberto Hernandez	84	59.2	12.7
Mark Wohlers	90	64.2	12.5
Randy Johnson	294	214.1	12.3
Troy Percival	94	74.0	11.4
Hideo Nomo	236	191.1	11.1
Jeff Nelson	96	78.2	11.0
Sid Fernandez	110	92.2	10.7
Alejandro Pena	64	55.1	10.4
Eric Plunk	71	64.0	10.0
Curt Leskanic	107	98.0	9.8

Minimum 50 innings pitched.

The chart lists the pitchers with the highest strikeout ratios last year, and most of these guys can throw some serious heat: consider Randy Johnson, Mark Wohlers and Troy Percival, to name three. On the other hand, Sid Fernandez and Hideo Nomo are two pitchers who use good movement and a tricky delivery, rather than sheer velocity, to record their high strikeout totals.

Whatever method the pitchers used to get their Ks, there's no question that the strikeout pitch was alive and well in 1995. We've been running this article for seven years now, and in the six seasons from 1989 through 1994, only one pitcher each year was able to average 12 strikeouts per nine innings (minimum 50 innings pitched). But in 1995, *three* pitchers averaged a dozen Ks per nine innings: Johnson, Wohlers and Roberto Hernandez. In addition, Johnson's '95 average of 12.4 strikeouts per nine marked the first time in baseball history that an ERA qualifier averaged at least 12 strikeouts per nine innings. And if that still doesn't convince you, here's yet another sign of the growth of the strikeout: the number of pitchers who averaged at least one K per inning jumped from 14 in 1994 to 20 in 1995.

Of course not everybody's a strikeout king. The following pitchers averaged the *fewest* strikeouts per nine innings last year. . . but as the last column shows, it's tough to post a good ERA if you're not able to punch out the hitters:

Fewest Strikeouts per Nine Innings, 1995				
Pitcher, Team	IP	K	K/9 IP	ERA
Bob Scanlan, Mil	83.1	29	3.1	6.59
Mark Gubicza, KC	213.1	81	3.4	3.75
Chris Haney, KC	81.1	31	3.4	3.65
Brian Maxcy, Det	52.1	20	3.4	6.88
Ricky Bones, Mil	200.1	77	3.5	4.63
Tim Pugh, Cin	98.1	38	3.5	3.84
Roger Bailey, Col	81.1	33	3.7	4.98
John Doherty, Det	113.0	46	3.7	5.10
Bob Tewksbury, Tex	129.2	53	3.7	4.58
Brad Radke, Min	181.0	75	3.7	5.32

(Minimum 50 innings pitched)

We don't want to unnerve Bob Scanlan and his cohorts, but if the past is any indication, several of these hurlers will be out of baseball by the time the '96 season ends. Among the pitchers featured on the fewest-Ks-per-nine-innings list in last year's *Scoreboard* were Rick Sutcliffe, Scott Sanderson, Mike Moore and Mark Williamson. Adios, amigos!

But interestingly, even *this* list shows how strikeouts are on the rise. 1995 marked the first time in the seven years we've been tracking this stat that no pitcher—not one—averaged less than three strikeouts per nine innings (minimum 50 IP). Yes, the K is king.

— Don Zminda

A complete listing for this category can be found on page 278.

How Does a Pitcher Do In the Start Following a No-Hitter?

It's probably safe to say that the most recognized streaks in baseball history belong to hitters. Who has the most consecutive games with a base hit? Joe DiMaggio, of course, with 56 back in 1941. Who has the most consecutive games with a home run? Pittsburgh's Dale Long first set the standard with eight back in 1956, a mark since equaled by Don Mattingly (1987) and Ken Griffey Jr. (1993). If you hear the phrase "three homers on three swings," Reggie Jackson immediately comes to mind, terrorizing the Dodgers in Game 6 of the 1977 World Series.

Batting streaks catch our eye because the next act in the drama is just around the corner—another at-bat today, another game tomorrow. Starting pitchers don't have that luxury. Even if Mike Mussina hurls a four-hit shutout, he doesn't get to strut his stuff again for another four or five days. It's awfully tough to remain "in the zone" with that amount of time separating your performances. With that in mind, we thought it would be interesting to take a look at no-hitters—in particular, how a pitcher fares in the start *following* his no-no. Did his no-hitter give him any momentum heading into his next start?

For the sake of simplicity, we considered nine-inning no-hit victories since 1987 only, eliminating flukes such as Andy Hawkins' eight-inning no-hit loss against the White Sox in 1990. With that criteria, we turned up 21 "traditional" no-hitters, beginning with one by Milwaukee's Juan Nieves in April of 1987 at Baltimore (with some big help from Robin Yount, whose diving catch in the outfield ended the game) and finishing with one by Ramon Martinez, who no-hit the Marlins last July at Dodger Stadium.

To start with, here is the average season pitching line for the 21 pitcher-seasons (just 20 total pitchers, since Nolan Ryan threw no-hitters in both 1990 and 1991) in the season they threw their no-hitter:

W	L	IP	H	ER	BB	K	ERA
13	9	189.0	166	75	67	135	3.55

Fans, that's an *unbelievable* season line for a population of 21 pitchers. Ask 30 major league general managers if they want a pitcher with those numbers next season, and you'll hear "yes" 30 times. As Bill James said in *The Baseball Book 1992*. . .

The number one factor in determining where and when a no-hitteroccurs is the quality of the pitcher on the mound. That's the numberone thing—not the weather, not the ballpark, not the losing team,not anything else but the man on the mound.

Look at the names of some of the pitchers who have thrown a no-hittersince 1987: Nolan Ryan, Fernando Valenzuela, Dave Stewart, DennisMartinez, Bret Saberhagen, Kenny Rogers, Ramon Martinez and RandyJohnson. If that doesn't emphasize Bill's point, I don't know whatpossibly could. For every Bobo Holloman or Mike Warren on the no-hitroll, you'll find dozens of pitchers with solid major league careers.

We know now that most of the no-hitters were thrown by quality pitchers,so let's get back to the original question. How did the pitchers doin the start following their no-hitter? Here are the cumulative totalsfor the 21 games following the no-hitters, as well as the averagestart:

	IP	H	ER	BB	K	ERA	W	L	ND
Total	138.1	135	57	37	92	3.71	6	8	7
Average	6.2	6.4	2.7	1.8	4.4	3.71			

A quick look at the ERA figure (3.71 vs 3.55 for the season) and youcan conclude that pitchers tend to drop off a bit after a no-hitter—whichisn't really a surprise. Everything in baseball gravitates towardcenter. Losing teams tend to improve the next season while winningteams tend to decline. Younger teams improve while older teams decline.Indeed, what goes up must come down.

For the record, the best start following a no-hitter in the groupwas turned in by Philadelphia's Tommy Greene. After no-hitting theExpos in Montreal on May 23, 1991, Greene shut down the same teamfive days later in Philadelphia, throwing a three-hit shutout, strikingout nine and walking no one. Oakland's Dave Stewart wasn't as fortunate.After he no-hit the Blue Jays in Toronto on June 29, 1990 (the sameday Fernando Valenzuela of the Dodgers threw *his* no-hitter),Stewart was shelled at Milwaukee in his next start: six earned runsin 2.1 innings, including three homers.

Although the pitchers dropped off a bit in the games following theirno-hitters, they somewhat surprisingly showed better control, walkingfewer batters per nine innings than during the season as a whole.

	BB/9	K/BB
Games Following No-Hitter	2.41	2.49
Seasons of No-Hitter	3.20	2.00

You can probably account for this in several ways—overly aggressive hitters trying to show up the no-hit king, a new respect from the home-plate umpire, or maybe just an injection of confidence by the pitcher himself. But whatever the case, the better control *didn't* yield better overall results.

A couple of more thoughts on no-hitters. . . Although it's clear that the quality of the starting pitcher is the most important ingredient in a no-hitter, the no-no has still eluded some of the game's best pitchers—Greg Maddux and Roger Clemens among them. Clemens' 1980s contemporary, Dwight Gooden, never got one either, despite several seasons as one of the National League's best pitchers.

So who had the best all-time "follow-up" game after a no-hitter? Cincinnati's Johnny Vander Meer, of course, who threw *another* no-hitter in his next start back in June of 1938. Vander Meer's feat might also stand as baseball's most unbreakable record, as a pitcher would have to hurl *three* straight no-hitters to better him. You'll see the Republican party nominate Barbara Streisand for President, with Snoop Doggy Dogg as a running mate, before *that* happens.

— Scott McDevitt

A complete listing for this category can be found on page 280.

Was That a "Quality" Start, or Just a Maddux Start?

If you look at the definition of a "quality start", the term itself seems awfully tough to defend. A quality start is any start in which a pitcher works six or more innings, while allowing three or fewer earned runs. Consequently, a pitcher meeting the minimum requirement for a quality start would have a "game ERA" of 4.50—three earned runs in six innings. Is that something to celebrate? It might not be for the pitcher, but it certainly is for his club. Remember, the ultimate goal of a starting pitcher is not to rack up strikeouts, lower his ERA or anything else—it's to *give his team a chance to win*. Even a six-inning, three-run performance will give a team an excellent chance. And year after year, teams which get a quality start from their pitchers wind up winning well over 80 percent of the time.

To the surprise of absolutely no one, Atlanta's Greg Maddux, en route to his fourth straight Cy Young Award, led the majors once again in quality-start percentage in 1995, at 78.6% (22 in 28 outings). In 1994 he was even better—24 quality starts in 25 outings (96.0%). But don't think for a second that Maddux is slipping, as the mark he set in '94 will likely last forever. Appropriately, the league's Cy Young Award winners finished one-two last season, with Seattle's Randy Johnson following Maddux.

Highest Percentage of Quality Starts—1995

Pitcher, Team	GS	QS	Pct
Greg Maddux, Atl	28	22	78.6
Randy Johnson, Sea	30	23	76.7
Dennis Martinez, Cle	28	21	75.0
David Wells, Det-Cin	29	21	72.4
Jaime Navarro, Cubs	29	21	72.4
Ramon Martinez, LA	30	21	70.0
Tom Candiotti, LA	30	21	70.0
Denny Neagle, Pit	31	21	67.7
Tim Wakefield, Bos	27	18	66.7
Ismael Valdes, LA	27	18	66.7
John Smiley, Cin	27	18	66.7

(Minimum 20 starts)

The rest of the list isn't nearly as glamorous, but it's still interesting to say the least. Cleveland's 40-year-old wonder, Dennis Martinez, finished third in quality-start percentage, fueled by an awesome first half. And what can you say about the Los Angeles Dodgers? Ramon Martinez, Tom Candiotti and Ismael Valdes *all* made the top 10, ahead of staff ace Hideo Nomo (64.3). It's frightening to think how many more games Los Angeles might have won with just *a little* run support.

But all of the accomplishments by the league's other pitchers are simply dwarfed by the Mad Dog. It's nearly impossible to comprehend how dominant Maddux has been over the last four seasons. Not only is he posting Walter Johnson-like ERAs, but he's doing it in a great offensive era. Unbelievably, his 78.6 quality-start percentage last season is his *worst* mark since 19912. Think about that. Last season, Maddux allowed no earned runs in eight starts, one in 10 starts and two in six starts. So in 24 of the 28 games he pitched, he allowed zero, one or two earned runs—and that's the *worst* he's been in four years. Here are the quality start breakdowns for his four Cy Young campaigns:

Greg Maddux, 1992-1995

Year	GS	QS	Pct
1995	28	22	78.6
1994	25	24	96.0
1993	36	29	80.6
1992	35	30	85.7
Total	124	105	84.7

Take a good look at that chart, because you probably won't see anything like it again. Okay, enough about Maddux. Although he has very little room to improve, you can't say that about the pitchers on the following chart. Here are the hurlers with the worst quality-start percentages in 1995:

Lowest Percentage of Quality Starts—1995

Pitcher, Team	GS	QS	Pct
Mike Moore, Det	25	6	24.0
Jason Bere, WSox	27	7	25.9
Ron Darling, Oak	21	6	28.6
Brad Radke, Min	28	8	28.6
Chris Bosio, Sea	31	9	29.0
Juan Guzman, Tor	24	7	29.2
Mark Clark, Cle	21	7	33.3
Paul Quantrill, Phi	29	10	34.5
Shawn Boskie, Cal	20	7	35.0
Mike Harkey, Oak-Cal	20	7	35.0

That doesn't say much for the American League, now does it? Only Philadelphia's Paul Quantrill prevented an A.L. "sweep" in the category. It's hard to believe that the Tigers gave Mike Moore 25 starts (in which he posted a 7.53 ERA) before letting him go in early September. The most curious name on the list is probably Juan Guzman, who looked like Hall-of-Fame material after his first three seasons, going 40-11 with a 3.28 ERA. He's simply fallen apart over the last two years, as have the Blue Jays.

—Scott McDevitt

A complete listing for this category can be found on page 281.

Which Pitchers Can Rest in Peace?

Roger Clemens of the Red Sox posted a 4.18 ERA in 1995. Darryl Kile of the Astros posted a 4.96 ERA. Yet—putting aside differences in park and league—you could argue that there really wasn't much difference in the way Clemens and Kile pitched. . . and even that Kile pitched better. The reason for the big ERA difference? Clemens was helped by his bullpen last year; Kile was hurt by his.

The reason we know this is that we keep a stat known as "bequeathed runners." It's pretty simple, really. Pitchers often leave a game with runners on base. To the reliever coming into the game, these are "inherited runners"; to the man departing, they're "bequeathed runners." Either way, if they happen to score, they'll get charged against the ERA of the pitcher who originally put them on base. And Clemens and Kile had totally different experiences with their bequeathed runners last year. Kile left a total of 23 men on base for his relievers; the Astro bullpen permitted 18 of those runners (78.3 percent) to score. Clemens, on the other hand, left games with a total of 21 men on base, and the Boston bullpen permitted just one of them (4.8 percent) to score.

Let's repeat a little exercise we perform every year, and swap the bullpen performances of Kile and Clemens. If Kile's pen had stranded his runners the way Clemens' did, he would have allowed 17 fewer earned runs. Instead of a 4.96 ERA, his ERA would have dropped more than a run to 3.76. On the other hand, had Clemens been saddled with the sort of bullpen work that Kile received, he would have allowed 15 *more* earned runs, and his ERA would have soared from 4.18 to 5.14. Now Kile not only looks like a better pitcher, he looks like a *much* better pitcher. What if each pitcher had received average bullpen performance? Well, last year major league relievers allowed 32.9 percent of all inherited runners to score. Bullpen work like that would have saved Kile 10 earned runs instead of 17, but it still would have lowered his ERA to 4.25. Average bullpen work on behalf of Clemens would have meant six more earned runs, and an ERA of 4.56.

Clemens and Kile are extreme cases, of course. As you can see from the chart, no 1995 pitcher was victimized more by his bullpen than Kile; no pitcher was *helped* by his pen more than Clemens (Cleveland's Eric Plunk had the same percentage of bequeathed runners scoring as Clemens did). It is undeniable that some pitchers are greatly helped—or hurt—by their bullpens, and that's why it's useful to study these figures.

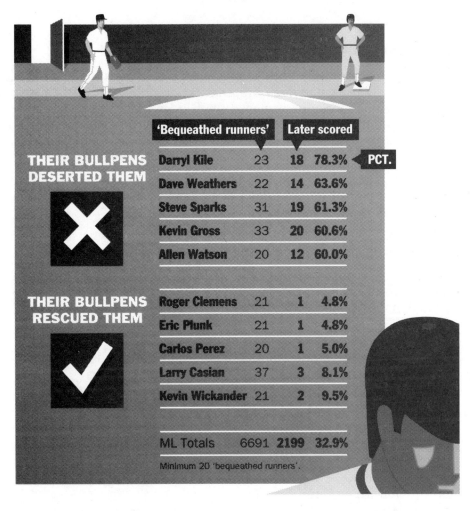

	'Bequeathed runners'		Later scored	
THEIR BULLPENS DESERTED THEM	Darryl Kile	23	18	78.3% ◀ PCT.
	Dave Weathers	22	14	63.6%
	Steve Sparks	31	19	61.3%
	Kevin Gross	33	20	60.6%
	Allen Watson	20	12	60.0%
THEIR BULLPENS RESCUED THEM	Roger Clemens	21	1	4.8%
	Eric Plunk	21	1	4.8%
	Carlos Perez	20	1	5.0%
	Larry Casian	37	3	8.1%
	Kevin Wickander	21	2	9.5%
	ML Totals	6691	2199	32.9%

Minimum 20 'bequeathed runners'.

A year ago, we singled out Denny Neagle as the pitcher who was most hurt by his bullpen in 1994, and stated that Neagle's 5.12 ERA gave a false impression about how well he'd pitched. In 1995, Neagle's ERA was an excellent 3.43. The main difference was that he pitched better, but he was also helped by far better bullpen support (4 of 14 bequeathed runners scoring) than he had in '94.

So next year when you're studying pitchers' ERAs, do yourself a favor: pick up a *Scoreboard* and take a look at the bequeathed runner stats. They'll tell you a bit more about how your favorites *really* pitched.

— Don Zminda

A complete listing for this category can be found on page 282.

Who Has the "Quick Hook"?

My baseball memory only goes back about 20-odd years, but even I can remember the relish with which broadcasters described Sparky Anderson as "Captain Hook" when he managed the Big Red Machine in the 1970s. Sparky had some starters who were pretty good but not particularly durable, and he also had a solid bullpen. As a result, Anderson wasn't the least bit shy about pulling his starter at the first hint of late-inning trouble.

A decade or so later, Bill James attempted to quantify managers' use of the "hook" with a pair of terms: "quick hook" and "slow hook." The definitions are as follows:

Quick Hook: The manager removes a starting pitcher who has pitched fewer than six innings, while allowing three or fewer runs.

Slow Hook: The manager leaves a starter in the game who has either pitched more than nine innings, given up seven or more runs, or whose combined innings pitched and runs allowed totals 13 or more.

Quick and Slow Hooks—American League, 1995

Quick Hooks		Slow Hooks	
Tigers	31	Blue Jays	27
White Sox	26	Brewers	21
Mariners	25	Athletics	20
Royals	22	Rangers	19
Brewers	20	Yankees	19
Red Sox	18	White Sox	17
Athletics	18	Twins	16
Angels	16	Angels	15
Orioles	16	Mariners	15
Blue Jays	15	Royals	14
Indians	13	Red Sox	14
Rangers	13	Tigers	14
Yankees	12	Indians	7
Twins	11	Orioles	3

In 1994, Sparky Anderson ranked around the middle in the quick hooks category. But in 1995, he lived up to his Captain Hook reputation by leading the American League with 31 quick hooks. Given the state of his rotation, can you blame him? The White Sox' pitching struggles are exemplified here, as Gene Lamont and Terry Bevington combined for 26 quick hooks, and that was after Lamont employed a mere *four* quick hooks in 1994.

On the other hand, the quick hook isn't necessarily the hallmark of a weak rotation; sometimes it's the result of a strong bullpen. In Seattle, Lou Piniella employed 25 quick hooks. True, aside from Randy Johnson the Mariner rotation wasn't outstanding. But Piniella has a history of fine bullpen tactics, and many times he was simply going to his strength, as Jeff Nelson and Norm Charlton both posted overpowering numbers.

Quick and Slow Hooks—National League, 1995

Quick Hooks		Slow Hooks	
Rockies	32	Rockies	15
Marlins	28	Giants	14
Braves	25	Dodgers	13
Padres	21	Mets	12
Reds	21	Pirates	12
Expos	20	Padres	11
Cubs	15	Cardinals	11
Astros	15	Marlins	9
Giants	15	Cubs	8
Phillies	15	Astros	7
Cardinals	15	Reds	7
Dodgers	14	Phillies	6
Pirates	13	Braves	3
Mets	9	Expos	3

Well, you certainly can't accuse Rockies manager Don Baylor of being a push-button manager. Yes, he led the National League in quick hooks last season with 32. But he also topped the loop with 15 *slow* hooks. Baylor's decisions obviously were based on more than the immediate situation.

We're a little surprised to see Bobby Cox and the Atlanta Braves at or near the extremes here, considering the quality of their pitching rotation. But Cox has always been careful with his starters' arms, and his willingness to call on the bullpen reflects that caution, along with plenty of confidence in his relief corps. Whatever works. . .

— Rob Neyer

Which Pitchers "Scored" the Best?

If you're a fan of Bill James and/or this book, you're probably familiar with "game scores," a James-designed tool used to quantify how well a starter did in a single game. To refresh your memory, here's how a game score is figured:

(1) Start with 50.

(2) Add 1 point for each hitter the pitcher retires, i.e. 1 point for each third of an inning pitched.

(3) Add 2 points for each inning the pitcher completes after the fourth.

(4) Add 1 point for each strikeout.

(5) Subtract 1 point for each walk.

(6) Subtract 2 points for each hit.

(7) Subtract 4 points for each earned run.

(8) Subtract 2 points for each unearned run.

The genius of this method is that the results are so easy to understand. A game score of 50 is about average, while anything in the 90's is outstanding. If you score 100, you're talking immortality. Since 1987, only two pitchers have hit the century mark: Jose DeLeon (103) and Nolan Ryan (101, twice). Ryan, incidentally, owns four of the top eight game scores of the last nine years despite retiring in 1993.

The fun thing about game scores is that you can use them to answer a lot of different questions. Who pitched the best games last year? Which were the best pitcher's duels? Who pitched the worst games? And on and on. Let's answer some of those questions. . .

Who pitched the best games in 1995? The short answer is "Chuck Finley and Frank Castillo." The long answer is the chart on the next page, which lists all starts which resulted in a game score of 90 or better:

Top Game Scores of 1995

Pitcher, Team	Date	Opp	W/L	IP	H	R	ER	BB	K	Score
Chuck Finley, Cal	05/23	Yanks	W	9.0	2	0	0	2	15	96
Frank Castillo, Cubs	09/25	StL	W	9.0	1	0	0	2	13	96
Randy Johnson, Sea	07/15	Tor	W	9.0	3	0	0	2	16	95
Pedro Martinez, Mon	06/03	SD	W	9.0	1	0	0	0	9	94
Ramon Martinez, LA	07/14	Fla	W	9.0	0	0	0	1	8	94
Hideo Nomo, LA	06/24	SF	W	9.0	2	0	0	3	13	93
Hideo Nomo, LA	08/05	SF	W	9.0	1	0	0	3	11	93
Paul Wagner, Pit	08/29	Col	W	9.0	1	0	0	3	11	93
Kevin Appier, KC	09/15	Cal	W	9.0	3	0	0	1	13	93
Randy Johnson, Sea	06/05	Bal	W	9.0	3	0	0	1	12	92
Todd Stottlemyre, Oak	06/16	KC	-	10.0	5	1	1	1	15	92
Greg Maddux, Atl	08/20	StL	W	9.0	2	0	0	0	9	92
Ismael Valdes, LA	09/17	StL	W	9.0	2	0	0	0	9	92
Kirk Rueter, Mon	08/27	SF	W	9.0	1	0	0	1	7	91
Pat Rapp, Fla	09/17	Col	W	9.0	1	0	0	1	7	91
Steve Ontiveros, Oak	05/27	Yanks	W	9.0	1	0	0	2	7	90
Doug Drabek, Hou	07/25	LA	W	9.0	3	0	0	0	9	90

For the third year in a row, Randy Johnson appears on the list twice. But it looks like the Big Unit might have a challenger for game-score supremacy, because Hideo Nomo also racked up a pair of 90-plus starts. He tossed two 93 games against the Giants, who are surely hoping that Nomo returns soon to his native Japan. And speaking of pairs, it was a nice game-score season for the Martinez brothers, each of whom posted a 94 start. Ramon's was the campaign's only no-hitter, while Pedro had a no-hitter of his own until the 10th inning.

Of course, for every pitching gem there's a lump of coal, so let's look at the five starts last year which resulted in a game score below 2. . .

Worst Game Scores of 1995

Pitcher, Team	Date	Opp	W/L	IP	H	R	ER	BB	K	Score
Tom Gordon, KC	10/01	Cle	L	1.0	9	10	10	4	1	-8
Sid Roberson, Mil	07/28	Cal	L	3.1	12	10	10	2	2	-4
Ricky Bones, Mil	09/29	Bos	L	3.0	10	10	10	3	1	-3
Brian Givens, Mil	06/29	WSox	L	4.2	13	9	9	3	2	1
Tom Candiotti, LA	08/04	SF	L	4.0	10	10	10	2	1	1

Ouch. The end of the month was not kind to Milwaukee starters, who sported three of the five worst game scores in the majors last year. But the title goes to Tom Gordon, who was pummeled by the Indians on the last day of the season. A day or two before that start, the newspapers reported some derogatory things Gordon had to say about the Kansas City organization, and it looked to this writer like that Cleveland pounding was related somehow. Gordon's -8 game score was the worst by a major league pitcher since David Wells posted a -14 in 1992.

Well, we're always hearing that there's too much negativity in the media, so let's shift back to the positive. The pitchers below boasted the highest *average* game scores in 1995:

Top Average Game Scores — 1995

Pitcher	Avg Gm Scr
Greg Maddux	69.1
Randy Johnson	66.4
Hideo Nomo	64.5
Ismael Valdes	58.4
David Cone	58.1
Pete Schourek	58.1
Mike Mussina	57.9
John Smoltz	57.9
Tim Wakefield	57.5
Pedro Martinez	57.3
(minimum 144 innings pitched)	

What do you know, the top two game-score pitchers also happened to win Cy Young Awards (Maddux and Johnson, by the way, are also the top two game scorers over the last three seasons, at 66.0 and 64.3, respectively.)

There aren't really any surprises on this list. However, if we drop the requirement for inclusion to 15 starts, Phillies righthander Curt Schilling ties for fourth with a 58.4 average game score, something to think about if you're drafting a fantasy team this spring.

Now we come to my favorite use of game scores: identifying the top duels of last season. Unfortunately, 1995 wasn't a good season for those nail-biters, as only two games featured a pair of starters with 80-plus game scores. Here they are:

Top Pitchers' Duels of 1995

Pitcher, Team	Date	W/L	IP	H	R	ER	BB	K	Score	Total
Joey Hamilton, SD	06/03	-	9.0	3	0	0	2	2	81	
Pedro Martinez, Mon		W	9.0	1	0	0	0	9	94	175
Tim Wakefield, Bos	06/04	W	10.0	6	1	0	2	5	81	
Tim Belcher, Sea		-	9.0	5	0	0	1	5	81	162

It wasn't a good year for pitching duels. There were four such games in the much-abbreviated 1994 but only two in 1995, and both of those came in a two-day span. On June 3, hard-luck Joey Hamilton was the victim of Pedro Martinez' near no-hitter. And the very next day, Tim Belcher went against knuckleballer Tim Wakefield. We like offense as much as anyone, but the occasional 1-0 squeaker can be a lot of fun, too. So major league pitchers, get it together this season!

— Rob Neyer

A complete listing for this category can be found on page 284.

V. QUESTIONS ON DEFENSE

Which Shortstops Are the Best "DP Middle Men"?

For several years the *Scoreboard* has presented stats on how well major league second basemen perform on the double-play pivot. However, we all know that many times it's the shortstop—not the second sacker—who plays the role of DP "middle man." So we thought it would be fun to see which shortstops are best, and worst, at handling the middle-man role (we can't call this a "pivot percentage," since shortstops *don't* pivot.)

First, let's get an overview on the subject. Last year major league shortstops had a total of 1,974 opportunities to turn a DP after getting the throw from another infielder (usually the second baseman). They succeeded in recording a twin killing a little less than 56 percent of the time (1,103 DPs turned). How does this compare with second basemen? Well, as you'd expect, second sackers get more opportunities to play the middle-man role than shortstops do—a total of 2,514 chances for second basemen last season. But we were surprised to discover that second basemen have a higher success rate in turning the DP than shortstops do—59.5 percent last year (1,495 DPs turned). We had thought that shortstops, who don't have to make the difficult pivot-and-throw in turning a DP that second basemen do, would succeed *more* often, not less. But that isn't the case. One reason might be that a left-handed hitter is more likely to hit a ball to the right side than a righty swinger, and left-handed hitters have a shorter distance to run to first, and thus a little better opportunity to reach the bag before the shortstop's throw arrives. Or there could be other factors involved. Whatever the reason, second basemen clearly complete more DPs than shortstops do, at least on average.

There are, of course, wide variations in how well individual shortstops complete the double play. Here are the top 10 from 1995, in a minimum of 30 DP opportunities:

Top DP Middle Men—1995 Shortstops

Player, Team	Opp	DP	Pct
Tony Fernandez, Yanks	39	28	.718
Jose Valentin, Mil	61	40	.656
Greg Gagne, KC	60	39	.650
Benji Gil, Tex	82	52	.634
John Valentin, Bos	75	46	.613
Jose Vizcaino, Mets	63	37	.587
Walt Weiss, Col	74	43	.581
Kevin Stocker Phi	42	24	.571
Kurt Abbott, Fla	51	29	.569
Omar Vizquel, Cle	81	46	.568

More surprises. Before looking at the data, we had thought that big, strong-armed shortstops—Cal Ripken and Jeff Blauser come to mind—would have the advantage, since they throw hard and are strong enough to handle a runner coming in to break up the DP. But neither made the top 10. The leader was veteran shortstop Tony Fernandez, who ranked well ahead of the pack with an excellent 72-percent rate last year. And there's no particular bias toward big guys on the list. Ripken ranked right in the middle of the park (40 for 71, 56.3 percent). Blauser, meanwhile, turned out to be one of the *worst* middle men, as did the rifle-armed Shawon Dunston. Here's the 1995 trailers list:

Worst DP Middle Men—1995 Shortstops			
Player, Team	Opp	DP	Pct
Alex Gonzalez, Tor	39	15	.385
Gary DiSarcina, Cal	45	18	.400
Jeff Blauser, Atl	56	24	.429
Shawon Dunston, Cubs	54	24	.444
Andujar Cedeno, SD	50	24	.480

Young Alex Gonzalez of the Blue Jays was the worst in the majors at completing the DP—perhaps not surprising since he's considered talented but still very raw. Blauser and Dunston were major surprises, as noticed, and so was Gary DiSarcina, who's earned a lot of praise from us for his other skills. In DiSarcina's defense, it's not easy working out a double-play rhythm when you have to work with several different second basemen over the course of a year. On the other hand, that didn't seem to bother Tony Fernandez. . .

These figures are based on 1995 only, and the number of opportunities isn't all that large. So we expanded the study to the last five years, with a minimum of 100 DP opportunities. Here's the top 10 among players who were still active in 1995:

Top DP Middle Men—1991-95 Shortstops

Player	Opp	DP	Pct
Alvaro Espinoza	115	81	.704
Rey Sanchez	102	68	.667
Jose Valentin	106	69	.651
John Valentin	217	139	.641
Travis Fryman	133	84	.632
Greg Gagne	301	187	.621
Ozzie Smith	241	149	.618
Cal Ripken	332	204	.614
Randy Velarde	101	62	.614
Omar Vizquel	335	203	.606

(1995 active players; minimum 100 opportunities)

Ripken *does* make this list, though only in eighth place. The leader was Alvaro Espinoza of the Indians, a veteran utility player who handles his DP responsibilities very well when given the chance. Next comes Rey Sanchez, who's been mostly a second baseman the last couple of years, but who's expected to be the Cubs' number-one shortstop this year. Clearly he has at least *one* of the skills.

Tony Fernandez appears to be a one-year fluke: over the last five seasons, he succeeded on only 54.5 percent of his DP opportunities, which is below average. Dunston's low ranking, though, *wasn't* a fluke: his DP conversion rate of 45.1 percent was the second worst among players with 100 or more opportunities, topping only Spike Owen (45.0). And Blauser remained one of the worst at 48.9 percent.

Given the high ranking of guys like Espinoza (utility man), Sanchez (sometimes a second baseman), Travis Fryman (now a third baseman) and Randy Velarde (another career utility man), we'd have to say that being a good middle man on the DP is probably not among a shortstop's most important skills. If you're good at it, that's a plus, but good range, a reliable arm and the ability to *start* a double play would have to be considered more important components in the makeup of a good shortstop.

— Don Zminda

A complete listing for this category can be found on page 285.

Did Ivan's Arm Come Back, or Did He Just Get a Little More Help?

Like many baseball statistics, catchers' throwing stats can be deceptive. Some catchers are blessed with pitchers who know how to hold runners, and that gives them an edge when they're trying to gun down a runner. Other receivers aren't as fortunate. Even a guy with an incredible arm like Ivan Rodriguez of the Rangers needs a *little* help from his pitchers. After throwing out a major league-leading 49 percent of opposing basestealers in 1992, Rodriguez slipped below the 40 percent mark in each of the next two years. Was there something wrong with his arm or his mechanics? Probably not; the difference undoubtedly was that he just wasn't blessed with a staff that could hold runners effectively.

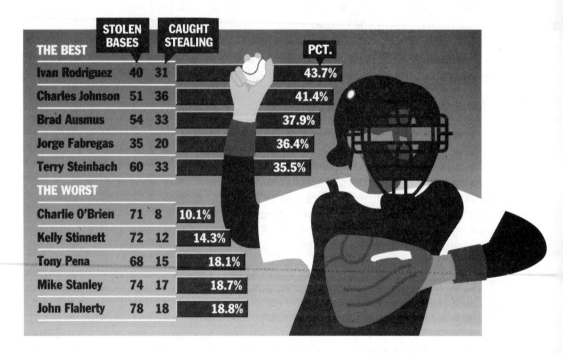

THE BEST	STOLEN BASES	CAUGHT STEALING	PCT.
Ivan Rodriguez	40	31	43.7%
Charles Johnson	51	36	41.4%
Brad Ausmus	54	33	37.9%
Jorge Fabregas	35	20	36.4%
Terry Steinbach	60	33	35.5%
THE WORST			
Charlie O'Brien	71	8	10.1%
Kelly Stinnett	72	12	14.3%
Tony Pena	68	15	18.1%
Mike Stanley	74	17	18.7%
John Flaherty	78	18	18.8%

In 1995 the Rangers changed managers, with Johnny Oates taking over the club. Oates is a former catcher, and he seemed to put renewed emphasis on the importance of holding baserunners. And as the chart shows, Rodriguez jumped to the top of the throw-out list again last year. Finishing a close second was Florida Marlin rookie Charles Johnson, whom some people are calling the best young defensive catcher to enter the majors since Rodriguez in 1991. Both Rodriguez and Johnson have the arms to dominate this list for years to come. . . but of course they'll need some support from their pitching staffs.

The trailer on the list, Charlie O'Brien, saw his throw-out rate tumble from a respectable 31.4 percent in 1994 to a pathetic 10.1 percent in 1995. O'Brien is considered an excellent handler of pitchers, and Greg Maddux even chose him as his "personal catcher" last year. But a 10-percent throw-out rate is hard to accept, whatever a catcher's other skills are, and that's a big reason why the Braves let O'Brien go after the season.

We like to compare the throw-out rates for catchers on the same team. The differences are often striking, as these examples show:

1995 Catcher Teammates

Catcher, Team	Innings	SB	CS	Pct
Terry Steinbach, Oak	916.2	60	33	35.5
Eric Helfand, Oak	254.0	21	5	19.2
Lance Parrish, Tor	467.2	38	25	39.7
Sandy Martinez, Tor	472.2	20	13	39.4
Randy Knorr, Tor	352.1	40	10	20.0
Ivan Rodriguez, Tex	1065.0	40	31	43.7
Dave Valle, Tex	197.0	12	3	20.0
Javy Lopez, Atl	756.2	61	17	21.8
Charlie O'Brien, Atl	510.0	71	8	10.1
Carlos Hernandez, LA	241.2	12	11	47.8
Mike Piazza, LA	941.0	87	27	23.7
Jeff Reed, SF	245.2	16	12	42.9
Kirt Manwaring, SF	971.2	70	21	23.1

As you can see, the Braves had problems controlling the running game no matter *who* was behind the plate last year. . . but even so, their throw-out rate was more than twice as high with Javy Lopez catching than it was with O'Brien. The Brave staff seems to take its cue from Greg Maddux, a pitcher who prefers to concentrate on the hitter and not worry too much about opposing basestealers. Indeed, opposing basestealers went 26-for-32 with Maddux on the mound last year. . . but then, not many of them came around to score. As long as they continue to win, the Braves probably won't worry too much about Javy's throw-out rate—unless, of course, it dips down to 10 percent or so.

— Don Zminda

A complete listing for this category can be found on page 286.

Who Are the Prime Pivot Men?

We've come a long way with fielding stats. Range factor continues to make inroads, and someday STATS' own zone ratings might be the standard yardstick for measuring fielding range. But there's more work to be done. Take double plays, for instance. Every baseball fan knows that twin killings are a crucial part of the game. But aside from the occasional "He turns the double play well," we hear very little from diamond pundits about the subject.

So how do you evaluate a player's ability to turn the twin killing? Well, we could just count them, but of course that's going to leave us subject to playing-time and pitching-staff differences. The next step would be to compute double plays per game, which isn't bad. But like range factor, DP/G can be heavily influenced by pitchers. Two second basemen with similar ability might sport much different DP numbers if one plays behind a staff of groundball pitchers and the other doesn't.

To avoid those influences, we use a tool called "pivot percentage." We simply record all situations in which a double-play pivot is possible: man on first, ball hit to another infielder, and the second baseman takes a throw. Divide the number of double plays turned by the opportunities, and you've got pivot percentage.

Here are the top five N.L. second basemen on the double-play pivot in 1995 (minimum 50 opportunities):

Best Pivot Men — 1995 National League

Player, Team	DP	Opp	Pct
Bret Boone, Reds	56	80	70.0
Mark Lemke, Braves	38	55	69.1
Mickey Morandini, Phillies	48	72	66.7
Jeff Kent, Mets	38	57	66.7
Carlos Garcia, Pirates	46	74	62.2

Yes, Bret Boone is one of the better-hitting second basemen in the National League. But did you know he's one of the better fielders, too? Boone's range is at least adequate and, like many slugging keystoners, he's got an arm to match his strong bat. Robby Thompson, who used to rule this list, would have ranked just ahead of Carlos Garcia, but he missed the 50-opportunity cutoff.

Here are the American League leaders:

Best Pivot Men — 1995 American League

Player, Team	DP	Opp	Pct
Fernando Vina, Brewers	48	59	81.4
Luis Alicea, Red Sox	54	78	69.2
Brent Gates, A's	45	73	61.6
Carlos Baerga, Indians	50	88	56.8
Chuck Knoblauch, Twins	54	96	56.3

He barely qualified, so perhaps we shouldn't give this much weight, but Milwaukee's Fernando Vina easily led the major leagues in pivot percentage. Carlos Baerga appears among the A.L. leaders almost annually, and here he is again. As we note elsewhere in this book, this is truly an era of great second basemen, with keystoners who both hit and field with great skill.

The single-season DP numbers aren't huge samples, so it's instructive to look at the numbers over the last five seasons. Here are the active pivot-percentage leaders since 1991 (minimum 175 opportunities):

Best Pivot Men — 1991-1995

Second Baseman	DP	Opp	Pct
Bret Boone	131	191	68.6
Jeff Kent	123	186	66.1
Luis Alicea	136	210	64.8
Scott Fletcher	161	251	64.1
Robby Thompson	193	305	63.3

Bret Boone is obviously no one-year wonder, and his presence at the top of this list makes a good case for him to be considered as one of the top all-around second basemen in the game. And just below him is Jeff Kent, another power hitter. Some have suggested that Kent be shifted to third base, but his ability to turn the double play argues otherwise.

— Rob Neyer

A complete listing for this category can be found on page 287.

Which Catchers Pick Off the Most Runners?

When I was a church-league softball player (fast-pitch), fielders who liked to throw the ball around always made me nervous. . . especially catchers. It seemed to me that for every snap throw to first base that nailed a dozing baserunner, there were five that sailed into right field. Of course, on the 10 uneventful throws in between, the catcher always got lots of shouts of "Nice throw!" from my teammates. . . as long as the ball didn't get away. The whole thing never made sense to me. An unnecessary throw always seemed to be a *bad* throw in my estimation—whether or not it turned out that way.

I always wondered whether my small-time theory held true in the big time. In the major leagues, where catchers are much more experienced and have superior throwing arms and instincts, do the majority of those snap throws result in success, or disaster? We took all the major league catchers in 1995 and totaled both their pickoffs and the throwing errors that resulted from snap throws. In the chart below are all catchers who had more than one pickoff or throw-away or combination of the two. We subtracted throw-aways from pickoffs for a net result.

Catcher Pickoffs—1995

Catcher, Team	Pkoff	ThA	Net
Ivan Rodriguez, Tex	6	2	4
Javy Lopez, Atl	4	1	3
Mike Matheny, Mil	3	0	3
Mike Macfarlane, Bos	2	0	2
Barry Lyons, WSox	2	0	2
Angelo Encarnacion, Pit	2	1	1
Tony Pena, Cle	2	1	1
Greg Zaun, Bal	1	1	0
Joe Oliver, Mil	1	2	-1

Is my theory right or wrong? I'm stuck in the middle. To be sure, there certainly are *not* five throws into right field for every caught runner. I was so amazed by the small numbers of errant throws (and the number of successful catcher pickoffs, for that matter) that I hand-checked all the errors of five catchers, just to make sure our reporters hadn't neglected to designate any plays as a catcher pickoff throw. Happily, I can report that these numbers are right on. On the other hand, the surprising lack of results from snap throws tells me that perhaps once a catcher has reached the majors, he has realized that the snap throw can easily result in disaster and is a weapon to be used carefully and sparingly.

As for the individuals on the list, some are expected and some are not. Though he came up short in some of the other defensive areas in which we examined him this year (see the Texas Ranger essay), Ivan Rodriguez sure looked like a Gold Glover in *this* category. His total of six pickoffs, albeit with two throw-aways, outdistances everyone else in the study by quite a bit. (I'm sure he heard lots of "Nice throw!" yells in between, also.) Javy Lopez, who ranked second, is establishing himself as a young catcher who's not afraid to gamble. As a matter of fact, most of the throwers on the list are young, with the exception of 39-year-old Tony Pena and 36-year-old Barry Lyons. Not counting Pena and Lyons, the average age of the other seven is 26 years young. I guess that old catchers never die, they just don't make snap throws anymore.

Mike Matheny, the young Brewer backstop, deserves special mention. His perfect record of three runners caught with no mistakes—in only 460 innings behind the plate—stands out as perhaps the best performance on the list. Matheny's defensive prowess could be a big reason the Brewers don't seem apprehensive about entering 1996 with only Matheny and defensive nightmare Matt Nokes as potential catchers. (Joe Oliver could return, but is testing the free-agent waters at this writing.)

Finally, I just have to recount the play-by-play of an "adventurous" first inning Matheny experienced last June 14 in Milwaukee against the Texas Rangers. I came across the inning while researching catcher errors for this article: "Nixon was out bunting to pitcher Roberson. McLemore was hit by a pitch. On Matheny's passed ball, McLemore to second. Clark walked on a full count. McLemore stole third on catcher Matheny's throwing error, Clark to second. Gonzalez hit a sacrifice fly to second baseman Vina. McLemore scored. On catcher Matheny's fielding error, Clark to third. Tettleton grounded out to third baseman Seitzer." A passed ball, a stolen base allowed, a throwing error and a fielding error, all in one inning. Only a catcher's interference kept Matheny from the "catcher's nightmare cycle."

Nice throw!

— Steve Moyer

A complete listing for this category can be found on page 288.

Who's Best in the Infield Zone?

Zone ratings for infielders and outfielders have been an annual highlight of this publication for years, and most of you are probably familiar with them by now. If not, there's nothing complicated about them. STATS reporters record the direction and distance of every batted ball, and from that we can compute how many balls were hit into each fielder's "zone"—the area he normally patrols. The zone rating is simply the percentage of those balls the fielder turned into outs (including double plays started). The results can sometimes be surprising, even to us, and we don't rely on zone ratings alone in evaluating a fielder. However, we've found them to be both consistent and reliable, and one of the best defensive measuring sticks around.

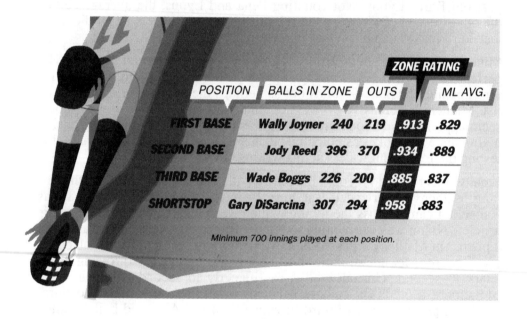

POSITION	BALLS IN ZONE	OUTS	ZONE RATING	ML AVG.
FIRST BASE	Wally Joyner 240	219	.913	.829
SECOND BASE	Jody Reed 396	370	.934	.889
THIRD BASE	Wade Boggs 226	200	.885	.837
SHORTSTOP	Gary DiSarcina 307	294	.958	.883

Minimum 700 innings played at each position.

The chart above lists the top zone-rating players at each infield position, and it's a pretty good looking group. Though only Boggs has ever won an official Gold Glove, Joyner and Reed and DiSarcina are all highly-regarded defenders. But these outstanding fielders are just the very best. Let's look at more zone-rating leaders. We'll show you the top five at each position (minimum 700 innings played), plus the player with the lowest rating.

First Basemen—1995 Zone Ratings

Wally Joyner, KC	.913
Eric Karros, LA	.904
Jeff Bagwell, Hou	.879
Andres Galarraga, Col	.865
David Segui, Mets-Mon	.853
Worst	
J.T., Snow Cal	.796

Wally Joyner has never won a Gold Glove in his career, but that's mostly because he's spent his career in the American League during the same period that Don Mattingly was manning the position. But Joyner does have a good defensive reputation, and perhaps now that he's in the National League as a member of the Padres, he'll get a little more recognition—but of course, he'll be dueling with a new set of fine first sackers like Eric Karros, Jeff Bagwell, Andres Galarraga, David Segui and Mark Grace. (With Mattingly at least temporarily retired, maybe Joyner would have been better off staying in the A.L. . .) The shocker in the ratings is the low mark for American League Gold Glove winner J.T. Snow. We watched Snow play a few times last year, and he sure *looked* like an outstanding first baseman, making a number of acrobatic plays. That's why we rely on more than zone ratings alone when evaluating a fielder. However, given his extremely low zone rating and his 1995 total of only 56 assists—less than half the number compiled by Joyner, Bagwell, Grace and Galarraga—we'd have to question Snow's selection for a Gold Glove.

Second Basemen—1995 Zone Ratings

Jody Reed, SD	.934
Mickey Morandini, Phi	.932
Damion Easley, Cal	.927
Quilvio Veras, Fla	.927
Delino DeShields, LA	.920
Worst	
Joey Cora, WSox	.815

Like Joyner, Jody Reed is a solid veteran infielder who's never won a Gold Glove, despite the fact that he does almost everything well. Given his 1995 stats—along with a splendid zone rating, he committed only four errors and ranked near the top in range factor (plays per nine innings)—

we'd say he was long overdue. The American League zone ratings leaders were notable, as usual, for the absence of perennial Gold Glove winner Roberto Alomar—he ranked a little below the middle of the pack with an .872 zone rating. This subject consumed us so much that we've devoted an entire essay to it, so for more on Alomar, turn to page 212.

Third Basemen—1995 Zone Ratings

Wade Boggs, Yanks	.885
Charlie Hayes, Phi	.876
Chipper Jones, Atl	.870
Travis Fryman, Det	.870
Tim Naehring, Bos	.857
Worst	
Mike Blowers, Sea	.755

Has the aging Wade Boggs deserved the Gold Gloves he's won each of the last two years? Our stats say he's a worthy choice, but last year we were even more impressed with Travis Fryman of the Tigers, who had an excellent zone rating, a fine range factor, and in addition participated in an impressive 38 double plays—13 more than any other third sacker. With Matt Williams missing considerable time due to injuries, the National League leader was the always-solid Charlie Hayes.

Those Dodger Stadium boo-birds who made life miserable for Jose Offerman probably can't *wait* to see Mike Blowers at third this year.

Shortstops—1995 Zone Ratings

Gary DiSarcina, Cal	.958
Mike Bordick, Oak	.954
Cal Ripken, Bal	.942
Kevin Stocker, Phi	.937
Greg Gagne, KC	.925
Worst	
Wil Cordero, Mon	.817

Lots of fine players here, with one of our favorites, Gary DiSarcina, topping the charts for the second year in a row. Gold Glove winners Omar Vizquel and Barry Larkin were well down the list with zone ratings of .873 and .869. Yes, we like them, too, but not as much as we like DiSarcina.

Like most statistics, zone ratings are most useful when studied over time. Here are the top three at each infield position over the last three years (minimum 1,000 innings played). A few surprises here, but also a number of players who have dominated the zone ratings year after year:

1993-95 Infield Zone Ratings Leaders

First Base		Second Base		Third Base		Shortstop	
Kevin Young	.887	Quilvio Veras	.927	Matt Williams	.898	Gary DiSarcina	.944
Jeff Bagwell	.882	Damion Easley	.923	Wade Boggs	.883	Ozzie Guillen	.922
Wa. Joyner	.881	Scott Fletcher	.923	Gary Gaetti	.877	Cal Ripken	.920

(Minimum 1,000 innings played)

As usual, we finish the article with our choices for the STATS infield Gold Gloves. Zone ratings play a big part, but so do other defensive stats and intelligent observation as well. And unlike those other Gold Gloves, you don't need to be a good hitter to qualify. Here are our picks:

First Base. Wally Joyner, A.L., and Jeff Bagwell, N.L. Sort of a going-away present for Joyner, who will now battle Bagwell and others in the N.L. We'll consider J.T. Snow next year, but only if his stats (and not just his zone ratings) improve.

Second Base. Carlos Baerga, A.L., and Jody Reed, N.L. Neither of the "official" Gold Glove winners, Alomar and Craig Biggio, had impressive numbers, and that goes for a lot of stats *besides* their zone ratings. We gave the A.L. award to the Tribe's Baerga, whose solid numbers (including a .911 zone rating) carried more weight with us than his 19 errors. The N.L. winner, Reed, won the STATS Gold Glove in 1994 as a Brewer.

Third Base. Travis Fryman, A.L., and Charlie Hayes, N.L. Boggs would have been a worthy winner in the American League, but we gave the nod to Fryman, whose overall numbers were a little more impressive. Matt Williams is usually an automatic choice in the N.L., but he missed too much time to injuries last year, and official Gold Glove winner Ken Caminiti showed decent range, but fielded at a sloppy .936 clip last year. So we'll go with Charlie Hayes, who's been a fine third sacker for years.

Shortstop. Gary DiSarcina, A.L., and Royce Clayton, N.L. We like Omar Vizquel, but our hunch is that if people saw DiSarcina on national television night after night the way they did Omar last year, we wouldn't be the only ones raving about the Angel shortstop. We thought about Larkin in the N.L., but Stocker ranked ahead of Larkin in everything except hitting. . . and that doesn't count in *these* awards.

— Don Zminda

A complete listing for this category can be found on page 289.

Who Makes Those "Home-Run-Saving Catches"?

There are few things in baseball more dramatic than a leaping catch at the wall to prevent a home run. But how often do those catches really occur? Leave it to STATS to provide the answer. Our reporters keep track of everything that happens during a major league game, and that includes a coding for each catch that prevented a home run. Let's look at the results.

The first thing we discovered was that those highlight-film catches don't happen very often. Our reporters counted a total of 64 home-run-saving catches last year, not a lot considering that there were more than 2,000 major league games played. There's a good reason why more of these catches don't take place: in all or part of many major league stadiums, the fences are simply too high. Even Michael Jordan would find it next to impossible to leap high enough to prevent a home run in a stadium where the fences are 12 feet high or more.

With that in mind, here are the 1995 leaders in home-run-saving catches:

Most Home-Run-Saving Catches—1995

Player, Team	Catches
Mark Whiten, Bos-Phi	3
Stan Javier, Oak	3
Jim Edmonds, Cal	2
Lou Frazier, Mon-Tex	2
Bernie Williams, Yanks	2
Bobby Bonilla, Mets-Bal	2
Lee Tinsley, Bos	2
Steve Finley, SD	2
Otis Nixon, Tex	2
Troy O'Leary, Bos	2
Curtis Goodwin, Bal	2
Raul Mondesi, LA	2

We were a little surprised that no one made more than three of these catches in 1995, but that was the case. There are a number of athletic players on the list who can leap up and snare a ball, but just as big a factor was where the player played his home games. For instance, the fences at the Oakland Coliseum, where Stan Javier played last year, are eight feet high all the way around. Not everyone was that lucky.

We also looked at the leaders for the last three years combined. No one had more than six home-run saving catches, and there was a three-way tie for the top spot:

Most Home Run Saving Catches—1993-95

Player	Catches
Stan Javier	6
Tim Salmon	6
Kenny Lofton	6
Devon White	5
Brady Anderson	5
Rickey Henderson	5
Otis Nixon	5
Mark McLemore	4
Lance Johnson	4
Jim Edmonds	4
Lou Frazier	4

Somehow we were not surprised to find players like Kenny Lofton, Devon White and Lance Johnson on this list. As for the others, they tend to share two traits: they're fast and they can jump high. Oh, and one more thing: they usually happen to play in front of a fence where such catches are possible.

— Don Zminda

A complete listing for this category can be found on page 291.

Who's Best in the Outfield Zone?

Zone ratings are nothing new for most of you, so we'll skip the detailed explanation. Simply, it measures the number of outs recorded by a fielder in relation to the number of balls hit to his fielding area, as measured by our reporters. This method eliminates the pitching-staff bias of range factor (plays per nine innings). Let's look at the 1995 zone-rating leaders at each outfield spot (minimum 700 innings), beginning in left:

Left Field—1995 Zone Ratings

Marty Cordova, Min	.867
Albert Belle, Cle	.853
Garret Anderson, Cal	.842
Luis Gonzalez, Hou-Cubs	.832
Joe Carter, Tor	.826
Worst	
Dante Bichette, Col	.723

We should probably wait a year to say for sure, but it looks like A.L. Rookie of the Year Marty Cordova might be the complete ballplayer. He hit 24 homers, he stole 20 bases, and he finished with the best zone rating among major league left fielders. Two spots below Cordova is Rookie of the Year runner-up Garret Anderson.

Center Field—1995 Zone Ratings

Jim Edmonds, Cal	.879
Bernie Williams, Yanks	.871
Steve Finley, SD	.867
Curtis Goodwin, Bal	.856
Marquis Grissom, Atl	.846
Worst	
Mike Kingery, Col	.684

Like his teammate Garret Anderson, Jim Edmonds combined a potent bat with excellent outfield range. The fact that Rockies outfielders Bichette and Kingery both compiled poor zone ratings might be a coincidence. However, as it does with so many other statistics, Coors Field might be exerting its powerful influence here. Larry Walker, generally considered a solid right fielder, finished with a .751 zone rating, second-worst in the majors.

Right Field—1995 Zone Ratings

Sammy Sosa, Cubs	.887
Reggie Sanders, Cin	.873
Tony Gwynn, SD	.854
Brian Jordan, StL	.841
Tony Tarasco, Mon	.840
Worst	
Jay Buhner, Sea	.747

Of the top five right fielders, only Reggie Sanders also ranked among the top five a year ago. His 1995 playoff woes aside, Sanders has to be considered among the game's best all-around right fielders, right up there with Sammy Sosa and Larry Walker. Jay Buhner, as usual, displayed little range for Seattle, though as we'll see later he is hindered by the Kingdome.

Unlike the "official" Rawlings Gold Gloves, the STATS Gold Gloves are awarded two each to left, center and right fielders. We base our awards on zone ratings, throwing arms and observation:

Left Field: Garret Anderson, A.L., and Luis Gonzalez, N.L. Rookie Garret Anderson was the only American League left fielder who combined an excellent zone rating with a solid throwing arm. Luis Gonzalez has always had fine numbers in left field, and that didn't change as he moved from the Astrodome to Wrigley Field last year. Gonzalez just edges Barry Bonds, runner-up for the second straight season.

Center Field: Jim Edmonds, A.L., and Marquis Grissom, N.L. Another young California outfielder, another STATS Gold Glove. Edmonds' zone rating topped the majors, he registered eight baserunner kills, and he made just one error. Grissom's bat was a disappointment for Atlanta, but his glove was as good as advertised.

Right Field: Tim Salmon, A.L., and Reggie Sanders, N.L. Yes, it's a clean sweep for those "Angels in the Outfield." We didn't plan it this way, but the numbers say what the numbers say, and all three have good reputations besides. Salmon's zone rating was .827, better than average, and his arm was solid. In the senior circuit, Sanders wins in a photo finish over Sammy Sosa. Their numbers were nearly identical, but just as in boxing, a tie goes to the defending champion, so Sanders takes his second straight STATS Gold Glove.

— Rob Neyer

A complete listing for this category can be found on page 292.

Who Led the League in Fumbles?

When I was beginning to follow baseball in the 1950s, the baseball cards had two kinds of averages on them: batting averages and fielding averages. So naturally I was convinced that anyone with a high batting average was a good hitter, and anyone with a high fielding average was a good fielder. Dick Groat hit over .300 a few times—what a great hitter he must be! Forget that he seldom hit a homer or drew a walk. Ted Kluszewski was a .995 fielder at first base—he must be awesome! Never mind that he couldn't move three feet off the bag.

Well, the study of baseball statistics has gotten a little more sophisticated over the years, and so have I. Now we all know that batting average and fielding average are good, but limited, stats, and that other numbers often tell us more about how much a player contributes on offense or defense. Still, both stats have their usefulness. And so this essay is a study of fielding average. . . but with a twist.

STONE HANDS		Games per error*	SOFT HANDS		
P	Bobby Jones	3.6	P	Mark Gubicza	0 in 23.7
C	John Flaherty	9.3	C	Chris Hoiles	32.3
1B	Andres Galarraga	10.5	1B	Rico Brogna	40.4
2B	Joey Cora	4.6	2B	Bret Boone	33.7
3B	Chipper Jones	4.7	3B	Wade Boggs	20.8
SS	Jose Offerman	3.1	SS	Cal Ripken	19.8
LF	Joe Carter	15.0	LF	Brady Anderson	52.2
CF	Kenny Lofton	13.5	CF	Jim Edmonds	132.3
RF	Sammy Sosa	10.9	RF	Brian Jordan	108.6

*A 'game' is equivalent to 9 defensive innings played; minimum 850 defensive innings (ERA qualifiers for pitchers).

What we do in this annual essay is look at the major league regulars who commit the most—and fewest—errors at each position. We *could* show you their fielding averages, but we think you'll get a better feel for how often they commit a miscue if we show you how many games, on the average, elapse between each of their errors. For instance, Cal Ripken committed an error about once every 20 games last year, which is good; Jose Offerman committed an error about every three games, which is very, very bad.

Looking at the "Soft Hands" list, it's obvious that these are not necessarily the *best* fielders at each position. . . just the steadiest. And in fact only one player on the list, Wade Boggs, made a Gold Glove team last year. But steadiness *does* count for something. A pitcher with Ripken or Bret Boone behind him in the infield can be pretty sure that they won't mess up the routine plays. A pitcher working in front of Offerman or Joey Cora has no such assurance.

One interesting thing about the two lists is the number of players known as "great athletes" who are on the "Stone Hands" list—Chipper Jones, Kenny Lofton, Sammy Sosa. Jones had the excuses of being a rookie and inexperienced at third base last year, but Lofton and Sosa have been around for several seasons. It's quite possible that, *being* great athletes, they sometimes try to make plays they shouldn't be attempting. . . and as a result, kick or throw the ball away. Often players settle down a bit after a year in which they commit too many errors, and stop trying to do the impossible. One example is Greg Maddux. Though he's a perennial Gold Glove winner, Maddux committed four errors in 1994—a high number for a pitcher, especially in a year that was considerably shortened by the strike. In 1995, Maddux committed *no* errors.

Sometimes too many errors are a sign a player needs a position switch. Offerman is one possibility, though his new team, the Royals, seems committed to giving him another shot at shortstop. A few other examples, though these players were not on the "Stone Hands" list:

Mike Piazza. Piazza averaged an error every 11.6 games behind the plate, which is bad. He's also had problems with his throwing, and some people in the Dodger organization have questioned his pitch selection. A good-hitting catcher is great to have, but only if he's good on defense. Why not shift Piazza—a major offensive talent—to a less demanding position?

Javy Lopez. Like Piazza, Lopez is a great-hitting catcher who's had problems with his throwing, and he averaged an error every 10.5 games behind the plate last year. He's young, and the Braves seem convinced he has the defensive skills. But if his problems continue, expect a switch.

Kurt Abbott. A shortstop with pop (17 homers last year) is an asset, but not if he's going to average an error every 5.7 games. The Marlins may need to find Abbott another position.

Gary Sheffield. He couldn't play shortstop, he couldn't play third base, and last year he averaged an error every 11.3 games in right field, though he didn't play enough innings to make our chart. DH is not an option, so that leaves left field or first base. The Marlins already have a first baseman, Jeff Conine, trying to play left. Since that's Greg Colbrunn—not Lou Gehrig—manning first for the Fish, we know what *we'd* do.

Bobby Bonilla. He still can't play third, averaging an error every 4.0 games there last year—though, like Sheffield, he didn't play enough innings to make the "Stone Hands" list. Isn't it about time to give up on this idea?

— Don Zminda

A complete listing of this category can be found on page 294.

Who Are Baseball's Best "Goalies"?

Which catchers are the best at blocking errant pitches? One way to begin to find the answer is to rate receivers on how many wild pitches and passed balls they allow per inning caught. A system like this can't be perfect, of course, since it's obvious that many wild pitches are entirely the pitcher's fault, and also that any catcher handling a knuckleballer is going to commit more passed balls. We'll take up some of the individual cases at the end of the article; in the meantime, here are the top "goalies" among catchers who caught at least 550 innings in 1995:

1995 Leaders—Errant Pitches Per 100 Innings Caught			
Catcher, Team	Innings	PB+WP	PB+WP/100 Inn
Chris Hoiles, Bal	871.2	22	2.52
Darrin Fletcher, Mon	767.0	22	2.87
Brent Mayne, KC	817.1	25	3.06
Scott Servais, Hou/Cubs	672.0	23	3.42
Charles Johnson, Fla	844.2	30	3.55
Todd Hundley, Mets	680.1	26	3.82
Kirt Manwaring, SF	971.2	38	3.91
Ron Karkovice, WSox	867.0	36	4.15
Tony Pena, Cle	703.0	30	4.27
Dan Wilson, Sea	1017.0	44	4.33

(Minimum 550 innings caught)

The results are really not too surprising. As their reputations suggest, guys like Brent Mayne, Kirt Manwaring and Ron Karkovice help justify their spots in the lineup with good glove work—including the ability to block a pitch. The biggest surprise is leader Chris Hoiles, who has always been known more for his hitting than his defense. Todd Hundley, who seems like an old veteran even though he's only 27, could still turn out to be a gem after years of disappointment.

Now let's look at the trailers list:

1995 Trailers—Errant Pitches Per 100 Innings Caught

Catcher, Team	Innings	PB+WP	PB+WP/100 Inn
Mike Macfarlane, Bos	899.2	74	8.23
Mark Parent, Pit-Cubs	634.0	43	6.78
Joe Oliver, Mil	730.1	46	6.30
Benito Santiago, Cin	606.0	36	5.94
Ivan Rodriguez, Tex	1065.0	57	5.35
Joe Girardi, Col	1044.1	55	5.27

Unexpected members of the trailer list are new Yankee backstop Joe Girardi and perennial Gold Glover Ivan Rodriguez. Each is reputed to be among the best defensive catchers in the game, but these numbers indicate a real weakness at blocking pitches. Benito Santiago is either a wonderful or terrible defensive catcher, depending on who you talk to (the Phillies, his new club, presumably think he's wonderful. . . for now). Santiago's ranking here shouldn't help his reputation any.

But as with almost everything in baseball, one has to consider every piece of the puzzle before evaluating the picture. As we noted earlier, the pitchers each catcher handled often have a profound effect on their numbers. For instance, former Brave and new Jay Charlie O'Brien just missed topping the list—and only because he didn't catch enough innings—with his total of eight errant pitches in 510 innings for a minuscule 1.57 chasers per 100 innings caught. That's great, but we have to point out that Charlie was the personal catcher last year for both Greg Maddux and Steve Avery. Avery threw just three wild pitches in 173.1 innings pitched, while Maddux uncorked only a single wild pitch in his league-leading 209.2 innings pitched. With Maddux' pinpoint control, he could probably be caught with a kiddie glove.

On the other hand, Mike Macfarlane, who had the worst record, spent lots of innings with knuckleballer Tim Wakefield on the mound. And the Blue Jay catchers—most notably Sandy Martinez, who had an astonishing 38 wild pitches and 14 passed balls in 472.2 innings—all ranked poorly as a result of having to wrestle with the arsenals of wild men Al Leiter and Juan Guzman. So, to borrow a football analogy from Rob Neyer, is it Steve Young or Jerry Rice who makes the tandem great? Charlie O'Brien's wife may find her husband a lot dirtier and more irritable when he comes home from work in 1996.

— Steve Moyer

A complete listing for this category can be found on page 296.

Which Outfielders Have the Cannons?

If you take a look at the outfield Gold Glove winners from year to year, you'll more than likely see players with high assist totals. The voters seem to love them, and assist totals alone can go a long way toward developing a player's defensive reputation—even if his range or fielding skill are less than stellar. Nothing impresses voters more than a good arm. Roberto Clemente was charged with 140 outfield errors in his major league career (an *incredibly* high total), yet still won 12 Gold Gloves. Why? You know why—Clemente had a cannon, racking up an amazing 266 lifetime outfield assists, including 27 in 1961. How remarkable was that? As the data below shows, no *two* right fielders were able to match in 1995 what Clemente did by himself in 1961.

1995 Outfield Assists Leaders

Left Field		Center Field		Right Field	
Barry Bonds, SF	12	Rich Becker, Min	11	Raul Mondesi, LA	13
Marty Cordova, Min	11	Kenny Lofton, Cle	11	Sammy Sosa, Cubs	13
Bernard Gilkey, StL	10	Marquis Grissom, Atl	9	Larry Walker, Col	13
Mike Greenwell, Bos	10				

Marquis Grissom, Kenny Lofton and Raul Mondesi were all awarded with Gold Gloves in 1995, and both Barry Bonds and Larry Walker have won previously. As we said earlier, the voters *love* assist totals, but are they the best way to measure an outfielder's throwing ability? We don't think so, choosing instead to put our faith in outfielder hold percentage. What is it? Simply put, it's the number of extra bases (first to third on a single, first to home on a double, etc.) taken against each outfielder per opportunity. For example, if a batter singles to right with a runner on first, we'll charge the right fielder with an "extra base taken" if the runner goes to third. If the runner stops at second, the fielder is credited with one opportunity and no extra bases taken—a hold.

Here are the 1995 leaders in outfielder hold percentage. As is always the case, left fielders have the best hold percentage and center fielders the worst, since left fielders typically have the shortest throws to make in extra-base situations, while center fielders have the longest.

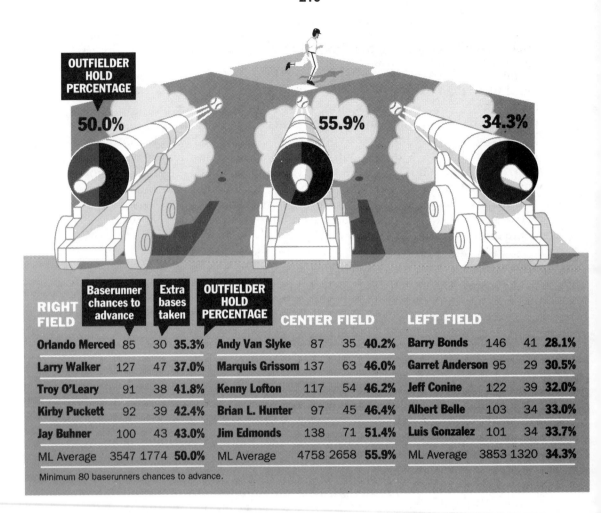

RIGHT FIELD	Baserunner chances to advance	Extra bases taken	OUTFIELDER HOLD PERCENTAGE	CENTER FIELD				LEFT FIELD			
Orlando Merced	85	30	35.3%	Andy Van Slyke	87	35	40.2%	Barry Bonds	146	41	28.1%
Larry Walker	127	47	37.0%	Marquis Grissom	137	63	46.0%	Garret Anderson	95	29	30.5%
Troy O'Leary	91	38	41.8%	Kenny Lofton	117	54	46.2%	Jeff Conine	122	39	32.0%
Kirby Puckett	92	39	42.4%	Brian L. Hunter	97	45	46.4%	Albert Belle	103	34	33.0%
Jay Buhner	100	43	43.0%	Jim Edmonds	138	71	51.4%	Luis Gonzalez	101	34	33.7%
ML Average	3547	1774	50.0%	ML Average	4758	2658	55.9%	ML Average	3853	1320	34.3%

Minimum 80 baserunners chances to advance.

It's hard to argue that Bonds shouldn't have won his sixth Gold Glove in 1995. Not only did he lead all left fielders in assists, but he also led the majors in hold percentage. It doesn't necessarily take a throw to stop a runner from taking the extra base; often the *threat* of a throw is enough, and Bonds has clearly established himself as a threat in the outfield. Unfortunately, Tony Gwynn can't say the same thing. Gwynn, with five Gold Gloves to his credit, allowed a whopping 68 extra bases in 117 opportunities while manning right field last season (58.1%). Only Toronto's Shawn Green (59.1%) was worse at that position among qualifiers.

It should come as no surprise that Bonds also leads all left fielders in hold percentage over the previous *three* seasons as well. In all, the top nine outfielders listed below have combined to win 24 Gold Gloves in their careers. The data seems to more than justify their reputations.

Outfielder Hold Percentage, 1993-95

Left Field	Pct	Center Field	Pct	Right Field	Pct
Barry Bonds	26.0	Marquis Grissom	43.8	Larry Walker	38.3
Albert Belle	30.6	Kenny Lofton	47.4	Mark Whiten	39.4
Luis Gonzalez	31.2	Andy Van Slyke	47.4	Kirby Puckett	39.5
Trailer		**Trailer**		**Trailer**	
Tim Raines	38.6	Alex Cole	64.9	Dante Bichette	58.3

(Minimum 200 baserunner chances to advance)

Could Bichette be overrated in *two* areas of his game? We hate to pick on Dante, but it's just too easy. Not only are his power numbers largely inflated by Coors Field, but the data shows that his throwing arm isn't scaring anybody. Don Baylor would be wise to keep Bichette in left field for good.

— Scott McDevitt

A complete listing for this category can be found on page 297.

Why Can't Roberto Alomar Zone In?

If you've gotten this far in the book, you're probably quite familiar with zone rating, the fielding statistic which we're certain is the most reliable barometer of a player's defensive range. One of the many reasons we're so confident about zone ratings is this: the players with the best zone ratings generally have fine reputations totally aside from the statistics. Perennial Gold Glovers like Devon White and Ryne Sandberg and Ozzie Smith have traditionally posted fine zone ratings. And conversely, those players regarded as poor fielders generally don't have good zone ratings.

But since we've been doing this book, there have been two major exceptions to the rule, and as a result some "experts" question the credibility of zone ratings. Those exceptions are two guys who between them have accounted for 11 Gold Gloves in the last six seasons: Ken Griffey and Roberto Alomar.

Both Griffey and Alomar post mediocre or poor zone ratings season after season, 1995 being no exception. A year ago, we devoted six pages to the possibility that maybe we were wrong about Griffey, that perhaps something in our methodology was penalizing Junior unfairly. Well, we looked at it every way we could think of, almost hoping to find something wrong. . . but our conclusion was no different: Griffey simply isn't as good as people think.

With Griffey out of the way, we decided to turn our attention to Roberto Alomar. After all, he's garnered every American League Gold Glove since joining the Toronto Blue Jays back in 1991. Yet in 1995 he compiled an .872 zone rating at second base, *below* the league average and consistent with his past performance. What's going on here?

First, let's explain once more how zone rating works. STATS has multiple reporters covering each major league game. The field is divided into wedges—down the left-field line is wedge C, straightaway center is M and N, and so on—and each batted ball is assigned a location based on both distance and direction, with the direction dictated by wedge. For the purposes of zone rating, each fielder is assigned a number of wedges as his responsibility. Zone rating is simply the total number of outs recorded by a fielder on line drives and ground balls as a percentage of total balls hit in his area of responsibility.

As we've noted many times before, the beauty of zone rating is that all pitching-staff biases—lefty/righty, flyball/groundball, etc.—are removed from the equation.

Before we continue, let's examine Alomar's fielding stats over the last five years. We'll look at both range factor (raw number of plays made per nine innings) and zone rating:

Year	Range	ML Range	Zone Rtng	ML Zone	Zone Rank*
1991	4.95	5.17	.875	.891	19th
1992	4.68	5.19	.890	.891	12th
1993	4.77	5.14	.863	.895	24th
1994	4.65	5.12	.854	.889	20th
1995	5.10	5.17	.872	.889	17th

(* Zone Rankings minimum 600 innings for '91-'93 and '95, 450 innings for '94)

Except for 1992, when he was about average, Alomar's zone ratings have consistently been well below average. Not what you expect from a perennial Gold Glover.

Take a look at those range factors, too. While the major league average for second basemen has hovered around the 5.15 mark for the last five seasons, Alomar's range factor has typically been well below that. Interestingly, up until 1995, Alomar had never led his league's second basemen in anything except errors. . . something that's highly unusual for someone considered a great fielder. Last season was his best in that span, as he did lead the A.L. in both putouts and fielding percentage. But his range factor was still below average even though American Leaguers have an advantage because their games feature more batters.

So the question remains, are the numbers painting the complete picture? Is there some bias or biases in our statistics that for some reason affect Alomar in particular?

The first thing we often think of is reporter bias. Could one reporter, with either a grudge against Alomar or simply a lack of knowledge, screw up Alomar's zone rating by mis-coding batted balls? Well, it's basically impossible. First of all, we've used a number of different reporters in Toronto over the years. Second, we have a backup system that would raise a red flag if there was consistent mis-reporting. Third, half the Blue Jays games are on the road, so literally hundreds of different reporters have been tracking Alomar's fielding stats. And fourth, our reporters are all fair-minded, talented individuals who have never held a grudge in their life. Or so they tell us.

That brings us to John Olerud, Alomar's teammate since 1989. Though he's not considered one of the better defensive first basemen in the American League, Olerud consistently posts high zone ratings. Given the fact that Alomar's zone ratings are worse than his reputation and Olerud's are better than his, we wondered if there might be some weird relationship between the two. Perhaps Olerud plays further off the bag than most first basemen, and as a result makes plays in what would normally be the second baseman's area, in essence "stealing" plays from Alomar.

There's an easy way to test this theory. If Olerud makes a lot of plays outside a first baseman's normal area of responsibility—in other words, if he makes a lot of plays to his right—he might be taking plays from Alomar. We looked at the 20 first basemen with at least 2,000 innings in the field over the last three seasons. Olerud ranked seventh with 11.4 percent of his outs recorded outside his zone. (By the way, Frank Thomas, generally regarded as an awful fielder, ranked last by a wide margin at 5.6 percent).

So Olerud does make more than his fair share of plays outside his zone. Is he encroaching in Alomar's territory? Well, we checked the same numbers for Alomar at second base, and guess what. . . He also makes a bunch of plays outside his zone. Here are the top five "outside-zone percentage" second basemen over the last three seasons:

Second Baseman	Total Plays	Outside Zone	Outside Zone%
Brent Gates	984	248	25.2
Robby Thompson	692	172	24.9
Bret Boone	731	180	24.6
Craig Biggio	1152	282	24.5
Roberto Alomar	1015	235	23.2

Among the 18 second basemen who have totaled at least 2,000 innings over the last three seasons, Alomar ranks fifth in terms of plays made outside his normal zone. Where is he making those plays? From 1993 through 1995, only 22 of them came to his right, or toward second base. A whopping 213 of those 235 "extra" plays were to his left, or toward first base. . . and Olerud. This is no surprise to those of us who have seen Alomar range into short right field to snag a grounder, then whirl and fire to Olerud just in time to retire a shocked hitter.

But with all those plays to his left comes a price: plays to his right. We already know that Olerud makes a lot of plays to *his* right, and we know that Alomar makes a lot of plays to his left. Sounds like overkill to us, and the result seems to be that Alomar *isn't* making plays to his right that other second basemen might. It's possible that he simply hasn't been positioning himself effectively.

Conclusion? Alomar looks quick because he *is* quick. Unfortunately, he's apparently wasting much of his quickness on plays that the first baseman could make, and the result is too many grounders squirting past the pitchers and on to center field for base hits. If Alomar wants *our* vote for the Gold Glove, he'll simply have to make more plays. Perhaps new teammate Cal Ripken will help him do just that.

— Rob Neyer

A complete listing for this category can be found on page 298.

Which Fielders Have the Best "Defensive Batting Average"?

Reading the fielding section of the *Scoreboard* will give you a pretty good idea of who the best fielders are. But it's nice to have *one* rating system that combines factors like zone ratings, pivot or outfield arm ratings and fielding average into one easy-to-understand number. For that we offer the "defensive batting average," or DBA. Just as with batting averages, a player with a .300 defensive batting average is a pretty good fielder, while one with a .210 DBA is a candidate for a full-time job as a designated hitter.

We won't bore you with the complex formulas used to compute defensive batting averages, but the ratings for the infield and outfield positions are weighted as follows:

Pos	Weighting
1B	Zone Rating 75%, Fielding Pct. 25%
2B	Zone Rating 60%, Fielding Pct. 15%, Pivot Rating 25%
3B	Zone Rating 60%, Fielding Pct. 40%
SS	Zone Rating 80%, Fielding Pct. 20%
LF	Zone Rating 65%, Fielding Pct. 15%, OF Arm 20%
CF	Zone Rating 55%, Fielding Pct. 15%, OF Arm 30%
RF	Zone Rating 50%, Fielding Pct. 15%, OF Arm 35%

Now for the fun part. Let's look at the five best and single worst players in defensive batting average at each infield and outfield spot last year. To qualify, a player needed to play at least 700 innings at that position.

First Base	Zone	FPct	DBA
Wally Joyner, KC	.329	.315	.325
Eric Karros, LA	.324	.289	.315
Jeff Bagwell, Hou	.308	.280	.301
David Segui, Mets-Mon	.290	.308	.295
Hal Morris, Cin	.299	.281	.295
Worst			
Frank Thomas, WSox	.218	.253	.226

The DBA for first basemen is heavily weighted by zone ratings, so this list is pretty much the same one you saw in the zone rating article. The only exceptions are David Segui, who sneaked into fourth place, and Frank Thomas, who ranked last here instead of J.T. Snow. We've been keeping DBAs for three years, and Thomas has ranked last every time. Well, at least he's got a great *offensive* batting average.

Second Base	Zone	FPct	Pivot	DBA
Mickey Morandini, Phi	.314	.296	.296	.306
Jody Reed, SD	.316	.315	.269	.304
Mark Lemke, Atl	.304	.302	.305	.304
Damion Easley, Cal	.309	.269	.285	.297
Quilvio Veras, Fla	.309	.286	.271	.296
Worst				
Joey Cora, Sea	.222	.182	.231	.218

Mickey Morandini and Jody Reed have ranked in the top five in defensive batting average for second basemen two years in a row, and we'd have to say that's a sign that they're pretty good second sackers. Mark Lemke, another good one, also had a good DBA—in fact, he topped the .300 mark in all three categories, which is pretty impressive. Joey Cora of the Mariners is a scrappy ballplayer with a lot of skills, but most of them are in areas other than defense.

Third Base	Zone	FPct	DBA
Wade Boggs, Yanks	.307	.335	.318
Travis Fryman, Det	.297	.313	.303
Charlie Hayes, Phi	.301	.302	.302
Tim Wallach, LA	.282	.326	.300
Tim Naehring, Bos	.288	.285	.287
Worst			
Dave Magadan, Hou	.236	.229	.233

We gave the STATS Gold Glove at third base to Travis Fryman, while acknowledging that Wade Boggs would have been a worthy choice. Boggs has the better defensive batting average, though Fryman was solid also. However, one category not factored into DBA for third basemen is double plays, and Fryman had a huge edge there (38 to 10). Let's just say it was a close decision. Charlie Hayes was our National League choice for the STATS Gold Glove, and the numbers back it up. And in case you're wondering, Hayes ranked second to Fryman in DPs by a third baseman with 25.

Shortstop	Zone	FPct	DBA
Gary DiSarcina, Cal	.335	.316	.331
Mike Bordick, Oak	.332	.308	.327
Cal Ripken, Bal	.323	.323	.323
Kevin Stocker, Phi	.319	.271	.309
Greg Gagne, KC	.309	.271	.301
Worst			
Jose Offerman, LA	.229	.173	.218

We keep talking up the defensive skills of Gary DiSarcina, and one of these years someone else east of Anaheim is going to take notice. Mike Bordick is also a fine glove man, and how about that Ripken kid? Kevin Stocker of the Phillies had the top DBA among National League shortstops, but he'll have a new rival this year in Greg Gagne, who's taking Jose Offerman's place as the Dodger shortstop.

Left Field	Zone	FPct	OF Arm	DBA
Marty Cordova, Min	.324	.299	.237	.303
Albert Belle, Cle	.314	.279	.285	.303
Garret Anderson, Cal	.305	.271	.297	.298
Luis Gonzalez, Hou-Cubs	.298	.270	.281	.290
Brady Anderson, Bal	.292	.303	.270	.289
Worst				
Ryan Klesko, Atl	.231	.174	.274	.231

As we mentioned in the outfield zone-rating essay, American League Rookie of the Year Marty Cordova appears to be a fine all-around player. His arm is a little on the weak side, but that's not terribly important for a left fielder. Albert Belle, clearly a better fielder than he looks, was solid in every category and tied Cordova for the top DBA. Luis Gonzalez of the Cubs and Astros topped National League left fielders, while the Braves' Ryan Klesko continued to show he's a first baseman playing out of position.

Center Field	Zone	FPct	OF Arm	DBA
Jim Edmonds, Cal	.326	.316	.292	.314
Marquis Grissom, Atl	.301	.304	.317	.306
Steve Finley, SD	.317	.251	.264	.291
Bernie Williams, Yanks	.320	.266	.243	.289
Darren Lewis, SF-Cin	.283	.305	.291	.289
Worst				
Mike Kingery, Col	.182	.256	.280	.223

Jim Edmonds of the Angels came out of nowhere to have a great year with the bat, and these stats show that he excelled on defense as well. The top National Leaguer was Gold Glove winner (theirs *and* ours) Marquis Grissom, who's ranked in the top five in DBA among center fielders each of the last three years. Last for the second year in a row was Mike Kingery, a guy who just doesn't have the skills to handle center field at the major league level.

Right Field	Zone	FPct	OF Arm	DBA
Orlando Merced, Pit	.285	.273	.341	.303
Reggie Sanders, Cin	.314	.294	.287	.302
Sammy Sosa, Cubs	.324	.239	.284	.297
Mark Whiten, Bos-Phi	.288	.274	.303	.291
Brian Jordan, StL	.293	.324	.270	.289
Worst				
Derek Bell, Hou	.248	.196	.254	.243

Orlando Merced surprisingly led the right fielders, mostly because of his awesome throwing record. But Merced's name shouldn't be such a shock, as he ranked in the top five in DBA in 1994 as well. National Leaguers dominated this position; the top-ranking player who played at least 700 innings in the A.L. last year was Tim Salmon of the Angels, who had a DBA of .282.

Derek Bell: he proved he couldn't play center field in 1994, and in 1995 he proved he couldn't play right. Ah, but he *can* hit.

— Don Zminda

A complete listing for this category can be found on page 299.

Which Players Cleaned Up At the Awards Banquet?

In the 1993 and 1995 *Scoreboards*, we ran a summary of past studies. For a change of pace this year, we decided to run a summary of past STATS award winners. STATS awards, that is, like the FlatBat (best bunter), Slidin' Billy Trophy (best leadoff man), STATS Gold Gloves, and more. Let's jump right in. . .

STATS FlatBat

The STATS FlatBat is awarded to our pick as the best bunter in the major leagues. We consider sacrifice bunts and bunt hits, and we look at both the raw numbers and the success rates. Here are the annual winners:

1989	Brett Butler
1990	Brett Butler
1991	Steve Finley
1992	Brett Butler
1993	Omar Vizquel
1994	Kenny Lofton
1995	Otis Nixon

Brett Butler has three FlatBats on his mantle, but in recent years others have taken turns with the award. Who will it be in 1996? Two nations await the answer. . .

Slidin' Billy Trophy

The Slidin' Billy Trophy, named in honor of premier 19th-century leadoff man Slidin' Billy Hamilton, goes to the top leadoff hitter each season. The most important factors are, of course, on-base percentage and runs scored, with stolen bases serving as a tiebreaker. Here are the annual winners:

1989	Rickey Henderson
1990	Rickey Henderson
1991	Paul Molitor
1992	Brady Anderson
1993	Lenny Dykstra
1994	Kenny Lofton
1995	Chuck Knoblauch

Since Rickey Henderson gave up the cup after 1990—largely because of his injury problems—a different leadoff man has taken the honors each season. Chuck Knoblauch gets to carry the traveling trophy on road trips in 1996, but he'll have a tough time keeping it. . .

Hottest Heaters

"Hottest Heaters" refers not to fastball velocity, but rather to strikeouts per nine innings. Not coincidentally, it works out about the same:

Year	Pitcher	K/9
1989	Rob Dibble	12.8
1990	Rob Dibble	12.5
1991	Rob Dibble	13.6
1992	Rob Dibble	14.1
1993	Duane Ward	12.2
1994	Bobby Ayala	12.1
1995	Roberto Hernandez	12.7

Dibble was really one of a kind, and the Heaters just haven't been as Hot since his downfall. Mortals like Duane Ward and Bobby Ayala were awesome, but 14.1 K's per nine? Wow.

Red Barrett Trophy

The Red Barrett Trophy goes to the hurler each season who uses the fewest pitches in a nine-inning game. No one has matched Barrett's 1944 feat of needing only 58 pitches to complete a game, but these guys gave it a shot:

Year	Pitcher	#Pitches
1989	Frank Viola	85
1990	Bob Tewksbury	76
1991	Chris Bosio	82
1992	John Smiley	80
1993	Tom Glavine	79
1994	Bobby Munoz	80
1995	Greg Maddux	88

Hey, what's Bobby Munoz doing on a list with all those pitchers?

STATS Gold Gloves

Now we come to the famous STATS Gold Gloves. It takes more than a few flashy plays and a great reputation to win one of these babies; it takes flashy plays, a good reputation, *and* quality defensive stats (not just fielding percentage, either). Everything counts.

First Base

Year	American	National
1989	Don Mattingly	Will Clark
1990	Mark McGwire	Sid Bream
1991	Don Mattingly	Mark Grace
1992	Wally Joyner	Mark Grace
1993	Don Mattingly	Mark Grace
1994	Don Mattingly	Jeff Bagwell
1995	Wally Joyner	Jeff Bagwell

You see a lot of the same names on the first-base lists. Of the 14 STATS Gold Gloves, 11 have gone to Don Mattingly (4), Mark Grace (3), Wally Joyner (2) and Jeff Bagwell (2). But with Joyner going to the Padres and Mattingly apparently in retirement, the American League will be wide open in 1996.

Second Base

Year	American	National
1989	Harold Reynolds	Ryne Sandberg
1990	Billy Ripken	Ryne Sandberg
1991	Mike Gallego	Ryne Sandberg
1992	Carlos Baerga	Ryne Sandberg
1993	Harold Reynolds	Robby Thompson
1994	Jody Reed	Mickey Morandini
1995	Carlos Baerga	Jody Reed

Aside from Sandberg's four-year run, we've seen a lot of different winners here. Jody Reed might be getting up there in years, but he can still pick it. Reed, by the way, is the only player to win a STATS Gold Glove in both leagues.

Third Base

Year	American	National
1989	Gary Gaetti	Tim Wallach
1990	Gary Gaetti	Charlie Hayes
1991	Wade Boggs	Steve Buechele
1992	Robin Ventura	Terry Pendleton
1993	Robin Ventura	Matt Williams
1994	Wade Boggs	Matt Williams
1995	Travis Fryman	Charlie Hayes

Wade Boggs didn't garner his first Rawlings Gold Glove until 1994, but we recognized his defensive excellence way back in 1991. Matt Williams would be a three-time winner, but he missed enough time last season to disqualify himself.

Shortstop

Year	American	National
1989	Ozzie Guillen	Ozzie Smith
1990	Ozzie Guillen	Ozzie Smith
1991	Cal Ripken	Ozzie Smith
1992	Cal Ripken	Ozzie Smith
1993	Ozzie Guillen	Ozzie Smith
1994	Gary DiSarcina	Barry Larkin
1995	Gary DiSarcina	Kevin Stocker

Not many different names here, as eight of the 14 winners were named "Ozzie." American League managers and coaches give the "real" award to the flashy Omar Vizquel these days, but we prefer California's steady Gary DiSarcina.

Left Field

Year	American	National
1989	Rickey Henderson	Barry Bonds
1990	Rickey Henderson	Barry Bonds
1991	Dan Gladden	Bernard Gilkey
1992	Greg Vaughn	Barry Bonds
1993	Greg Vaughn	Barry Bonds
1994	Tony Phillips	Moises Alou
1995	Garret Anderson	Luis Gonzalez

One nice thing about our outfield Gold Gloves (we say, modestly) is that we reserve one for each position. It's a little silly, we think, to give all three Gold Gloves to center fielders, as the American League does nearly every season. How else would Dan Gladden win anything?

Center Field

Year	American	National
1989	Devon White	Eric Davis
1990	Gary Pettis	Lenny Dykstra
1991	Devon White	Brett Butler
1992	Devon White	Darrin Jackson
1993	Kenny Lofton	Darren Lewis
1994	Devon White	Marquis Grissom
1995	Jim Edmonds	Marquis Grissom

Just as they do in real life, Devon White, Kenny Lofton and Marquis Grissom fare quite well here. Remember when Eric Davis was Eric Davis?

Right Field

Year	American	National
1989	Jesse Barfield	Andre Dawson
1990	Jesse Barfield	Tony Gwynn
1991	Joe Carter	Larry Walker
1992	Mark Whiten	Larry Walker
1993	Paul O'Neill	Tony Gwynn
1994	Paul O'Neill	Reggie Sanders
1995	Tim Salmon	Reggie Sanders

Right field is a position for strong-armed gardeners, and that's obvious when you look at our Gold Glove winners over the last seven years. Barfield, Walker, Dawson, Whiten. . . bazooka throwing arms all. Reggie Sanders looks like the right fielder of the moment.

So there they are, the honored few. We should give special mention to the amazing Kenny Lofton, who has captured three different STATS awards: best bunter, best leadoff man, and best center fielder. And he's still only 28; could the Hottest Heater be coming up next?

— Rob Neyer

APPENDIX

After years as a devoted reader of STATS, Inc. products, this is my first attempt at preparing some of the data which appears in the annual edition of the *Scoreboard*. The old adage, "If it ain't broke, don't fix it", applies in this circumstance, and I promise you that I've tried my best not to mess up what has heretofore been a successful enterprise.

Most of the following explanation will sound familiar to longtime readers of the *Scoreboard*. If it doesn't, then I've done something wrong.

Each Appendix is keyed twice. The "Title" key attempts to convey the topic being covered, and matches the corresponding title in the Table of Contents. The "Page" key refers, appropriately enough, to the page number where you'll be able to locate the corresponding essay. Most appendices will be accompanied by labels describing how the list has been ordered, as well as the minimum requirements necessary to appear.

— Jim Henzler

The team abbreviation following a player's name refers to the team with which he accumulated the most playing time. Here are the abbreviations:

American League Teams		National League Teams	
Bal	Baltimore Orioles	Atl	Atlanta Braves
Bos	Boston Red Sox	ChN	Chicago Cubs
Cal	California Angels	Cin	Cincinnati Reds
ChA	Chicago White Sox	Col	Colorado Rockies
Cle	Cleveland Indians	Fla	Florida Marlins
Det	Detroit Tigers	Hou	Houston Astros
KC	Kansas City Royals	LA	Los Angeles Dodgers
Mil	Milwaukee Brewers	Mon	Montreal Expos
Min	Minnesota Twins	NYN	New York Mets
NYA	New York Yankees	Phi	Philadelphia Phillies
Oak	Oakland Athletics	Pit	Pittsburgh Pirates
Sea	Seattle Mariners	StL	St. Louis Cardinals
Tex	Texas Rangers	SD	San Diego Padres
Tor	Toronto Blue Jays	SF	San Francisco Giants

Baltimore Orioles: How Amazing is Ripken's Streak? (p. 4)

Shortstops Who Have Played the Entire Season
Both Leagues—Listed Chronologically

Player	Team	Year	G	SS Games	Player	Team	Year	G	SS Games
Sadie Houck	Det	1883	101	101	Ray Chapman	Cle	1915	154	154
Bill Gleason	STL	1884	110	110	Dave Bancroft	Phi	1915	153	153
Sadie Houck	Phi	1884	108	108	Jimmy Esmond	New	1915	155	155
Bill Gleason	STL	1885	112	112	Honus Wagner	Pit	1915	156	131
Jack Glasscock	StL	1885	111	110	Everett Scott	Bos	1917	157	157
Frank Fennelly	Cin	1885	112	112	Ray Chapman	Cle	1917	156	156
Chippy McGarr	Phi	1887	137	137	Ivy Olson	Bro	1918	126	126
Monte Ward	NYG	1887	129	129	C. Hollocher	ChN	1918	131	131
Ned Williamson	ChN	1887	127	127	Everett Scott	Bos	1918	126	126
Bill Kuehne	Pit	1888	138	63	Donie Bush	Det	1918	128	128
Shorty Fuller	STL	1889	140	140	Dave Bancroft	Phi	1918	125	125
Ollie Beard	Cin	1889	141	141	Art Fletcher	NYG	1918	124	124
Frank Fennelly	Phi	1889	138	138	Everett Scott	Bos	1919	138	138
Bob Allen	Phi	1890	133	133	Wally Gerber	STL	1919	140	140
Germany Smith	Bro	1890	129	129	Wally Gerber	STL	1920	154	154
Billy Shindle	Phi	1890	132	130	Everett Scott	Bos	1920	154	154
Frank Scheibeck	Tol	1890	134	134	Everett Scott	Bos	1921	154	154
Ed McKean	Cle	1890	136	134	Joe Sewell	Cle	1921	154	154
Ed McKean	Cle	1891	141	141	Dave Bancroft	NYG	1921	153	153
Germany Smith	Cin	1891	138	138	Chick Galloway	Phi	1922	155	155
Ed McKean	Cle	1894	130	130	Everett Scott	NYA	1922	154	154
Ed McKean	Cle	1895	131	131	Topper Rigney	Det	1922	155	155
Hughie Jennings	Bal	1895	131	131	Dave Bancroft	NYG	1922	156	156
G. DeMontreville	Was	1896	133	133	Everett Scott	NYA	1923	152	152
G. DeMontreville	Was	1897	133	99	Joe Sewell	Cle	1923	153	151
Billy Clingman	Lou	1898	154	74	Wally Gerber	STL	1923	154	154
Monte Cross	Phi	1899	154	154	Joe Sewell	Cle	1924	153	153
Honus Wagner	Pit	1901	140	61	Everett Scott	NYA	1924	153	153
Freddy Parent	Bos	1901	138	138	Glenn Wright	Pit	1924	153	153
Freddy Parent	Bos	1902	138	138	Glenn Wright	Pit	1925	153	153
Monte Cross	Phi	1902	137	137	Joe Sewell	Cle	1925	155	153
Monte Cross	Phi	1903	137	137	T. Thevenow	StL	1926	156	156
Lee Tannehill	ChA	1903	138	138	Joe Sewell	Cle	1926	154	154
Bobby Wallace	STL	1905	156	156	Joe Sewell	Cle	1927	153	153
Freddy Parent	Bos	1905	153	153	Joe Sewell	Cle	1928	155	137
Mickey Doolan	Phi	1906	154	154	Bill Cissell	ChA	1929	152	152
G. Schaefer	Det	1908	153	68	Joe Cronin	Was	1930	154	154
George McBride	Was	1908	155	155	T. Thevenow	Phi	1930	156	156
George McBride	Was	1909	156	156	Woody English	ChN	1930	156	78
George McBride	Was	1911	154	154	Red Kress	STL	1930	154	123
Donie Bush	Det	1913	153	152	Joe Cronin	Was	1931	156	155
Donie Bush	Det	1914	157	157	Woody English	ChN	1931	156	138
R. Peckinpaugh	NYA	1914	157	157	Lyn Lary	NYA	1931	155	155

Player	Team	Year	G	SS Games	Player	Team	Year	G	SS Games
Dick Bartell	Phi	1932	154	154	Ernie Banks	ChN	1955	154	154
Billy Rogell	Det	1933	155	155	Ernie Banks	ChN	1957	156	100
Dick Bartell	Phi	1933	152	152	Ernie Banks	ChN	1958	154	154
Luke Appling	ChA	1933	151	151	Ernie Banks	ChN	1959	155	154
Billy Rogell	Det	1934	154	154	Ernie Banks	ChN	1960	156	156
Luke Appling	ChA	1935	153	153	Maury Wills	LA	1962	165	165
Arky Vaughan	Pit	1936	156	156	Dick Groat	Pit	1962	161	161
Lyn Lary	STL	1936	155	155	Leo Cardenas	Cin	1964	163	163
Leo Norris	Phi	1936	154	121	Ron Hansen	ChA	1965	162	161
Lyn Lary	Cle	1937	156	156	Leo Cardenas	Cin	1966	160	160
Luke Appling	ChA	1937	154	154	Jim Fregosi	Cal	1966	162	162
Frankie Crosetti	NYA	1938	157	157	Ed Brinkman	Det	1972	156	156
Frankie Crosetti	NYA	1939	152	152	Roger Metzger	Hou	1972	153	153
Arky Vaughan	Pit	1940	156	155	Ed Brinkman	Det	1973	162	162
Lou Boudreau	Cle	1940	155	155	Bill Russell	LA	1973	162	162
Marty Marion	StL	1941	155	155	Larry Bowa	Phi	1974	162	162
W. Wietelmann	Bos	1943	153	153	Toby Harrah	Tex	1974	161	158
Luke Appling	ChA	1943	155	155	Robin Yount	Mil	1976	161	161
Eddie Miller	Cin	1944	155	155	Roy Smalley	Min	1979	162	161
Eddie Lake	Det	1946	155	155	Ozzie Smith	SD	1981	110	110
Eddie Lake	Det	1947	158	158	Ivan DeJesus	ChN	1981	106	106
Stan Rojek	Pit	1948	156	156	Alfredo Griffin	Tor	1982	162	162
Vern Stephens	Bos	1948	155	155	Cal Ripken	Bal	1983	162	162
Granny Hamner	Phi	1949	154	154	Alfredo Griffin	Tor	1983	162	157
Vern Stephens	Bos	1949	155	155	Cal Ripken	Bal	1984	162	162
Roy Smalley	ChN	1950	154	154	Alfredo Griffin	Oak	1985	162	162
Granny Hamner	Phi	1950	157	157	Tony Fernandez	Tor	1985	161	160
Al Dark	NYG	1950	154	154	Cal Ripken	Bal	1985	161	161
Sam Dente	Was	1950	155	128	Cal Ripken	Bal	1986	162	162
Phil Rizzuto	NYA	1950	155	155	Alfredo Griffin	Oak	1986	162	162
Roy McMillan	Cin	1952	154	154	Tony Fernandez	Tor	1986	163	163
Billy Hunter	STL	1953	154	152	Cal Ripken	Bal	1987	162	162
Roy McMillan	Cin	1953	155	155	Cal Ripken	Bal	1988	161	161
Al Dark	NYG	1953	155	110	Cal Ripken	Bal	1989	162	162
Johnny Logan	Mil	1954	154	154	Cal Ripken	Bal	1990	161	161
Ernie Banks	ChN	1954	154	154	Cal Ripken	Bal	1991	162	162
C. Carrasquel	ChA	1954	155	155	Cal Ripken	Bal	1992	162	162
Al Dark	NYG	1954	154	154	Cal Ripken	Bal	1993	162	162
Roy McMillan	Cin	1954	154	154	Mike Bordick	Oak	1994	114	112
Harvey Kuenn	Det	1954	155	155	Cal Ripken	Bal	1994	112	112
Johnny Logan	Mil	1955	154	154	Cal Ripken	Bal	1995	144	144

Chicago White Sox: Is Thomas Too Selective in RBI Situations? (p. 13)

Walks per Plate Appearance With Runners in Scoring Position, 1993-95
(Minimum 475 Plate Appearances)

Player	Avg	OBP	Slg	AB	H	2B	3B	HR	RBI	BB	K	BB/PA
Barry Bonds	.327	.527	.590	324	106	20	4	19	169	150	50	.306
Frank Thomas	.305	.465	.563	387	118	29	1	23	209	141	56	.250
John Olerud	.321	.475	.468	380	122	33	1	7	176	119	47	.231
Robin Ventura	.279	.413	.448	451	126	23	1	17	202	116	75	.196
Rafael Palmeiro	.287	.416	.516	376	108	25	2	19	173	94	53	.191
Mo Vaughn	.338	.471	.606	396	134	30	2	24	216	98	105	.188
Jeff Bagwell	.300	.419	.497	390	117	22	2	17	199	92	68	.179
Tim Salmon	.303	.428	.562	370	112	28	1	22	179	85	89	.178
Jay Buhner	.279	.402	.515	402	112	18	1	25	196	91	90	.176
Chili Davis	.306	.418	.560	382	117	22	0	25	205	83	82	.173
Albert Belle	.299	.413	.623	422	126	30	1	35	233	92	82	.170
Larry Walker	.280	.404	.491	389	109	27	8	13	178	82	72	.165
Cecil Fielder	.269	.387	.482	442	119	16	0	26	201	90	97	.164
Ken Caminiti	.281	.389	.459	438	123	31	1	15	184	85	78	.159
Fred McGriff	.289	.399	.543	387	112	16	2	26	186	76	70	.158
Paul Molitor	.369	.459	.506	417	154	23	2	10	182	79	40	.153
Todd Zeile	.263	.367	.453	411	108	24	0	18	177	74	68	.146
Will Clark	.306	.392	.439	385	118	23	5	6	187	67	55	.140
Cal Ripken	.298	.387	.489	423	126	21	3	18	196	70	37	.136
Luis Gonzalez	.285	.379	.452	396	113	27	6	9	165	66	62	.134
Jeff Conine	.313	.390	.482	425	133	22	1	16	204	66	99	.128
Bernie Williams	.279	.362	.425	409	114	16	4	12	163	57	58	.120
Jeff King	.277	.355	.401	404	112	29	3	5	178	57	44	.117
Eric Karros	.276	.347	.455	409	113	18	2	17	165	52	75	.108
Ruben Sierra	.291	.349	.505	422	123	21	0	23	216	53	71	.105
Joe Carter	.268	.338	.476	466	125	20	1	25	213	57	92	.102
Charlie Hayes	.300	.366	.489	427	128	29	2	16	194	50	71	.101
Sammy Sosa	.282	.354	.497	443	125	15	4	24	178	49	102	.097
Derek Bell	.279	.351	.413	419	117	16	2	12	168	44	89	.090
Carlos Baerga	.324	.373	.501	441	143	24	3	16	220	44	45	.085
Ed Sprague	.211	.288	.317	426	90	21	3	6	144	40	91	.081
Dante Bichette	.321	.355	.572	439	141	23	3	27	222	25	79	.051

Cleveland Indians: How Good *Was* Belle Last Year? (p. 16)

Highest Single Season Double Plus Home Runs Totals

Player	Team	Year	2B	HR	2B+HR	Player	Team	Year	2B	HR	2B+HR
Babe Ruth	NYA	1921	44	59	103	Joe DiMaggio	NYA	1937	35	46	81
Albert Belle	Cle	1995	52	50	102	H Greenberg	Det	1938	23	58	81
Chuck Klein	Phi	1930	59	40	99	Cal Ripken	Bal	1991	46	34	80
Lou Gehrig	NYA	1927	52	47	99	J Bench	Cin	1970	35	45	80
Hack Wilson	ChN	1930	35	56	91	R Hornsby	StL	1925	41	39	80
H Greenberg	Det	1940	50	41	91	Hal Trosky	Cle	1934	45	35	80
Jimmie Foxx	Phi	1932	33	58	91	Duke Snider	Bro	1953	38	42	80
F Robinson	Cin	1962	51	39	90	Earl Averill	Cle	1934	48	31	79
Babe Ruth	NYA	1920	36	54	90	J Gonzalez	Tex	1993	33	46	79
Babe Ruth	NYA	1927	29	60	89	Rudy York	Det	1940	46	33	79
H Greenberg	Det	1934	63	26	89	Duke Snider	Bro	1954	39	40	79
Lou Gehrig	NYA	1934	40	49	89	George Bell	Tor	1987	32	47	79
H Greenberg	Det	1937	49	40	89	Mel Ott	NYG	1929	37	42	79
R Hornsby	StL	1922	46	42	88	E Mathews	Mil	1953	31	47	78
Chuck Klein	Phi	1932	50	38	88	D Bichette	Col	1995	38	40	78
Chuck Klein	Phi	1929	45	43	88	John Olerud	Tor	1993	54	24	78
Joe Medwick	StL	1937	56	31	87	W McCovey	SF	1970	39	39	78
Hal Trosky	Cle	1936	45	42	87	Jim Rice	Bos	1979	39	39	78
Willie Stargell	Pit	1973	43	44	87	Babe Ruth	NYA	1931	31	46	77
Lou Gehrig	NYA	1936	37	49	86	F Thomas	ChA	1993	36	41	77
Babe Ruth	NYA	1923	45	41	86	Ernie Banks	ChN	1957	34	43	77
R Hornsby	ChN	1929	47	39	86	M McGwire	Oak	1987	28	49	77
Babe Ruth	NYA	1924	39	46	85	Stan Musial	StL	1949	41	36	77
Willie Mays	SF	1962	36	49	85	Babe Ruth	NYA	1926	30	47	77
Hank Aaron	Mil	1959	46	39	85	Lou Gehrig	NYA	1931	31	46	77
Jimmie Foxx	Phi	1933	37	48	85	Babe Ruth	NYA	1930	28	49	77
Stan Musial	StL	1948	46	39	85	Johnny Mize	NYG	1947	26	51	77
Don Mattingly	NYA	1986	53	31	84	T Kluszewski	Cin	1954	28	49	77
Barry Bonds	SF	1993	38	46	84	Al Simmons	Phi	1930	41	36	77
Babe Ruth	NYA	1928	29	54	83	H Johnson	NYN	1989	41	36	77
Lou Gehrig	NYA	1930	42	41	83	Willie Mays	SF	1959	43	34	77
Babe Herman	Bro	1930	48	35	83	Roger Maris	NYA	1961	16	61	77
G Foster	Cin	1977	31	52	83	R Palmeiro	Tex	1993	40	37	77
Don Mattingly	NYA	1985	48	35	83	Duke Snider	Bro	1956	33	43	76
Ken Griffey Jr	Sea	1993	38	45	83	Hank Aaron	Atl	1967	37	39	76
F Robinson	Bal	1966	34	49	83	Billy Williams	ChN	1970	34	42	76
Stan Musial	StL	1953	53	30	83	Dave Parker	Cin	1985	42	34	76
Jimmie Foxx	Bos	1938	33	50	83	Chick Hafey	StL	1929	47	29	76
R Jackson	Oak	1969	36	47	83	J Canseco	Oak	1988	34	42	76
Ted Williams	Bos	1949	39	43	82	Lou Gehrig	NYA	1932	42	34	76
Joe Medwick	StL	1936	64	18	82	Tris Speaker	Cle	1923	59	17	76
H Greenberg	Det	1935	46	36	82	J Frederick	Bro	1929	52	24	76
Earl Webb	Bos	1931	67	14	81	Cecil Fielder	Det	1990	25	51	76
E Martinez	Sea	1995	52	29	81	Duke Snider	Bro	1955	34	42	76
Fred Lynn	Bos	1979	42	39	81	Stan Musial	StL	1954	41	35	76
Kevin Mitchell	SF	1989	34	47	81	J Canseco	Oak	1991	32	44	76

Minnesota Twins: Is It Tougher to "Zone In" in a Domed Stadium? (p. 26)

Outfielder Zone Ratings — Dome Vs. Outdoors
(Minimum 100 Chances in Domes, 1993-95)

Player	Domes	Outdoors	Diff	Min	Sea	Tor	Hou	Mon
Moises Alou	.843	.815	.028	—	—	—	.778	.847
Eric Anthony	.818	.802	.016	1.000	.784	1.000	.810	1.000
Rich Becker	.808	.848	-.041	.795	.857	1.000	—	—
Derek Bell	.762	.840	-.077	—	—	—	.756	.808
Jay Buhner	.732	.799	-.067	.765	.736	.563	—	—
Joe Carter	.766	.820	-.054	.842	.647	.772	—	—
Alex Cole	.801	.789	.012	.797	.750	.667	.895	.800
Marty Cordova	.848	.867	-.018	.834	1.000	—	—	—
Steve Finley	.842	.838	.004	—	—	—	.840	.857
Luis Gonzalez	.820	.824	-.004	—	—	—	.810	.964
Ken Griffey Jr	.752	.800	-.048	.767	.760	.526	—	—
Marquis Grissom	.832	.856	-.024	—	—	—	.824	.833
Shane Mack	.826	.856	-.030	.829	.810	.500	—	—
James Mouton	.876	.813	.063	—	—	—	.888	.667
Pedro Munoz	.767	.777	-.010	.769	.714	.800	—	—
Kirby Puckett	.774	.793	-.019	.780	.660	1.000	—	—
Tony Tarasco	.854	.840	.015	—	—	—	1.000	.852
Larry Walker	.862	.804	.058	—	—	—	.778	.868
Devon White	.869	.840	.030	.844	.867	.872	—	—
Rondell White	.839	.805	.034	—	—	—	.926	.827
Total, All OF	**.803**	**.823**	**-.019**	**.791**	**.763**	**.821**	**.806**	**.850**

New York Yankees: Is Mattingly a Hall of Famer? (p. 29)

Similar Players to Don Mattingly
(Minimum Similarity Score of 800)

Player	G	AB	R	H	2B	3B	HR	RBI	BB	K	SB	Avg	Slg	Score
Don Mattingly	1785	7003	1007	2153	442	20	222	1099	588	444	14	.307	.471	1000
Cecil Cooper	1896	7349	1012	2192	415	47	241	1125	448	911	89	.298	.465	943
Hal McRae	2084	7218	940	2091	484	66	191	1097	648	779	109	.289	.454	887
Kirby Puckett	1783	7244	1071	2304	414	57	207	1085	450	965	134	.318	.476	883
Tony Oliva	1676	6301	870	1917	329	48	220	947	448	645	86	.304	.476	861
Carl Furillo	1806	6378	895	1910	324	56	192	1058	514	436	48	.299	.458	855
Jim Bottomley	1991	7471	1177	2313	465	151	219	1422	664	591	58	.309	.500	853
K Hernandez	2088	7370	1124	2182	426	60	162	1071	1070	1012	98	.296	.436	853
Cy Williams	2002	6780	1024	1981	306	74	251	1005	690	721	115	.292	.470	852
Bob Watson	1832	6185	802	1826	307	41	184	989	653	796	27	.295	.447	847
Kent Hrbek	1747	6192	903	1749	312	18	293	1086	838	798	37	.282	.480	846
Del Ennis	1903	7254	985	2063	358	69	288	1284	597	719	45	.284	.471	844
Harold Baines	2183	7871	1033	2271	387	48	301	1261	804	1163	30	.288	.464	840
T Kluszewski	1718	5929	848	1766	290	29	279	1028	492	365	20	.297	.497	838
M Minoso	1835	6579	1136	1963	336	83	186	1023	814	584	205	.298	.459	835
Bill Terry	1721	6428	1120	2193	373	112	154	1078	537	449	56	.341	.505	834
G Hendrick	2048	7129	941	1980	343	27	267	1111	567	1013	59	.277	.445	832
C Chambliss	2175	7571	912	2109	392	42	185	972	632	926	40	.278	.414	829
P Guerrero	1536	5392	730	1618	267	29	215	898	609	862	97	.300	.479	824
C Cedeno	2006	7310	1084	2087	436	60	199	976	664	938	550	.285	.443	823
Bill White	1673	5972	843	1706	278	65	202	870	596	927	103	.285	.455	820
George Kelly	1622	5993	819	1778	337	76	148	1020	386	694	65	.296	.452	818
Bing Miller	1821	6212	947	1937	389	95	117	990	383	340	128	.311	.461	818
Felipe Alou	2082	7339	985	2101	359	49	206	852	423	706	107	.286	.432	816
George Scott	2034	7433	957	1992	306	60	271	1051	699	1418	69	.267	.434	816
Chet Lemon	1988	6868	973	1875	396	61	215	884	749	1024	58	.273	.442	816
Fred Lynn	1969	6925	1063	1960	388	43	306	1111	857	1116	72	.283	.484	815
Dusty Baker	2039	7117	964	1981	320	23	242	1013	762	926	137	.278	.431	812
George Burns	1866	6573	901	2018	444	72	72	948	363	433	153	.307	.429	812
Joe Adcock	1959	6606	823	1832	295	35	336	1122	594	1059	20	.277	.485	811
Chili Davis	1970	7087	1026	1934	348	29	270	1100	936	1385	127	.272	.444	811
Steve Garvey	2332	8835	1143	2599	440	43	272	1308	479	1003	83	.294	.446	810
Roy Sievers	1887	6387	945	1703	292	42	318	1147	841	920	14	.266	.474	809
Reggie Smith	1987	7033	1123	2020	363	57	314	1092	890	1030	137	.287	.488	808
Andy Pafko	1852	6292	844	1796	264	62	213	976	561	477	38	.285	.448	807
Ken Singleton	2082	7189	985	2029	317	25	246	1065	1263	1246	21	.282	.435	806
Rudy York	1603	5891	876	1621	291	52	277	1152	791	867	38	.275	.483	806
Dixie Walker	1905	6740	1037	2064	376	96	105	1023	817	325	59	.306	.437	804
Greg Luzinski	1821	6505	880	1795	344	24	307	1128	845	1495	37	.275	.477	803
Will Clark	1393	5112	845	1543	300	42	205	881	645	853	57	.301	.497	803
George Bell	1587	6123	814	1702	308	34	265	1002	331	771	67	.277	.469	803
Bobby Murcer	1908	6730	972	1862	285	45	252	1043	862	841	127	.276	.444	803
G Matthews	2033	7147	1083	2011	319	51	234	978	940	1125	183	.281	.438	802
Hal Trosky	1347	5161	835	1561	331	58	228	1012	545	440	28	.302	.521	802
Rico Carty	1651	5606	712	1677	278	17	204	890	642	663	21	.299	.463	802
Gus Bell	1741	6478	865	1823	311	66	206	942	470	636	30	.281	.445	802
Lee May	2071	7609	959	2031	340	31	354	1244	487	1570	39	.266	.459	800
Vic Wertz	1862	6099	867	1692	289	42	266	1178	828	842	9	.277	.469	800

Oakland Athletics: Did McGwire Have the Best Home-Run Season Ever? (p. 33)

Smallest Single-Season At Bat to Home Run Ratio
(Minimum 300 At Bats)

Player	Team	Year	AB	HR	Ratio	Player	Team	Year	AB	HR	Ratio
M McGwire	Oak	1995	317	39	8.128	Mike Schmidt	Phi	1981	354	31	11.419
Babe Ruth	NYA	1920	458	54	8.481	Ted Williams	Bos	1955	320	28	11.429
Babe Ruth	NYA	1927	540	60	9.000	H Killebrew	Min	1963	515	45	11.444
Babe Ruth	NYA	1921	540	59	9.153	Albert Belle	Cle	1994	412	36	11.444
M Mantle	NYA	1961	514	54	9.519	Johnny Mize	NYG	1947	586	51	11.490
H Greenberg	Det	1938	556	58	9.586	Babe Ruth	NYA	1924	529	46	11.500
Roger Maris	NYA	1961	590	61	9.672	H Killebrew	Min	1962	552	48	11.500
Hank Aaron	Atl	1973	392	40	9.800	Kevin Mitchell	SF	1989	543	47	11.553
Babe Ruth	NYA	1928	536	54	9.926	Babe Ruth	NYA	1922	406	35	11.600
Jimmie Foxx	Phi	1932	585	58	10.086	Babe Ruth	NYA	1931	534	46	11.609
Ralph Kiner	Pit	1949	549	54	10.167	Ralph Kiner	Pit	1950	547	47	11.638
M Mantle	NYA	1956	533	52	10.250	J Gonzalez	Tex	1993	536	46	11.652
Jeff Bagwell	Hou	1994	400	39	10.256	R Jackson	Oak	1969	549	47	11.681
Kevin Mitchell	Cin	1994	310	30	10.333	T Kluszewski	Cin	1954	573	49	11.694
Matt Williams	SF	1994	445	43	10.349	Barry Bonds	SF	1993	539	46	11.717
Hack Wilson	ChN	1930	585	56	10.446	Jay Buhner	Sea	1995	470	40	11.750
F Thomas	ChA	1994	399	38	10.500	F Robinson	Bal	1966	576	49	11.755
Hank Aaron	Atl	1971	495	47	10.532	H Killebrew	Min	1961	541	46	11.761
Babe Ruth	NYA	1926	495	47	10.532	H Killebrew	Min	1964	577	49	11.776
Jim Gentile	Bal	1961	486	46	10.565	Lou Gehrig	NYA	1934	579	49	11.816
Barry Bonds	SF	1994	391	37	10.568	Lou Gehrig	NYA	1936	579	49	11.816
Babe Ruth	NYA	1930	518	49	10.571	G Foster	Cin	1977	615	52	11.827
Willie Stargell	Pit	1971	511	48	10.646	Willie Stargell	Pit	1973	522	44	11.864
Ted Williams	Bos	1960	310	29	10.690	H Greenberg	Det	1946	523	44	11.886
Rudy York	Det	1937	375	35	10.714	E Mathews	Mil	1954	476	40	11.900
Willie Mays	SF	1965	558	52	10.731	G Sheffield	Fla	1994	322	27	11.926
Ken Griffey Jr	Sea	1994	433	40	10.825	R Colavito	Cle	1958	489	41	11.927
Babe Ruth	NYA	1929	499	46	10.848	Ted Williams	Bos	1950	334	28	11.929
Boog Powell	Bal	1964	424	39	10.872	Jimmie Foxx	Phi	1933	573	48	11.938
W McCovey	SF	1969	491	45	10.911	Joe Adcock	Mil	1956	454	38	11.947
Albert Belle	Cle	1995	546	50	10.920	Jack Clark	StL	1987	419	35	11.971
Ted Williams	Bos	1957	420	38	11.053	Mike Schmidt	Phi	1979	541	45	12.022
Ralph Kiner	Pit	1947	565	51	11.078	E Mathews	Mil	1955	499	41	12.171
D Kingman	ChN	1979	532	48	11.083	Jimmie Foxx	Phi	1934	539	44	12.250
M McGwire	Oak	1992	467	42	11.119	Rob Deer	Det	1992	393	32	12.281
Babe Ruth	NYA	1932	457	41	11.146	Ken Phelps	Sea	1987	332	27	12.296
Cecil Fielder	Det	1990	573	51	11.235	Willie Mays	SF	1964	578	47	12.298
Jimmie Foxx	Bos	1938	565	50	11.300	E Mathews	Mil	1953	579	47	12.319
H Killebrew	Min	1969	555	49	11.327	Ted Williams	Bos	1941	456	37	12.324
M McGwire	Oak	1987	557	49	11.367	F Thomas	ChA	1995	493	40	12.325
Willie Mays	NYG	1955	580	51	11.373	F Howard	Was	1969	592	48	12.333
Mike Schmidt	Phi	1980	548	48	11.417	M Mantle	NYA	1958	519	42	12.357

Seattle Mariners: Should Edgar Have Been the MVP? (p. 36)

Players Ranking in Top Two of Avg, OBP, and Slg

Year	League	Player	Team	BA	OBP	Slg	Year	League	Player	Team	BA	OBP	Slg
1995	AL	Martinez	Sea	1	1	2	1931	AL	Ruth	NYA	2	1	1
1994	NL	Bagwell	Hou	2	2	1		NL	Hafey	StL	1	1	2
1990	AL	Henderson	Oak	2	1	2	1930	AL	Gehrig	NYA	2	2	2
1985	AL	Brett	KC	2	2	1	1928	NL	Hornsby	Bos	1	1	
	NL	Guerrero	LA	2	1	1	1927	NL	Hornsby	NYG	2	1	1
1980	AL	Brett	KC	1	1	1	1926	AL	Ruth	NYA	2	1	1
1979	AL	Lynn	Bos	1	2	1		NL	Waner	Pit	1	1	2
1978	NL	Parker	Pit	1	2	1	1925	NL	Hornsby	StL	1	1	1
1977	AL	Carew	Min	1	1	2	1924	AL	Ruth	NYA	1	1	1
1972	NL	Williams	ChN	1	2	1		NL	Hornsby	StL	1	1	1
1971	AL	Murcer	NYA	2	1	2	1923	AL	Ruth	NYA	2	1	1
1970	AL	Yastrzemski	Bos	2	1	1			Heilmann	Det	1	2	2
1967	AL	Yastrzemski	Bos	1	1	1		NL	Hornsby	StL	1	1	1
1966	AL	Robinson	Bal	1	1	1	1922	NL	Hornsby	StL	1	1	1
1965	AL	Yastrzemski	Bos	2	1	1			Grimes	ChN	2	2	2
1962	AL	Mantle	NYA	2	1	1	1921	NL	Hornsby	StL	1	1	1
	NL	Robinson	Cin	2	1	1	1920	NL	Hornsby	StL	1	1	1
1961	AL	Cash	Det	1	1	2	1918	AL	Cobb	Det	1	1	1
1959	NL	Aaron	Mil	1	2	1	1917	AL	Cobb	Det	1	1	1
1957	AL	Williams	Bos	1	1	1		NL	Hornsby	StL	2	2	1
		Mantle	NYA	2	2	2	1916	AL	Speaker	Cle	1	1	1
	NL	Musial	StL	1	1	2	1915	Fed	Kauff	Bro	1	1	1
		Mays	NYG	2	2	1		AL	Cobb	Det	1	1	2
1956	AL	Mantle	NYA	1	2	1		NL	Luderus	Phi	2	2	2
		Williams	Bos	2	1	2	1914	Fed	Kauff	Ind	1	1	2
1955	AL	Kaline	Det	1	2	2		AL	Speaker	Bos	2	2	1
1953	AL	Rosen	Cle	2	2	1	1913	AL	Cobb	Det	1	1	2
1952	NL	Musial	StL	1	2	1			Jackson	Cle	2	2	1
1951	NL	Musial	StL	1	2	2		NL	Cravath	Phi	2	2	1
1950	NL	Musial	StL	1	2	1	1912	AL	Jackson	Cle	2	2	2
1949	AL	Williams	Bos	2	1	1	1911	AL	Cobb	Det	1	2	1
	NL	Musial	StL	2	1	2			Jackson	Cle	2	1	2
1948	AL	Williams	Bos	1	1	1	1910	AL	Cobb	Det	2	1	1
	NL	Musial	StL	1	1	1			Lajoie	Cle	1	2	2
1947	AL	Williams	Bos	1	1	1		NL	Magee	Phi	1	1	1
1946	AL	Williams	Bos	2	1	1	1909	AL	Cobb	Det	1	1	1
	NL	Musial	StL	1	2	1		NL	Wagner	Pit	1	1	1
1944	NL	Musial	StL	2	1	1	1908	NL	Wagner	Pit	1	1	1
1943	NL	Musial	StL	1	1	1	1907	NL	Wagner	Pit	1	1	1
1942	AL	Williams	Bos	1	1	1			Magee	Phi	2	2	2
1941	AL	Williams	Bos	1	1	1	1906	AL	Stone	StL	1	1	1
1939	AL	Foxx	Bos	2	1	1			Lajoie	Cle	2	2	2
	NL	Mize	StL	1	2	1		NL	Wagner	Pit	1	2	2
1938	AL	Foxx	Bos	1	1	1	1905	AL	Flick	Cle	1	2	1
1937	NL	Mize	StL	2	2	2		NL	Seymour	Cin	1	1	1
1935	NL	Vaughan	Pit	1	1	1			Wagner	Pit	2	2	2
1934	AL	Gehrig	NYA	1	1	1	1904	AL	Lajoie	Cle	1	1	1
1933	AL	Foxx	Phi	1	2	1		NL	Wagner	Pit	1	1	1
	NL	Klein	Phi	1	1	1	1902	AL	Delehanty	Was	1	1	1
1932	AL	Foxx	Phi	1	2	1	1901	AL	Lajoie	Phi	1	1	1

Florida Marlins: What Kind Of Career Will Sheffield Have? (p. 58)

Similar Players to Gary Sheffield — Through Age 26
(Minimum Similarity Score of 900)

Player	G	AB	R	H	2B	3B	HR	RBI	BB	K	SB	Avg	Slg	Score
Gary Sheffield	730	2696	399	774	139	12	117	430	298	295	96	.287	.477	1000
Andre Dawson	729	2829	414	795	140	40	110	387	175	468	145	.281	.475	968
Reggie Smith	768	2890	438	810	156	27	107	393	289	386	66	.280	.464	959
Vic Wertz	663	2392	390	693	128	27	87	461	344	313	4	.289	.474	956
Bobby Murcer	642	2365	378	659	103	22	108	359	300	347	49	.278	.477	953
Bobby Bonds	704	2837	537	779	132	30	126	385	318	734	179	.274	.475	952
Ellis Valentine	686	2520	312	711	144	12	100	379	155	368	56	.282	.467	951
Billy Williams	658	2484	360	725	117	29	107	379	248	323	32	.291	.491	950
Harold Baines	847	3184	420	908	153	36	119	501	225	450	27	.285	.467	948
Kent Hrbek	761	2816	405	815	156	15	117	474	319	415	11	.289	.480	945
Dave Winfield	796	2842	413	796	127	23	100	421	299	431	95	.280	.446	945
Jack Clark	852	3036	482	837	163	29	132	485	380	448	54	.275	.478	941
Sixto Lezcano	785	2722	360	749	130	22	102	374	333	524	34	.275	.451	937
Dale Murphy	714	2591	381	686	97	11	128	407	283	568	63	.264	.458	936
Steve Kemp	684	2504	378	711	114	18	89	422	375	362	24	.283	.450	935
Ellis Burks	656	2559	405	725	152	24	85	357	226	402	88	.283	.461	932
Willie Horton	735	2582	334	694	102	18	141	461	240	515	11	.268	.486	932
Gary Matthews	742	2730	407	781	125	29	81	360	342	402	75	.286	.442	932
B Thomson	599	2274	366	628	107	24	99	351	173	250	16	.276	.474	931
Gus Bell	849	3329	489	959	175	46	114	511	256	346	15	.288	.471	931
Richie Hebner	777	2754	415	791	137	31	98	374	295	336	8	.287	.466	928
Jesse Barfield	715	2325	371	634	112	19	128	376	238	578	45	.272	.502	926
Chet Lemon	785	2794	403	804	178	29	73	348	281	377	45	.287	.450	926
Al Oliver	725	2770	366	798	148	25	75	405	139	245	21	.288	.440	924
D Tartabull	603	2122	316	601	120	13	106	375	295	552	26	.283	.501	924
Jim Ray Hart	770	2813	416	799	109	26	139	449	268	424	17	.284	.489	921
Jimmy Wynn	713	2587	389	666	120	21	112	354	343	586	92	.257	.449	920
E Slaughter	666	2531	421	780	150	54	63	391	267	184	24	.308	.484	920
T Conigliaro	855	3164	456	842	138	23	164	507	279	620	19	.266	.479	920
R Jackson	775	2712	434	700	128	20	157	419	371	780	79	.258	.493	919
Tommy Davis	721	2686	365	814	98	21	83	438	138	285	62	.303	.447	918
George Bell	574	2129	297	610	112	21	92	319	117	282	43	.286	.488	917
Tony Oliva	631	2443	394	761	150	27	90	366	178	269	55	.311	.505	913
Leon Durham	568	1980	312	564	110	29	75	318	246	354	89	.284	.483	912
J Callison	940	3413	529	933	155	65	134	467	330	599	41	.273	.474	911
Del Ennis	883	3407	487	1000	188	40	130	558	306	336	24	.293	.486	910
John Olerud	795	2705	405	801	188	6	91	410	454	393	2	.296	.470	910
Sammy Sosa	802	2881	419	738	110	27	131	423	198	719	159	.256	.449	909
Sam Chapman	531	1964	319	557	96	25	80	308	199	301	22	.283	.480	908
B Campbell	597	2166	334	640	143	31	54	361	211	301	26	.295	.464	906
Will Clark	736	2700	452	815	150	27	117	447	319	503	34	.301	.507	905
Alvin Davis	599	2204	310	628	122	7	92	366	335	301	6	.284	.471	902
Larry Doby	573	1968	386	586	101	22	83	324	345	330	31	.297	.497	901

Houston Astros: Should a Fast Catcher Be Shifted to a New Position? (p. 60)

Young Catchers with 15+ Steals in a Season
(Age 27 or Younger; Minimum 60 Games Caught)

Player	Team	Year	G	SB	Age	Player	Team	Year	G	SB	Age
Brad Ausmus	SD	1995	100	16	26	John Grim	Lou	1893	92	15	25
Craig Biggio	Hou	1991	139	19	25	Con Daily	Bro	1892	68	18	27
B.J. Surhoff	Mil	1990	125	18	25	John Grim	Lou	1892	69	18	24
Craig Biggio	Hou	1990	113	25	24	Doggie Miller	Pit	1892	63	28	27
Craig Biggio	Hou	1989	125	21	23	Jack Boyle	STL	1891	91	19	25
B.J. Surhoff	Mil	1988	106	21	23	Morgan Murphy	Bos	1891	104	17	24
Benito Santiago	SD	1988	136	15	23	Tom Daly	Bro	1890	69	20	24
Benito Santiago	SD	1987	146	21	22	Herman Pitz	Syr	1890	61	39	24
John Stearns	NYN	1979	121	15	27	Jack O'Connor	Col	1890	106	29	21
John Stearns	NYN	1978	141	25	26	Connie Mack	Buf	1890	112	16	27
Fran Healy	KC	1974	138	16	27	Wilbert Robinson	Bal	1890	93	21	27
Ray Schalk	ChA	1917	139	19	24	Morgan Murphy	Bos	1890	67	16	23
Eddie Ainsmith	Was	1917	119	16	25	Doggie Miller	Pit	1889	76	16	24
Ray Schalk	ChA	1916	124	30	23	Jack O'Connor	Col	1889	84	26	20
Ray Schalk	ChA	1915	134	15	22	Doggie Miller	Pit	1888	68	27	23
Ivy Wingo	StL	1914	70	15	23	Connie Mack	Was	1888	79	31	25
Jeff Sweeney	NYA	1914	78	19	25	Connie Mack	Was	1887	76	26	24
Ray Schalk	ChA	1914	125	24	21	Tom Daly	ChN	1887	64	29	21
Eddie Ainsmith	Was	1913	79	17	21	Wilbert Robinson	Phi	1887	67	15	24
Ivy Wingo	StL	1913	98	18	22	Doggie Miller	Pit	1887	73	33	22
Red Dooin	Phi	1906	107	15	27	Chris Fulmer	Bal	1886	68	29	27
Roger Bresnahan	NYG	1906	82	25	27	Fred Carroll	Pit	1886	70	20	21
Red Dooin	Phi	1904	96	15	25	Wilbert Robinson	Phi	1886	61	33	23
Johnny Kling	ChN	1902	112	24	27	John Kerins	Lou	1886	65	26	27
O Schreckengost	StL	1899	64	18	24	Jimmy Peoples	Bro	1886	76	20	22
John Warner	NYG	1899	82	15	26	Doggie Miller	Pit	1886	61	35	21

L.A. Dodgers: Did Teams Catch Up with Nomo the Second Time Around? (p. 63)

Nomo's Record Versus Teams He Faced More Than Once

Nomo's Record the First Time Around the League

Opponent	GS	IP	H	AB	Avg	R	HR	W	L	ERA
Cubs	1	6.2	11	28	.393	5	0	1	0	5.40
Expos	1	6.1	4	23	.174	3	0	0	1	4.26
Mets	1	6.0	8	25	.320	4	1	0	0	4.50
Phillies	1	3.0	6	15	.400	7	1	0	1	18.00
Pirates	1	7.0	2	22	.091	0	0	0	0	0.00
Cardinals	1	4.0	0	14	.000	3	0	0	0	2.25
Padres	1	5.0	3	17	.176	2	0	1	0	1.80
Giants	1	5.0	1	15	.067	0	0	0	0	0.00
Rockies	1	4.2	9	23	.391	7	3	0	0	13.50
Marlins	1	9.0	3	28	.107	1	0	1	0	1.00
Total : 1st Games	10	56.2	47	210	.224	32	5	3	2	4.13

Nomo's Record Second Time Around the League

Opponent	GS	IP	H	AB	Avg	R	HR	W	L	ERA
Cubs	1	8.0	6	29	.207	1	0	1	0	1.13
Expos	1	8.0	6	30	.200	1	1	1	0	1.13
Mets	3	22.1	10	76	.132	6	4	1	1	2.42
Phillies	1	5.0	3	16	.188	1	0	0	0	1.80
Pirates	1	8.0	6	30	.200	3	0	1	0	2.25
Cardinals	2	16.1	9	57	.158	4	2	1	1	1.65
Padres	1	8.0	6	28	.214	2	0	1	0	1.13
Giants	3	23.0	10	76	.132	6	0	2	1	2.35
Rockies	1	9.0	6	31	.194	0	0	1	0	0.00
Marlins	1	8.0	4	27	.148	2	1	0	0	2.25
Total : 2nd+ Games	15	115.2	66	400	.165	26	8	9	3	1.79

New York Mets: How Do Their Hurlers Compare With '69? (p. 68)

1969 Mets Pitching Staff

Seaver, Tom
B:R, T:R, Born: 11/17/1944 (25 in 1969)

YR	TEAM	LG	W	L	G	IP	H	R	ER	TBB	SO	ERA
1966	Jacksonville	AAA	12	12	34	210.0	184	87	73	66	188	3.13
1967	Mets	MLB	16	13	35	251.0	224	85	77	78	170	2.76
1968	Mets	MLB	16	12	36	278.0	224	73	68	48	205	2.20
1969	Mets	MLB	25	7	36	273.0	202	75	67	82	208	2.21
Totals			311	205	656	4782.0	3971	1674	1521	1390	3640	2.86

Koosman, Jerry
B:R, T:L, Born: 12/23/1942 (26 in 1969)

YR	TEAM	LG	W	L	G	IP	H	R	ER	TBB	SO	ERA
1965	Greenville	A	5	11	27	107.0	101	70	56	56	128	4.71
	Williamsport	AA	0	2	2	12.0	11	7	5	11	11	3.75
1966	Auburn	A	12	7	24	170.0	109	43	26	43	174	1.38
1967	Mets	MLB	0	2	9	22.0	22	17	15	19	11	6.14
	Jacksonville	AAA	11	10	25	178.0	137	60	48	46	183	2.43
1968	Mets	MLB	19	12	35	264.0	221	72	61	69	178	2.08
1969	Mets	MLB	17	9	32	241.0	187	66	61	68	180	2.28
Totals			222	209	612	3839.1	3635	1608	1433	1198	2556	3.36

Gentry, Gary
B:R, T:R, Born: 10/6/1946 (22 in 1969)

YR	TEAM	LG	W	L	G	IP	H	R	ER	TBB	SO	ERA
1967	Williamsport	AA	4	4	11	79.0	62	18	14	35	77	1.59
1968	Jacksonville	AAA	12	8	30	198.0	142	73	64	87	156	2.91
1969	Mets	MLB	13	12	35	234.0	192	94	89	81	154	3.42
Totals			46	49	157	903.0	770	400	57	369	615	3.56

McAndrew, Jim
B:R, T:R, Born: 1/11/1944 (25 in 1969)

YR	TEAM	LG	W	L	G	IP	H	R	ER	TBB	SO	ERA
1965	Auburn	A	5	5	11	67.0	72	50	40	20	69	5.37
	Marion	R	1	0	2	13.0	8	4	4	3	17	2.77
1966	Auburn	A	11	7	26	162.0	171	84	65	52	154	3.61
1967	Williamsport	AA	10	8	25	153.0	119	43	25	42	120	1.47
1968	Jacksonville	AAA	8	3	23	117.0	101	34	33	30	117	2.54
	Mets	MLB	4	7	12	79.0	66	20	20	17	46	2.28
1969	Mets	MLB	6	7	27	135.0	112	57	52	44	90	3.47
Totals			37	53	161	771.0	712	348	13	213	424	3.65

Ryan, Nolan
B:R, T:R, Born: 1/31/1947 (22 in 1969)

YR	TEAM	LG	W	L	G	IP	H	R	ER	TBB	SO	ERA
1965	Marion	R	3	6	13	78.0	61	47	38	56	115	4.38
1966	Greenville	A	17	2	29	183.0	109	59	51	127	272	2.51
	Williamsport	AA	0	2	3	19.0	9	6	2	12	35	0.95
	Mets	MLB	0	1	2	3.0	5	5	5	3	6	5.00
1967	Winter Haven	A	0	0	1	4.0	1	1	1	2	5	2.25
	Jacksonville	AAA	1	0	3	7.0	3	1	0	3	18	0.00
1968	Mets	MLB	6	9	21	134.0	93	50	46	75	133	3.09
1969	Mets	MLB	6	3	25	89.0	60	38	35	53	92	3.54
Totals			324	292	807	5386.2	3923	2178	1911	2795	5714	3.19

1995 Mets Pitching Staff

Jones, Bobby
B:R, T:R, Born: 2/10/1970 (26 in 1996)

YR	TEAM	LG	W	L	G	IP	H	R	ER	TBB	SO	ERA
1991	Columbia	A	3	1	5	24.1	20	5	5	3	35	1.85
1992	Binghamton	AA	12	4	24	158.0	118	40	33	43	143	1.88
1993	Norfolk	AAA	12	10	24	166.0	149	72	67	32	126	3.63
	Mets	MLB	2	4	9	61.2	61	35	25	22	35	3.65
1994	Mets	MLB	12	7	24	160.0	157	75	56	56	80	3.15
1995	Mets	MLB	10	10	30	195.2	209	107	91	53	127	4.19
Totals			24	21	63	417.1	427	217	172	131	242	3.71

Pulsipher, Bill
B:L, T:L, Born: 10/9/1973 (22 in 1996)

YR	TEAM	LG	W	L	G	IP	H	R	ER	TBB	SO	ERA
1992	Pittsfield	A	6	3	14	95.0	88	40	30	56	83	2.84
1993	Capital City	A	2	3	6	43.1	34	17	10	12	29	2.08
	St. Lucie	A	7	3	13	96.1	63	27	24	39	102	2.24
1994	Binghamton	AA	14	9	28	201.0	179	90	72	89	171	3.22
1995	Norfolk	AAA	6	4	13	91.2	84	36	32	33	63	3.14
	Mets	MLB	5	7	17	126.2	122	58	56	45	81	3.98
Totals			5	7	17	126.2	122	58	56	45	81	3.98

Isringhausen, Jason
B:R, T:R, Born: 9/7/1972 (23 in 1996)

YR	TEAM	LG	W	L	G	IP	H	R	ER	TBB	SO	ERA
1992	Mets	R	2	4	6	29.0	26	19	14	17	25	4.34
	Kingsport	R	4	1	7	36.0	32	22	13	12	24	3.25
1993	Pittsfield	A	7	4	15	90.1	68	45	33	28	104	3.29
1994	St. Lucie	A	6	4	14	101.0	76	31	25	27	59	2.23
	Binghamton	AA	5	4	14	92.1	78	35	31	23	69	3.02
1995	Binghamton	AA	2	1	6	41.0	26	15	13	12	59	2.85
	Norfolk	AAA	9	1	12	87.0	64	17	15	24	75	1.55
	Mets	MLB	9	2	14	93.0	88	29	29	31	55	2.81
Totals			9	2	14	93.0	88	29	29	31	55	2.81

Acevedo, Juan
B:R, T:R, Born: 5/5/1970 (26 in 1996)

YR	TEAM	LG	W	L	G	IP	H	R	ER	TBB	SO	ERA
1992	Bend	A	0	0	1	2.0	4	3	3	1	3	3.50
	Visalia	A	3	4	12	64.2	75	46	39	33	37	5.43
1993	Central Vly	A	9	8	27	118.2	119	68	58	58	107	4.40
1994	New Haven	AA	17	6	26	174.2	142	56	46	38	161	2.37
1995	Col Springs	AAA	1	1	3	14.2	18	11	10	7	7	6.14
	Rockies	MLB	4	6	17	65.2	82	53	47	20	40	6.44
	Norfolk	AAA	0	0	2	3.0	0	0	0	1	2	0.00
Totals			4	6	17	65.2	82	53	47	20	40	6.44

Wilson, Paul
B:R, T:R, Born: 3/28/1973 (23 in 1996)

YR	TEAM	LG	W	L	G	IP	H	R	ER	TBB	SO	ERA
1994	Mets	R	0	2	3	12.0	8	4	4	4	13	3.00
	St. Lucie	A	0	5	8	37.1	32	23	21	17	37	5.06
1995	Binghamton	AA	6	3	16	120.1	89	34	29	24	127	2.17
	Norfolk	AAA	5	3	10	66.1	59	25	21	20	67	2.85
Totals			11	13	37	236.0	188	86	75	65	244	2.86

Philadelphia Phillies: What Happened After June 25? (p. 72)

Phillie Stats Before and After June Peak

Through 6/25/95

Player	Avg	OBP	Slg	AB	H	2B	3B	HR	RBI	BB	K
Jim Eisenreich	.377	.438	.530	151	57	12	1	3	23	17	15
Darren Daulton	.246	.350	.409	171	42	10	0	6	31	27	26
Mariano Duncan	.278	.279	.381	126	35	5	1	2	13	0	24
Lenny Dykstra	.257	.348	.301	136	35	6	0	0	9	19	16
Gregg Jefferies	.262	.317	.405	168	44	12	0	4	16	14	8
Charlie Hayes	.316	.399	.474	196	62	9	2	6	44	28	28
Dave Hollins	.248	.412	.409	137	34	8	1	4	17	40	24
Mickey Morandini	.289	.351	.428	187	54	15	1	3	22	13	29
Kevin Stocker	.219	.328	.252	155	34	5	0	0	18	23	22
Phillies Total :	.274	.349	.390	1868	512	101	7	34	238	210	298
League Average :	.261	.330	.403	1894	494	92	10	51	239	185	359

Player	G	GS	CG	IP	H	R	ER	BB	K	W	L	S	ERA
Norm Charlton	19	0	0	17.1	17	14	14	12	10	2	4	0	7.27
Curt Schilling	12	12	1	83.0	69	36	33	12	76	5	2	0	3.58
Gene Harris	21	0	0	19.0	19	9	9	8	9	2	2	0	4.26
Heathcliff Slocumb	27	0	0	27.2	17	3	3	14	19	1	0	19	0.98
Mike Williams	10	3	0	29.2	28	15	13	11	21	0	1	0	3.94
Paul Quantrill	12	12	0	74.0	77	37	33	14	44	7	2	0	4.01
Tyler Green	12	12	4	80.2	70	27	26	36	51	7	4	0	2.90
Toby Borland	16	0	0	21.0	33	21	16	16	13	0	0	1	6.86
Ricky Bottalico	22	0	0	29.1	16	4	4	15	24	3	1	1	1.23
Michael Mimbs	10	10	2	62.1	52	22	21	27	38	6	1	0	3.03
Phillies Total :	181	55	7	492.2	438	207	191	191	337	37	18	21	3.49
League Average :	203	55	3	497.2	9494	254	230	185	359	27	27	14	4.18

After 6/25/95

Player	Avg	OBP	Slg	AB	H	2B	3B	HR	RBI	BB	K
Jim Eisenreich	.274	.333	.420	226	62	10	1	7	32	21	29
Darren Daulton	.251	.368	.392	171	43	9	3	3	24	28	26
Andy Van Slyke	.240	.325	.337	208	50	10	2	2	14	25	40
Lenny Dykstra	.271	.358	.415	118	32	9	1	2	9	14	12
Gregg Jefferies	.330	.367	.471	312	103	19	2	7	40	21	18
Charlie Hayes	.252	.302	.366	333	84	21	1	5	41	22	60
Lenny Webster	.284	.361	.459	109	31	7	0	4	11	13	17
Mark Whiten	.269	.365	.481	212	57	10	1	11	37	31	63
Mickey Morandini	.280	.349	.410	307	86	19	6	3	27	29	51
Kevin Stocker	.218	.289	.288	257	56	9	3	1	14	20	53
Phillies Total :	.254	.322	.380	3082	784	162	23	60	338	287	586
League Average :	.265	.332	.410	3037	803	148	19	85	385	290	590

Player	G	GS	CG	IP	H	R	ER	BB	K	W	L	S	ERA
Sid Fernandez	11	11	0	64.2	48	25	24	21	79	6	1	0	3.34
Tommy Greene	11	6	0	33.2	45	32	31	20	24	0	5	0	8.29
Heathcliff Slocumb	34	0	0	37.2	47	23	18	21	44	4	6	13	4.30
Jeff Juden	13	10	1	62.2	53	31	28	31	47	2	4	0	4.02
Russ Springer	14	0	0	26.2	22	11	11	10	32	0	0	0	3.71
Mike Williams	23	5	0	58.0	50	22	19	18	36	3	2	0	2.95
Paul Quantrill	21	17	0	105.1	135	65	60	30	59	4	10	0	5.13
Tyler Green	14	13	0	60.0	87	59	57	30	34	1	5	0	8.55
Paul Fletcher	10	0	0	13.1	15	8	8	9	10	1	0	0	5.40
Toby Borland	34	0	0	53.0	48	16	15	21	46	1	3	5	2.55
Ricky Bottalico	40	0	0	58.1	34	21	20	27	63	2	2	0	3.09
Michael Mimbs	25	9	0	74.1	75	48	42	48	55	3	6	1	5.09
Phillies Total :	304	89	1	797.2	803	451	412	347	643	32	57	20	4.65
League Average :	312	88	5	792.1	803	411	368	290	590	44	44	22	4.19

Pittsburgh Pirates: Is a Four-Man Rotation the Right One? (p. 75)

Pirate Starters' Performance on Various Days Rest

John Ericks

Category	GS	W	L	IP	H	R	ER	HR	BB	K	ERA
0-3 Days Rest	6	2	3	37.2	32	16	14	2	14	31	3.35
4 Days Rest	8	0	3	44.2	52	30	27	4	20	26	5.44
5+ Days Rest	4	1	3	22.0	23	13	13	1	16	20	5.32

Jon Lieber

Category	GS	W	L	IP	H	R	ER	HR	BB	K	ERA
0-3 Days Rest	5	2	3	23.1	39	25	24	3	4	13	9.26
4 Days Rest	3	1	1	16.2	24	10	9	0	2	8	4.86
5+ Days Rest	4	0	3	20.2	28	16	16	4	5	16	6.97

Esteban Loaiza

Category	GS	W	L	IP	H	R	ER	HR	BB	K	ERA
0-3 Days Rest	8	5	1	49.1	54	28	26	7	11	27	4.74
4 Days Rest	17	2	6	96.2	112	63	51	10	34	48	4.75
5+ Days Rest	6	1	2	23.2	36	24	22	4	10	9	8.37

Denny Neagle

Category	GS	W	L	IP	H	R	ER	HR	BB	K	ERA
0-3 Days Rest	8	4	2	55.2	56	17	13	4	5	42	2.10
4 Days Rest	17	6	4	114.1	127	55	52	15	30	79	4.09
5+ Days Rest	6	3	2	39.2	38	19	15	1	10	29	3.40

Steve Parris

Category	GS	W	L	IP	H	R	ER	HR	BB	K	ERA
0-3 Days Rest	3	1	1	19.0	20	6	6	1	4	15	2.84
4 Days Rest	7	3	4	41.2	45	28	28	7	18	25	6.05
5+ Days Rest	5	2	1	21.1	24	15	15	4	11	21	6.33

Paul Wagner

Category	GS	W	L	IP	H	R	ER	HR	BB	K	ERA
0-3 Days Rest	7	1	6	42.1	38	20	17	4	25	36	3.61
4 Days Rest	12	2	4	70.2	81	44	42	7	28	44	5.35
5+ Days Rest	6	1	4	34.0	33	21	20	6	15	27	5.29

Pittsburgh Pirates

Category	GS	W	L	IP	H	R	ER	HR	BB	K	ERA
0-3 Days Rest	38	15	17	232.1	245	116	102	21	66	166	3.95
4 Days Rest	71	14	25	417.1	476	257	233	48	141	246	5.02
5+ Days Rest	35	10	15	182.0	211	117	109	20	73	135	5.39

San Diego Padres: Can Gwynn Keep Winning Batting Crowns? (p. 81)

Players 36 or Older Who Hit .330 or Better
(Minimum 400 Plate Appearances)

Player	Team	Year	Avg	Age
Cap Anson	ChN	1896	.331	44
Cap Anson	ChN	1895	.335	43
Stan Musial	StL	1962	.330	41
Ty Cobb	Phi	1927	.357	40
Sam Rice	Was	1930	.349	40
Eddie Collins	ChA	1926	.344	39
Jim O'Rourke	NY	1890	.360	39
Nap Lajoie	Cle	1913	.335	38
Pete Rose	Phi	1979	.331	38
Bill Terry	NYG	1935	.341	38
Jake Daubert	Cin	1922	.336	38
Ted Williams	Bos	1957	.388	38
Eddie Collins	ChA	1925	.346	38
Ty Cobb	Det	1925	.378	38
Zack Wheat	Bro	1925	.359	37
Eddie Collins	ChA	1924	.349	37
Stan Musial	StL	1958	.337	37
Tris Speaker	Cle	1925	.389	37
Ty Cobb	Det	1924	.338	37
Rod Carew	Cal	1983	.339	37
Ted Williams	Bos	1956	.345	37
Babe Ruth	NYA	1932	.341	37
Nap Lajoie	Cle	1912	.368	37
Honus Wagner	Pit	1911	.334	37
Bill Terry	NYG	1934	.354	37
Paul Molitor	Tor	1994	.341	37
Sam Rice	Was	1926	.337	36
Roberto Clemente	Pit	1971	.341	36
Wade Boggs	NYA	1994	.342	36
Lave Cross	Phi	1902	.342	36
Cap Anson	ChN	1888	.344	36
Ted Williams	Bos	1955	.356	36
Tris Speaker	Cle	1924	.344	36
Ty Cobb	Det	1923	.340	36
Earl Averill	Cle	1938	.330	36
Zack Wheat	Bro	1924	.375	36
Babe Ruth	NYA	1931	.373	36
Paul Molitor	Tor	1993	.332	36
Stan Musial	StL	1957	.351	36
Eddie Collins	ChA	1923	.360	36
Dan Brouthers	Bal	1894	.347	36

San Francisco Giants: Is Bonds the Best Clutch Hitter? (p. 83)

Top Players in OBP+Slg With Runners in Scoring Position and in Late and Close Situations, 1991-95

Runners in Scoring Position (Min 350 PA)			Late & Close (Min 250 PA)		
Player	OBP+Slg	PA	Player	OBP+Slg	PA
Bonds, SF	1.129	877	Bonds, SF	1.063	512
Thomas, ChA	1.006	988	Martinez, Sea	1.063	366
Vaughn, Bos	1.005	715	Griffey Jr, Sea	.956	426
Piazza, LA	.992	460	Canseco, Bos	.949	366
Sheffield, Fla	.989	543	Gwynn, SD	.947	459
McGwire, Oak	.976	513	Bagwell, Hou	.945	483
Martinez, Sea	.971	641	Sheffield, Fla	.934	323
Belle, Cle	.970	870	Tettleton, Tex	.933	422
McGriff, Atl	.970	869	Thomas, ChA	.930	515
Salmon, Cal	.969	508	Blowers, Sea	.918	201
Griffey Jr, Sea	.968	816	Salmon, Cal	.914	258
Tartabull, Oak	.967	734	McGriff, Atl	.908	455
Justice, Atl	.963	806	Grace, ChN	.902	558
Gwynn, SD	.951	672	Dunston, ChN	.895	278
Tettleton, Tex	.943	792	Belle, Cle	.894	466
Molitor, Tor	.933	898	Davis, Cal	.885	416
Canseco, Bos	.932	714	Alomar, Tor	.885	453
Davis, Cal	.931	857	Bonilla, Bal	.882	493
Whitaker, Det	.925	568	O'Neill, NYA	.882	396
Blowers, Sea	.918	390	Puckett, Min	.882	466
Puckett, Min	.913	953	Tartabull, Oak	.882	396
Clark, Tex	.910	816	McGwire, Oak	.878	272
Merced, Pit	.908	718	Valentin, Bos	.878	250
Alou, Mon	.903	587	Clark, Tex	.872	434
Stanley, NYA	.899	481	Mattingly, NYA	.869	434
Valentin, Bos	.898	500	Dykstra, Phi	.867	346
Larkin, Cin	.897	714	Walker, Col	.865	458
Murray, Cle	.897	822	Butler, LA	.854	569
Daulton, Phi	.894	709	Henderson, Oak	.854	375
Buhner, Sea	.891	825	Olerud, Tor	.852	450
Gant, Cin	.890	741	Martinez, Sea	.852	385
Ventura, ChA	.885	965	Buhner, Sea	.848	454
Lankford, StL	.884	790	Justice, Atl	.847	398
Raines, ChA	.884	676	Jaha, Mil	.844	230
Conine, Fla	.882	542	Jose, ChN	.844	390
Bonilla, Bal	.880	780	Snow, Cal	.842	203
Fielder, Det	.876	978	Sorrento, Cle	.842	309
Bagwell, Hou	.874	936	Piazza, LA	.836	274
Ripken, Bal	.871	887	Hamilton, Mil	.834	318
Gonzalez, Tex	.870	834	Stanley, NYA	.834	261
Sierra, NYA	.870	908	Bichette, Col	.833	402
Walker, Col	.868	830	Gant, Cin	.831	366
Joyner, KC	.861	772	Phillips, Cal	.831	434
Henderson, Oak	.860	580	Kruk, ChA	.828	414
Surhoff, Mil	.860	632	Maldonado, Tex	.828	249
Gilkey, StL	.859	574	Gilkey, StL	.827	426
Palmeiro, Bal	.859	859	Lansing, Mon	.827	234
Olerud, Tor	.858	830	Greenwell, Bos	.824	352
Martinez, Sea	.856	575	Molitor, Tor	.824	492
Lofton, Cle	.852	467	Merced, Pit	.819	430
Grace, ChN	.849	796	Joyner, KC	.815	428
Pendleton, Fla	.848	813	Alou, Mon	.813	277
Baines, Bal	.847	670	Seitzer, Mil	.810	365
Kent, NYN	.847	522	Slaught, Pit	.808	264
Gibson, Det	.844	450	Palmeiro, Bal	.807	455
Jaha, Mil	.844	375	Gallego, Oak	.803	255

Which Manages Use the Hit-and-Run Most Effectively? (p. 88)

Manager, Team	Attempts	Success %	Favorite Count
Anderson, Sparky, Det	59	28.8	2-1
Bevington, Terry, ChA	83	31.3	2-1
Boone, Bob, KC	79	34.2	1-1
Garner, Phil, Mil	67	40.3	2-1
Gaston, Cito, Tor	20	25.0	2-1
Hargrove, Mike, Cle	50	30.0	2-1
Kelly, Tom, Min	109	43.1	2-1
Kennedy, Kevin, Box	57	38.6	2-1
La Russa, Tony, Oak	105	33.3	1-0
Lachemann, Marcel, Cal	77	32.5	1-1
Lamont, Gene, ChA	15	26.7	0-1
Oates, Johnny, Tex	74	37.8	2-2
Piniella, Lou, Sea	77	36.4	2-1
Regan, Phil, Bal	70	38.6	2-1
Showalter, Buck, NYA	47	46.8	2-2
Alou, Felipe, Mon	104	23.1	2-1
Baker, Dusty, SF	128	38.3	1-1
Baylor, Don, Col	91	36.3	0-0
Bochy, Bruce, SD	108	52.8	2-1
Collins, Terry, Hou	130	40.8	2-1
Cox, Bobby, Atl	64	50.0	1-1
Fregosi, Jim, Phi	49	36.7	2-1
Green, Dallas, NYN	83	43.4	2-1
Johnson, Davey, Cin	78	29.5	2-1
Jorgensen, Mike, StL	47	42.6	2-1
Lachemann, Rene, Fla	70	30.0	2-2
Lasorda, Tom, LA	77	24.7	1-1
Leyland, Jim, Pit	94	33.0	1-0
Riggleman, Jim, ChN	104	32.7	1-0
Torre, Joe, Stl	18	27.8	2-2

Which Umps *Already* Speed Up the Game? (p. 90)

Average Game Time By Home-Plate Umpire — Nine- Inning Games
(Minimum 100 Games Umped, 1991-95)

Umpire	Games	Avg Time	Umpire	Games	Avg Time
Barnett, Larry	132	2:54	Bonin, Greg	135	2:44
Brinkman, Joe	150	2:52	Crawford, Jerry	150	2:50
Clark, Al	142	2:52	Darling, Gary	142	2:44
Coble, Drew	130	2:52	Davidson, Bob	147	2:43
Cousins, Derryl	137	2:57	Davis, Gerry	152	2:48
Craft, Terry	120	2:54	DeMuth, Dana	141	2:44
Denkinger, Don	128	2:52	Froemming, Bruce	137	2:47
Evans, Jeff	140	2:58	Gregg, Eric	110	2:42
Evans, Jim	140	2:58	Hallion, Tom	125	2:46
Ford, Dale	135	2:50	Hirschbeck, Mark	116	2:41
Garcia, Rich	144	2:51	Hohn, Bill	139	2:45
Hendry, Ted	144	2:51	Layne, Jerry	132	2:46
Hirschbeck, John	122	2:51	Marsh, Randy	139	2:47
Johnson, Mark	120	2:55	McSherry, John	127	2:47
Joyce, Jim	133	2:56	Montague, Ed	130	2:44
Kaiser, Ken	129	2:50	Pulli, Frank	134	2:41
Kosc, Greg	147	2:52	Quick, Jim	123	2:46
McClelland, Tim	140	2:54	Rapuano, Ed	140	2:45
McCoy, Larry	128	2:53	Reliford, Charlie	133	2:48
McKean, Jim	125	2:52	Rippley, Steve	141	2:44
Meriwether, Chuck	128	2:54	Runge, Paul	121	2:45
Merrill, Durwood	150	2:52	Tata, Terry	144	2:45
Morrison, Dan	139	2:55	Wendelstedt, Harry	129	2:46
Phillips, Dave	137	2:55	West, Joe	146	2:43
Reed, Rick	144	2:58	Williams, Charles	140	2:47
Reilly, Mike	140	2:52	Winters, Mike	143	2:45
Roe, Rocky	141	2:57	**NL Average**	**4382**	**2:45**
Scott, Dale	136	2:52			
Shulock, John	144	2:55			
Tschida, Tim	146	2:55			
Welke, Tim	141	2:49			
Young, Larry	148	2:58			
AL Average	**4733**	**2:54**			

Who Had the Best Months of the Year? (p. 92)

The Top Batting and Pitching Months of 1995

Batting (75 or more Plate Appearances)

Player	Month	AVG	SLG	OBP	AB	R	H	2B	3B	HR	RBI	SB	BB
Klesko, Atl	June	.435	.841	.481	69	12	30	7	0	7	22	1	7
Ausmus, SD	August	.424	.627	.514	59	13	25	4	1	2	15	6	13
Magadan, Hou	Sep-Oct	.419	.527	.506	74	9	31	8	0	0	18	0	14
Anderson G, Cal	July	.410	.686	.422	105	22	43	8	0	7	31	0	3
Eisenreich, Phi	May	.406	.580	.475	69	11	28	7	1	1	14	1	10
Young E, Col	July	.406	.554	.469	101	23	41	3	3	2	8	12	11
Gwynn T, SD	Sep-Oct	.405	.517	.439	116	19	47	8	1	1	15	7	7
Williams M, SF	May	.405	.811	.451	111	23	45	7	1	12	31	1	10
Young E, Col	Sep-Oct	.404	.629	.470	89	20	36	7	2	3	12	7	10
Martinez E, Sea	June	.402	.761	.537	92	24	37	9	0	8	32	1	28
Gwynn T, SD	July	.400	.518	.419	110	14	44	7	0	2	24	3	5
Mayne, KC	Sep-Oct	.400	.523	.480	65	5	26	8	0	0	8	0	9
Piazza, LA	August	.400	.696	.440	115	24	46	7	0	9	25	0	9
Seitzer, Mil	May	.398	.568	.465	88	7	35	9	0	2	19	0	10
Martinez E, Sea	August	.398	.786	.560	98	31	39	11	0	9	33	0	31
Ramirez, Cle	May	.394	.808	.459	99	23	39	8	0	11	27	1	12
Cora, Sea	August	.392	.570	.456	79	16	31	7	2	1	10	3	9
Butler, LA	July	.388	.500	.445	116	24	45	2	4	1	6	10	12
Knoblauch, Min	August	.384	.643	.444	112	24	43	8	3	5	19	12	12
Bichette, Col	May	.382	.618	.412	110	22	42	8	0	6	23	4	6
Morris, Cin	August	.381	.600	.449	105	26	40	9	1	4	15	1	13
Belle, Cle	August	.381	.847	.456	118	28	45	13	0	14	30	1	16
Davis C, Cal	May	.379	.621	.481	103	27	39	7	0	6	27	1	23
Hunter B, Hou	June	.378	.488	.433	82	18	31	2	2	1	10	10	7
Bonilla, Bal	Sep-Oct	.378	.604	.417	111	26	42	6	2	5	27	0	8
Salmon, Cal	August	.378	.757	.453	111	25	42	5	2	11	22	1	14
Kingery, Col	May	.377	.638	.469	69	17	26	4	1	4	13	6	12

Pitching (25 or more Innings Pitched)

Pitcher	Month	ERA	W	L	S	IP	H	R	ER	BB	K
Maddux G, Atl	Sep-Oct	0.29	4	0	0	31.0	21	1	1	3	29
Rogers K, Tex	May	0.65	5	1	0	41.1	32	6	3	15	32
Nomo, LA	June	0.89	6	0	0	50.1	25	7	5	16	60
Mussina, Bal	August	1.15	3	2	0	47.0	36	11	6	10	35
Maddux G, Atl	June	1.18	3	0	0	38.0	33	5	5	2	27
Ashby, SD	June	1.20	3	1	0	45.0	34	9	6	8	38
Fernandez A, ChA	Sep-Oct	1.21	3	0	0	52.0	35	8	7	9	42
Rapp, Fla	Sep-Oct	1.24	5	0	0	43.2	24	6	6	15	29
Maddux G, Atl	July	1.27	4	0	0	49.2	33	7	7	5	49
Candiotti, LA	June	1.43	2	2	0	44.0	32	9	7	11	32
Glavine, Atl	August	1.45	4	0	0	37.1	28	11	6	9	22
Erickson, Bal	Sep-Oct	1.47	4	0	0	43.0	32	7	7	10	28
Hamilton, SD	June	1.50	3	0	0	48.0	27	13	8	15	19
Wakefield, Bos	July	1.53	6	0	0	47.0	41	9	8	14	34
Schourek, Cin	May	1.54	3	1	0	35.0	24	6	6	10	32
Leiter M, SF	August	1.65	4	2	0	49.0	31	12	9	13	34
Green, Phi	June	1.66	4	1	0	48.2	33	9	9	21	28
Reynolds, Hou	July	1.72	2	1	0	47.0	36	14	9	3	43
Johnson, Sea	Sep-Oct	1.74	5	0	0	46.2	29	9	9	15	65
Isringhausen, NYN	Sep-Oct	1.74	5	0	0	41.1	42	8	8	12	22
Perez C, Mon	May	1.75	4	0	0	25.2	22	5	5	5	25
Ogea, Cle	June	1.77	4	0	0	35.2	27	8	7	6	18
Hampton, Hou	June	1.78	1	1	0	25.1	19	10	5	5	19
Portugal, Cin	Sep-Oct	1.80	3	1	0	35.0	27	7	7	10	11
Pavlik, Tex	Sep-Oct	1.90	4	1	0	47.1	25	10	10	18	48
Wakefield, Bos	June	1.91	3	1	0	47.0	38	15	10	13	27

How Often Does a Leadoff Walk Really Score? (p. 96)

Both Leagues — Listed Alphabetically
(1995 Pitchers with a minimum of 10 Leadoff Walks)

Player	BB	Scored	Pct	Player	BB	Scored	Pct
Abbott, Jim	18	7	38.9	Kile, Darryl	22	11	50.0
Belcher, Tim	13	7	53.8	Langston, Mark	13	4	30.8
Benes, Andy	10	3	30.0	Leiter, Al	31	6	19.4
Bere, Jason	24	15	62.5	Leiter, Mark	10	4	40.0
Bergman, Sean	14	4	28.6	Lira, Felipe	11	7	63.6
Bones, Ricky	12	4	33.3	Loaiza, Esteban	14	7	50.0
Bosio, Chris	12	4	33.3	Martinez, Pedro	22	6	27.3
Bullinger, Jim	11	1	9.1	Martinez, Ramon	15	7	46.7
Burkett, John	13	5	38.5	McDowell, Jack	23	6	26.1
Candiotti, Tom	10	3	30.0	Mercker, Kent	10	4	40.0
Carrasco, Hector	10	6	60.0	Mimbs, Michael	15	4	26.7
Clark, Mark	11	5	45.5	Moore, Mike	10	5	50.0
Clemens, Roger	17	7	41.2	Moyer, Jamie	10	2	20.0
Cone, David	12	4	33.3	Navarro, Jaime	13	5	38.5
DeLucia, Rich	12	4	33.3	Neagle, Denny	10	3	30.0
Ericks, John	14	5	35.7	Nomo, Hideo	13	4	30.8
Erickson, Scott	18	7	38.9	Oquist, Mike	10	3	30.0
Fassero, Jeff	17	9	52.9	Pavlik, Roger	18	6	33.3
Fernandez, Alex	13	5	38.5	Petkovsek, Mark	11	2	18.2
Fernandez, Sid	10	2	20.0	Pettitte, Andy	10	4	40.0
Finley, Chuck	12	6	50.0	Pulsipher, Bill	13	3	23.1
Fleming, Dave	16	6	37.5	Radke, Brad	14	6	42.9
Florie, Bryce	10	3	30.0	Rapp, Pat	19	7	36.8
Foster, Kevin	14	2	14.3	Rhodes, Arthur	12	6	50.0
Freeman, Marvin	14	5	35.7	Ritz, Kevin	16	7	43.8
Givens, Brian	12	2	16.7	Rodriguez, Frank	18	7	38.9
Glavine, Tom	13	6	46.2	Rogers, Kenny	18	3	16.7
Gordon, Tom	16	8	50.0	Schourek, Pete	10	4	40.0
Green, Tyler	17	7	41.2	Smoltz, John	22	8	36.4
Gross, Kevin	19	7	36.8	Sparks, Steve	18	9	50.0
Guardado, Eddie	10	3	30.0	Stottlemyre, Todd	16	4	25.0
Gubicza, Mark	10	5	50.0	Swift, Bill	11	5	45.5
Guzman, Juan	15	10	66.7	Tapani, Kevin	10	4	40.0
Hamilton, Joey	10	4	40.0	Torres, Salomon	12	7	58.3
Hammond, Chris	12	3	25.0	Trachsel, Steve	18	9	50.0
Hampton, Mike	16	5	31.3	Trombley, Mike	14	6	42.9
Hanson, Erik	13	4	30.8	Valdes, Ismael	15	7	46.7
Harkey, Mike	11	6	54.5	Van Poppel, Todd	13	5	38.5
Hentgen, Pat	17	8	47.1	Wagner, Paul	18	7	38.9
Hill, Ken	16	6	37.5	Wakefield, Tim	25	10	40.0
Hitchcock, Sterling	20	7	35.0	Watson, Allen	12	6	50.0
Hurtado, Edwin	12	3	25.0	Weathers, Dave	10	6	60.0
Jackson, Danny	14	5	35.7	Wegman, Bill	10	5	50.0
Jarvis, Kevin	11	9	81.8	Wells, David	11	6	54.5
Johns, Doug	10	5	50.0	Witt, Bobby	13	4	30.8
Johnson, Randy	15	5	33.3	**MLB Totals**	**3031**	**1171**	**38.6**
Jones, Bobby	14	9	64.3				

Who Were the Best Bargains—and Best Buys— of '95? (p. 100)

Ratio of Salary to BJFB Points
(Minimum 500 At Bats or 175 Innings Pitched)

Player, Team	Salary	Points	Ratio	Player, Team	Salary	Points	Ratio
Nomo, LA	109000	505.0	215.84	McRae, ChN	2650000	434.5	6098.97
Cordova, Min	109000	454.0	240.09	Nagy, Cle	1888889	302.5	6244.26
Jones, Atl	114000	427.5	266.67	Stottlemyre, Oak	2050000	325.5	6298.00
Edmonds, Cal	177500	573.0	309.77	Vizquel, Cle	2850000	428.0	6658.88
Valdes, LA	136000	432.0	314.81	Baerga, Cle	3650000	533.0	6848.03
Pettitte, NYA	109000	271.0	402.21	Anderson, Bal	3333333	484.5	6879.95
Wakefield, Bos	175000	413.5	423.22	Johnson, Sea	4675000	635.0	7362.21
Snow, Cal	200000	468.5	426.89	Biggio, Hou	4650000	624.0	7451.92
Hamilton, SD	170000	351.5	483.64	Erickson, Bal	1862500	249.0	7479.92
Reynolds, Hou	175000	355.5	492.26	Hentgen, Tor	1250000	156.5	7987.22
Berroa, Oak	235000	459.0	511.98	Grace, ChN	4375000	542.0	8071.96
Sparks, Mil	109000	208.0	524.04	Sosa, ChN	4300000	532.5	8075.12
Castilla, Col	265000	498.0	532.13	Galarraga, Col	3950000	483.5	8169.60
Gates, Oak	190000	343.5	553.13	Palmeiro, Bal	4906603	594.0	8260.28
Colbrunn, Fla	240000	397.0	604.53	Nixon, Tex	3150000	378.5	8322.33
Radke, Min	109000	169.5	643.07	Rogers, Tex	3700000	416.0	8894.23
Martinez, Mon	270000	404.0	668.32	Raines, ChA	3700000	412.5	8969.70
Castillo, ChN	250000	360.5	693.48	Bonilla, NYN	5000950	557.0	8978.37
Williams, NYA	400000	515.0	776.70	Gwynn, SD	4608334	512.0	9000.65
Jones, NYN	220000	277.5	792.79	Phillips, Cal	4366667	485.0	9003.44
Boone, Cin	400000	460.0	869.57	McGriff, Atl	4275000	474.0	9018.99
Pavlik, Tex	255000	284.5	896.31	Fernandez, ChA	3250000	352.5	9219.86
Mondesi, LA	435000	482.5	901.55	Caminiti, SD	4550000	485.5	9371.78
Valentin, Bos	612500	642.5	953.31	Maddux, Atl	6375000	676.5	9423.50
Cordero, Mon	315000	300.5	1048.25	Fryman, Det	4150000	437.5	9485.71
Quantrill, Phi	242500	210.5	1152.02	Martinez, LA	3925000	409.0	9596.58
Salmon, Cal	900000	652.0	1380.37	Abbott, ChA	2775000	289.0	9602.08
Clayton, SF	475000	331.5	1432.88	Finley, SD	4450000	440.5	10102.17
Schourek, Cin	762777	466.0	1636.86	Bell, Pit	4400000	422.5	10414.21
Neagle, Pit	740000	390.0	1897.44	Alvarez, ChA	2250000	212.0	10613.22
Martinez, Sea	1025000	537.5	1906.98	Alomar, Tor	5525000	513.0	10769.99
Ashby, SD	755000	379.0	1992.09	Appier, KC	4387500	399.5	10982.49
Gaetti, KC	940000	452.0	2079.65	Molitor, Tor	4500000	385.5	11673.16
Sprague, Tor	760000	357.0	2128.85	Martinez, Cle	4550000	384.5	11833.56
Leiter, SF	700000	316.5	2211.69	Glavine, Atl	4975000	417.5	11916.18
Gubicza, KC	750000	303.5	2471.17	Smoltz, Atl	4894444	405.5	12070.16
Bones, Mil	531945	199.5	2666.39	Puckett, Min	6300000	515.5	12221.15
Leiter, Tor	795000	276.5	2875.23	Bonds, SF	8000183	644.5	12413.02
Belcher, Sea	580000	188.0	3085.11	Burkett, Fla	3350000	260.0	12884.63
Navarro, ChN	1400000	400.0	3500.00	Kelly, LA	3733334	289.0	12918.12
Vizcaino, NYN	1355000	378.5	3579.92	Benes, SD	3400000	256.5	13255.37
Hayes, Phi	1500000	377.5	3973.51	Ripken, Bal	6650000	487.0	13655.04
Curtis, Det	1900000	460.5	4125.95	Smiley, Cin	4975000	362.0	13743.10
Pendleton, Fla	1600000	377.0	4244.03	Portugal, SF	3977777	282.0	14105.60
Hanson, Bos	1450000	335.5	4321.91	Grissom, Atl	4900000	344.5	14223.52
Karros, LA	2350000	535.5	4388.42	Finley, Cal	4875000	336.5	14487.38
Vaughn, Bos	2725000	607.5	4485.60	McDowell, NYA	5400000	368.5	14654.01
Knoblauch, Min	2987500	621.5	4806.92	Gordon, KC	3300000	218.5	15102.98
Wells, Det	2000000	413.5	4836.76	Candiotti, LA	4450000	292.5	15213.68
Martinez, Sea	3591667	714.5	5026.83	Langston, Cal	5000000	314.0	15923.58
Bichette, Col	3375000	657.0	5136.99	Cone, Tor	8000000	460.5	17372.43
Butler, NYN	2000000	380.5	5256.24	Tapani, Min	3600000	198.5	18136.03
Johnson, ChA	2666667	470.5	5667.73	Drabek, Hou	5000000	256.5	19493.19
Mussina, Bal	2925000	500.0	5850.00	Carter, Tor	7500000	376.5	19920.33
Fassero, Mon	1500000	255.0	5882.35	Hill, StL	4525000	214.0	21144.87
Belle, Cle	4375000	725.5	6030.32	Gross, Tex	2889000	125.0	23112.01

Who Hits Who? (p. 109)

How Hitters Fare Against Good/Average/Poor Pitchers
(1995 Hitters with at Least 446 Plate Appearances)

Player, Team	Avg	Vs. Good	Vs. Ave	Vs. Poor	Player, Team	Avg	Vs. Good	Vs. Ave	Vs. Poor
Abbott, Fla	.255	.152	.270	.320	DeShields, LA	.256	.221	.290	.238
Alicea, Bos	.270	.252	.257	.281	Dunston, ChN	.296	.248	.342	.280
Alomar, Tor	.300	.258	.288	.361	Durham, ChA	.257	.235	.222	.333
Anderson, Bal	.262	.194	.307	.288	Edmonds, Cal	.290	.235	.286	.345
Baerga, Cle	.314	.280	.307	.342	Fielder, Det	.243	.182	.297	.208
Bagwell, Hou	.290	.207	.312	.350	Finley, SD	.297	.275	.302	.284
Baines, Bal	.299	.242	.243	.404	Fryman, Det	.275	.286	.258	.271
Bell, Hou	.334	.279	.372	.307	Gaetti, KC	.261	.224	.276	.273
Bell, Pit	.262	.228	.259	.307	Gagne, KC	.256	.235	.215	.360
Belle, Cle	.317	.264	.332	.357	Galarraga, Col	.280	.243	.287	.323
Berroa, Oak	.278	.210	.321	.284	Gant, Cin	.276	.295	.240	.313
Bichette, Col	.340	.288	.338	.410	Gates, Oak	.254	.233	.253	.263
Biggio, Hou	.302	.258	.280	.363	Gilkey, StL	.298	.242	.286	.373
Blauser, Atl	.211	.169	.212	.246	Girardi, Col	.262	.222	.271	.311
Blowers, Sea	.257	.239	.244	.284	Gomez, Det	.223	.132	.236	.311
Boggs, NYA	.324	.276	.360	.306	Gonzalez, ChN	.276	.265	.269	.307
Bonds, SF	.294	.251	.292	.331	Goodwin, KC	.288	.248	.317	.300
Boone, Cin	.267	.175	.288	.336	Grace, ChN	.326	.340	.284	.329
Bordick, Oak	.264	.205	.318	.272	Greenwell, Bos	.297	.260	.299	.318
Brogna, NYN	.289	.255	.280	.338	Greer, Tex	.271	.172	.294	.319
Buhner, Sea	.262	.205	.259	.306	Grissom, Atl	.258	.271	.270	.241
Butler, NYN	.300	.226	.337	.320	Gwynn, SD	.368	.372	.354	.353
Caminiti, SD	.302	.222	.302	.364	Hamilton, Mil	.271	.305	.269	.240
Canseco, Bos	.306	.299	.308	.302	Hayes, Phi	.276	.248	.299	.273
Carter, Tor	.253	.222	.290	.231	Henderson, Oak	.300	.273	.273	.384
Castilla, Col	.309	.263	.316	.314	Higginson, Det	.224	.225	.201	.250
Clark, Tex	.302	.318	.300	.289	Hill, SF	.264	.237	.254	.319
Clayton, SF	.244	.231	.246	.254	Javier, Oak	.278	.258	.292	.278
Colbrunn, Fla	.277	.225	.281	.333	Jefferies, Phi	.306	.305	.247	.372
Coleman, KC	.288	.283	.242	.398	Johnson, ChA	.306	.247	.302	.380
Conine, Fla	.302	.191	.342	.372	Jones, Atl	.265	.214	.219	.329
Cora, Sea	.297	.263	.252	.429	Jordan, StL	.296	.250	.289	.369
Cordero, Mon	.286	.341	.218	.346	Joyner, KC	.310	.265	.302	.353
Cordova, Min	.277	.229	.310	.295	Justice, Atl	.253	.250	.224	.286
Curtis, Det	.268	.254	.266	.260	Karros, LA	.298	.287	.263	.382
Davis, Cal	.318	.248	.365	.273	Kelly, LA	.278	.270	.254	.338

Player, Team	Avg	Vs. Good	Vs. Ave	Vs. Poor	Player, Team	Avg	Vs. Good	Vs. Ave	Vs. Poor
Kent, NYN	.278	.225	.262	.396	Ramirez, Cle	.308	.233	.340	.333
King, Pit	.265	.207	.309	.279	Reed, SD	.256	.233	.228	.288
Knoblauch, Min	.333	.291	.382	.347	Ripken, Bal	.262	.204	.318	.253
Lankford, StL	.277	.284	.279	.271	Rodriguez, Tex	.303	.271	.315	.331
Lansing, Mon	.255	.212	.280	.277	Salmon, Cal	.330	.310	.301	.390
Larkin, Cin	.319	.285	.342	.308	Sanders, Cin	.306	.248	.316	.372
Lemke, Atl	.253	.203	.286	.244	Segui, Mon	.309	.230	.309	.398
Lewis, SF	.250	.215	.282	.252	Seitzer, Mil	.311	.291	.309	.363
Lofton, Cle	.310	.286	.235	.412	Sierra, Oak	.263	.236	.286	.242
Martin, Pit	.282	.284	.270	.281	Snow, Cal	.289	.203	.321	.343
Martinez, Sea	.293	.285	.274	.308	Sosa, ChN	.268	.306	.249	.253
Martinez, Sea	.356	.316	.400	.374	Sprague, Tor	.244	.230	.226	.272
Mattingly, NYA	.288	.270	.293	.299	Stanley, NYA	.268	.250	.255	.314
McGriff, Atl	.280	.240	.249	.325	Stocker, Phi	.218	.252	.230	.189
McLemore, Tex	.261	.266	.243	.288	Surhoff, Mil	.320	.277	.341	.361
McRae, ChN	.288	.202	.329	.311	Tarasco, Mon	.249	.172	.272	.293
Merced, Pit	.300	.236	.306	.336	Tettleton, Tex	.238	.215	.249	.231
Molitor, Tor	.270	.228	.261	.323	Thomas, ChA	.308	.296	.297	.321
Mondesi, LA	.285	.207	.266	.382	Thome, Cle	.314	.261	.290	.403
Morandini, Phi	.283	.192	.326	.315	Valentin, Bos	.298	.226	.321	.338
Murray, Cle	.323	.301	.312	.336	Vaughn, Bos	.300	.265	.279	.376
Naehring, Bos	.307	.263	.374	.283	Vaughn, Mil	.224	.184	.258	.250
Nixon, Tex	.295	.266	.296	.331	Ventura, ChA	.295	.234	.325	.315
O'Neill, NYA	.300	.240	.290	.347	Veras, Fla	.261	.236	.264	.294
Offerman, LA	.287	.228	.284	.328	Vizcaino, NYN	.287	.247	.311	.321
Olerud, Tor	.291	.289	.280	.308	Vizquel, Cle	.266	.217	.269	.322
Palmeiro, Bal	.310	.273	.310	.338	Walker, Col	.306	.254	.335	.315
Pendleton, Fla	.290	.245	.315	.336	Weiss, Col	.260	.274	.225	.297
Phillips, Cal	.261	.206	.254	.340	White, Mon	.295	.253	.311	.295
Piazza, LA	.346	.290	.321	.446	White, Tor	.283	.263	.289	.302
Puckett, Min	.314	.264	.324	.371	Williams, NYA	.307	.266	.347	.293
Raines, ChA	.285	.272	.267	.294	Zeile, ChN	.246	.212	.250	.257

Which Young Hitters Will Finish with "Immortal" Numbers? (p. 112)

Players With At Least a 1% Chance at 3000 Hits

Player	Age	Current Hits	Proj. Hits	Chance
Paul Molitor	39.6	2789	3070	83.20
Tony Gwynn	35.9	2401	2936	39.24
Kirby Puckett	35.0	2304	2870	31.37
Roberto Alomar	28.2	1329	2574	24.53
Carlos Baerga	27.4	971	2457	23.25
Cal Ripken	35.6	2371	2830	22.94
Chuck Knoblauch	27.7	822	2245	15.36
Travis Fryman	27.0	848	2211	13.35
Rafael Palmeiro	31.5	1455	2427	12.91
Gregg Jefferies	28.7	1106	2289	12.43
Frank Thomas	27.8	893	2208	12.41
Ivan Rodriguez	24.3	569	2033	10.21
Ruben Sierra	30.5	1547	2395	8.38
Craig Biggio	30.3	1105	2200	7.76
Wil Cordero	24.5	425	1907	7.55
Sammy Sosa	27.4	738	2030	7.12
John Olerud	27.7	801	2038	6.25
Mark Grace	31.8	1333	2270	6.20
Albert Belle	29.6	827	2041	5.88
Jeff Bagwell	27.8	771	2013	5.70
Wade Boggs	37.8	2541	2796	5.66
Ken Griffey Jr	26.4	1039	2128	5.52
Brian McRae	28.6	794	2019	5.52
Bernie Williams	27.5	592	1920	5.15
Marquis Grissom	29.0	889	2050	4.98
Don Mattingly	34.9	2153	2616	4.64
Barry Bonds	31.7	1436	2289	4.51
Kenny Lofton	28.8	673	1941	4.50
Andre Dawson	41.7	2758	2887	3.49
Chad Curtis	27.4	553	1839	2.56
Will Clark	32.0	1543	2306	2.37
Derek Bell	27.3	471	1778	1.70
Mo Vaughn	28.3	587	1826	1.35
Mike Piazza	27.6	469	1763	1.14

Players With At Least a 1% Chance at 500 Home Runs

Player	Age	Current HR	Proj. HR	Chance
Eddie Murray	40.1	479	515	95.53
Frank Thomas	27.8	182	525	57.95
Albert Belle	29.6	194	514	54.53
Barry Bonds	31.7	292	509	54.32
Ken Griffey Jr	26.4	189	481	44.04
Matt Williams	30.3	225	453	32.92
Fred McGriff	32.4	289	458	30.26
Juan Gonzalez	26.5	167	425	27.41
Sammy Sosa	27.4	131	414	26.77
Jose Canseco	31.7	300	447	23.38
Mo Vaughn	28.3	111	384	20.25
Mark McGwire	32.5	277	425	16.41
Rafael Palmeiro	31.5	194	392	14.61
Mike Piazza	27.6	92	353	14.04
Cecil Fielder	32.5	250	409	13.68
Tim Salmon	27.6	90	351	13.55
Jeff Bagwell	27.8	113	356	12.84
Larry Walker	29.3	135	345	7.49
Manny Ramirez	23.8	50	304	6.37
Jay Buhner	31.6	169	354	5.83
Jim Edmonds	25.8	38	276	1.49
Ruben Sierra	30.5	220	363	1.16

Who Are the "Perfect Offensive Players"? (p. 114)

Active Players With A .300 Avg, .400 OBP, and a .500 Slg
(Minimum 400 Plate Appearances)

Player	Team	Year	Avg	OBP	Slg
Manny Ramirez	Cle	1995	.308	.402	.558
Mike Piazza	LA	1995	.346	.400	.606
Tim Salmon	Cal	1995	.330	.429	.594
Jim Thome	Cle	1995	.314	.438	.558
Frank Thomas	ChA	1995	.308	.454	.606
Albert Belle	Cle	1995	.317	.401	.690
Edgar Martinez	Sea	1995	.356	.479	.628
Chili Davis	Cal	1995	.318	.429	.514
Kenny Lofton	Cle	1994	.349	.412	.536
Mo Vaughn	Bos	1994	.310	.408	.576
Jeff Bagwell	Hou	1994	.368	.451	.750
Frank Thomas	ChA	1994	.353	.487	.729
Albert Belle	Cle	1994	.357	.438	.714
Dave Justice	Atl	1994	.313	.427	.531
Ken Griffey Jr	Sea	1994	.323	.402	.674
Will Clark	Tex	1994	.329	.431	.501
Barry Bonds	SF	1994	.312	.426	.647
Paul O'Neill	NYA	1994	.359	.460	.603
Tony Gwynn	SD	1994	.394	.454	.568
Chili Davis	Cal	1994	.311	.410	.561
Paul Molitor	Tor	1994	.341	.410	.518
Frank Thomas	ChA	1993	.317	.426	.607
John Olerud	Tor	1993	.363	.473	.599
Chris Hoiles	Bal	1993	.310	.416	.585
Ken Griffey Jr	Sea	1993	.309	.408	.617
Barry Bonds	SF	1993	.336	.458	.677
Andres Galarraga	Col	1993	.370	.403	.602
Paul Molitor	Tor	1993	.332	.402	.509
Frank Thomas	ChA	1992	.323	.439	.536
Edgar Martinez	Sea	1992	.343	.404	.544
Barry Bonds	Pit	1992	.311	.456	.624
Frank Thomas	ChA	1991	.318	.453	.553
Barry Bonds	Pit	1990	.301	.406	.565
Fred McGriff	Tor	1990	.300	.400	.530
Rickey Henderson	Oak	1990	.325	.439	.577
Eddie Murray	LA	1990	.330	.414	.520
Will Clark	SF	1989	.333	.407	.546
Mike Greenwell	Bos	1988	.325	.416	.531
Randy Ready	SD	1987	.309	.423	.520
Tony Gwynn	SD	1987	.370	.447	.511
Wade Boggs	Bos	1987	.363	.461	.588
Tim Raines	Mon	1987	.330	.429	.526
Paul Molitor	Mil	1987	.353	.438	.566
Alan Trammell	Det	1987	.343	.402	.551
Rickey Henderson	NYA	1985	.314	.419	.516
Eddie Murray	Bal	1984	.306	.410	.509

Who Soared to the Skies—and Who Crashed and Burned—in 1995.
(p. 118)

Both Leagues — Listed Alphabetically
(Minimum 350 PA in 1994 and 1995)

Player, Team	94	95	+/-	Player, Team	94	95	+/-	Player, Team	94	95	+/-
Abbott, Fla	.249	.255	+6	Gaetti, KC	.287	.261	-26	Murray, Cle	.254	.323	+69
Alomar R, Tor	.306	.300	-6	Gagne, KC	.259	.256	-3	Nixon, Tex	.274	.295	+21
Alou, Mon	.339	.273	-66	Galarraga, Col	.319	.280	-39	O'Neill, NYA	.359	.300	-59
Anderson B, Bal	.263	.262	-1	Garcia C, Pit	.277	.294	+17	Olerud, Tor	.297	.291	-6
Ausmus, SD	.251	.293	+42	Gilkey, StL	.253	.298	+45	Palmeiro R, Bal	.319	.310	-9
Baerga, Cle	.314	.314	+0	Girardi, Col	.276	.262	-14	Phillips T, Cal	.281	.261	-20
Bagwell, Hou	.368	.290	-78	Gonzalez J, Tex	.275	.295	+20	Piazza, LA	.319	.346	+27
Baines, Bal	.294	.299	+5	Gonzalez L, ChN	.273	.276	+3	Puckett, Min	.317	.314	-3
Bell D, Hou	.311	.334	+23	Grace, ChN	.298	.326	+28	Raines, ChA	.266	.285	+19
Bell J, Pit	.276	.262	-14	Greenwell, Bos	.269	.297	+28	Reed J, SD	.271	.256	-15
Belle, Cle	.357	.317	-40	Grissom, Atl	.288	.258	-30	Ripken C, Bal	.315	.262	-53
Berroa, Oak	.306	.278	-28	Guillen, ChA	.288	.248	-40	Rodriguez I, Tex	.298	.303	+5
Bichette, Col	.304	.340	+36	Gwynn T, SD	.394	.368	-26	Salmon, Cal	.287	.330	+43
Biggio, Hou	.318	.302	-16	Hayes, Phi	.288	.276	-12	Sanders D, SF	.283	.268	-15
Blauser, Atl	.258	.211	-47	Henderson, Oak	.260	.300	+40	Sanders R, Cin	.263	.306	+43
Boggs, NYA	.342	.324	-18	Hoiles, Bal	.247	.250	+3	Segui, Mon	.241	.309	+68
Bonds, SF	.312	.294	-18	Javier, Oak	.272	.278	+6	Sierra, NYA	.268	.263	-5
Bonilla, Bal	.290	.329	+39	Jefferies, Phi	.325	.306	-19	Sorrento, Cle	.280	.235	-45
Boone, Cin	.320	.267	-53	Johnson L, ChA	.277	.306	+29	Sosa, ChN	.300	.268	-32
Bordick, Oak	.253	.264	+11	Joyner, KC	.311	.310	-1	Sprague, Tor	.240	.244	+4
Brosius, Oak	.238	.262	+24	Justice, Atl	.313	.253	-60	Steinbach, Oak	.285	.278	-7
Buhner, Sea	.279	.262	-17	Karros, LA	.266	.298	+32	Tettleton, Tex	.248	.238	-10
Butler, LA	.314	.300	-14	Kelly R, LA	.293	.278	-15	Thomas, ChA	.353	.308	-45
Caminiti, SD	.283	.302	+19	Kent, NYN	.292	.278	-14	Thome, Cle	.268	.314	+46
Canseco, Bos	.282	.306	+24	King, Pit	.263	.265	+2	Valentin J, Bos	.316	.298	-18
Carr, Fla	.263	.227	-36	Knoblauch, Min	.312	.333	+21	Vaughn G, Mil	.254	.224	-30
Carter, Tor	.271	.253	-18	Lankford, StL	.267	.277	+10	Vaughn M, Bos	.310	.300	-10
Cedeno A, SD	.263	.210	-53	Lansing, Mon	.266	.255	-11	Ventura, ChA	.282	.295	+13
Clark W, Tex	.329	.302	-27	Larkin, Cin	.279	.319	+40	Vizcaino, NYN	.256	.287	+31
Clayton, SF	.236	.244	+8	Leius, Min	.246	.247	+1	Walbeck, Min	.204	.257	+53
Coleman, Sea	.240	.288	+48	Lemke, Atl	.294	.253	-41	Walker, Col	.322	.306	-16
Conine, Fla	.319	.302	-17	Lewis D, Cin	.257	.250	-7	Wallach, LA	.280	.266	-14
Cooper, StL	.282	.230	-52	Lofton, Cle	.349	.310	-39	Weiss, Col	.251	.260	+9
Cora, Sea	.276	.297	+21	Macfarlane, Bos	.255	.225	-30	White D, Tor	.270	.283	+13
Cordero, Mon	.294	.286	-8	Manwaring, SF	.250	.251	+1	Whiten, Phi	.293	.241	-52
Curtis, Det	.256	.268	+12	Martinez E, Sea	.285	.356	+71	Williams B, NYA	.289	.307	+18
Davis C, Cal	.311	.318	+7	Martinez T, Sea	.261	.293	+32	Zeile, ChN	.267	.246	-21
DeShields, LA	.250	.256	+6	Mattingly, NYA	.304	.288	-16	**AL Avg**	**.273**	**.270**	**-3**
DiSarcina, Cal	.260	.307	+47	McGriff, Atl	.318	.280	-38	**NL Avg**	**.267**	**.263**	**-4**
Dunston, ChN	.278	.296	+18	McLemore, Tex	.257	.261	+4				
Easley, Cal	.215	.216	+1	McRae, ChN	.273	.288	+15				
Fernandez, NYA	.279	.245	-34	Merced, Pit	.272	.300	+28				
Fielder, Det	.259	.243	-16	Molitor, Tor	.341	.270	-71				
Finley, SD	.276	.297	+21	Mondesi, LA	.306	.285	-21				
Fryman, Det	.263	.275	+12	Morris, Cin	.335	.279	-56				

He Can Slug, So Why Can't He Walk? (p. 121)

Smallest Single Season Walk to Home Run Ratios
(Minimum 20 Home Runs)

Player	Year	BB	HR	BB/HR	Player	Year	BB	HR	BB/HR
Dante Bichette	1995	22	40	.550	Joe Pepitone	1963	23	27	.852
Andres Galarraga	1994	19	31	.613	Hal Trosky	1936	36	42	.857
Fred Whitfield	1965	16	26	.615	Joe Pepitone	1964	24	28	.857
Juan Gonzalez	1995	17	27	.630	Tony Armas	1981	19	22	.864
Abner Dalrymple	1884	14	22	.636	Pete Incaviglia	1993	21	24	.875
Andre Dawson	1987	32	49	.653	Albert Belle	1991	25	28	.893
Cory Snyder	1986	16	24	.667	Butch Hobson	1977	27	30	.900
Bob Horner	1979	22	33	.667	Carl Reynolds	1930	20	22	.909
Walker Cooper	1947	24	35	.686	Al Simmons	1929	31	34	.912
Dante Bichette	1994	19	27	.704	Buck Freeman	1899	23	25	.920
Lee May	1974	17	24	.708	George Bell	1984	24	26	.923
Andre Dawson	1991	22	31	.710	Joe Pepitone	1966	29	31	.935
Matt Williams	1993	27	38	.711	Mack Jones	1965	29	31	.935
Tony Armas	1984	32	43	.744	Vinny Castilla	1995	30	32	.938
Dave Kingman	1976	28	37	.757	Dave Kingman	1979	45	48	.938
Bill Robinson	1976	16	21	.762	Cory Snyder	1987	31	33	.939
Matt Williams	1994	33	43	.767	Dave Kingman	1986	33	35	.943
Bob Horner	1980	27	35	.771	Dave Kingman	1975	34	36	.944
Don Demeter	1964	17	22	.773	Rip Repulski	1957	19	20	.950
Felipe Alou	1966	24	31	.774	Greg Colbrunn	1995	22	23	.957
Tony Armas	1985	18	23	.783	Kirby Puckett	1988	23	24	.958
Juan Gonzalez	1993	37	46	.804	Bill Robinson	1977	25	26	.962
Tony Armas	1983	29	36	.806	Matt Williams	1991	33	34	.971
Dave Roberts	1973	17	21	.810	Dick Stuart	1961	34	35	.971
Willie Stargell	1964	17	21	.810	Bill Robinson	1979	24	24	1.000
Ernie Banks	1962	30	37	.811	Cecil Cooper	1982	32	32	1.000
Juan Gonzalez	1992	35	43	.814	Matt Williams	1990	33	33	1.000
Jesse Barfield	1983	22	27	.815	Charley Smith	1964	20	20	1.000
Joe DiMaggio	1936	24	29	.828	Brian Jordan	1995	22	22	1.000
Tony Armas	1980	29	35	.829	Larry Sheets	1987	31	31	1.000
George Bell	1987	39	47	.830	Sammy Sosa	1994	25	25	1.000
Wes Covington	1958	20	24	.833	Fred Whitfield	1966	27	27	1.000
Joe Adcock	1956	32	38	.842	Gus Zernial	1955	30	30	1.000
Ernie Banks	1968	27	32	.844	Fred Pfeffer	1884	25	25	1.000
Joe Carter	1987	27	32	.844	Ruben Sierra	1994	23	23	1.000
Orlando Cepeda	1961	39	46	.848	Bo Jackson	1988	25	25	1.000

Which Teams Had the Most "Heart"? (p. 124)

Team total statistics for the Number 3, 4, and 5 hitters

American League — Sorted by Most RBI

Team	Avg	HR	RBI	Slg	Main 3-4-5 Hitters
Seattle	.289	99	360	.543	Martinez E, Buhner, Buhner
Boston	.297	91	331	.520	Vaughn M, Canseco, Greenwell
Cleveland	.310	93	327	.540	Baerga, Belle, Murray
Texas	.274	80	299	.481	Clark W, Gonzalez J, Tettleton
California	.300	74	297	.494	Salmon, Davis C, Snow
Chicago	.295	79	296	.496	Thomas, Thomas, Ventura
Baltimore	.288	81	294	.499	Palmeiro R, Ripken C, Baines
Oakland	.278	88	285	.493	Berroa, McGwire, Steinbach
New York	.277	52	279	.439	O'Neill, Sierra, Mattingly
Minnesota	.283	63	263	.459	Puckett, Munoz P, Cordova
Kansas City	.256	65	257	.435	Joyner, Gaetti, Lockhart
Milwaukee	.277	54	251	.436	Seitzer, Vaughn G, Vaughn G
Detroit	.257	66	230	.431	Fryman, Fielder, Gibson
Toronto	.267	42	193	.397	Alomar R, Carter, Olerud
AL Average	**.282**	**73**	**283**	**.476**	

National League — Sorted by Most RBI

Team	Avg	HR	RBI	Slg	Main 3-4-5 Hitters
Colorado	.304	112	350	.565	Bichette, Walker, Galarraga
San Francisco	.286	93	321	.525	Bonds, Williams M, Hill
Los Angeles	.296	93	313	.517	Piazza, Karros, Mondesi
Cincinnati	.286	80	312	.514	Gant, Sanders R, Morris
Florida	.287	78	311	.485	Conine, Pendleton, Colbrunn
Houston	.295	50	301	.445	Bagwell, Bell D, Magadan
Chicago	.277	70	283	.469	Grace, Sosa, Zeile
San Diego	.308	55	281	.466	Gwynn T, Caminiti, Williams E
Atlanta	.268	79	278	.471	Jones C, McGriff, Justice
Pittsburgh	.272	51	268	.427	Merced, King, King
New York	.279	70	256	.467	Brogna, Bonilla, Brogna
St. Louis	.271	60	252	.446	Lankford, Lankford, Jordan B
Philadelphia	.275	44	237	.424	Jefferies, Hollins, Daulton
Montreal	.284	48	223	.434	Cordero, Alou, Fletcher D
NL Average	**.285**	**70**	**285**	**.476**	

Which Baserunners Generate the Most Pickoff Attempts? (p. 126)

Pickoff Throws per Stolen Base
(Minimum 40 Pickoff Throws in 1995)

Player	PkOf	SB	Ratio	Player	PkOf	SB	Ratio
Abbott, Fla	43	4	10.8	Curtis, Det	194	22	8.8
Alexander, Bal	63	10	6.3	Damon, KC	41	6	6.8
Alfonzo, NYN	42	1	42.0	DeShields, LA	162	31	5.2
Alicea, Bos	137	10	13.7	Devereaux, ChA/Atl	53	8	6.6
Alomar, Tor	99	21	4.7	Diaz, Sea	59	11	5.4
Alou, Mon	66	2	33.0	DiSarcina, Cal	40	6	6.7
Amaral, Sea	82	12	6.8	Duncan, Phi/Cin	46	1	46.0
Anderson, Bal	211	23	9.2	Dunston, ChN	106	8	13.3
Ausmus, SD	53	11	4.8	Durham, ChA	101	15	6.7
Baerga, Cle	51	9	5.7	Dykstra, Phi	80	7	11.4
Bagwell, Hou	65	12	5.4	Easley, Cal	89	5	17.8
Bass, Bal	60	7	8.6	Edmonds, Cal	67	1	67.0
Bates, Col	46	3	15.3	Eisenreich, Phi	47	9	5.2
Becker, Min	76	7	10.9	Everett, NYN	65	1	65.0
Bell, Hou	159	17	9.4	Fernandez, NYA	68	5	13.6
Bell, Pit	73	1	73.0	Finley, SD	185	24	7.7
Belle, Cle	41	5	8.2	Fonville, Mon/LA	106	19	5.6
Bichette, Col	77	8	9.6	Frazier, Mon/Tex	65	10	6.5
Biggio, Hou	172	23	7.5	Frye, Tex	42	2	21.0
Blauser, Atl	72	7	10.3	Fryman, Det	51	3	17.0
Blowers, Sea	43	2	21.5	Gagne, KC	57	2	28.5
Bonds, SF	135	25	5.4	Gant, Cin	114	20	5.7
Boone, Cin	70	3	23.3	Garcia, Pit	55	8	6.9
Bordick, Oak	96	9	10.7	Gates, Oak	113	2	56.5
Brosius, Oak	56	2	28.0	Gibson, Det	50	6	8.3
Brumfield, Pit	117	18	6.5	Gil, Tex	43	2	21.5
Buford, Bal/NYN	48	9	5.3	Gilkey, StL	85	11	7.7
Burks, Col	47	7	6.7	Girardi, Col	64	3	21.3
Butler, NYN/LA	174	25	7.0	Gomez, Det	49	3	16.3
Caminiti, SD	44	10	4.4	Gonzalez, Tor	86	3	28.7
Cangelosi, Hou	99	19	5.2	Gonzalez, Hou/ChN	99	6	16.5
Carr, Fla	161	20	8.1	Goodwin, Bal	106	21	5.0
Castilla, Col	55	2	27.5	Goodwin, KC	160	35	4.6
Cirillo, Mil	70	7	10.0	Grace, ChN	43	5	8.6
Clayton, SF	114	21	5.4	Green, Tor	48	1	48.0
Colbrunn, Fla	42	10	4.2	Greenwell, Bos	51	7	7.3
Coleman, KC/Sea	216	26	8.3	Grissom, Atl	195	23	8.5
Cora, Sea	83	16	5.2	Guillen, ChA	56	5	11.2
Cordero, Mon	97	9	10.8	Gwynn, SD	60	11	5.5
Cordova, Min	103	19	5.4	Hamilton, Mil	88	11	8.0

Player	PkOf	SB	Ratio	Player	PkOf	SB	Ratio
Hammonds, Bal	50	4	12.5	Nunnally, KC	48	1	48.0
Hayes, Phi	54	4	13.5	O'Leary, Bos	48	5	9.6
Henderson, Oak	115	21	5.5	Offerman, LA	124	2	62.0
Hill, SF	86	22	3.9	Orsulak, NYN	54	1	54.0
Howard, Cin	74	13	5.7	Pendleton, Fla	48	1	48.0
Hulse, Mil	59	14	4.2	Phillips, Cal	147	11	13.4
Hunter, Hou	122	17	7.2	Polonia, NYA/Atl	104	13	8.0
Javier, Oak	106	25	4.2	Puckett, Min	57	3	19.0
Jefferies, Phi	93	9	10.3	Raines, ChA	92	10	9.2
Johnson, ChA	133	29	4.6	Ramirez, Cle	61	6	10.2
Jones, Atl	62	6	10.3	Reboulet, Min	51	1	51.0
Jordan, StL	135	18	7.5	Reed, SD	80	4	20.0
Justice, Atl	53	4	13.3	Roberts, SD	138	14	9.9
Karros, LA	44	4	11.0	Salmon, Cal	79	2	39.5
Kelly, Atl	40	7	5.7	Sanchez, ChN	66	4	16.5
Kelly, NYA	52	6	8.7	Sanders, Cin/SF	152	15	10.1
Kelly, Mon/LA	105	17	6.2	Sanders, Cin	127	29	4.4
Kent, NYN	55	2	27.5	Segui, NYN/Mon	46	2	23.0
Kingery, Col	81	11	7.4	Sheffield, Fla	87	16	5.4
Kirby, Cle	50	9	5.6	Sierra, Oak/NYA	47	5	9.4
Knoblauch, Min	184	36	5.1	Smith, StL	41	4	10.3
Lankford, StL	160	16	10.0	Snow, Cal	41	2	20.5
Lansing, Mon	66	18	3.7	Sojo, Sea	40	3	13.3
Larkin, Cin	127	34	3.7	Sosa, ChN	133	31	4.3
Leius, Min	46	1	46.0	Tarasco, Mon	96	21	4.6
Lewis, SF/Cin	167	29	5.8	Tavarez, Fla	57	5	11.4
Liriano, Pit	49	2	24.5	Thompson, NYN	48	3	16.0
Listach, Mil	75	9	8.3	Tinsley, Bos	70	13	5.4
Lofton, Cle	194	39	5.0	Tucker, KC	46	2	23.0
Martin, Pit	144	15	9.6	Valentin, Bos	90	20	4.5
Martin, ChA	46	4	11.5	Valentin, Mil	57	14	4.1
Martinez, ChA	47	5	9.4	Vaughn, Mil	40	6	6.7
McGee, Bos	45	5	9.0	Vaughn, Bos	47	11	4.3
McLemore, Tex	115	18	6.4	Velarde, NYA	58	4	14.5
McRae, ChN	184	20	9.2	Veras, Fla	195	42	4.6
Meares, Min	76	9	8.4	Vina, Mil	94	5	18.8
Merced, Pit	58	5	11.6	Vizcaino, NYN	94	2	47.0
Mieske, Mil	47	1	47.0	Vizquel, Cle	105	23	4.6
Molitor, Tor	75	8	9.4	Walker, Col	76	7	10.9
Mondesi, LA	176	24	7.3	Weiss, Col	123	11	11.2
Morandini, Phi	93	6	15.5	White, Tor	68	10	6.8
Mouton, Hou	112	22	5.1	White, Mon	156	20	7.8
Naehring, Bos	61	0	—	Williams, NYA	141	7	20.1
Nixon, Tex	228	35	6.5	Young, Col	169	23	7.3

Who Gets the "Slidin' Billy Trophy"? (p. 128)

Both Leagues — Listed Alphabetically
(Players with 100+ Plate Appearances Batting Leadoff in 1995)

Player, Team	OBP	AB	R	H	BB	HBP	SB
Amaral, Sea	.328	159	28	42	15	0	11
Anderson B, Bal	.356	425	77	111	57	6	17
Biggio, Hou	.423	85	17	21	21	5	4
Boggs, NYA	.420	203	39	68	32	0	0
Brumfield, Pit	.333	377	61	100	34	5	22
Buford, NYN	.328	101	17	21	15	4	5
Butler, LA	.375	512	77	153	66	0	31
Cangelosi, Hou	.454	120	30	37	31	1	12
Coleman, Sea	.343	453	64	130	37	2	40
Cora, Sea	.332	189	28	54	11	2	6
Curtis, Det	.350	585	96	157	70	7	27
Damon, KC	.345	163	29	49	11	1	6
DeShields, LA	.320	241	35	56	30	1	18
Dykstra, Phi	.354	253	36	67	33	3	10
Finley, SD	.405	304	62	103	32	3	27
Fonville, LA	.350	125	19	36	12	0	12
Gilkey, StL	.344	332	46	98	22	3	3
Goodwin C, Bal	.281	131	16	32	7	0	6
Grissom, Atl	.299	509	73	122	42	3	26
Hamilton, Mil	.333	108	15	29	10	1	1
Henderson, Oak	.408	401	65	120	72	4	32
Howard T, Cin	.355	141	22	44	10	0	11
Hunter B, Hou	.345	288	48	86	20	2	19
Johnson L, ChA	.354	521	91	166	29	1	34
Kingery, Col	.357	109	19	28	17	0	0
Kirby, Cle	.202	107	11	18	4	1	3
Knoblauch, Min	.423	530	105	175	77	10	45
Lewis D, Cin	.305	371	50	92	25	6	23
Listach, Mil	.270	183	20	40	13	0	5
Lofton, Cle	.363	480	92	149	40	1	52
Martin A, Pit	.363	175	32	52	17	1	8
McGee, Bos	.316	149	27	42	8	0	3
McRae, ChN	.349	579	92	167	47	7	27
Morandini, Phi	.353	266	33	72	27	7	4
Mouton J, Hou	.315	116	18	29	8	3	15
Nixon, Tex	.356	589	86	174	57	0	50
O'Leary, Bos	.300	95	17	25	5	0	4
Pena G, StL	.386	95	20	27	16	1	3
Phillips T, Cal	.396	517	118	136	111	3	13
Polonia, Atl	.319	250	36	64	25	0	10
Roberts, SD	.333	270	37	80	13	2	20
Sanders D, SF	.320	320	43	85	24	2	20
Tarasco, Mon	.333	169	32	45	17	0	8
Tinsley, Bos	.346	252	44	68	29	1	13
Veras, Fla	.387	429	85	114	77	9	54
Vina, Mil	.295	155	27	32	14	6	2
Walton, Cin	.349	128	20	34	13	4	10
Weiss, Col	.390	78	14	18	19	2	5
White D, Tor	.335	426	61	121	29	5	11
White R, Mon	.375	245	44	76	25	1	16
Williams B, NYA	.345	149	23	40	16	2	0
Young E, Col	.402	339	64	107	44	5	30
AL Team Avg	**.350**	**609**	**100**	**169**	**65**	**4**	**31**
NL Team Avg	**.349**	**605**	**96**	**166**	**64**	**7**	**35**

Who Puts Their Teams Ahead? (p. 132)

In the chart below, **Tot RBI** is a player's Total RBI for the season; **GA RBI** is his total number of RBI in plate appearances in which he drove in the go-ahead run; **GA Opp** is the number of times a player drove in the go-ahead run plus the number of times he stranded the go-ahead run in scoring position; **GA DI** is the number of times the player drove in the go-ahead run; **DI%** is the percentage if times a player drove in the go-ahead run divided by his opportunities (**GA Opp**).

Both Leagues — Listed Alphabetically
(Minimum 50 Total RBI in 1995)

Player, Team	Tot RBI	GA RBI	GA Opp	GA DI	DI%	Player, Team	Tot RBI	GA RBI	GA Opp	GA DI	DI%
Abbott, Fla	60	23	49	13	27	Cordova, Min	84	19	86	15	17
Alomar R, Tor	66	11	82	10	12	Curtis, Det	67	7	73	7	10
Alou, Mon	58	19	62	14	23	Daulton, Phi	55	15	70	13	19
Anderson B, Bal	64	22	81	12	15	Davis C, Cal	86	34	73	19	26
Anderson G, Cal	69	18	57	10	18	Devereaux, Atl	63	16	71	14	20
Baerga, Cle	90	26	87	22	25	Dunston, ChN	69	31	78	20	26
Bagwell, Hou	87	23	93	16	17	Durham, ChA	51	6	76	5	7
Baines, Bal	63	13	54	9	17	Edmonds, Cal	107	22	84	16	19
Bell D, Hou	86	28	110	20	18	Eisenreich, Phi	55	11	60	9	15
Bell J, Pit	55	10	91	8	9	Eusebio, Hou	58	12	68	8	12
Belle, Cle	126	38	98	24	24	Everett, NYN	54	19	60	12	20
Berroa, Oak	88	28	99	18	18	Fielder, Det	82	25	91	15	16
Berry, Mon	55	9	47	7	15	Fryman, Det	81	31	103	21	20
Bichette, Col	128	58	118	37	31	Gaetti, KC	96	31	110	21	19
Biggio, Hou	77	26	110	19	17	Galarraga, Col	106	30	100	22	22
Blowers, Sea	96	31	77	18	23	Gant, Cin	88	31	82	23	28
Boggs, NYA	63	17	50	13	26	Garcia C, Pit	50	8	59	7	12
Bonds, SF	104	54	105	38	36	Gates, Oak	56	7	85	7	8
Bonilla, Bal	99	39	123	30	24	Gilkey, StL	69	18	76	16	21
Boone, Cin	68	18	64	11	17	Girardi, Col	55	19	80	15	19
Brogna, NYN	76	19	97	14	14	Gomez C, Det	50	12	72	9	13
Buhner, Sea	121	42	110	22	20	Gonzalez J, Tex	82	25	68	17	25
Caminiti, SD	94	22	96	17	18	Gonzalez L, ChN	69	18	78	13	17
Canseco, Bos	81	24	55	16	29	Grace, ChN	92	33	95	28	29
Carreon, SF	65	25	75	18	24	Green, Tor	54	21	75	15	20
Carter, Tor	76	27	121	18	15	Greenwell, Bos	76	20	73	16	22
Castilla, Col	90	15	70	12	17	Greer, Tex	61	26	71	19	27
Clark W, Tex	92	34	96	28	29	Gwynn T, SD	90	28	92	21	23
Clayton, SF	58	10	78	7	9	Hayes, Phi	85	25	109	19	17
Colbrunn, Fla	89	21	88	15	17	Henderson, Oak	54	20	53	13	25
Conine, Fla	105	35	110	25	23	Hill, SF	86	24	112	17	15

Player, Team	Tot RBI	GA RBI	GA Opp	GA DI	DI%	Player, Team	Tot RBI	GA RBI	GA Opp	GA DI	DI%
Hoiles, Bal	58	17	61	12	20	Oliver, Mil	51	22	55	13	24
Hundley, NYN	51	19	40	12	30	Palmeiro R, Bal	104	35	97	25	26
Jaha, Mil	65	25	55	11	20	Pendleton, Fla	78	23	79	16	20
Javier, Oak	56	7	87	7	8	Phillips T, Cal	61	11	68	9	13
Jefferies, Phi	56	13	87	11	13	Piazza, LA	93	30	74	21	28
Johnson L, ChA	57	13	77	11	14	Puckett, Min	99	39	126	28	22
Jones C, Atl	86	37	90	29	32	Raines, ChA	67	20	86	17	20
Jordan B, StL	81	30	89	21	24	Ramirez, Cle	107	29	74	19	26
Joyner, KC	83	26	91	22	24	Ripken C, Bal	88	25	97	20	21
Justice, Atl	78	39	71	24	34	Rodriguez I, Tex	67	18	85	14	16
Karkovice, ChA	51	13	65	7	11	Salmon, Cal	105	25	81	19	23
Karros, LA	105	34	99	23	23	Sanders R, Cin	99	31	86	23	27
Kelly R, LA	57	11	76	8	11	Segui, Mon	68	26	88	17	19
Kent, NYN	65	11	82	9	11	Seitzer, Mil	69	23	93	22	24
King, Pit	87	23	106	17	16	Sierra, NYA	86	33	98	20	20
Klesko, Atl	70	19	50	13	26	Snow, Cal	102	22	88	14	16
Knoblauch, Min	63	25	81	17	21	Sorrento, Cle	79	13	45	9	20
Lankford, StL	82	30	93	18	19	Sosa, ChN	119	41	104	29	28
Lansing, Mon	62	16	63	12	19	Sprague, Tor	74	21	106	16	15
Larkin, Cin	66	22	66	14	21	Stanley, NYA	83	22	62	11	18
Lofton, Cle	53	15	49	11	22	Steinbach, Oak	65	23	63	13	21
Lopez, Atl	51	12	46	10	22	Surhoff, Mil	73	18	69	11	16
Macfarlane, Bos	51	11	54	8	15	Tettleton, Tex	78	25	66	16	24
Magadan, Hou	51	16	68	12	18	Thomas, ChA	111	40	105	31	30
Martinez E, Sea	113	28	100	19	19	Thome, Cle	73	20	66	13	20
Martinez T, Sea	111	24	93	17	18	Valentin J, Bos	102	31	89	23	26
May, Hou	50	15	74	13	18	Vaughn G, Mil	59	14	63	10	16
McGriff, Atl	93	28	82	19	23	Vaughn M, Bos	126	34	94	25	27
McGwire, Oak	90	39	59	20	34	Ventura, ChA	93	20	100	17	17
Merced, Pit	83	29	109	19	17	Vizcaino, NYN	56	20	81	15	19
Molitor, Tor	60	11	84	9	11	Vizquel, Cle	56	15	84	15	18
Mondesi, LA	88	27	82	16	20	Walker, Col	101	35	90	24	27
Morris, Cin	51	11	68	10	15	White D, Tor	53	8	44	7	16
Munoz P, Min	58	23	80	16	20	White R, Mon	57	18	60	13	22
Murray, Cle	82	20	65	17	26	Williams B, NYA	82	27	77	21	27
Naehring, Bos	57	20	63	15	24	Williams M, SF	65	25	55	17	31
Nilsson, Mil	53	16	54	11	20	Wilson D, Sea	51	13	53	9	17
O'Neill, NYA	96	31	86	23	27	Zeile, ChN	52	12	66	10	15
Olerud, Tor	54	15	97	12	12						

Who's the Best Bunter? (p. 134)

The following table shows: **SH** = Sac Hits, **FSH** = Failed Sac Hits; and **BH**= Bunt Hits, **FBH** = Failed Bunt Hits

Both Leagues — Listed Alphabetically
(minimum 10 bunts in play)

Batter, Team	SH	FSH	%	BH	FBH	%	Batter, Team	SH	FSH	%	BH	FBH	%
Alicea, Bos	13	2	87	2	3	40	Lemke, Atl	7	2	78	1	0	100
Alomar R, Tor	6	1	86	10	6	62	Lewis D, Cin	12	1	92	9	11	45
Ashby, SD	16	1	94	1	0	100	Listach, Mil	6	2	75	2	8	20
Ausmus, SD	4	1	80	5	2	71	Loaiza, Pit	6	4	60	0	0	0
Avery, Atl	8	2	80	0	0	0	Lofton, Cle	4	2	67	10	9	53
Bautista, Det	6	1	86	3	3	50	Maddux G, Atl	6	4	60	1	0	100
Biggio, Hou	11	0	100	9	1	90	Martinez D, ChA	9	0	100	7	2	78
Bordick, Oak	7	0	100	2	1	67	Martinez R, LA	13	2	87	0	0	0
Browne, Fla	8	0	100	1	1	50	Mayne, KC	11	1	92	0	1	0
Buford, NYN	3	1	75	4	3	57	McLemore, Tex	10	0	100	1	5	17
Butler, LA	10	1	91	20	15	57	McRae, ChN	3	2	60	7	13	35
Carr, Fla	6	2	75	5	12	29	Mercker, Atl	6	3	67	1	2	33
Coleman, Sea	5	3	62	11	8	58	Mimbs, Phi	8	2	80	0	0	0
Cora, Sea	13	0	100	2	2	50	Mlicki, NYN	12	1	92	0	0	0
DeShields, LA	3	1	75	5	5	50	Molitor, Tor	3	3	50	4	1	80
Diaz A, Sea	4	0	100	4	2	67	Mouton J, Hou	3	1	75	3	6	33
DiSarcina, Cal	7	0	100	2	3	40	Nixon, Tex	6	0	100	23	23	50
Dunston, ChN	7	0	100	8	2	80	Offerman, LA	9	5	64	6	3	67
Durham, ChA	5	3	62	10	9	53	Polonia, Atl	3	0	100	6	3	67
Easley, Cal	5	1	83	4	3	57	Portugal, Cin	8	3	73	0	0	0
Fassero, Mon	8	7	53	1	0	100	Rapp, Fla	9	3	75	0	0	0
Fermin, Sea	8	2	80	0	1	0	Reynolds, Hou	10	0	100	0	0	0
Fernandez, NYA	3	0	100	3	8	27	Ritz, Col	11	3	79	1	0	100
Finley, SD	4	3	57	5	3	62	Sanchez, ChN	8	3	73	6	11	35
Fonville, LA	6	3	67	18	9	67	Sanders D, SF	3	0	100	12	6	67
Gagne, KC	7	0	100	0	5	0	Schourek, Cin	12	2	86	0	1	0
Gil, Tex	10	5	67	1	2	33	Segui, Mon	8	0	100	2	0	100
Girardi, Col	12	0	100	5	2	71	Stocker, Phi	10	1	91	4	5	44
Glavine, Atl	8	2	80	2	0	100	Tarasco, Mon	3	2	60	8	6	57
Gonzalez A, Tor	9	1	90	4	0	100	Tavarez, Fla	3	2	60	5	5	50
Goodwin C, Bal	7	2	78	5	10	33	Tinsley, Bos	9	0	100	0	1	0
Goodwin T, KC	13	6	68	12	10	55	Valdes I, LA	7	3	70	0	0	0
Green, Phi	8	2	80	0	0	0	Valentin J, Mil	7	0	100	5	4	56
Hamilton, Mil	8	2	80	4	5	44	Veras, Fla	7	7	50	6	9	40
Howard D, KC	6	4	60	4	5	44	Vina, Mil	4	2	67	5	14	26
Javier, Oak	5	0	100	10	10	50	Vizcaino, NYN	13	1	93	5	2	71
Johnson L, ChA	2	0	100	5	6	45	Vizquel, Cle	10	0	100	9	4	69
Jones B, NYN	18	2	90	1	0	100	Walton, Cin	3	1	75	3	6	33
Karkovice, ChA	9	1	90	5	1	83	Weiss, Col	6	1	86	2	3	40
Kelly P, NYA	10	0	100	5	2	71	Young E, Col	3	0	100	8	6	57
Kingery, Col	6	2	75	1	1	50	**MLB Avg.**	1465	330	82	530	457	54
Leiter M, SF	9	1	90	0	0	0							

Who's First in the Secondary? (p. 136)

Both Leagues — Listed Alphabetically
(minimum 300 plate appearances in 1995)

Player, Team	SA	Player, Team	SA	Player, Team	SA	Player, Team	SA
Abbott, Fla	.286	DiSarcina, Cal	.215	Karkovice, ChA	.288	Phillips T, Cal	.419
Alfonzo, NYN	.140	Dunston, ChN	.208	Karros, LA	.348	Piazza, LA	.353
Alicea, Bos	.263	Durham, ChA	.221	Kelly P, NYA	.200	Polonia, Atl	.223
Alomar R, Tor	.292	Easley, Cal	.182	Kelly R, LA	.157	Puckett, Min	.307
Alou, Mon	.273	Edmonds, Cal	.332	Kent, NYN	.248	Raines, ChA	.299
Anderson B, Bal	.374	Eisenreich, Phi	.276	King, Pit	.321	Ramirez, Cle	.405
Anderson G, Cal	.246	Eusebio, Hou	.190	Kingery, Col	.294	Reed J, SD	.209
Ausmus, SD	.247	Everett, NYN	.301	Klesko, Atl	.444	Ripken C, Bal	.253
Baerga, Cle	.217	Fernandez, NYA	.211	Knoblauch, Min	.351	Roberts, SD	.186
Bagwell, Hou	.397	Fielder, Det	.379	Lankford, StL	.400	Rodriguez I, Tex	.175
Baines, Bal	.418	Finley, SD	.270	Lansing, Mon	.246	Salmon, Cal	.434
Bass, Bal	.173	Flaherty, Det	.212	Larkin, Cin	.389	Sanchez, ChN	.119
Bates, Col	.273	Fletcher D, Mon	.249	Leius, Min	.237	Sanders D, SF	.254
Becker, Min	.143	Fonville, LA	.138	Lemke, Atl	.213	Sanders R, Cin	.465
Bell D, Hou	.221	Frye, Tex	.176	Lewis D, Cin	.148	Segui, Mon	.228
Bell J, Pit	.240	Fryman, Det	.249	Leyritz, NYA	.265	Seitzer, Mil	.244
Belle, Cle	.513	Gaetti, KC	.348	Listach, Mil	.141	Servais, ChN	.352
Berroa, Oak	.293	Gagne, KC	.202	Lockhart, KC	.234	Sierra, NYA	.284
Berry, Mon	.274	Galarraga, Col	.307	Lofton, Cle	.308	Snow, Cal	.274
Bichette, Col	.325	Gant, Cin	.495	Lopez, Atl	.222	Sojo, Sea	.201
Biggio, Hou	.371	Garcia C, Pit	.204	Mabry, StL	.152	Sorrento, Cle	.433
Blauser, Atl	.269	Gates, Oak	.177	Macfarlane, Bos	.286	Sosa, ChN	.383
Blowers, Sea	.339	Gil, Tex	.186	Magadan, Hou	.293	Sprague, Tor	.274
Boggs, NYA	.259	Gilkey, StL	.292	Manwaring, SF	.156	Stanley, NYA	.356
Bonds, SF	.561	Girardi, Col	.160	Martin A, Pit	.280	Steinbach, Oak	.236
Bonilla, Bal	.336	Gomez C, Det	.234	Martinez D, ChA	.254	Stocker, Phi	.172
Boone, Cin	.250	Gonzalez A, Tor	.275	Martinez E, Sea	.501	Surhoff, Mil	.270
Bordick, Oak	.187	Gonzalez J, Tex	.347	Martinez T, Sea	.378	Tarasco, Mon	.320
Branson, Cin	.311	Gonzalez L, ChN	.295	Mattingly, NYA	.207	Tartabull, Oak	.289
Brogna, NYN	.275	Goodwin C, Bal	.183	May, Hou	.241	Tettleton, Tex	.522
Brosius, Oak	.301	Goodwin T, KC	.217	Mayne, KC	.153	Thomas, ChA	.576
Brumfield, Pit	.214	Grace, ChN	.315	McGriff, Atl	.326	Thome, Cle	.460
Buhner, Sea	.430	Green, Tor	.272	McGwire, Oak	.688	Thompson R, SF	.238
Burks, Col	.385	Greenwell, Bos	.249	McLemore, Tex	.244	Tinsley, Bos	.261
Butler, LA	.253	Greer, Tex	.290	McRae, ChN	.266	Valentin J, Bos	.419
Caminiti, SD	.356	Griffey Jr, Sea	.431	Meares, Min	.215	Valentin J, Mil	.317
Canseco, Bos	.366	Grissom, Atl	.240	Merced, Pit	.285	Van Slyke, Phi	.264
Carr, Fla	.279	Guillen, ChA	.099	Mieske, Mil	.285	Vaughn G, Mil	.339
Carreon, SF	.245	Gwynn T, SD	.204	Miller O, Hou	.179	Vaughn M, Bos	.411
Carter, Tor	.262	Hamilton, Mil	.261	Molitor, Tor	.291	Velarde, NYA	.275
Castilla, Col	.300	Hayes, Phi	.233	Mondesi, LA	.315	Ventura, ChA	.358
Cedeno A, SD	.174	Henderson, Oak	.378	Morandini, Phi	.225	Veras, Fla	.373
Cirillo, Mil	.323	Higginson, Det	.324	Morris, Cin	.253	Vina, Mil	.191
Clark W, Tex	.326	Hill, SF	.338	Mouton J, Hou	.255	Vizcaino, NYN	.157
Clayton, SF	.202	Hoiles, Bal	.403	Munoz P, Min	.231	Vizquel, Cle	.227
Colbrunn, Fla	.233	Howard T, Cin	.203	Murray, Cle	.291	Walbeck, Min	.127
Coleman, Sea	.248	Hulse, Mil	.183	Naehring, Bos	.314	Walker, Col	.427
Conine, Fla	.358	Hundley, NYN	.360	Nixon, Tex	.190	Wallach, LA	.245
Cooper, StL	.206	Hunter B, Hou	.212	Nunnally, KC	.403	Weiss, Col	.319
Cora, Sea	.187	Jaha, Mil	.383	O'Leary, Bos	.261	White D, Tor	.237
Cordero, Mon	.212	Javier, Oak	.290	O'Neill, NYA	.378	White R, Mon	.297
Cordova, Mil	.336	Jefferies, Phi	.223	Offerman, LA	.238	Whiten, Phi	.306
Cromer, StL	.139	Johnson C, Fla	.298	Olerud, Tor	.285	Williams B, NYA	.316
Curtis, Det	.307	Johnson L, ChA	.227	Oliver, Mil	.240	Williams E, SD	.243
Daulton, Phi	.322	Jones C, Atl	.332	Orsulak, NYN	.148	Williams M, SF	.424
Davis C, Cal	.406	Jordan B, StL	.267	Palmeiro R, Bal	.388	Wilson D, Sea	.223
DeShields, LA	.320	Joyner, KC	.288	Paquette, Oak	.244	Young E, Col	.352
Devereaux, Atl	.227	Justice, Atl	.409	Pendleton, Fla	.220	Zeile, ChN	.232

Did the Moon-Shot Boom Continue Last Season? (p. 138)

Both Leagues — 1995 Home Runs Listed by Distance (450+ Feet)

Dir	Dis	Batter	Pitcher	Date	Site
G	510	Mondesi, LA	Olivares, Col	5/5	@Col
E	490	Canseco, Bos	Tewksbury, Tex	7/13	@Bos
J	480	Buhner, Sea	Radke, Min	9/11	@Sea
L	470	Fielder, Det	Baldwin, ChA	5/28	@Det
G	470	McGwire, Oak	Boskie, Cal	9/20	@Oak
J	460	Ashley, LA	Loaiza, Pit	5/18	@LA
H	460	Jordan B, StL	Saberhagen, NYN	4/28	@NYN
H	460	Piazza, LA	Bautista, SF	6/22	@LA
V	460	Anthony, Cin	Mathews T, Fla	6/25	@Cin
M	460	Sosa, ChN	Bailey R, Col	8/17	@Col
G	460	Hill, SF	Cornelius, NYN	8/22	@NYN
E	460	Bichette, Col	Valenzuela, SD	8/4	@Col
T	460	Griffey Jr, Sea	Wells D, Det	4/29	@Sea
L	460	Fielder, Det	Eldred, Mil	5/9	@Mil
N	460	McGwire, Oak	Tapani, Min	5/12	@Min
F	460	Thomas, ChA	Sanderson, Cal	5/20	@ChA
T	460	Phillips T, Cal	Mahomes, Min	5/18	@Min
G	460	Martinez E, Sea	Rivera M, NYA	6/11	@NYA
O	460	Martinez T, Sea	MacDonald, NYA	6/11	@NYA
E	460	McGwire, Oak	Gordon, KC	9/12	@Oak
R	450	Walker, Col	Mathews T, Fla	6/20	@Col
I	450	Galarraga, Col	Gomez, SF	5/11	@Col
L	450	Abbott, Fla	Thompson, Col	5/12	@Fla
U	450	Jones C, Atl	Nen, Fla	5/20	@Atl
F	450	Sanders R, Cin	Perez C, Mon	6/18	@Cin
D	450	Galarraga, Col	Valenzuela, SD	6/25	@SD
F	450	Hill, SF	Reynolds, Hou	7/23	@Hou
L	450	Grissom, Atl	Nen, Fla	5/4	@Fla
E	450	Owens J, Col	Florie, SD	8/6	@Col
P	450	McGriff, Atl	Drabek, Hou	8/21	@Hou
T	450	Klesko, Atl	Jones B, NYN	9/29	@NYN
L	450	Belle, Cle	Pena, Bos	5/20	@Bos
F	450	McGwire, Oak	Smith L, Cal	6/30	@Oak
S	450	Macfarlane, Bos	Key, NYA	5/1	@NYA
N	450	Fielder, Det	Rodriguez F, Bos	5/7	@Det
L	450	Buhner, Sea	Erickson, Min	5/20	@Min
H	450	Williams G, NYA	Fleming, Sea	6/11	@NYA
F	450	Brosius, Oak	Carrara, Tor	7/29	@Tor
K	450	McGwire, Oak	Givens, Mil	7/4	@Oak
M	450	Belle, Cle	Stottlemyre, Oak	7/21	@Oak
C	450	Canseco, Bos	Harris G, Min	7/22	@Bos
I	450	Ramirez, Cle	Moyer, Bal	8/14	@Bal

Who Are the Real RBI Kings? (p. 140)

Both Leagues — Sorted by RBI Percentage
(minimum 500 RBI Opportunities)

Player, Team	Opp	RBI	Pct	Player, Team	Opp	RBI	Pct
Mark McGwire, Oak	549	90	16.4	Ruben Sierra, Oak-NYA	838	86	10.3
Jay Buhner, Sea	854	121	14.2	Chipper Jones, Atl	847	86	10.2
Albert Belle, Cle	916	126	13.8	Tony Gwynn, SD	889	90	10.1
Mo Vaughn, Bos	918	126	13.7	Orlando Merced, Pit	822	83	10.1
Edgar Martinez, Sea	839	113	13.5	Brian Jordan, StL	808	81	10.0
Juan Gonzalez, Tex	612	82	13.4	Cecil Fielder, Det	819	82	10.0
Paul Sorrento, Cle	591	79	13.4	Carlos Baerga, Cle	900	90	10.0
Dante Bichette, Col	960	128	13.3	Harold Baines, Bal	631	63	10.0
Ron Gant, Cin	668	88	13.2	Greg Colbrunn, Fla	898	89	9.9
Frank Thomas, ChA	851	111	13.0	Moises Alou, Mon	586	58	9.9
Manny Ramirez, Cle	827	107	12.9	Glenallen Hill, SF	871	86	9.9
Mike Piazza, LA	725	93	12.8	Raul Mondesi, LA	896	88	9.8
Barry Bonds, SF	814	104	12.8	Mark Carreon, SF	667	65	9.7
Sammy Sosa, ChN	936	119	12.7	Marty Cordova, Min	863	84	9.7
Ryan Klesko, Atl	560	70	12.5	Chris Hoiles, Bal	599	58	9.7
John Jaha, Mil	520	65	12.5	Jim Thome, Cle	757	73	9.6
Jeff Conine, Fla	841	105	12.5	Geronimo Berroa, Oak	914	88	9.6
Larry Walker, Col	809	101	12.5	Terry Steinbach, Oak	678	65	9.6
Mike Blowers, Sea	769	96	12.5	Bernard Gilkey, StL	723	69	9.5
Reggie Sanders, Cin	807	99	12.3	Javy Lopez, Atl	542	51	9.4
Jose Canseco, Bos	661	81	12.3	Rico Brogna, NYN	813	76	9.3
Tino Martinez, Sea	913	111	12.2	Cal Ripken, Bal	948	88	9.3
Mike Stanley, NYA	695	83	11.9	David Segui, NYN-Mon	737	68	9.2
John Valentin, Bos	861	102	11.8	Mike Greenwell, Bos	824	76	9.2
Will Clark, Tex	779	92	11.8	Joe Oliver, Mil	554	51	9.2
Chili Davis, Cal	729	86	11.8	Jason Bates, Col	502	46	9.2
Tim Salmon, Cal	902	105	11.6	Eddie Williams, SD	516	47	9.1
Dave Justice, Atl	680	78	11.5	Darren Daulton, Phi	606	55	9.1
Andres Galarraga, Col	927	106	11.4	Terry Pendleton, Fla	862	78	9.0
Eddie Murray, Cle	719	82	11.4	Pedro Munoz, Min	641	58	9.0
Eric Karros, LA	923	105	11.4	Ron Karkovice, ChA	565	51	9.0
Rafael Palmeiro, Bal	920	104	11.3	Kurt Abbott, Fla	665	60	9.0
Paul O'Neill, NYA	852	96	11.3	Rickey Henderson, Oak	601	54	9.0
Mickey Tettleton, Tex	693	78	11.3	Charlie Hayes, Phi	949	85	9.0
Jim Edmonds, Cal	954	107	11.2	Tony Eusebio, Hou	648	58	9.0
Jeff King, Pit	776	87	11.2	Derrick May, Mil-Hou	559	50	8.9
Kirby Puckett, Min	893	99	11.1	Mike Devereaux, ChA-Atl	712	63	8.8
Gary Gaetti, KC	874	96	11.0	Bernie Williams, NYA	930	82	8.8
Jeff Bagwell, Hou	796	87	10.9	Travis Fryman, Det	924	81	8.8
Wally Joyner, KC	765	83	10.8	Barry Larkin, Cin	754	66	8.8
Bobby Bonilla, NYN-Bal	921	99	10.7	Greg Vaughn, Mil	677	59	8.7
Carl Everett, NYN	503	54	10.7	Shawon Dunston, ChN	793	69	8.7
B.J. Surhoff, Mil	686	73	10.6	Kevin Seitzer, Mil	800	69	8.6
Derek Bell, Hou	810	86	10.6	Rusty Greer, Tex	708	61	8.6
Vinny Castilla, Col	850	90	10.6	Luis Gonzalez, Hou-ChN	806	69	8.6
Sean Berry, Mon	520	55	10.6	Dave Magadan, Hou	596	51	8.6
J.T. Snow, Cal	965	102	10.6	Mark Whiten, Bos-Phi	551	47	8.5
Ken Caminiti, SD	890	94	10.6	Craig Biggio, Hou	905	77	8.5
Garret Anderson, Cal	656	69	10.5	Jose Valentin, Mil	577	49	8.5
Mark Grace, ChN	875	92	10.5	Shawn Green, Tor	640	54	8.4
Fred McGriff, Atl	889	93	10.5	Devon White, Tor	632	53	8.4
Ray Lankford, StL	787	82	10.4	Wade Boggs, NYA	752	63	8.4
Robin Ventura, ChA	896	93	10.4	Hal Morris, Cin	609	51	8.4

Player, Team	Opp	RBI	Pct	Player, Team	Opp	RBI	Pct
Carlos Garcia, Pit	599	50	8.3	Matt Walbeck, Min	650	44	6.8
Jim Eisenreich, Phi	660	55	8.3	Orlando Miller, Hou	534	36	6.7
Tim Raines, ChA	811	67	8.3	Mike Kingery, Col	550	37	6.7
Ed Sprague, Tor	901	74	8.2	Brad Ausmus, SD	514	34	6.6
David Hulse, Mil	577	47	8.1	Mickey Morandini, Phi	743	49	6.6
Mike Macfarlane, Bos	630	51	8.1	Eric Young, Col	547	36	6.6
Jeff Kent, NYN	805	65	8.1	John Olerud, Tor	821	54	6.6
Mike Lansing, Mon	769	62	8.1	Jay Bell, Pit	837	55	6.6
Joe Carter, Tor	947	76	8.0	Scott Cooper, StL	609	40	6.6
Dan Wilson, Sea	638	51	8.0	Omar Vizquel, Cle	855	56	6.5
Jeff Branson, Cin	564	45	8.0	Brent Gates, Oak	857	56	6.5
Bret Boone, Cin	858	68	7.9	Bob Higginson, Det	661	43	6.5
Roberto Alomar, Tor	838	66	7.9	Mike Bordick, Oak	686	44	6.4
Tony Phillips, Cal	775	61	7.9	Ray Durham, ChA	811	51	6.3
Ivan Rodriguez, Tex	859	67	7.8	Luis Alicea, Bos	701	44	6.3
Chad Curtis, Det	863	67	7.8	Al Martin, Pit	658	41	6.2
Rondell White, Mon	736	57	7.7	Lance Johnson, ChA	918	57	6.2
Charles Johnson, Fla	506	39	7.7	Wil Cordero, Mon	795	49	6.2
Todd Zeile, StL-ChN	675	52	7.7	Tony Tarasco, Mon	655	40	6.1
Troy O'Leary, Bos	640	49	7.7	Ozzie Guillen, ChA	672	41	6.1
Darrin Fletcher, Mon	589	45	7.6	Don Mattingly, NYA	817	49	6.0
Tim Naehring, Bos	747	57	7.6	Mark Lemke, Atl	638	38	6.0
Randy Velarde, NYA	605	46	7.6	Delino DeShields, LA	626	37	5.9
Brady Anderson, Bal	842	64	7.6	Brian McRae, ChN	819	48	5.9
Chuck Knoblauch, Min	830	63	7.6	Kirt Manwaring, SF	617	36	5.8
Edgardo Alfonzo, NYN	542	41	7.6	Joey Cora, Sea	675	39	5.8
Jeff Cirillo, Mil	518	39	7.5	Jeff Frye, Tex	505	29	5.7
Pat Meares, Min	654	49	7.5	Jody Reed, SD	698	40	5.7
Stan Javier, Oak	754	56	7.4	Damion Easley, Cal	613	35	5.7
Paul Molitor, Tor	808	60	7.4	Mark McLemore, Tex	740	41	5.5
Lee Tinsley, Bos	554	41	7.4	Marquis Grissom, Atl	769	42	5.5
Kenny Lofton, Cle	719	53	7.4	Steve Finley, SD	816	44	5.4
Scott Brosius, Oak	625	46	7.4	Brent Mayne, KC	503	27	5.4
Joe Girardi, Col	749	55	7.3	Rich Becker, Min	639	33	5.2
Alex Gonzalez, Tor	575	42	7.3	Jose Offerman, LA	642	33	5.1
Luis Sojo, Sea	538	39	7.2	Brett Butler, NYN-LA	755	38	5.0
John Flaherty, Det	552	40	7.2	Otis Nixon, Tex	896	45	5.0
Tim Wallach, LA	525	38	7.2	Quilvio Veras, Fla	645	32	5.0
Chris Gomez, Det	695	50	7.2	Andujar Cedeno, SD	628	31	4.9
Gregg Jefferies, Phi	780	56	7.2	Pat Listach, Mil	512	25	4.9
Darryl Hamilton, Mil	615	44	7.2	Jeff Blauser, Atl	638	31	4.9
Gary DiSarcina, Cal	575	41	7.1	Kevin Stocker, Phi	694	32	4.6
Scott Leius, Min	635	45	7.1	Jacob Brumfield, Pit	576	26	4.5
Royce Clayton, SF	824	58	7.0	Vince Coleman, KC-Sea	653	29	4.4
Roberto Kelly, Mon-LA	816	57	7.0	Rey Sanchez, ChN	643	27	4.2
Tony Fernandez, NYA	650	45	6.9	Tom Goodwin, KC	729	28	3.8
Benji Gil, Tex	672	46	6.8	Walt Weiss, Col	660	25	3.8
Jose Vizcaino, NYN	819	56	6.8	Darren Lewis, SF-Cin	673	24	3.6
Greg Gagne, KC	722	49	6.8	Tripp Cromer, StL	533	18	3.4
John Mabry, StL	605	41	6.8	**MLB Avg**			**9.0**

Who Are the Human Air Conditioners? (p. 142)

The table below shows swings missed (**Sw**) as a % of total pitches swung at (**Pit**).

Both Leagues — Listed Alphabetically
(minimum 350 plate appearances in 1995)

Player, Team	Sw	Pit	%	Player, Team	Sw	Pit	%	Player, Team	Sw	Pit	%
Abbott, Fla	236	860	27	Carter, Tor	251	1287	20	Galarraga, Col	360	1225	29
Alfonzo, NYN	78	573	14	Castilla, Col	260	997	26	Gant, Cin	232	815	28
Alicea, Bos	108	810	13	Cedeno A, SD	253	856	30	Garcia C, Pit	90	656	14
Alomar R, Tor	98	944	10	Cirillo, Mil	82	591	14	Gates, Oak	127	931	14
Alou, Mon	170	728	23	Clark W, Tex	120	879	14	Gil, Tex	332	905	37
Anderson B, Bal	170	996	17	Clayton, SF	241	1068	23	Gilkey, StL	167	886	19
Anderson G, Cal	169	742	23	Colbrunn, Fla	194	1035	19	Girardi, Col	207	896	23
Ausmus, SD	93	579	16	Coleman, Sea	135	865	16	Gomez C, Det	150	805	19
Baerga, Cle	110	948	12	Conine, Fla	181	965	19	Gonzalez A, Tor	204	723	28
Bagwell, Hou	225	902	25	Cooper, StL	142	756	19	Gonzalez J, Tex	146	655	22
Baines, Bal	120	719	17	Cora, Sea	51	786	6	Gonzalez L,ChN	130	903	14
Bates, Col	122	577	21	Cordero, Mon	193	988	20	Goodwin T, KC	131	813	16
Becker, Min	161	709	23	Cordova, Min	291	1064	27	Grace, ChN	101	948	11
Bell D, Hou	216	931	23	Cromer, StL	141	631	22	Green, Tor	174	742	23
Bell J, Pit	205	1045	20	Curtis, Det	154	982	16	Greenwell, Bos	107	842	13
Belle, Cle	188	1008	19	Daulton, Phi	126	642	20	Greer, Tex	137	781	18
Berroa, Oak	260	1123	23	Davis C, Cal	200	872	23	Grissom, Atl	156	980	16
Bichette, Col	278	1206	23	DeShields, LA	110	726	15	Guillen, ChA	78	742	11
Biggio, Hou	175	1042	17	Devereaux, Atl	142	689	21	Gwynn T, SD	50	837	6
Blauser, Atl	179	815	22	DiSarcina, Cal	57	548	10	Hamilton, Mil	63	725	9
Blowers, Sea	233	841	28	Dunston, ChN	222	983	23	Hayes, Phi	231	1023	23
Boggs, NYA	42	798	5	Durham, ChA	193	952	20	Henderson, Oak	109	777	14
Bonds, SF	141	942	15	Easley, Cal	90	611	15	Higginson, Det	177	773	23
Bonilla, Bal	214	1140	19	Edmonds, Cal	245	1125	22	Hill, SF	276	989	28
Boone, Cin	187	924	20	Eisenreich, Phi	80	642	12	Hoiles, Bal	163	673	24
Bordick, Oak	77	733	11	Eusebio, Hou	140	716	20	Hulse, Mil	128	696	18
Branson, Cin	156	733	21	Fernandez, NYA	75	728	10	Jaha, Mil	131	614	21
Brogna, NYN	262	996	26	Fielder, Det	312	1086	29	Javier, Oak	144	823	17
Brosius, Oak	167	831	20	Finley, SD	135	968	14	Jefferies, Phi	40	779	5
Brumfield, Pit	140	735	19	Flaherty, Det	86	613	14	Johnson C, Fla	178	653	27
Buhner, Sea	257	868	30	Fletcher D, Mon	64	589	11	Johnson L, ChA	77	945	8
Butler, LA	52	942	6	Fonville, LA	57	519	11	Jones C, Atl	213	972	22
Caminiti, SD	227	1005	23	Frye, Tex	71	573	12	Jordan B, StL	228	937	24
Canseco, Bos	182	783	23	Fryman, Det	195	1079	18	Joyner, KC	133	851	16
Carr, Fla	132	660	20	Gaetti, KC	291	1101	26	Justice, Atl	169	848	20
Carreon, SF	89	752	12	Gagne, KC	153	869	18	Karkovice, ChA	187	696	27

Player, Team	Sw	Pit	%	Player, Team	Sw	Pit	%	Player, Team	Sw	Pit	%
Karros, LA	219	1131	19	Oliver, Mil	161	682	24	Wallach, LA	179	699	26
Kelly R, LA	223	1010	22	Palmeiro R, Bal	148	1051	14	Weiss, Col	86	720	12
Kent, NYN	231	971	24	Pendleton, Fla	230	1070	21	White D, Tor	233	913	26
King, Pit	124	829	15	Phillips T, Cal	273	1069	26	White R, Mon	194	845	23
Kingery, Col	74	621	12	Piazza, LA	224	889	25	Whiten, Phi	147	568	26
Klesko, Atl	176	653	27	Puckett, Min	240	1020	24	Williams B, NYA	180	1015	18
Knoblauch, Min	148	1073	14	Raines, ChA	97	889	11	Wilson D, Sea	141	747	19
Lankford, StL	229	1006	23	Ramirez, Cle	192	938	20	Young E, Col	63	623	10
Lansing, Mon	112	812	14	Reed J, SD	48	706	7	Zeile, ChN	143	757	19
Larkin, Cin	99	956	10	Ripken C, Bal	135	1002	13	**MLB Average**			20
Leius, Min	98	640	15	Rodriguez I, Tex	162	991	16				
Lemke, Atl	74	647	11	Salmon, Cal	231	1072	22				
Lewis D, Cin	58	775	7	Sanchez, ChN	103	766	13				
Listach, Mil	110	651	17	Sanders D, SF	110	591	19				
Lofton, Cle	87	829	10	Sanders R, Cin	294	978	30				
Lopez, Atl	144	628	23	Segui, Mon	119	873	14				
Mabry, StL	110	688	16	Seitzer, Mil	97	957	10				
Macfarlane, Bos	190	733	26	Sierra, NYA	167	871	19				
Magadan, Hou	90	621	14	Snow, Cal	145	1004	14				
Manwaring, SF	152	781	19	Sojo, Sea	41	569	7				
Martin A, Pit	246	870	28	Sorrento, Cle	128	574	22				
Martinez E, Sea	115	867	13	Sosa, ChN	377	1258	30				
Martinez T, Sea	194	1005	19	Sprague, Tor	192	1024	19				
Mattingly, NYA	90	779	12	Stanley, NYA	199	791	25				
McGriff, Atl	219	979	22	Steinbach, Oak	192	824	23				
McGwire, Oak	173	629	28	Stocker, Phi	125	807	15				
McLemore, Tex	115	792	15	Surhoff, Mil	81	710	11				
McRae, ChN	208	1157	18	Tarasco, Mon	132	743	18				
Meares, Min	169	749	23	Tettleton, Tex	189	780	24				
Merced, Pit	162	914	18	Thomas, ChA	148	959	15				
Miller O, Hou	166	633	26	Thome, Cle	235	916	26				
Molitor, Tor	148	1036	14	Thompson R,SF	147	664	22				
Mondesi, LA	304	1101	28	Tinsley, Bos	147	636	23				
Morandini, Phi	133	905	15	Valentin J, Bos	127	994	13				
Morris, Cin	111	699	16	Valentin J, Mil	160	708	23				
Munoz P, Min	230	835	28	Vaughn G, Mil	241	826	29				
Murray, Cle	228	883	26	Vaughn M, Bos	355	1125	32				
Naehring, Bos	104	759	14	Velarde, NYA	120	678	18				
Nixon, Tex	128	1129	11	Ventura, ChA	192	968	20				
Nunnally, KC	209	680	31	Veras, Fla	82	788	10				
O'Leary, Bos	151	750	20	Vizcaino, NYN	128	956	13				
O'Neill, NYA	163	876	19	Vizquel, Cle	100	947	11				
Offerman, LA	114	770	15	Walbeck, Min	123	760	16				
Olerud, Tor	101	822	12	Walker, Col	205	972	21				

Sure Belle Was Great, But Did He Create the Most Runs? (p. 145)

In the chart below, **RC** stands for Runs Created, and **OW%** stands for Offensive Winning Percentage.

Both Leagues — Listed Alphabetically
(minimum 350 plate appearances in 1995)

Player, Team	RC	OW%	Player, Team	RC	OW%	Player, Team	RC	OW%
Abbott, Fla	61.0	.539	Carter, Tor	72.0	.439	Galarraga, Col	92.0	.620
Alfonzo, NYN	37.4	.416	Castilla, Col	94.9	.660	Gant, Cin	90.5	.728
Alicea, Bos	61.7	.472	Cedeno A, SD	30.6	.233	Garcia C, Pit	53.1	.559
Alomar R, Tor	84.3	.566	Cirillo, Mil	56.5	.589	Gates, Oak	55.3	.326
Alou, Mon	53.4	.580	Clark W, Tex	90.2	.672	Gil, Tex	38.0	.257
Anderson B, Bal	101.3	.618	Clayton, SF	53.6	.370	Gilkey, StL	80.1	.622
Anderson G, Cal	64.8	.621	Colbrunn, Fla	70.5	.508	Girardi, Col	48.3	.364
Ausmus, SD	49.7	.571	Coleman, Sea	62.9	.474	Gomez C, Det	44.5	.308
Baerga, Cle	87.8	.573	Conine, Fla	97.7	.712	Gonzalez A, Tor	48.1	.419
Bagwell, Hou	93.4	.722	Cooper, StL	38.6	.354	Gonzalez J, Tex	61.6	.602
Baines, Bal	81.8	.691	Cora, Sea	60.0	.481	Gonzalez L, ChN	73.7	.565
Bates, Col	48.3	.564	Cordero, Mon	73.0	.546	Goodwin T, KC	62.9	.437
Becker, Min	34.6	.244	Cordova, Min	89.7	.599	Grace, ChN	115.2	.746
Bell D, Hou	78.8	.665	Cromer, StL	26.5	.225	Green, Tor	62.3	.587
Bell J, Pit	70.5	.497	Curtis, Det	90.2	.519	Greenwell, Bos	72.7	.532
Belle, Cle	144.1	.784	Daulton, Phi	54.0	.589	Greer, Tex	65.0	.542
Berroa, Oak	87.3	.556	Davis C, Cal	97.8	.735	Grissom, Atl	68.3	.461
Bichette, Col	121.3	.745	DeShields, LA	60.9	.523	Guillen, ChA	31.9	.205
Biggio, Hou	121.2	.741	Devereaux, Atl	56.5	.519	Gwynn T, SD	100.6	.717
Blauser, Atl	50.5	.407	DiSarcina, Cal	54.5	.528	Hamilton, Mil	58.0	.499
Blowers, Sea	66.7	.507	Dunston, ChN	68.4	.552	Hayes, Phi	70.0	.494
Boggs, NYA	83.5	.643	Durham, ChA	57.3	.403	Henderson, Oak	81.3	.666
Bonds, SF	133.7	.806	Easley, Cal	31.3	.233	Higginson, Det	57.2	.452
Bonilla, Bal	114.5	.716	Edmonds, Cal	104.0	.640	Hill, SF	75.7	.569
Boone, Cin	71.2	.517	Eisenreich, Phi	68.9	.685	Hoiles, Bal	63.1	.595
Bordick, Oak	50.7	.394	Eusebio, Hou	51.8	.542	Hulse, Mil	35.3	.333
Branson, Cin	49.9	.552	Fernandez, NYA	41.4	.326	Jaha, Mil	71.0	.736
Brogna, NYN	80.9	.624	Fielder, Det	79.9	.537	Javier, Oak	67.1	.524
Brosius, Oak	62.9	.557	Finley, SD	90.9	.614	Jefferies, Phi	72.1	.580
Brumfield, Pit	52.2	.493	Flaherty, Det	39.5	.352	Johnson C, Fla	45.2	.516
Buhner, Sea	88.6	.619	Fletcher D, Mon	51.4	.554	Johnson L, ChA	92.4	.558
Butler, LA	82.0	.602	Fonville, LA	34.3	.397	Jones C, Atl	86.0	.606
Caminiti, SD	104.5	.710	Frye, Tex	39.9	.424	Jordan B, StL	81.2	.632
Canseco, Bos	84.6	.709	Fryman, Det	80.1	.488	Joyner, KC	86.7	.643
Carr, Fla	36.2	.397	Gaetti, KC	88.3	.582	Justice, Atl	77.5	.669
Carreon, SF	65.5	.638	Gagne, KC	49.7	.367	Karkovice, ChA	40.3	.378

Player, Team	RC	OW%	Player, Team	RC	OW%	Player, Team	RC	OW%
Karros, LA	107.2	.700	Oliver, Mil	46.1	.471	Wallach, LA	44.1	.504
Kelly R, LA	55.4	.400	Palmeiro R, Bal	123.6	.732	Weiss, Col	65.8	.570
Kent, NYN	70.4	.568	Pendleton, Fla	76.3	.582	White D, Tor	63.8	.535
King, Pit	70.4	.580	Phillips T, Cal	102.7	.646	White R, Mon	80.5	.637
Kingery, Col	52.4	.552	Piazza, LA	103.0	.806	Whiten, Phi	45.3	.490
Klesko, Atl	78.2	.780	Puckett, Min	102.3	.661	Williams B, NYA	109.3	.666
Knoblauch, Min	115.2	.707	Raines, ChA	85.1	.594	Wilson D, Sea	54.1	.469
Lankford, StL	91.1	.671	Ramirez, Cle	108.9	.721	Young E, Col	75.0	.724
Lansing, Mon	54.3	.423	Reed J, SD	54.0	.447	Zeile, ChN	51.8	.423
Larkin, Cin	108.0	.758	Ripken C, Bal	74.0	.456			
Leius, Min	43.6	.377	Rodriguez I, Tex	68.9	.509			
Lemke, Atl	44.1	.382	Salmon, Cal	142.0	.801			
Lewis D, Cin	44.1	.299	Sanchez, ChN	44.3	.376			
Listach, Mil	25.4	.192	Sanders D, SF	48.0	.520			
Lofton, Cle	82.7	.600	Sanders R, Cin	115.4	.775			
Lopez, Atl	52.2	.607	Segui, Mon	74.2	.613			
Mabry, StL	53.5	.550	Seitzer, Mil	85.1	.615			
Macfarlane, Bos	48.3	.431	Sierra, NYA	70.3	.503			
Magadan, Hou	63.5	.684	Snow, Cal	87.2	.561			
Manwaring, SF	40.6	.383	Sojo, Sea	45.9	.472			
Martin A, Pit	68.2	.589	Sorrento, Cle	55.0	.557			
Martinez E, Sea	161.1	.860	Sosa, ChN	99.4	.645			
Martinez T, Sea	107.5	.691	Sprague, Tor	70.9	.447			
Mattingly, NYA	61.4	.462	Stanley, NYA	69.8	.581			
McGriff, Atl	88.8	.612	Steinbach, Oak	54.7	.461			
McGwire, Oak	102.2	.831	Stocker, Phi	37.7	.291			
McLemore, Tex	59.9	.416	Surhoff, Mil	78.7	.666			
McRae, ChN	89.8	.589	Tarasco, Mon	64.1	.550			
Meares, Min	48.2	.402	Tettleton, Tex	95.3	.693			
Merced, Pit	84.7	.657	Thomas, ChA	144.4	.813			
Miller O, Hou	37.2	.421	Thome, Cle	117.7	.790			
Molitor, Tor	82.4	.547	Thompson R, SF	38.8	.404			
Mondesi, LA	90.2	.632	Tinsley, Bos	50.0	.494			
Morandini, Phi	71.4	.551	Valentin J, Bos	119.0	.729			
Morris, Cin	51.6	.550	Valentin J, Mil	42.6	.392			
Munoz P, Min	56.3	.531	Vaughn G, Mil	51.7	.423			
Murray, Cle	83.7	.672	Vaughn M, Bos	121.1	.713			
Naehring, Bos	81.7	.644	Velarde, NYA	58.1	.550			
Nixon, Tex	76.8	.453	Ventura, ChA	98.7	.675			
Nunnally, KC	53.1	.580	Veras, Fla	72.3	.575			
O'Leary, Bos	68.0	.607	Vizcaino, NYN	60.8	.445			
O'Neill, NYA	90.2	.644	Vizquel, Cle	70.2	.428			
Offerman, LA	66.6	.583	Walbeck, Min	36.3	.285			
Olerud, Tor	81.0	.581	Walker, Col	114.1	.770			

Who Gets the Easy Saves? (p. 149)

Both Leagues — Listed Alphabetically
(1995 Relievers with a minimum of 3 Save Opportunities)

Reliever	Easy	Regular	Tough	Reliever	Easy	Regular	Tough
Acre, Oak	0/2	0/1	0/1	Leskanic, Col	1/2	6/7	3/7
Aguilera, Bos	17/17	12/13	3/6	Lilliquist, LA	0/0	0/0	0/3
Aquino, SF	0/0	1/2	1/2	Lira, Det	0/0	1/3	0/0
Arocha, StL	0/1	0/5	0/1	Lloyd, Mil	1/1	2/2	1/3
Ausanio, NYA	0/1	1/2	0/0	Mahomes, Min	0/0	3/4	0/3
Ayala, Sea	8/8	7/12	4/7	Mathews T, Fla	0/0	2/3	1/4
Barton, SF	0/0	1/2	0/2	McCaskill, ChA	0/1	1/1	1/3
Beck, SF	17/18	13/18	3/7	McDowell R, Tex	0/0	2/2	2/6
Belinda, Bos	6/6	3/6	1/2	McElroy, Cin	0/1	0/2	0/0
Benitez, Bal	1/1	1/1	0/3	McMichael, Atl	2/2	0/2	0/0
Berumen, SD	1/1	0/1	0/2	Meacham, KC	0/0	2/3	0/0
Bochtler, SD	0/0	1/3	0/1	Mesa, Cle	33/33	12/14	1/1
Boever, Det	0/0	3/4	0/2	Miceli, Pit	13/13	6/8	2/6
Borbon, Atl	0/0	1/1	1/3	Miranda, Mil	0/0	0/2	1/1
Borland, Phi	1/1	5/6	0/2	Montgomery, KC	12/12	16/22	3/4
Bottalico, Phi	0/1	1/2	0/2	Munoz M, Col	0/0	0/1	2/3
Brantley, Cin	10/10	17/19	1/3	Myers R, ChN	25/26	10/13	3/5
Brewer, KC	0/2	0/2	0/0	Nelson, Sea	0/0	2/3	0/1
Burrows, Tex	0/1	1/1	0/1	Nen, Fla	7/9	14/15	2/5
Carrasco, Cin	0/1	4/7	1/1	Olson, KC	0/0	1/2	2/3
Casian, ChN	0/0	0/0	0/3	Orosco, Bal	0/0	1/2	2/4
Castillo T, Tor	5/5	5/9	3/7	Percival, Cal	0/0	3/4	0/2
Charlton, Sea	5/5	6/8	3/3	Perez M, ChN	0/0	2/2	0/1
Christiansen, Pit	0/0	0/2	0/2	Perez Y, Fla	0/0	1/4	0/0
Clontz, Atl	2/2	2/3	0/1	Plesac, Pit	0/0	2/4	1/1
Corsi, Oak	0/0	2/4	0/0	Plunk, Cle	1/2	1/2	0/1
DeLeon, Mon	0/0	0/2	0/3	Radinsky, ChA	0/0	1/3	0/0
DiPoto, NYN	0/2	2/2	0/2	Reed S, Col	0/0	3/4	0/2
Doherty, Det	0/0	6/8	0/1	Rightnowar, Mil	1/1	0/2	0/1
Eckersley, Oak	20/21	7/14	2/3	Risley, Sea	1/2	0/2	0/3
Fetters, Mil	14/15	8/12	0/0	Rojas, Mon	7/8	22/28	1/3
Florie, SD	0/1	1/3	0/0	Ruffin B, Col	1/1	9/10	1/1
Franco, NYN	17/17	11/17	1/2	Russell, Tex	11/13	7/8	2/3
Gott, Pit	0/0	3/3	0/0	Ryan, Bos	1/1	6/9	0/0
Groom, Fla	0/0	1/1	0/2	Scott, Mon	1/1	1/2	0/2
Guardado, Min	1/1	1/1	0/3	Seanez, LA	1/1	0/0	2/3
Gunderson, Bos	0/0	0/1	0/2	Shaw, ChA	0/1	2/2	1/2
Hall, Tor	3/4	0/0	0/0	Slocumb, Phi	18/19	12/17	2/2
Hartgraves, Hou	0/0	0/0	0/3	Smith L, Cal	23/24	14/16	0/1
Henke, StL	19/19	12/14	5/5	Stanton, Bos	0/1	0/1	1/1
Henneman, Hou	14/14	10/12	2/3	Stevens, Min	4/4	3/4	3/4
Henry D, NYN	0/0	4/6	0/1	Tavarez, Cle	0/1	0/2	0/1
Henry D, Det	3/3	2/2	0/0	Timlin, Tor	0/0	4/4	1/5
Heredia G, Mon	0/0	1/1	0/2	Veres D, Hou	0/0	1/2	0/1
Hernandez R, ChA	17/17	13/19	2/6	Villone, SD	1/1	0/1	0/3
Hernandez X, Cin	0/0	3/4	0/0	Vosberg, Tex	1/1	3/4	0/3
Hickerson, Col	0/2	1/1	0/1	Walker M, ChN	0/0	1/2	0/1
Hoffman, SD	20/23	10/13	1/2	Wegman, Mil	0/0	2/2	0/1
Holmes, Col	9/10	2/4	3/4	Wetteland, NYA	22/23	6/11	3/3
Honeycutt, NYA	0/0	1/1	1/4	Whiteside M, Tex	1/1	2/3	0/0
Howe, NYA	1/1	1/1	0/1	Wickander, Mil	0/0	0/0	1/3
Hudek, Hou	3/3	1/3	3/3	Wickman, NYA	0/0	0/7	1/3
Hudson, Bos	0/0	1/3	0/1	Wohlers, Atl	9/9	13/15	3/5
Jackson M, Cin	1/1	1/1	0/2	Worrell T, LA	15/16	12/15	5/5
Jones D, Bal	10/10	12/14	0/1	**AL Totals**	**231/253**	**211/333**	**51/154**
Jones T, Hou	5/5	9/13	1/2	**NL Totals**	**217/246**	**240/351**	**56/146**
Leiper, Mon	0/0	1/2	1/1	**MLB Totals**	**320/364**	**355/530**	**102/274**

Who Pitched Better Last Year: Martinez or Candiotti? (p. 152)

In the table below, **Sup** stands for Run Support Per Nine Innings. **RS** is the total Runs In Support for that pitcher while he was in the game.

Both Leagues — Listed Alphabetically
(minimum 20 games started in 1995)

Pitcher, Team	W/L	ERA	Sup	IP	RS	Pitcher, Team	W/L	ERA	Sup	IP	RS
Abbott J, Cal	11-8	3.70	5.03	197.0	110	Leiter M, SF	10-11	3.68	3.73	193.0	80
Alvarez W, ChA	8-11	4.32	5.55	175.0	108	Lira, Det	7-10	4.30	3.63	121.1	49
Appier, KC	15-10	3.89	5.81	201.1	130	Loaiza, Pit	8-9	5.25	4.93	169.2	93
Ashby, SD	12-10	2.94	4.39	192.2	94	Maddux G, Atl	19-2	1.63	4.34	209.2	101
Avery, Atl	7-13	4.67	4.36	173.1	84	Martinez D, Cle	12-5	3.08	5.87	187.0	122
Belcher, Sea	10-12	4.52	4.37	179.1	87	Martinez P, Mon	14-10	3.51	4.30	194.2	93
Benes A, Sea	11-9	4.76	6.04	181.2	122	Martinez R, LA	17-7	3.66	5.32	206.1	122
Bere, ChA	8-15	7.19	5.56	137.2	85	McDowell J, NYA	15-10	3.93	5.17	217.2	125
Bergman, Det	7-10	5.12	5.25	135.1	79	Mercker, Atl	7-8	4.24	5.72	140.0	89
Bones, Mil	10-12	4.60	5.50	199.2	122	Mlicki, NYN	8-7	4.40	5.56	155.1	96
Bosio, Sea	10-8	4.92	6.46	170.0	122	Moore, Det	5-15	7.53	5.83	132.2	86
Boskie, Cal	7-7	5.64	5.00	111.2	62	Morgan, StL	7-7	3.56	4.25	131.1	62
Brown, Bal	10-9	3.60	4.91	172.1	94	Mulholland, SF	5-13	5.83	4.66	139.0	72
Bullinger, ChN	12-8	4.14	5.94	150.0	99	Mussina, Bal	19-9	3.29	4.91	221.2	121
Burkett, Fla	14-14	4.30	5.11	188.1	107	Nagy, Cle	16-6	4.55	8.14	178.0	161
Candiotti, LA	7-14	3.50	3.45	190.1	73	Navarro, ChN	14-6	3.28	4.90	200.1	109
Castillo F, ChN	11-10	3.21	4.16	188.0	87	Neagle, Pit	13-8	3.43	5.37	209.2	125
Clark M, Cle	8-7	5.43	4.98	119.1	66	Nomo, LA	13-6	2.54	4.75	191.1	101
Clemens, Bos	10-5	4.18	5.85	140.0	91	Ontiveros, Oak	9-6	4.37	5.62	129.2	81
Cone, NYA	18-8	3.57	6.51	229.1	166	Pavlik, Tex	10-10	4.37	4.41	191.2	94
Darling, Oak	4-7	6.23	5.37	104.0	62	Perez C, Mon	10-8	3.72	4.66	135.1	70
Drabek, Hou	10-9	4.77	5.35	185.0	110	Petkovsek, StL	5-6	4.16	4.02	125.1	56
Erickson, Bal	13-10	4.79	6.82	195.1	148	Pettitte, NYA	12-9	4.13	5.20	168.0	97
Fassero, Mon	13-14	4.33	5.52	189.0	116	Portugal, Cin	11-10	4.01	6.19	181.2	125
Fernandez A, ChA	12-8	3.80	5.79	203.2	131	Quantrill, Phi	10-12	4.86	4.65	172.1	89
Finley, Cal	15-12	4.21	6.65	203.0	150	Radke, Min	11-14	5.26	4.90	178.0	97
Foster, ChN	12-11	4.55	5.86	164.1	107	Rapp, Fla	14-7	3.44	6.19	167.1	115
Glavine, Atl	16-7	3.08	4.94	198.2	109	Reynolds, Hou	10-11	3.47	5.09	189.1	107
Gordon, KC	12-12	4.43	4.76	189.0	100	Ritz, Col	11-11	4.37	4.92	164.2	90
Green, Phi	8-9	5.18	4.92	139.0	76	Rogers K, Tex	17-7	3.38	5.41	208.0	125
Gross, Tex	9-15	5.58	5.18	180.2	104	Saberhagen, Col	7-6	4.18	5.24	153.0	89
Gubicza, KC	12-14	3.75	3.97	213.1	94	Schourek, Cin	18-7	3.22	5.49	190.1	116
Guzman, Tor	4-14	6.32	3.79	135.1	57	Smiley, Cin	12-5	3.43	4.66	175.2	91
Hamilton, SD	6-9	3.11	3.55	202.2	80	Smith Z, Bos	8-8	5.69	7.42	104.1	86
Hammond, Fla	9-6	3.83	5.75	159.2	102	Smoltz, Atl	12-7	3.18	4.81	192.2	103
Hampton, Hou	9-8	3.35	5.56	150.2	93	Sparks, Mil	9-11	4.62	5.21	183.0	106
Hanson, Bos	15-5	4.24	6.61	186.2	137	Stottlemyre, Oak	14-7	4.55	6.48	209.2	151
Harkey, Cal	7-8	5.70	4.95	107.1	59	Swindell, Hou	8-9	4.44	5.61	146.0	91
Henry B, Mon	7-9	2.84	4.05	126.2	57	Tapani, LA	10-13	4.99	5.32	187.2	111
Hentgen, Tor	10-14	5.11	5.11	200.2	114	Tewksbury, Tex	8-7	4.58	6.87	129.2	99
Hershiser, Cle	16-6	3.87	6.08	167.1	113	Trachsel, ChN	7-13	5.15	5.09	159.0	90
Hill, Cle	10-8	4.62	5.75	183.0	117	Valdes I, LA	13-11	3.06	4.16	188.0	87
Hitchcock, NYA	11-10	4.70	5.45	168.1	102	Wagner P, Pit	4-14	4.84	3.73	147.0	61
Johnson, Sea	18-2	2.48	5.12	214.1	122	Wakefield, Bos	16-8	2.95	4.98	195.1	108
Jones B, NYN	10-10	4.19	5.01	195.2	109	Wells D, Cin	16-8	3.24	5.28	203.0	119
Kile, Hou	4-12	4.87	4.13	122.0	56	Witt, Tex	5-11	4.13	3.77	172.0	72
Langston, Cal	15-7	4.63	7.19	200.1	160	**MLB Average**		4.53	5.17		
Leiter A, Tor	11-11	3.64	3.84	183.0	78						

Is Greg Maddux the Best. . . Ever? (p. 154)

Pitchers' Four-Year Relative ERA
(Minimum of 144 Innings per Season)

Pitcher	Years	ERA	League ERA	Ratio	Pitcher	Years	ERA	League ERA	Ratio
Walter Johnson	1910-13	1.43	3.03	.4719	Walter Johnson	1908-11	1.75	2.68	.6530
Walter Johnson	1912-15	1.45	2.98	.4866	Bob Gibson	1968-71	2.32	3.55	.6535
Walter Johnson	1911-14	1.53	3.08	.4968	Jim Palmer	1975-78	2.49	3.80	.6553
Greg Maddux	1992-95	1.98	3.98	.4975	Christy Mathewson	1902- 5	1.92	2.93	.6553
Three Finger Brown	1906- 9	1.31	2.51	.5219	Dwight Gooden	1984-87	2.46	3.75	.6560
Sandy Koufax	1963-66	1.86	3.49	.5330	Cy Young	1901- 4	1.96	2.98	.6577
Walter Johnson	1913-16	1.58	2.85	.5544	Kid Nichols	1896-99	2.64	4.01	.6584
Sandy Koufax	1962-65	2.02	3.58	.5642	Walter Johnson	1914-17	1.84	2.79	.6595
Christy Mathewson	1908-11	1.62	2.84	.5704	Juan Marichal	1963-66	2.31	3.49	.6619
Three Finger Brown	1905- 8	1.50	2.61	.5747	Jim Palmer	1972-75	2.37	3.58	.6620
Lefty Grove	1928-31	2.49	4.32	.5764	Ron Guidry	1977-80	2.67	4.03	.6625
Ed Walsh	1907-10	1.43	2.48	.5766	Tom Seaver	1969-72	2.42	3.65	.6630
Walter Johnson	1909-12	1.68	2.91	.5773	Dolf Luque	1922-25	2.69	4.05	.6642
Lefty Grove	1929-32	2.56	4.43	.5779	Hal Newhouser	1942-45	2.29	3.44	.6657
Three Finger Brown	1907-10	1.51	2.61	.5785	Rube Waddell	1904- 7	1.83	2.74	.6679
Christy Mathewson	1909-12	1.81	3.10	.5839	Joe Horlen	1964-67	2.30	3.44	.6686
Three Finger Brown	1904- 7	1.59	2.70	.5889	Dazzy Vance	1928-31	2.93	4.38	.6689
Ed Walsh	1908-11	1.58	2.68	.5896	Rube Waddell	1902- 5	1.88	2.81	.6690
Carl Hubbell	1931-34	2.25	3.78	.5952	Eddie Cicotte	1916-19	1.92	2.86	.6713
Lefty Grove	1930-33	2.65	4.45	.5955	Jim Palmer	1973-76	2.48	3.69	.6721
Lefty Grove	1936-39	2.87	4.77	.6017	Roger Clemens	1988-91	2.67	3.97	.6725
Walter Johnson	1916-19	1.73	2.86	.6049	Juan Marichal	1964-67	2.37	3.51	.6752
Lefty Grove	1935-38	2.88	4.73	.6089	Lefty Grove	1937-40	3.11	4.60	.6761
Bob Gibson	1966-69	2.08	3.40	.6118	Dolf Luque	1923-26	2.70	3.99	.6767
Carl Hubbell	1933-36	2.38	3.86	.6166	Chief Bender	1909-12	1.97	2.91	.6770
Ed Walsh	1909-12	1.80	2.91	.6186	Rube Waddell	1903- 6	1.91	2.82	.6773
Ed Walsh	1906- 9	1.56	2.52	.6190	Lefty Grove	1926-29	2.78	4.10	.6780
Christy Mathewson	1907-10	1.62	2.61	.6207	Lefty Gomez	1935-38	3.21	4.73	.6786
Walter Johnson	1915-18	1.74	2.80	.6214	Doc White	1904- 7	1.86	2.74	.6788
Christy Mathewson	1910-13	2.02	3.25	.6215	Roger Clemens	1990-93	2.77	4.08	.6789
Greg Maddux	1991-94	2.41	3.86	.6244	Jose Rijo	1990-93	2.56	3.77	.6790
Hal Newhouser	1944-47	2.20	3.50	.6286	Jose Rijo	1991-94	2.63	3.86	.6813
Lefty Gomez	1934-37	2.93	4.65	.6301	Roger Clemens	1987-90	2.77	4.06	.6823
Dazzy Vance	1927-30	2.78	4.39	.6333	Old Hoss Radbourn	1883-86	2.09	3.06	.6830
Tom Seaver	1968-71	2.25	3.55	.6338	Red Ruffing	1937-40	3.15	4.60	.6848
Cy Young	1899- 2	2.31	3.64	.6346	Pete Alexander	1913-16	1.94	2.83	.6855
Addie Joss	1906- 9	1.60	2.52	.6349	Lefty Gomez	1936-39	3.27	4.77	.6855
Carl Hubbell	1932-35	2.43	3.82	.6361	Amos Rusie	1891-94	2.86	4.17	.6859
Old Hoss Radbourn	1882-85	1.88	2.95	.6373	Kevin Appier	1990-93	2.80	4.08	.6863
Three Finger Brown	1908-11	1.81	2.84	.6373	Cy Young	1900- 3	2.19	3.19	.6865
Hal Newhouser	1943-46	2.17	3.40	.6382	Whitey Ford	1953-56	2.72	3.96	.6869
Roger Clemens	1989-92	2.54	3.97	.6398	Kid Nichols	1897- 0	2.66	3.87	.6873
Hal Newhouser	1945-48	2.38	3.71	.6415	Carl Hubbell	1934-37	2.75	4.00	.6875
Pete Alexander	1914-17	1.74	2.71	.6421	Tim Keefe	1885-88	2.29	3.33	.6877
Bob Gibson	1967-70	2.27	3.53	.6431	Tom Seaver	1971-74	2.45	3.56	.6882
Three Finger Brown	1903- 6	1.86	2.89	.6436	Bob Gibson	1965-68	2.33	3.38	.6882
Old Hoss Radbourn	1881-84	1.90	2.95	.6441	Red Ruffing	1936-39	3.29	4.77	.6897
Doc White	1903- 6	1.82	2.82	.6454	Clark Griffith	1898- 1	2.56	3.71	.6900
Carl Hubbell	1930-33	2.60	4.01	.6484	Addie Joss	1904- 7	1.81	2.62	.6908
Kid Nichols	1895-98	2.75	4.24	.6486	Juan Marichal	1966-69	2.35	3.40	.6912
Cy Young	1898- 1	2.41	3.71	.6496	Bob Feller	1937-40	3.18	4.60	.6913
Lefty Grove	1927-30	2.77	4.26	.6502	Stan Coveleski	1917-20	2.16	3.12	.6923
Tom Seaver	1970-73	2.38	3.66	.6503	Cy Young	1892-95	3.09	4.46	.6928
Ed Reulbach	1905- 8	1.70	2.61	.6513	Harry Brecheen	1945-48	2.64	3.81	.6929
Sandy Koufax	1961-64	2.40	3.68	.6522	Orval Overall	1907-10	1.81	2.61	.6935
Addie Joss	1905- 8	1.67	2.56	.6523	Lefty Gomez	1933-36	3.17	4.57	.6937

Who Are Baseball's Best-Hitting Pitchers? (p. 158)

1995 Active Pitchers — Listed Alphabetically
(minimum 50 plate appearances lifetime)

Pitcher, Team	AVG	AB	H	HR	RBI	Pitcher, Team	AVG	AB	H	HR	RBI
Aguilera, Bos	.203	138	28	3	11	Mercker, Atl	.068	117	8	0	9
Arocha, StL	.103	68	7	0	3	Mlicki, NYN	.051	39	2	0	2
Ashby, SD	.146	157	23	0	5	Morgan, StL	.091	385	35	0	12
Astacio, LA	.121	157	19	0	3	Mulholland, SF	.081	405	33	1	9
Avery, Atl	.171	362	62	2	20	Myers R, ChN	.186	59	11	0	7
Banks, Phi	.179	67	12	0	1	Nabholz, ChN	.107	178	19	0	4
Bedrosian, Atl	.098	153	15	0	2	Navarro, ChN	.185	65	12	0	7
Benes A, Sea	.126	374	47	4	24	Neagle, Pit	.121	141	17	2	15
Blair, SD	.060	83	5	0	5	Nied, Col	.143	70	10	0	2
Bowen, Fla	.176	102	18	0	3	Nomo, LA	.091	66	6	0	4
Brantley, Cin	.119	67	8	0	5	Olivares, Phi	.229	201	46	4	21
Brocail, Hou	.196	56	11	0	1	Osborne, StL	.159	138	22	0	7
Bullinger, ChN	.156	90	14	1	11	Painter, Col	.175	40	7	0	3
Burba, Cin	.140	50	7	0	3	Palacios, StL	.045	88	4	0	0
Burkett, Fla	.076	367	28	0	13	Pena, Atl	.110	181	20	1	7
Candiotti, LA	.122	221	27	0	8	Perez C, Mon	.133	45	6	1	5
Castillo F, ChN	.114	211	24	0	6	Portugal, Cin	.197	345	68	2	31
Charlton, Sea	.093	86	8	0	1	Pugh, Cin	.202	109	22	0	4
Darling, Oak	.144	526	76	2	21	Quantrill, Phi	.100	60	6	0	0
DeLeon, Mon	.091	419	38	0	9	Rapp, Fla	.131	130	17	0	9
Deshaies, Phi	.088	373	33	0	12	Reynolds, Hou	.137	102	14	0	3
Drabek, Hou	.166	658	109	2	43	Reynoso, Col	.126	119	15	2	4
Eckersley, Oak	.133	180	24	3	12	Rijo, Cin	.193	429	83	2	29
Fassero, Mon	.070	143	10	0	1	Ritz, Col	.132	68	9	0	2
Fernandez S, Phi	.185	519	96	1	32	Rojas, Mon	.080	50	4	0	0
Foster, ChN	.191	89	17	1	9	Roper, SF	.177	62	11	0	4
Freeman, Col	.111	99	11	2	7	Rueter, Mon	.079	76	6	0	5
Gardner, Fla	.114	201	23	0	8	Ruffin B, Col	.082	294	24	0	7
Glavine, Atl	.187	556	104	1	41	Saberhagen, Col	.128	180	23	0	1
Gott, Pit	.178	73	13	4	5	Sanders, SD	.173	75	13	0	6
Green, Phi	.174	46	8	1	5	Schilling, Phi	.152	210	32	0	10
Greene, Phi	.219	210	46	4	18	Schourek, Cin	.163	178	29	1	13
Hamilton, SD	.067	105	7	0	4	Smiley, Cin	.141	396	56	2	27
Hammond, Fla	.215	214	46	4	14	Smith P, Cin	.116	233	27	0	11
Hampton, Hou	.143	49	7	0	0	Smoltz, Atl	.142	457	65	3	23
Harnisch, NYN	.125	264	33	0	14	Swift, Col	.211	199	42	1	13
Harris G, Mon	.221	68	15	0	4	Swindell, Hou	.188	234	44	0	13
Henry B, Mon	.139	151	21	1	12	Tewksbury, Tex	.152	309	47	0	16
Heredia G, Mon	.218	78	17	0	3	Trachsel, ChN	.224	98	22	0	6
Hickerson, Col	.149	74	11	0	7	Urbani, StL	.254	59	15	1	4
Hill, Cle	.148	324	48	1	19	Valdes I, LA	.094	64	6	0	1
Honeycutt, NYA	.133	181	24	0	8	Valenzuela, SD	.204	851	174	10	80
Jackson D, StL	.123	399	49	0	24	VanLandingham, SF	.117	77	9	1	4
Jones B, NYN	.123	122	15	0	3	Viola, Cin	.141	185	26	0	6
Kile, Hou	.102	206	21	1	12	Wagner P, Pit	.194	124	24	0	7
Leiter M, SF	.098	61	6	0	5	Watson, StL	.270	100	27	0	12
Lieber, Pit	.083	60	5	0	0	Weathers, Fla	.100	80	8	0	1
Loaiza, Pit	.192	52	10	0	2	West, Phi	.167	48	8	1	5
Maddux G, Atl	.182	716	130	2	35	Williams B, SD	.163	80	13	0	7
Maddux M, Bos	.068	88	6	0	4	Williams M, Phi	.180	50	9	0	6
Martinez P, Mon	.097	113	11	0	7	Wilson T, SF	.176	193	34	2	14
Martinez R, LA	.153	451	69	1	29	Young, ChN	.163	92	15	0	4
McMurtry, Hou	.098	153	15	0	4						

How Dominant Was Percival? (p. 160)

Lowest Hit to Innings Pitched Ratio
(Minimum 50 Innings Pitched)

Player	Year	Hits	Innings	Hits/9 IP
Troy Percival	1995	37	74.0	4.500
Mike Naymick	1943	32	63.0	4.571
Rob Murphy	1986	26	50.1	4.649
Vicente Romo	1968	44	84.0	4.714
Jim Brewer	1972	41	78.0	4.731
Ryne Duren	1958	40	76.0	4.737
Andy Messersmith	1968	44	81.0	4.889
Steve Mingori	1971	31	57.0	4.895
Dennis Eckersley	1989	32	57.2	4.994
Toad Ramsey	1885	44	79.0	5.013
Dennis Eckersley	1990	41	73.1	5.032
Ferdie Schupp	1916	79	140.0	5.079
J.R. Richard	1980	65	114.0	5.132
Ricky Bottalico	1995	50	87.2	5.133
Junior Thompson	1946	36	63.0	5.143
Moe Drabowsky	1968	35	61.0	5.164
John Shaffer	1886	40	69.0	5.217
Mitch Williams	1987	63	108.2	5.218
Tom Niedenfuer	1983	55	94.2	5.229
Nolan Ryan	1972	166	284.0	5.261
Goose Gossage	1977	78	133.0	5.278
Luis Tiant	1968	152	258.0	5.302
Nolan Ryan	1991	102	173.0	5.306
Tommy Byrne	1948	79	134.0	5.306
Ed Reulbach	1906	129	218.0	5.326
Bill Risley	1994	31	52.1	5.331
Nick Maddox	1907	32	54.0	5.333
Ken Tatum	1969	51	86.0	5.337
Dave LaRoche	1976	57	96.0	5.344
Ted Abernathy	1967	63	106.0	5.349
Jim Poole	1993	30	50.1	5.364
Bill Henry	1964	31	52.0	5.365
Don Mossi	1954	56	93.0	5.419
Don Carman	1985	52	86.1	5.421
Steve Ontiveros	1985	45	74.2	5.424
Mike Fetters	1992	38	62.2	5.457
Tom Hall	1970	94	155.0	5.458
Red Ruffing	1946	37	61.0	5.459
Ray Narleski	1956	36	59.0	5.492
Hoyt Wilhelm	1965	88	144.0	5.500
Willie Ramsdell	1952	41	67.0	5.507
Julio Solano	1984	31	50.2	5.507
Chris Nabholz	1990	43	70.0	5.529
Diego Segui	1968	51	83.0	5.530
Craig McMurtry	1988	37	60.0	5.550
Hoyt Wilhelm	1966	50	81.0	5.556
Dutch Leonard	1914	139	225.0	5.560
Joey Jay	1958	60	97.0	5.567
Jeff Russell	1989	45	72.2	5.573
Tom Hall	1972	77	124.0	5.589
Don McMahon	1967	68	109.1	5.598
Don McMahon	1969	38	61.0	5.607
Rob Dibble	1989	62	99.0	5.636
Jim Hearn	1950	84	134.0	5.642
Henry Porter	1884	32	51.0	5.647
Carl Lundgren	1907	130	207.0	5.652
Derek Lilliquist	1992	39	61.2	5.692
Jeff Gray	1991	39	61.2	5.692

Are High-Pitch Outings on the Way Out? (p. 162)

Most Pitches In a Game By Starting Pitchers in 1995

Date	Opp	Score	Pitcher	W/L	IP	H	R	ER	BB	SO	#Pit	Time
7/7	@Cle	5- 3	Johnson, Sea	W	9.0	8	3	2	0	13	161	3:11
6/12	NYA	6- 1	Wells D, Cin	W	8.2	4	1	1	5	7	158	3:07
8/17	Sea	3- 2	Van Poppel, Oak		7.0	6	2	2	3	5	153	3:13
7/3	SD	5- 2	Burkett, Fla	W	9.0	7	2	1	3	7	148	2:33
5/18	@ChA	2- 4	Stewart, Oak	L	7.0	9	4	4	3	6	148	2:49
9/22	Cal	8- 3	Rogers K, Tex	W	9.0	7	3	3	5	3	148	3:13
5/23	NYA	10- 0	Finley, Cal	W	9.0	2	0	0	2	15	147	3:10
8/4	@Cal	6- 4	Rogers K, Tex	W	7.2	7	4	4	3	8	147	3:07
8/24	NYA	9- 7	Benes A, Sea		7.0	8	7	7	6	5	147	3:00
5/21	Mil	6- 0	Rogers K, Tex	W	9.0	5	0	0	3	5	146	2:59
7/7	@Cal	9- 3	Sparks, Mil	W	9.0	4	3	2	7	3	146	2:52
8/10	@Mil	8- 4	Hentgen, Tor	W	8.0	9	3	2	2	6	144	3:12
8/6	LA	3- 1	Leiter M, SF	W	9.0	5	1	1	2	10	144	2:41
9/11	@Cle	4- 0	McDowell J, NYA	W	9.0	4	0	0	4	8	144	2:52
5/31	@Phi	4- 1	Martinez R, LA	W	9.0	3	1	1	7	6	143	3:05
6/28	@Min	4- 3	Bere, ChA	W	8.1	6	3	2	4	14	143	2:42
7/4	NYA	1- 4	Fernandez A, ChA	L	8.2	8	4	4	2	5	143	2:49
5/21	@Tex	0- 6	Scanlan, Mil	L	6.2	7	6	6	7	3	142	2:59
6/13	Fla	7- 3	Saberhagen, Col	W	8.0	8	3	3	2	10	142	2:48
9/20	SF	4- 2	Martinez R, LA	W	8.0	7	2	2	2	5	142	2:41
5/21	Bal	5- 0	Hitchcock, NYA	W	9.0	4	0	0	1	8	141	2:47
7/20	SF	11- 4	Drabek, Hou	W	8.2	9	4	3	2	6	141	2:59
6/5	@Bal	2- 0	Johnson, Sea	W	9.0	3	0	0	1	12	141	2:36
6/8	@SF	9- 6	Mlicki, NYN	W	7.1	8	5	5	3	6	141	3:18
6/19	@Col	7- 2	Hammond, Fla	W	9.0	12	2	2	5	3	141	2:47
7/15	Tor	3- 0	Johnson, Sea	W	9.0	3	0	0	2	16	141	2:46
7/16	@Det	6- 4	Finley, Cal	W	7.0	7	4	4	3	6	141	3:17
9/6	Cal	4- 2	Mussina, Bal	W	7.2	5	2	2	2	7	141	3:35
9/9	Bos	9- 1	Pettitte, NYA	W	8.2	7	1	1	1	7	141	2:39
9/17	Mil	5- 0	Leiter A, Tor	W	9.0	6	0	0	2	10	141	2:27
9/23	@Min	14- 4	Alvarez W, ChA	W	9.0	7	4	3	3	5	141	3:04
5/16	@Mil	5- 0	Hanson, Bos	W	9.0	4	0	0	0	10	140	2:35
6/10	@NYA	3- 2	Johnson, Sea		7.0	5	2	2	4	12	140	3:03
6/14	@Sea	2- 1	Appier, KC	W	6.2	6	1	1	4	11	140	3:04
9/23	Det	5- 2	Cone, NYA	W	8.0	4	2	2	6	10	140	2:44
8/12	Cle	3- 2	McDowell J, NYA	W	9.0	7	2	2	3	4	140	2:53

Fewest Pitches In a 9-Inning Complete Game By Starting Pitchers in 1995

Date	Opp	Score	Pitcher	W/L	IP	H	R	ER	BB	SO	#Pit	Time
6/15	@Mon	2- 0	Maddux G, Atl	W	9.0	7	0	0	0	3	88	2:25
8/20	@StL	1- 0	Maddux G, Atl	W	9.0	2	0	0	0	9	88	1:50
8/31	Hou	5- 2	Maddux G, Atl	W	9.0	6	2	2	1	4	88	2:28
8/6	@Min	11- 1	Gubicza, KC	W	9.0	4	1	1	0	1	89	2:17
9/27	@Tor	7- 0	Erickson, Bal	W	9.0	3	0	0	0	5	91	2:20
6/14	@StL	3- 0	Hamilton, SD	W	9.0	2	0	0	2	3	92	1:59
6/23	@Atl	9- 3	Saberhagen, Col	W	9.0	6	3	3	0	3	93	2:16
8/27	SF	1- 0	Rueter, Mon	W	9.0	1	0	0	1	7	94	1:54
9/8	@Mon	5- 0	Jones B, NYN	W	9.0	3	0	0	2	6	95	2:23
7/7	NYA	10- 0	Tewksbury, Tex	W	9.0	6	0	0	0	5	96	2:23
9/19	StL	12- 1	Wagner P, Pit	W	9.0	7	1	1	2	4	96	2:18
5/28	@Hou	3- 1	Maddux G, Atl	W	9.0	1	1	1	1	7	97	2:19
9/2	NYN	5- 3	Valdez S, SF	W	9.0	4	3	3	0	4	98	2:00
9/18	Cal	4- 0	Johns, Oak	W	9.0	2	0	0	2	2	98	2:29
7/18	@NYA	9- 4	Abbott J, Cal	W	9.0	13	4	4	0	4	99	2:57
6/18	@StL	6- 1	Portugal, Cin	W	9.0	5	1	1	2	4	99	2:08
7/6	Sea	8- 1	Ogea, Cle	W	9.0	3	1	1	0	3	99	2:13
8/7	Bal	3- 0	McDowell J, NYA	W	9.0	3	0	0	3	5	99	2:24
10/1	Bos	8- 1	Karl, Mil	W	9.0	6	1	1	0	2	99	1:57
9/24	ChA	4- 3	Hawkins, Min	W	9.0	5	3	3	0	4	100	2:24

What Relievers *Really* Put Out the Fires? (p. 164)

The table below shows the percentage (%) of Inherited Runners (**IR**) each relief pitcher allowed to score (**SC**)

Both Leagues — Listed Alphabetically
(minimum 20 inherited runners in 1995)

Pitcher, Team	IR	SC	%	Pitcher, Team	IR	SC	%	Pitcher, Team	IR	SC	%
Abbott K, Phi	20	5	25.0	Franco, NYN	21	5	23.8	Nelson, Sea	57	14	24.6
Acre, Oak	37	16	43.2	Gardner, Fla	21	2	9.5	Oquist, Bal	32	18	56.3
Aquino, SF	31	17	54.8	Groom, Fla	27	13	48.1	Orosco, Bal	66	15	22.7
Assenmacher, Cle	28	3	10.7	Guardado, Min	40	14	35.0	Painter, Col	27	6	22.2
Ausanio, NYA	20	7	35.0	Gunderson, Bos	47	16	34.0	Patterson B, Cal	66	14	21.2
Ayala, Sea	34	16	47.1	Guthrie, LA	42	10	23.8	Percival, Cal	53	9	17.0
Barton, SF	53	14	26.4	Habyan, Cal	37	8	21.6	Perez M, ChN	53	16	30.2
Bautista, SF	32	13	40.6	Harris G, Mon	38	11	28.9	Perez Y, Fla	42	6	14.3
Beck, SF	34	9	26.5	Hartgraves, Hou	39	11	28.2	Plesac, Pit	40	11	27.5
Bedrosian, Atl	30	16	53.3	Henneman, Hou	24	16	66.7	Plunk, Cle	26	5	19.2
Belinda, Bos	52	16	30.8	Henry D, NYN	22	11	50.0	Poole, Cle	27	4	14.8
Benitez, Bal	46	16	34.8	Hernandez R, ChA	33	16	48.5	Radinsky, ChA	48	10	20.8
Blair, SD	22	10	45.5	Hernandez X, Cin	21	10	47.6	Reed S, Col	53	13	24.5
Bochtler, SD	32	7	21.9	Hickerson, Col	31	11	35.5	Reyes C, Oak	26	11	42.3
Boever, Det	53	24	45.3	Holmes, Col	33	8	24.2	Rightnowar, Mil	35	9	25.7
Bohanon, Det	44	17	38.6	Honeycutt, NYA	41	13	31.7	Risley, Sea	34	16	47.1
Borbon, Atl	29	5	17.2	Hook, SF	29	13	44.8	Rojas, Mon	23	8	34.8
Bottalico, Phi	36	13	36.1	Howe, NYA	36	14	38.9	Russell, Tex	24	9	37.5
Brewer, KC	49	18	36.7	Hudson, Bos	32	15	46.9	Schullstrom, Min	36	15	41.7
Briscoe, Oak	22	9	40.9	Ignasiak, Mil	24	13	54.2	Scott, Mon	56	7	12.5
Brocail, Hou	22	9	40.9	James, Cal	42	15	35.7	Seanez, LA	22	10	45.5
Burba, Cin	24	8	33.3	Jones T, Hou	35	11	31.4	Shaw, ChA	29	3	10.3
Burrows, Tex	26	6	23.1	Jordan, Tor	21	12	57.1	Springer R, Phi	21	8	38.1
Butcher, Cal	35	17	48.6	Karchner, ChA	26	9	34.6	Stanton, Bos	33	9	27.3
Casian, ChN	41	11	26.8	Lee, Bal	39	6	15.4	Stevens, Min	40	12	30.0
Castillo T, Tor	55	26	47.3	Leiper, Mon	34	12	35.3	Tabaka, Hou	30	7	23.3
Charlton, Sea	38	8	21.1	Leskanic, Col	46	8	17.4	Tavarez, Cle	36	7	19.4
Christiansen, Pit	46	16	34.8	Lilliquist, LA	23	9	39.1	Timlin, Tor	27	12	44.4
Christopher, Det	33	3	9.1	Lloyd, Mil	23	7	30.4	Veres D, Hou	48	16	33.3
Clark T, Bal	39	11	28.2	MacDonald, NYA	25	9	36.0	Veres R, Fla	43	15	34.9
Clontz, Atl	33	10	30.3	Maddux M, Bos	25	13	52.0	Villone, SD	23	12	52.2
Cook, Tex	47	18	38.3	Magnante, KC	37	14	37.8	Vosberg, Tex	49	14	28.6
Cormier, Bos	29	6	20.7	Mahomes, Min	39	16	41.0	Walker M, ChN	35	11	31.4
Corsi, Oak	20	3	15.0	Mathews T, Fla	35	13	37.1	Watkins, Min	29	8	27.6
Cummings, LA	30	6	20.0	Maxcy, Det	39	14	35.9	Wells B, Sea	28	6	21.4
Daal, LA	28	8	28.6	McCaskill, ChA	41	9	22.0	Wendell, ChN	35	12	34.3
DeLeon, Mon	45	12	26.7	Mccurry, Pit	37	10	27.0	Wetteland, NYA	24	7	29.2
DeLucia, StL	28	11	39.3	McDowell R, Tex	66	15	22.7	Whiteside M, Tex	36	7	19.4
Dewey, SF	23	9	39.1	McElroy, Cin	37	16	43.2	Wickander, Mil	32	10	31.3
Dibble, Mil	34	11	32.4	McMichael, Atl	22	3	13.6	Wickman, NYA	53	15	28.3
DiPoto, NYN	29	7	24.1	Meacham, KC	40	23	57.5	Williams M, Phi	28	7	25.0
Doherty, Det	27	7	25.9	Miceli, Pit	24	11	45.8	Williams M, Cal	20	10	50.0
Dougherty, Hou	49	16	32.7	Mills, Bal	24	12	50.0	Wohlers, Atl	28	9	32.1
Dyer, Pit	39	9	23.1	Miranda, Mil	20	4	20.0	Worrell T, LA	26	10	38.5
Embree, Cle	20	2	10.0	Mohler, Oak	29	7	24.1	Young, ChN	22	7	31.8
Eversgerd, Mon	25	10	40.0	Montgomery, KC	20	10	50.0	**MLB Avg**			**32.9**
Florie, SD	35	12	34.3	Munoz M, Col	43	10	23.3				
Fortugno, Cal	29	5	17.2	Myers R, ChN	37	10	27.0				
Fossas, StL	51	12	23.5	Nabholz, ChN	33	8	24.2				

Who Holds the Fort? (p. 166)

A Hold (**H**) is a Save Opportunity passed on to the next pitcher. If a pitcher comes into the game in a Save Situation and leaves the game having gotten at least one out and without having blown the lead, this is a "passed on" Save Opportunity and the pitcher is credited with a Hold.

Both Leagues — Listed By Most Holds
(minimum 2 Holds in 1995)

Pitcher, Team	H	Pitcher, Team	H	Pitcher, Team	H	Pitcher, Team	H
Percival, Cal	29	Hickerson, Col	9	Seanez, LA	6	Eversgerd, Mon	3
Wickman, NYA	21	Jackson M, Cin	9	Shaw, ChA	6	Fortugno, Cal	3
Bottalico, Phi	20	Lloyd, Mil	9	Villone, SD	6	Fraser, Mon	3
McMichael, Atl	20	Mahomes, Min	9	Bailey R, Col	5	Gohr, Det	3
Fossas, StL	19	McDowell R, Tex	9	Bautista, SF	5	Gott, Pit	3
Leskanic, Col	19	Veres R, Fla	9	Berumen, SD	5	Harris G, Mon	3
Scott, Mon	19	Bochtler, SD	8	Burba, Cin	5	Ignasiak, Mil	3
Tavarez, Cle	19	DiPoto, NYN	8	Castillo T, Tor	5	James, Cal	3
Veres D, Hou	19	Hudson, Bos	8	Christopher, Det	5	Lieber, Pit	3
Belinda, Bos	17	Jones T, Hou	8	Dewey, SF	5	Martinez P, Hou	3
Perez M, ChN	16	McCaskill, ChA	8	Doherty, Det	5	McElroy, Cin	3
Perez Y, Fla	16	Nabholz, ChN	8	Dougherty, Hou	5	Miranda, Mil	3
Guthrie, LA	15	Radinsky, ChA	8	Guardado, Min	5	Pierce, Bos	3
Orosco, Bal	15	Stanton, Bos	8	Guetterman, Sea	5	Rojas, Mon	3
Arocha, StL	14	Brewer, KC	7	Lee, Bal	5	Simas, ChA	3
Nelson, Sea	14	Clark T, Bal	7	Magnante, KC	5	Slocumb, Phi	3
Corsi, Oak	13	Dibble, Mil	7	Mccurry, Pit	5	Wendell, ChN	3
Holmes, Col	13	Leiper, Mon	7	Stevens, Min	5	Young, ChN	3
Karchner, ChA	13	Mathews T, StL	7	Tabaka, Hou	5	Acre, Oak	2
Risley, Sea	13	Meacham, KC	7	Vosberg, Tex	5	Aquino, SF	2
Charlton, Sea	12	Parrett, StL	7	Wegman, Mil	5	Astacio, LA	2
Christiansen, Pit	12	Pichardo, KC	7	Wickander, Mil	5	Ayala, Sea	2
Habyan, Cal	12	Service, SF	7	Boever, Det	4	Cornett, Tor	2
Honeycutt, NYA	12	Watkins, Min	7	Casian, ChN	4	Fetters, Mil	2
Munoz M, Col	12	Whiteside M, Tex	7	Daal, LA	4	Florence, NYN	2
Patterson B, Cal	12	Williams B, SD	7	Frey, Phi	4	Hall, Tor	2
Borland, Phi	11	Benitez, Bal	6	Gardner, Fla	4	Hammaker, ChA	2
Carrasco, Cin	11	Borbon, Atl	6	Hartgraves, Hou	4	Haney, KC	2
Mathews T, Fla	11	Burrows, Tex	6	MacDonald, NYA	4	Keyser, ChA	2
Osuna, LA	11	Clontz, Atl	6	Mohler, Oak	4	Kiefer, Mil	2
Pena, Atl	11	Cook, Tex	6	Painter, Col	4	Maxcy, Det	2
Plesac, Pit	11	Cummings, LA	6	Reyes A, Mil	4	Miceli, Pit	2
Reed S, Col	11	Dyer, Pit	6	Reyes C, Oak	4	Minor, NYN	2
Barton, SF	10	Embree, Cle	6	Timlin, Tor	4	Olson, KC	2
Bohanon, Det	10	Gunderson, Bos	6	Walker M, ChN	4	Powell J, Fla	2
Howe, NYA	10	Henry D, NYN	6	Williams M, Cal	4	Thomas L, ChA	2
Plunk, Cle	10	Hernandez X, Cin	6	Bedrosian, Atl	3	Thompson, Col	2
Assenmacher, Cle	9	Hook, SF	6	Blair, SD	3	Valdes I, LA	2
Cormier, Bos	9	Maddux M, Bos	6	Butcher, Cal	3	Valenzuela, SD	2
DeLucia, StL	9	Poole, Cle	6	Byrd, NYN	3	Wohlers, Atl	2
Florie, SD	9	Rightnowar, Mil	6	Cox, Tor	3		
Harris G, Bal	9	Ruffin B, Col	6	DeLeon, Mon	3		

Which Relievers Have the Best Conversion Rates? (p. 168)

The table below lists a relievers Holds (**H**), Saves (**Sv**), Blown Saves (**BS**), and Hold + Save Percentage (**%**), which is Holds plus Saves divided by Holds plus Saves plus Blown Saves.

Both Leagues — Listed Alphabetically
(minimum 5 Holds+Saves+Blown Saves in 1995)

Pitcher	H	Sv	BS	%	Pitcher	H	Sv	BS	%	Pitcher	H	Sv	BS	%
Acre, Oak	2	0	4	33	Gardner, Fla	4	1	0	100	Olson, KC	2	3	2	71
Aguilera, Bos	0	32	4	89	Gott, Pit	3	3	0	100	Orosco, Bal	15	3	3	86
Aquino, SF	2	2	2	67	Guardado, Min	5	2	3	70	Osuna, LA	11	0	2	85
Arocha, StL	14	0	7	67	Guetterman, Sea	5	1	1	86	Painter, Col	4	1	0	100
Assenmacher, Cle	9	0	1	90	Gunderson, Bos	6	0	3	67	Parrett, StL	7	0	2	78
Ayala, Sea	2	19	8	72	Guthrie, LA	15	0	2	88	Patterson B, Cal	12	0	1	92
Bailey R, Col	5	0	0	100	Habyan, Cal	12	0	2	86	Pena, Atl	11	0	1	92
Barton, SF	10	1	3	79	Hall, Tor	2	3	1	83	Percival, Cal	29	3	3	91
Bautista, SF	5	0	0	100	Harris G, Bal	9	0	2	82	Perez M, ChN	16	2	1	95
Beck, SF	0	33	10	77	Hartgraves, Hou	4	0	3	57	Perez Y, Fla	16	1	3	85
Bedrosian, Atl	3	0	2	60	Henke, StL	0	36	2	95	Pichardo, KC	7	1	1	89
Belinda, Bos	17	10	4	87	Henneman, Hou	1	26	3	90	Plesac, Pit	11	3	2	88
Benitez, Bal	6	2	3	73	Henry D, NYN	6	4	3	77	Plunk, Cle	10	2	3	80
Berumen, SD	5	1	3	67	Henry D, Det	0	5	0	100	Poole, Cle	6	0	0	100
Bochtler, SD	8	1	3	75	Hernandez R, ChA	0	32	10	76	Radinsky, ChA	8	1	2	82
Boever, Det	4	3	3	70	Hernandez X, Cin	6	3	1	90	Reed S, Col	11	3	3	82
Bohanon, Det	10	1	0	100	Hickerson, Col	9	1	3	77	Reyes A, Mil	4	1	0	100
Borbon, Atl	6	2	2	80	Hoffman, SD	0	31	7	82	Reyes C, Oak	4	0	1	80
Borland, Phi	11	6	3	85	Holmes, Col	13	14	4	87	Rightnowar, Mil	6	1	3	70
Bottalico, Phi	20	1	4	84	Honeycutt, NYA	12	2	3	82	Risley, Sea	13	1	6	70
Brantley, Cin	0	28	4	88	Hook, SF	6	0	0	100	Rojas, Mon	3	30	9	79
Brewer, KC	7	0	4	64	Howe, NYA	10	2	1	92	Ruffin B, Col	6	11	1	94
Burba, Cin	5	0	1	83	Hudek, Hou	0	7	2	78	Russell, Tex	1	20	4	84
Burrows, Tex	6	1	2	78	Hudson, Bos	8	1	3	75	Ryan, Bos	0	7	3	70
Butcher, Cal	3	0	2	60	Jackson M, Cin	9	2	2	85	Scott, Mon	19	2	3	88
Carrasco, Cin	11	5	4	80	James, Cal	3	1	1	80	Seanez, LA	6	3	1	90
Casian, ChN	4	0	3	57	Jones D, Bal	0	22	3	88	Service, SF	7	0	0	100
Castillo T, Tor	5	13	8	69	Jones T, Hou	8	15	5	82	Shaw, ChA	6	3	2	82
Charlton, Sea	12	14	2	93	Karchner, ChA	13	0	0	100	Slocumb, Phi	3	32	6	85
Christiansen, Pit	12	0	4	75	Lee, Bal	5	1	1	86	Smith L, Cal	0	37	4	90
Christopher, Det	5	1	1	86	Leiper, Mon	7	2	1	90	Stanton, Bos	8	1	2	82
Clark T, Bal	7	1	0	100	Leskanic, Col	19	10	6	83	Stevens, Min	5	10	2	88
Clontz, Atl	6	4	2	83	Lloyd, Mil	9	4	2	87	Tabaka, Hou	5	0	1	83
Cook, Tex	6	2	0	100	MacDonald, NYA	4	0	1	80	Tavarez, Cle	19	0	4	83
Cormier, Bos	9	0	2	82	Maddux M, Bos	6	1	0	100	Timlin, Tor	4	5	4	69
Corsi, Oak	13	2	2	88	Magnante, KC	5	0	1	83	Veres D, Hou	19	1	2	91
Cox, Tor	3	0	2	60	Mahomes, Min	9	3	4	75	Veres R, Fla	9	1	1	91
Cummings, LA	6	0	0	100	Mathews T, StL	7	2	0	100	Villone, SD	6	1	4	64
Daal, LA	4	0	1	80	Mathews T, Fla	11	3	4	78	Vosberg, Tex	5	4	4	69
DeLeon, Mon	3	0	5	38	McCaskill, ChA	8	2	3	77	Walker M, ChN	4	1	2	71
DeLucia, StL	9	0	1	90	Mccurry, Pit	5	1	1	86	Watkins, Min	7	0	2	78
Dewey, SF	5	0	0	100	McDowell R, Tex	9	4	4	76	Wegman, Mil	5	2	1	88
Dibble, Mil	7	1	1	89	McElroy, Cin	3	0	3	50	Wetteland, NYA	0	31	6	84
DiPoto, NYN	8	2	4	71	McMichael, Atl	20	2	2	92	Whiteside M, Tex	7	3	1	91
Doherty, Det	5	6	3	79	Meacham, KC	7	2	1	90	Wickander, Mil	5	1	2	75
Dougherty, Hou	5	0	2	71	Mesa, Cle	0	46	2	96	Wickman, NYA	21	1	9	71
Dyer, Pit	6	0	2	75	Miceli, Pit	2	21	6	79	Williams B, SD	7	0	2	78
Eckersley, Oak	0	29	9	76	Miranda, Mil	3	1	2	67	Williams M, Cal	4	0	1	80
Embree, Cle	6	1	0	100	Mohler, Oak	4	1	1	83	Wohlers, Atl	2	25	4	87
Fetters, Mil	2	22	5	83	Montgomery, KC	0	31	7	82	Worrell T, LA	1	32	4	89
Florie, SD	9	1	3	77	Munoz, Col	12	2	2	88	Young, ChN	3	2	0	100
Fossas, StL	19	0	0	100	Myers R, ChN	0	38	6	86					
Franco, NYN	0	29	7	81	Nabholz, ChN	8	0	0	100					
Fraser, Mon	3	2	0	100	Nelson, Sea	14	2	2	89					
Frey, Phi	4	1	0	100	Nen, Fla	0	23	6	79					

Whose Heater is Hottest? (p. 170)

Both Leagues — Listed Alphabetically
(minimum 100 innings pitched or 50 relief games)

Pitcher,Team	IP	K	K/9	Pitcher,Team	IP	K	K/9
Abbott J, Cal	197.0	86	3.9	Eckersley, Oak	50.1	40	7.2
Aguilera, Bos	55.1	52	8.5	Ericks, Pit	106.0	80	6.8
Alvarez W, ChA	175.0	118	6.1	Erickson, Bal	196.1	106	4.9
Appier, KC	201.1	185	8.3	Fassero, Mon	189.0	164	7.8
Ashby, SD	192.2	150	7.0	Fernandez A, ChA	203.2	159	7.0
Astacio, LA	104.0	80	6.9	Finley, Cal	203.0	195	8.6
Avery, Atl	173.1	141	7.3	Fossas, StL	36.2	40	9.8
Ayala, Sea	71.0	77	9.8	Foster, ChN	167.2	146	7.8
Barton, SF	44.1	22	4.5	Gardner, Fla	102.1	87	7.7
Bautista, SF	100.2	45	4.0	Givens, Mil	107.1	73	6.1
Beck, SF	58.2	42	6.4	Glavine, Atl	198.2	127	5.8
Belcher, Sea	179.1	96	4.8	Gordon, KC	189.0	119	5.7
Belinda, Bos	69.2	57	7.4	Green, Phi	140.2	85	5.4
Benes A, Sea	181.2	171	8.5	Gross, Tex	183.2	106	5.2
Bere, ChA	137.2	110	7.2	Gubicza, KC	213.1	81	3.4
Bergman, Det	135.1	86	5.7	Guthrie, LA	62.0	67	9.7
Blair, SD	114.0	83	6.6	Guzman, Tor	135.1	94	6.3
Boever, Det	98.2	71	6.5	Habyan, Cal	73.1	60	7.4
Bohanon, Det	105.2	63	5.4	Hamilton, SD	204.1	123	5.4
Bones, Mil	200.1	77	3.5	Hammond, Fla	161.0	126	7.0
Borland, Phi	74.0	59	7.2	Hampton, Hou	150.2	115	6.9
Bosio, Sea	170.0	85	4.5	Hanson, Bos	186.2	139	6.7
Boskie, Cal	111.2	51	4.1	Harkey, Cal	127.1	56	4.0
Bottalico, Phi	87.2	87	8.9	Harnisch, NYN	110.0	82	6.7
Brantley, Cin	70.1	62	7.9	Henke, StL	54.1	48	8.0
Brown, Bal	172.1	117	6.1	Henneman, Hou	50.1	43	7.7
Bullinger, ChN	150.0	93	5.6	Henry B, Mon	126.2	60	4.3
Burba, Cin	106.2	96	8.1	Henry D, NYN	67.0	62	8.3
Burkett, Fla	188.1	126	6.0	Hentgen, Tor	200.2	135	6.1
Candiotti, LA	190.1	141	6.7	Heredia G, Mon	119.0	74	5.6
Carrasco, Cin	87.1	64	6.6	Hernandez R, ChA	59.2	84	12.7
Castillo F, ChN	188.0	135	6.5	Hernandez X, Cin	90.0	84	8.4
Castillo T, Tor	72.2	38	4.7	Hershiser, Cle	167.1	111	6.0
Charlton, Sea	69.2	70	9.0	Hickerson, Col	48.1	40	7.4
Christiansen, Pit	56.1	53	8.5	Hill, Cle	185.0	98	4.8
Clark M, Cle	124.2	68	4.9	Hitchcock, NYA	168.1	121	6.5
Clemens, Bos	140.0	132	8.5	Hoffman, SD	53.1	52	8.8
Clontz, Atl	69.0	55	7.2	Holmes, Col	66.2	61	8.2
Cone, NYA	229.1	191	7.5	Honeycutt, NYA	45.2	21	4.1
Cormier, Bos	115.0	69	5.4	Howe, NYA	49.0	28	5.1
Darling, Oak	104.0	69	6.0	Jackson D, StL	100.2	52	4.6
DeLucia, StL	82.1	76	8.3	Jacome, KC	105.0	50	4.3
DiPoto, NYN	78.2	49	5.6	Johnson, Sea	214.1	294	12.3
Doherty, Det	113.0	46	3.7	Jones B, NYN	195.2	127	5.8
Dougherty, Hou	67.2	49	6.5	Jones D, Bal	46.2	42	8.1
Drabek, Hou	185.0	143	7.0	Jones T, Hou	99.2	96	8.7
Dyer, Pit	74.2	53	6.4	Karl, Mil	124.0	59	4.3

Pitcher,Team	IP	K	K/9	Pitcher,Team	IP	K	K/9
Kile, Hou	127.0	113	8.0	Petkovsek, StL	137.1	71	4.7
Langston, Cal	200.1	142	6.4	Pettitte, NYA	175.0	114	5.9
Leiper, Mon	44.2	22	4.4	Plesac, Pit	60.1	57	8.5
Leiter A, Tor	183.0	153	7.5	Plunk, Cle	64.0	71	10.0
Leiter M, SF	195.2	129	5.9	Portugal, Cin	181.2	96	4.8
Leskanic, Col	98.0	107	9.8	Pulsipher, NYN	126.2	81	5.8
Lira, Det	146.1	89	5.5	Quantrill, Phi	179.1	103	5.2
Loaiza, Pit	172.2	85	4.4	Radke, Min	181.0	75	3.7
Maddux G, Atl	209.2	181	7.8	Rapp, Fla	167.1	102	5.5
Martinez D, Cle	187.0	99	4.8	Reed S, Col	84.0	79	8.5
Martinez P, Mon	194.2	174	8.0	Reynolds, Hou	189.1	175	8.3
Martinez R, LA	206.1	138	6.0	Ritz, Col	173.1	120	6.2
Mathews T, Fla	82.2	72	7.8	Rodriguez F, Min	105.2	59	5.0
McCaskill, ChA	81.0	50	5.6	Rogers K, Tex	208.0	140	6.1
Mccurry, Pit	61.0	27	4.0	Rojas, Mon	67.2	61	8.1
McDowell J, NYA	217.2	157	6.5	Saberhagen, Col	153.0	100	5.9
McDowell R, Tex	85.0	49	5.2	Schilling, Phi	116.0	114	8.8
McMichael, Atl	80.2	74	8.3	Schourek, Cin	190.1	160	7.6
Mercker, Atl	143.0	102	6.4	Scott, Mon	63.1	57	8.1
Mesa, Cle	64.0	58	8.2	Shaw, ChA	72.0	51	6.4
Miceli, Pit	58.0	56	8.7	Slocumb, Phi	65.1	63	8.7
Mimbs, Phi	136.2	93	6.1	Smiley, Cin	176.2	124	6.3
Mlicki, NYN	160.2	123	6.9	Smith L, Cal	49.1	43	7.8
Montgomery, KC	65.2	49	6.7	Smith Z, Bos	110.2	47	3.8
Moore, Det	132.2	64	4.3	Smoltz, Atl	192.2	193	9.0
Morgan, StL	131.1	61	4.2	Sparks, Mil	202.0	96	4.3
Moyer, Bal	115.2	65	5.1	Stevens, Min	65.2	47	6.4
Mulholland, SF	149.0	65	3.9	Stottlemyre, Oak	209.2	205	8.8
Munoz M, Col	43.2	37	7.6	Swift, Col	105.2	68	5.8
Mussina, Bal	221.2	158	6.4	Swindell, Hou	153.0	96	5.6
Myers R, ChN	55.2	59	9.5	Tapani, LA	190.2	131	6.2
Nagy, Cle	178.0	139	7.0	Tavarez, Cle	85.0	68	7.2
Navarro, ChN	200.1	128	5.8	Tewksbury, Tex	129.2	53	3.7
Neagle, Pit	209.2	150	6.4	Trachsel, ChN	160.2	117	6.6
Nelson, Sea	78.2	96	11.0	Valdes I, LA	197.2	150	6.8
Nen, Fla	65.2	68	9.3	Van Poppel, Oak	138.1	122	7.9
Nomo, LA	191.1	236	11.1	VanLandingham, SF	122.2	95	7.0
Ogea, Cle	106.1	57	4.8	Veres D, Hou	103.1	94	8.2
Ontiveros, Oak	129.2	77	5.3	Wagner P, Pit	165.0	120	6.5
Orosco, Bal	49.2	58	10.5	Wakefield, Bos	195.1	119	5.5
Osborne, StL	113.1	82	6.5	Watson, StL	114.1	49	3.9
Parrett, StL	76.2	71	8.3	Wells D, Cin	203.0	133	5.9
Patterson B, Cal	53.1	41	6.9	Wetteland, NYA	61.1	66	9.7
Pavlik, Tex	191.2	149	7.0	Wickman, NYA	80.0	51	5.7
Percival, Cal	74.0	94	11.4	Witt, Tex	172.0	141	7.4
Perez C, Mon	141.1	106	6.8	Wohlers, Atl	64.2	90	12.5
Perez M, ChN	71.1	49	6.2	Worrell T, LA	62.1	61	8.8
Perez Y, Fla	46.2	47	9.1				

How Does a Pitcher Do In the Start Following a No-Hitter? (p. 172)

How Pitchers Fared in Games After No-Hitters and in Seasons of No-Hitters (Since 1987)

Pitcher	Date	IP	H	R	ER	BB	K	ERA
Ramon Martinez	7/14/95	7.0	9	5	0	1	5	0.00
		206.1	176	95	84	81	138	3.66
Kenny Rogers	7/28/94	5.1	6	5	4	3	2	6.75
		167.1	169	93	83	52	120	4.46
Scott Erickson	4/27/94	5.0	9	7	7	1	2	12.60
		144.0	173	95	87	59	104	5.44
Kent Mercker	4/ 8/94	7.0	6	1	1	3	8	1.29
		112.1	90	46	43	45	111	3.45
Darryl Kile	9/ 8/93	7.1	7	3	2	3	5	2.45
		171.2	152	73	67	69	141	3.51
Jim Abbott	9/ 4/93	7.0	10	4	4	1	1	5.14
		214.0	221	115	104	73	95	4.37
Chris Bosio	4/22/93	5.0	3	0	0	2	4	0.00
		164.1	138	75	63	59	119	3.45
Kevin Gross	8/17/92	8.0	6	3	3	1	6	3.38
		204.2	182	82	72	77	158	3.17
Bret Saberhagen	8/26/91	7.2	9	6	5	1	5	5.87
		196.1	165	76	67	45	136	3.07
Wilson Alvarez	8/11/91	4.1	8	3	3	1	1	6.23
		56.1	47	26	22	29	32	3.51
Dennis Martinez	7/28/91	7.0	6	4	4	2	4	5.14
		222.0	187	70	59	62	123	2.39
Tommy Greene	5/23/91	9.0	3	0	0	0	9	0.00
		207.2	177	85	78	66	154	3.38
Nolan Ryan	5/ 1/91	6.0	2	3	3	5	6	4.50
		173.0	102	58	56	72	203	2.91
Dave Stieb	9/ 2/90	8.0	6	0	0	2	3	0.00
		208.2	179	73	68	64	125	2.93
Terry Mulholland	8/15/90	8.1	8	2	2	1	4	2.16
		180.2	172	78	67	42	75	3.34
Dave Stewart	6/29/90	2.1	8	6	6	1	0	23.14
		267.0	226	84	76	83	166	2.56
Fernando Valenzuela	6/29/90	7.0	10	5	4	1	2	5.14
		204.0	223	112	104	77	115	4.59
Nolan Ryan	6/11/90	5.0	4	3	3	5	9	5.40
		204.0	137	86	78	74	232	3.44
Randy Johnson	6/ 2/90	9.0	5	1	1	1	10	1.00
		219.2	174	103	89	120	194	3.65
Tom Browning	9/16/88	8.0	5	1	1	1	4	1.13
		250.2	205	98	95	64	124	3.41
Juan Nieves	4/15/87	5.0	5	4	4	1	2	7.20
		195.2	199	112	106	100	163	4.88
Total: Games After No-Hitters		138.1	135	66	57	37	92	3.71
Total: Seasons of No-Hitters		3970.1	3494	1735	1568	1413	2828	3.55

Was That a "Quality" Start, Or Just a Maddux Start? (p. 175)

Both Leagues — Listed Alphabetically
(minimum 15 games started in 1995)

Player,Team	GS	QS	%	Player,Team	GS	QS	%	Player,Team	GS	QS	%
Abbott J, Cal	30	16	53.3	Hentgen, Tor	30	13	43.3	Reynolds, Hou	30	19	63.3
Alvarez W, ChA	29	12	41.4	Heredia G, Mon	18	6	33.3	Reynoso, Col	18	5	27.8
Anderson B, Cal	17	6	35.3	Hershiser, Cle	26	16	61.5	Ritz, Col	28	13	46.4
Appier, KC	31	17	54.8	Hill, Cle	29	15	51.7	Rodriguez F, Min	18	8	44.4
Ashby, SD	31	18	58.1	Hitchcock, NYA	27	15	55.6	Rogers K, Tex	31	18	58.1
Avery, Atl	29	11	37.9	Jackson D, StL	19	4	21.1	Saberhagen, Col	25	13	52.0
Banks, Phi	15	6	40.0	Jacome, KC	19	4	21.1	Sanders, SD	15	8	53.3
Belcher, Sea	28	13	46.4	Johnson, Sea	30	23	76.7	Schilling, Phi	17	11	64.7
Benes A, Sea	31	17	54.8	Jones B, NYN	30	16	53.3	Schourek, Cin	29	19	65.5
Bere, ChA	27	7	25.9	Kamieniecki, NYA	16	6	37.5	Smiley, Cin	27	18	66.7
Bergman, Det	28	10	35.7	Karl, Mil	18	12	66.7	Smith Z, Bos	21	8	38.1
Bones, Mil	31	14	45.2	Kile, Hou	21	12	57.1	Smoltz, Atl	29	16	55.2
Bosio, Sea	31	9	29.0	Langston, Cal	31	17	54.8	Sparks, Mil	27	11	40.7
Boskie, Cal	20	7	35.0	Leiter A, Tor	28	12	42.9	Stewart, Oak	16	5	31.3
Brown, Bal	26	14	53.8	Leiter M, SF	29	16	55.2	Stottlemyre, Oak	31	16	51.6
Bullinger, ChN	24	11	45.8	Lima, Det	15	6	40.0	Swift, Col	19	6	31.6
Burkett, Fla	30	15	50.0	Lira, Det	22	10	45.5	Swindell, Hou	26	16	61.5
Candiotti, LA	30	21	70.0	Loaiza, Pit	31	15	48.4	Tapani, LA	31	11	35.5
Castillo F, ChN	29	19	65.5	Maddux G, Atl	28	22	78.6	Tewksbury, Tex	21	10	47.6
Clark M, Cle	21	7	33.3	Martinez D, Cle	28	21	75.0	Trachsel, ChN	29	15	51.7
Clemens, Bos	23	13	56.5	Martinez P, Mon	30	17	56.7	Trombley, Min	18	5	27.8
Cone, NYA	30	16	53.3	Martinez R, LA	30	21	70.0	Valdes I, LA	27	18	66.7
Darling, Oak	21	6	28.6	McDowell J, NYA	30	19	63.3	Valenzuela, SD	15	3	20.0
Darwin, Tex	15	2	13.3	Mercker, Atl	26	11	42.3	VanL'nd'ngh'm,SF	18	11	61.1
Dishman, SD	16	6	37.5	Mimbs, Phi	19	10	52.6	Wagner P, Pit	25	12	48.0
Drabek, Hou	31	16	51.6	Mlicki, NYN	25	11	44.0	Wakefield, Bos	27	18	66.7
Ericks, Pit	18	9	50.0	Moore, Det	25	6	24.0	Watson, StL	19	7	36.8
Erickson, Bal	31	14	45.2	Morgan, StL	21	10	47.6	Weathers, Fla	15	4	26.7
Fassero, Mon	30	12	40.0	Moyer, Bal	18	7	38.9	Wells D, Cin	29	21	72.4
Fernandez A, ChA	30	18	60.0	Mulholland, SF	24	9	37.5	Wilson T, SF	17	9	52.9
Fernandez S, Phi	18	6	33.3	Mussina, Bal	32	20	62.5	Witt, Tex	29	16	55.2
Finley, Cal	32	16	50.0	Nagy, Cle	29	14	48.3	**MLB Avg**			**46.3**
Foster, ChN	28	13	46.4	Navarro, ChN	29	21	72.4				
Freeman, Col	18	7	38.9	Neagle, Pit	31	21	67.7				
Givens, Mil	19	8	42.1	Nitkowski, Det	18	3	16.7				
Glavine, Atl	29	19	65.5	Nomo, LA	28	18	64.3				
Gordon, KC	31	15	48.4	Ontiveros, Oak	22	10	45.5				
Green, Phi	25	13	52.0	Osborne, StL	19	10	52.6				
Gross, Tex	30	12	40.0	Parris, Pit	15	8	53.3				
Gubicza, KC	33	20	60.6	Pavlik, Tex	31	16	51.6				
Guzman, Tor	24	7	29.2	Perez C, Mon	23	12	52.2				
Hamilton, SD	30	19	63.3	Petkovsek, StL	21	12	57.1				
Hammond, Fla	24	12	50.0	Pettitte, NYA	26	14	53.8				
Hampton, Hou	24	13	54.2	Portugal, Cin	31	17	54.8				
Hanson, Bos	29	14	48.3	Pulsipher, NYN	17	7	41.2				
Harkey, Cal	20	7	35.0	Quantrill, Phi	29	10	34.5				
Harnisch, NYN	18	13	72.2	Radke, Min	28	8	28.6				
Henry B, Mon	21	12	57.1	Rapp, Fla	28	16	57.1				

Which Pitchers Can Rest in Peace? (p. 178)

The following table lists the Percentage (%) of baserunners that a pitcher "bequeathed" to his bullpen (Left), and those that subsequently scored (Sc).

Both Leagues — Listed Alphabetically
(minimum 15 runners bequeathed)

Pitcher	Left	Sc	%	Pitcher	Left	Sc	%
Abbott J, Cal	26	8	30.8	DeLeon, Mon	33	15	45.5
Acre, Oak	18	9	50.0	DeLucia, StL	22	9	40.9
Anderson B, Cal	15	8	53.3	Dibble, Mil	32	7	21.9
Appier, KC	22	10	45.5	DiPoto, NYN	15	7	46.7
Aquino, SF	22	5	22.7	Doherty, Det	24	12	50.0
Assenmacher, Cle	27	4	14.8	Dougherty, Hou	30	10	33.3
Astacio, LA	20	7	35.0	Drabek, Hou	22	3	13.6
Bailey R, Col	16	7	43.8	Dyer, Pit	22	8	36.4
Banks, Phi	22	7	31.8	Erickson, Bal	28	10	35.7
Barton, SF	28	12	42.9	Eversgerd, Mon	17	3	17.6
Bautista, SF	19	5	26.3	Fassero, Mon	19	7	36.8
Bedrosian, Atl	15	3	20.0	Fernandez S, Phi	15	3	20.0
Belcher, Sea	28	12	42.9	Finley, Cal	20	3	15.0
Belinda, Bos	25	7	28.0	Fleming, KC	20	8	40.0
Benes A, Sea	24	9	37.5	Fortugno, Cal	15	7	46.7
Benitez, Bal	24	11	45.8	Fossas, StL	19	0	0.0
Bere, ChA	28	13	46.4	Foster, ChN	18	9	50.0
Bergman, Det	27	6	22.2	Frey, Phi	18	5	27.8
Bielecki, Cal	19	9	47.4	Gardner, Fla	19	4	21.1
Boever, Det	19	8	42.1	Givens, Mil	15	6	40.0
Bohanon, Det	34	14	41.2	Gordon, KC	31	16	51.6
Bones, Mil	28	10	35.7	Green, Phi	18	6	33.3
Borbon, Atl	20	2	10.0	Groom, Fla	30	7	23.3
Borland, Phi	25	4	16.0	Gross, Tex	33	20	60.6
Bottalico, Phi	17	1	5.9	Guardado, Min	26	9	34.6
Brewer, KC	21	4	19.0	Gubicza, KC	24	5	20.8
Brown, Bal	26	10	38.5	Guetterman, Sea	26	8	30.8
Bullinger, ChN	20	4	20.0	Gunderson, Bos	36	10	27.8
Burba, Cin	18	6	33.3	Guthrie, LA	41	9	22.0
Burkett, Fla	18	6	33.3	Guzman, Tor	18	10	55.6
Burrows, Tex	31	5	16.1	Habyan, Cal	38	11	28.9
Butcher, Cal	19	10	52.6	Hamilton, SD	20	5	25.0
Carrasco, Cin	16	4	25.0	Hammond, Fla	18	5	27.8
Casian, ChN	37	3	8.1	Harkey, Cal	25	8	32.0
Castillo F, ChN	27	4	14.8	Hartgraves, Hou	26	7	26.9
Charlton, Sea	16	9	56.3	Hentgen, Tor	15	5	33.3
Christiansen, Pit	30	7	23.3	Heredia G, Mon	28	11	39.3
Clark M, Cle	16	5	31.3	Hernandez X, Cin	18	11	61.1
Clark T, Bal	16	4	25.0	Hickerson, Col	45	14	31.1
Clemens, Bos	21	1	4.8	Hill, Cle	19	3	15.8
Clontz, Atl	20	6	30.0	Hitchcock, NYA	26	13	50.0
Cook, Tex	28	4	14.3	Holmes, Col	20	5	25.0
Cormier, Bos	33	10	30.3	Hook, SF	30	8	26.7
Cummings, LA	21	11	52.4	Howe, NYA	19	5	26.3
Daal, LA	26	8	30.8	Hudson, Bos	19	6	31.6
Darling, Oak	18	5	27.8	James, Cal	29	9	31.0

Pitcher	Left	Sc	%	Pitcher	Left	Sc	%
Jarvis, Cin	16	9	56.3	Pichardo, KC	25	14	56.0
Jones B, NYN	22	8	36.4	Plesac, Pit	35	11	31.4
Keyser, ChA	19	5	26.3	Plunk, Cle	21	1	4.8
Kile, Hou	23	18	78.3	Portugal, Cin	21	7	33.3
Krueger, Sea	16	0	0.0	Powell R, Pit	19	6	31.6
Langston, Cal	24	7	29.2	Quantrill, Phi	20	8	40.0
Lee, Bal	35	6	17.1	Radinsky, ChA	26	8	30.8
Leiper, Mon	29	7	24.1	Reed S, Col	15	1	6.7
Leiter A, Tor	20	3	15.0	Reyes C, Oak	20	11	55.0
Leiter M, SF	25	6	24.0	Rhodes, Bal	15	8	53.3
Leskanic, Col	22	7	31.8	Rightnowar, Mil	16	5	31.3
Lieber, Pit	15	3	20.0	Rivera M, NYA	15	6	40.0
Lira, Det	19	7	36.8	Roberson, Mil	17	2	11.8
Loaiza, Pit	19	6	31.6	Robertson, Min	20	10	50.0
MacDonald, NYA	21	6	28.6	Rodriguez F, Min	16	12	75.0
Maddux M, Bos	20	9	45.0	Rogers K, Tex	30	7	23.3
Mahomes, Min	30	16	53.3	Rojas, Mon	16	4	25.0
Martinez P, Mon	17	5	29.4	Sanders, SD	15	6	40.0
Martinez P, Hou	21	4	19.0	Schullstrom, Min	22	8	36.4
Maxcy, Det	29	14	48.3	Scott, Mon	26	6	23.1
McCaskill, ChA	26	6	23.1	Seanez, LA	23	9	39.1
Mccurry, Pit	24	5	20.8	Shaw, ChA	39	17	43.6
McDowell J, NYA	19	3	15.8	Smith Z, Bos	16	9	56.3
McDowell R, Tex	37	12	32.4	Sparks, Mil	31	19	61.3
McElroy, Cin	19	5	26.3	Stanton, Bos	20	4	20.0
McMichael, Atl	25	10	40.0	Stevens, Min	17	2	11.8
Mercker, Atl	15	9	60.0	Stottlemyre, Oak	20	6	30.0
Mills, Bal	20	5	25.0	Swindell, Hou	22	3	13.6
Mimbs, Phi	23	8	34.8	Tabaka, Hou	26	6	23.1
Miranda, Mil	16	5	31.3	Tapani, LA	16	7	43.8
Mohler, Oak	22	5	22.7	Thompson, Col	18	6	33.3
Moore, Det	28	11	39.3	Torres D, KC	15	4	26.7
Moyer, Bal	25	10	40.0	Trachsel, ChN	30	15	50.0
Munoz M, Col	31	8	25.8	Valenzuela, SD	17	5	29.4
Mussina, Bal	15	7	46.7	Van Poppel, Oak	16	4	25.0
Nabholz, ChN	22	6	27.3	Veres D, Hou	27	8	29.6
Nagy, Cle	15	3	20.0	Villone, SD	30	8	26.7
Navarro, ChN	17	8	47.1	Vosberg, Tex	28	5	17.9
Nelson, Sea	23	9	39.1	Walker M, ChN	19	3	15.8
Nitkowski, Det	15	1	6.7	Watkins, Min	21	5	23.8
Oliver, Tex	19	4	21.1	Watson, StL	20	12	60.0
Ontiveros, Oak	15	8	53.3	Weathers, Fla	22	14	63.6
Oquist, Bal	27	9	33.3	Wegman, Mil	17	4	23.5
Orosco, Bal	29	7	24.1	Wells B, Sea	23	9	39.1
Painter, Col	16	0	0.0	Wendell, ChN	17	3	17.6
Parra, Min	16	8	50.0	Whiteside M, Tex	16	8	50.0
Parrett, StL	22	3	13.6	Wickander, Mil	21	2	9.5
Patterson B, Cal	37	7	18.9	Wickman, NYA	28	9	32.1
Pavlik, Tex	38	12	31.6	Williams B, SD	26	13	50.0
Percival, Cal	17	6	35.3	Williams M, Cal	29	7	24.1
Perez C, Mon	20	1	5.0	Wilson T, SF	16	12	75.0
Perez M, ChN	28	8	28.6	Witt, Tex	19	8	42.1
Perez Y, Fla	43	11	25.6	**MLB Avg**			**32.9**
Pettitte, NYA	19	6	31.6				

Which Pitchers "Scored" the Best? (p. 182)

1995 Games Scores of 85+ — Sorted by Game Score

Player, Team	Date	Opp	W/L	IP	H	R	ER	BB	K	Score
C Finley, Cal	5/23	NYA	W	9.0	2	0	0	2	15	96
F Castillo, ChN	9/25	StL	W	9.0	1	0	0	2	13	96
R Johnson, Sea	7/15	Tor	W	9.0	3	0	0	2	16	95
P Martinez, Mon	6/3	SD	W	9.0	1	0	0	0	9	94
R Martinez, LA	7/14	Fla	W	9.0	0	0	0	1	8	94
H Nomo, LA	6/24	SF	W	9.0	2	0	0	3	13	93
H Nomo, LA	8/5	SF	W	9.0	1	0	0	3	11	93
P Wagner, Pit	8/29	Col	W	9.0	1	0	0	3	11	93
K Appier, KC	9/15	Cal	W	9.0	3	0	0	1	13	93
R Johnson, Sea	6/5	Bal	W	9.0	3	0	0	1	12	92
T Stottlemyre, Oak	6/16	KC	ND	10.0	5	1	1	1	15	92
G Maddux, Atl	8/20	StL	W	9.0	2	0	0	0	9	92
I Valdes, LA	9/17	StL	W	9.0	2	0	0	0	9	92
K Rueter, Mon	8/27	SF	W	9.0	1	0	0	1	7	91
P Rapp, Fla	9/17	Col	W	9.0	1	0	0	1	7	91
S Ontiveros, Oak	5/27	NYA	W	9.0	1	0	0	2	7	90
D Drabek, Hou	7/25	LA	W	9.0	3	0	0	0	9	90
E Hanson, Bos	5/16	Mil	W	9.0	4	0	0	0	10	89
M Gubicza, KC	6/15	Oak	W	9.0	1	0	0	1	5	89
D Neagle, Pit	6/23	Mon	W	9.0	2	0	0	1	6	88
M Mussina, Bal	8/27	Cal	W	9.0	4	0	0	2	11	88
M Mussina, Bal	10/1	Det	W	9.0	2	0	0	2	7	88
R Johnson, Sea	10/2	Cal	W	9.0	3	1	1	1	12	88
G Maddux, Atl	5/28	Hou	W	9.0	1	1	1	1	7	87
C Schilling, Phi	6/7	SD	W	9.0	2	1	1	0	8	87
A Ashby, SD	6/18	Pit	W	9.0	4	0	0	2	10	87
H Nomo, LA	6/29	Col	W	9.0	6	0	0	1	13	87
M Langston, Cal	7/8	Mil	W	9.0	3	0	0	3	9	87
H Nomo, LA	7/15	Fla	W	9.0	3	1	1	0	10	87
M Leiter, SF	7/26	Cin	W	9.0	2	1	1	0	8	87
S Hitchcock, NYA	5/21	Bal	W	9.0	4	0	0	1	8	86
M Mimbs, Phi	5/26	SD	W	9.0	2	0	0	1	4	86
J Bullinger, ChN	7/30	Phi	W	9.0	3	0	0	3	8	86
A Ashby, SD	8/11	StL	W	9.0	5	0	0	2	11	86
S Erickson, Bal	9/5	Cal	W	9.0	3	0	0	4	9	86
S Erickson, Bal	9/27	Tor	W	9.0	3	0	0	0	5	86
P Schourek, Cin	6/4	StL	W	7.2	1	0	0	2	10	85
O Hershiser, Cle	6/5	Det	W	9.0	6	0	0	0	10	85
M Bielecki, Cal	7/2	Oak	W	8.0	2	0	0	2	9	85
M Rivera, NYA	7/4	ChA	W	8.0	2	0	0	4	11	85
P Martinez, Mon	7/4	StL	W	9.0	4	0	0	1	7	85
S Bergman, Det	8/2	Bos	W	9.0	4	0	0	1	7	85
B Jones, NYN	9/8	Mon	W	9.0	3	0	0	2	6	85

Which Shortstops Are the Best "DP Middle Men"? (p. 187)

Both Leagues — Listed Alphabetically
1995 Active Players with 10 or more DP Opportunities (1991-1995)

Player, Team	DP Opp	DP	Pct.	Player, Team	DP Opp	DP	Pct.
Abbott, Fla	100	58	.580	Gutierrez, Hou	95	44	.463
Amaral, Sea	16	10	.625	Hernandez J, ChN	39	21	.538
Arias, Fla	45	21	.467	Hocking, Min	11	7	.636
Bell J, Pit	332	174	.524	Holbert, SD	10	7	.700
Bell J, Bos	40	19	.475	Howard D, KC	85	51	.600
Belliard, Atl	110	59	.536	Huson, Bal	85	42	.494
Beltre, Tex	50	25	.500	Johnson H, ChN	14	9	.643
Benjamin, SF	37	20	.541	Lansing, Mon	18	12	.667
Blauser, Atl	190	93	.489	Larkin, Cin	267	141	.528
Bogar, NYN	35	21	.600	Lee, StL	154	73	.474
Bordick, Oak	254	152	.598	Lewis M, Cin	72	38	.528
Branson, Cin	37	18	.486	Liriano, Pit	18	9	.500
Castilla, Col	61	43	.705	Listach, Mil	138	76	.551
Cedeno A, SD	210	121	.576	Meares, Min	137	77	.562
Cedeno D, Tor	27	12	.444	Miller O, Hou	45	25	.556
Clayton, SF	242	131	.541	Naehring, Bos	20	18	.900
Cordero, Mon	130	64	.492	Offerman, LA	233	119	.511
Correia, Cal	15	9	.600	Oquendo, StL	26	8	.308
Cromer, StL	27	21	.778	Owen, Cal	160	72	.450
Diaz M, Fla	50	23	.460	Perez T, Tor	16	10	.625
DiSarcina, Cal	229	121	.528	Reboulet, Min	56	37	.661
Duncan, Phi-Cin	55	29	.527	Ripken B, Cle	10	8	.800
Dunston, ChN	182	82	.451	Ripken C, Bal	332	204	.614
Easley, Cal	22	9	.409	Rodriguez A, Sea	23	10	.435
Elster, NYA-Phi	56	25	.446	Rodriguez C, Bos	21	14	.667
Espinoza, Cle	115	81	.704	Sanchez, ChN	102	68	.667
Fermin, Sea	219	106	.484	Schofield, LA-Cal	186	95	.511
Fernandez, NYA	255	139	.545	Shipley, Hou	45	20	.444
Foley, Mon	20	15	.750	Smith O, StL	241	149	.618
Fonville, Mon-LA	13	6	.462	Sojo, Sea	38	24	.632
Fryman, Det	133	84	.632	Spiers, NYN	94	46	.489
Gagne, KC	301	187	.621	Stankiewicz, Hou	56	31	.554
Gallego, Oak	97	52	.536	Stocker, Phi	101	55	.545
Garcia C, Pit	10	4	.400	Trammell, Det	135	77	.570
Gil, Tex	90	57	.633	Valentin J, Bos	217	139	.641
Gomez C, Det	93	46	.495	Valentin J, Mil	106	69	.651
Gonzales, Cal	13	6	.462	Velarde, NYA	101	62	.614
Gonzalez A, Tor	43	18	.419	Vizcaino, NYN	187	101	.540
Grebeck, ChA	76	44	.579	Vizquel, Cle	335	203	.606
Grudzielanek, Mon	12	9	.750	Weiss, Col	254	148	.583
Guillen, ChA	196	91	.464	**MLB Avg**	9626	5301	.551

Did Ivan's Arm Come Back. . . or Did He Just Get a Little More Help? (p. 190)

The chart below lists the Stolen Bases (**SB**) while this catcher was behind the plate, the runners he caught stealing (**CCS**), that percentage (**CS%**), the runners he picked off (**CPk**), the SB allowed per 9 innings (**SB/9**), the runners caught stealing (**PCS**) and picked off (**PPk**) by his pitchers.

Both Leagues — Listed Alphabetically
(Minimum 500 Innings Caught)

Catcher, Team	SB	CCS	CS%	CPk	SB/9	PCS	PPk
Ausmus, SD	54	33	37.9	0	0.59	6	3
Daulton, Phi	74	25	25.3	0	0.82	2	4
Eusebio, Hou	66	18	21.4	1	0.72	11	5
Fabregas, Cal	35	20	36.4	1	0.56	2	2
Flaherty, Det	78	18	18.8	0	0.77	6	1
Fletcher D, Mon	83	25	23.1	0	0.97	11	5
Girardi, Col	88	26	22.8	0	0.76	7	9
Hoiles, Bal	64	22	25.6	0	0.66	10	2
Hundley, NYN	51	16	23.9	0	0.67	2	5
Johnson C, Fla	51	36	41.4	0	0.54	2	4
Karkovice, ChA	67	30	30.9	0	0.70	4	5
Lopez, Atl	61	17	21.8	4	0.73	0	4
Macfarlane, Bos	53	22	29.3	2	0.53	7	4
Manwaring, SF	70	21	23.1	1	0.65	7	5
Mayne, KC	55	15	21.4	0	0.61	0	2
O'Brien, Atl	71	8	10.1	1	1.25	12	4
Oliver, Mil	72	20	21.7	1	0.89	7	4
Pagnozzi, StL	48	26	35.1	0	0.83	2	1
Parent, ChN	54	29	34.9	0	0.77	6	2
Pena T, Cle	68	15	18.1	2	0.87	3	7
Piazza, LA	87	27	23.7	1	0.83	2	3
Rodriguez I, Tex	40	31	43.7	6	0.34	6	2
Santiago, Cin	34	10	22.7	1	0.50	3	1
Servais, ChN	73	23	24.0	0	0.98	3	1
Stanley, NYA	74	17	18.7	0	0.75	12	5
Steinbach, Oak	60	33	35.5	0	0.59	6	3
Stinnett, NYN	72	12	14.3	1	1.24	5	0
Walbeck, Min	64	19	22.9	1	0.62	1	2
Wilkins, Hou	44	22	33.3	1	0.77	1	1
Wilson D, Sea	67	30	30.9	0	0.59	9	0

Who Are the Prime Pivot Men? (p. 192)

Both Leagues — Listed Alphabetically
1995 Active Players with 10 or more DP Opportunities (1991-1995)

Player, Team	DP Opp	DP	Pct.	Player, Team	DP Opp	DP	Pct.
Alexander	42	30	.714	Jefferies	121	47	.388
Alicea	210	136	.648	Kelly P	278	167	.601
Alomar R	521	304	.583	Kent	186	123	.661
Amaral	79	46	.582	King	24	14	.583
Arias	24	13	.542	Knoblauch	418	258	.617
Baerga	426	271	.636	Lansing	139	83	.597
Barberie	160	98	.613	Lee	102	47	.461
Bates	38	28	.737	Lemke	338	200	.592
Bell D	21	13	.619	Lewis M	29	19	.655
Bell J	79	53	.671	Lind	486	261	.537
Belliard	43	26	.605	Liriano	210	108	.514
Benjamin	20	12	.600	Listach	34	21	.618
Biggio	289	151	.522	Lockhart	37	23	.622
Blauser	47	25	.532	Martin N	27	12	.444
Boone	191	131	.686	McLemore	177	115	.650
Bordick	64	42	.656	Mejia	53	24	.453
Branson	46	31	.674	Miller K	109	59	.541
Browne	198	91	.460	Morandini	282	162	.574
Brumley	20	18	.900	Naehring	57	28	.491
Caraballo	16	11	.688	Oquendo	271	157	.579
Cedeno D	18	11	.611	Patterson	74	41	.554
Cirillo	17	12	.706	Pena G	156	109	.699
Cora	235	150	.638	Phillips T	195	114	.585
DeShields	368	204	.554	Ready	65	29	.446
Duncan	178	95	.534	Reboulet	17	10	.588
Durham	78	41	.526	Reed J	509	325	.639
Easley	105	66	.629	Ripken B	299	195	.652
Espinoza	19	11	.579	Roberts	157	77	.490
Fermin	27	17	.630	Rodriguez C	17	12	.706
Fletcher S	385	257	.668	Samuel	228	99	.434
Foley	96	51	.531	Sanchez	79	45	.570
Fonville	23	10	.435	Scarsone	39	27	.692
Frye	127	67	.528	Sharperson	42	27	.643
Gallego	193	118	.611	Shipley	20	11	.550
Garcia C	239	149	.623	Shumpert	128	74	.578
Gates	171	106	.620	Sojo	182	113	.621
Gomez C	38	24	.632	Spiers	58	33	.569
Gonzales	80	53	.663	Stankiewicz	22	15	.682
Grebeck	29	18	.621	Strange	121	74	.612
Hale	20	13	.650	Thompson R	451	282	.625
Haney	19	7	.368	Treadway	217	123	.567
Harris	117	55	.470	Velarde	39	23	.590
Hernandez J	19	10	.526	Veras	70	42	.600
Howard D	31	14	.452	Vina	73	59	.808
Hudler	57	39	.684	Vizcaino	20	14	.700
Hulett	59	38	.644	Whitaker	506	275	.543
Huson	38	25	.658	Young E	94	55	.585
Ingram G	20	12	.600	**MLB Avg**	**12393**	**7315**	**.590**

Which Catchers Pick Off the Most Runners? (p. 194)

Both Leagues — Listed Alphabetically
(1995 Catchers With At Least One Pickoff Atttempt)

Catcher	Pickoffs	Pickoff Errors	Net
Encarnacion, Pit	2	1	1
Eusebio, Hou	1	0	1
Fabregas, Cal	1	0	1
Hemond, StL	1	0	1
Hernandez, LA	0	1	-1
Hundley, NYM	0	1	-1
Laker, Mon	1	0	1
Lopez, Atl	4	1	3
Lyons, CHA	2	0	2
MacFarlane, Bos	2	0	2
Manwaring, SF	1	0	1
Matheny, Mil	3	0	3
Mercedes, KC	1	0	1
O'Brien, Atl	1	0	1
Oliver, Mil	1	2	-1
Pena, Cle	2	1	1
Piazza, LA	1	0	1
Rodriguez, Tex	6	2	4
Santiago, Cin	1	0	1
Stinnett, NYN	1	0	1
Walbeck, Min	1	0	1
Wilkins, ChA	1	0	1
Zaun, Bal	1	1	0

Who's Best in the Infield Zone? (p. 196)

Zone Ratings — Infielders
(minimum 550 defensive innings in 1995)

FIRST BASE		1995			1993-94		
Player, Team	Innings	In Zone	Outs	Zone Rating	In Zone	Outs	Zone Rating
Jaha, Mil	658.0	142	131	.923	572	495	.865
Joyner, KC	1069.2	240	219	.913	696	613	.881
Karros, LA	1271.2	240	217	.904	790	675	.854
Bagwell, Hou	1048.1	215	189	.879	667	588	.882
Morris, Cin	790.2	148	128	.865	487	418	.858
Galarraga, Col	1229.1	293	250	.853	730	619	.848
Segui, Mon	877.2	181	154	.851	548	441	.805
Mabry, StL	566.1	109	92	.844	109	92	.844
Olerud, Tor	1173.0	246	206	.837	696	603	.866
Fielder, Det	635.2	153	128	.837	518	424	.819
Colbrunn, Fla	1163.2	242	202	.835	390	326	.836
Martinez T, Sea	1195.2	256	212	.828	568	464	.817
Mattingly, NYA	1038.0	203	166	.818	561	477	.850
Palmeiro R, Bal	1238.0	293	238	.812	797	646	.811
Vaughn M, Bos	1225.2	265	215	.811	672	543	.808
Sorrento, Cle	760.1	184	148	.804	595	481	.808
McGwire, Oak	754.2	193	155	.803	299	237	.793
Carreon, SF	670.1	146	117	.801	149	119	.799
Grace, ChN	1268.0	256	205	.801	714	601	.842
Clark W, Tex	1058.1	218	173	.794	617	491	.796
McGriff, Atl	1240.2	199	157	.789	588	493	.838
Williams E, SD	608.2	105	82	.781	185	142	.768
Brogna, NYN	1089.2	222	171	.770	268	211	.787
Thomas, ChA	772.1	145	106	.731	516	385	.746
Snow, Cal	1249.0	178	129	.725	458	348	.760

SECOND BASE		1995			1993-95		
Player, Team	Innings	In Zone	Outs	Zone Rating	In Zone	Outs	Zone Rating
Reed J, SD	1066.2	396	370	.934	1230	1123	.913
Morandini, Phi	1027.1	352	328	.932	910	836	.919
Easley, Cal	701.0	218	202	.927	443	409	.923
Veras, Fla	1001.0	354	328	.927	354	328	.927
DeShields, LA	968.1	363	334	.920	1096	1009	.921
Lemke, Atl	967.1	335	308	.919	1134	1024	.903
Sanchez, ChN	903.2	383	349	.911	552	503	.911
Baerga, Cle	1165.0	505	460	.911	1372	1239	.903
Lansing, Mon	1105.1	412	373	.905	707	628	.888
Kelly P, NYA	731.2	292	263	.901	958	875	.913
Alicea, Bos	1150.2	480	430	.896	946	846	.894
Boone, Cin	1214.1	401	359	.895	891	799	.897
Frye, Tex	688.2	285	255	.895	450	395	.878
Gates, Oak	1129.0	492	438	.890	1199	1041	.868
Kent, NYN	1045.2	399	351	.880	1139	1024	.899
Thompson R, SF	770.2	273	240	.879	818	744	.910
Alomar R, Tor	1126.2	446	389	.872	1272	1099	.864
Biggio, Hou	1273.1	481	419	.871	1372	1229	.896
Vina, Mil	626.2	237	206	.869	305	267	.875
Knoblauch, Min	1159.2	456	392	.860	1263	1097	.869
Young E, Col	617.2	265	227	.857	533	466	.874
Durham, ChA	1049.2	354	301	.850	354	301	.850
Garcia C, Pit	767.1	305	250	.820	1052	873	.830
Cora, Sea	919.2	346	282	.815	1029	865	.841
Alexander, Bal	564.0	187	151	.807	187	151	.807
Bates, Col	551.0	219	174	.795	219	174	.795

THIRD BASE

Player, Team	Innings	1995 In Zone	Outs	Zone Rating	1993-95 In Zone	Outs	Zone Rating
Branson, Cin	680.2	211	201	.953	253	237	.937
Cirillo, Mil	614.1	184	171	.929	261	243	.931
Boggs, NYA	935.0	226	200	.885	871	769	.883
Seitzer, Mil	660.0	208	184	.885	487	406	.834
Hayes, Phi	1255.0	339	297	.876	1006	852	.847
Jones C, Atl	1055.0	324	282	.870	324	282	.870
Fryman, Det	1275.0	438	381	.870	857	731	.853
Williams M, SF	642.1	221	191	.864	814	731	.898
Naehring, Bos	1077.2	322	276	.857	351	298	.849
Thome, Cle	1144.2	280	239	.854	613	520	.848
Gaetti, KC	1047.2	289	246	.851	648	568	.877
Wallach, LA	792.0	198	168	.848	724	602	.831
Berry, Mon	674.2	229	194	.847	660	542	.821
Caminiti, SD	1226.0	371	312	.841	973	825	.848
Cooper, StL	908.0	317	266	.839	953	771	.809
Bonilla, Bal	569.0	158	132	.835	594	481	.810
Sprague, Tor	1215.0	323	269	.833	839	701	.836
Ventura, ChA	1016.1	256	213	.832	835	711	.851
Pendleton, Fla	1129.1	334	276	.826	962	803	.835
King, Pit	684.0	213	176	.826	933	788	.845
Leius, Min	911.2	247	204	.826	495	402	.812
Castilla, Col	1175.2	337	268	.795	357	282	.790
Phillips T, Cal	734.2	238	186	.782	240	187	.779
Magadan, Hou	736.2	218	169	.775	550	434	.789
Zeile, ChN	641.1	180	137	.761	881	708	.804
Blowers, Sea	1008.2	220	166	.755	651	509	.782

SHORTSTOP

Player, Team	Innings	1995 In Zone	Outs	Zone Rating	1993-95 In Zone	Outs	Zone Rating
DiSarcina, Cal	864.0	307	294	.958	1123	1060	.944
Bordick, Oak	1073.1	392	374	.954	1246	1130	.907
Ripken C, Bal	1250.0	450	424	.942	1404	1292	.920
Stocker, Phi	1073.1	444	416	.937	1017	912	.897
Gagne, KC	1008.0	427	395	.925	1324	1194	.902
Cromer, StL	758.0	328	303	.924	354	326	.921
Valentin J, Mil	884.1	373	341	.914	775	702	.906
Fernandez, NYA	887.2	311	284	.913	824	733	.890
Gil, Tex	1100.2	451	411	.911	542	486	.897
Valentin J, Bos	1192.2	476	430	.903	1267	1146	.904
Blauser, Atl	997.0	408	362	.887	1265	1129	.892
Gonzalez A, Tor	841.0	253	223	.881	307	271	.883
Cedeno A, SD	944.1	362	318	.878	1153	966	.838
Gomez C, Det	798.0	339	297	.876	587	509	.867
Vizcaino, NYN	1119.2	474	414	.873	1123	988	.880
Vizquel, Cle	1187.0	472	412	.873	1279	1152	.901
Guillen, ChA	967.2	385	336	.873	1073	989	.922
Larkin, Cin	1090.2	398	346	.869	1091	965	.885
Sojo, Sea	635.2	211	183	.867	317	281	.886
Clayton, SF	1169.0	522	451	.864	1443	1245	.863
Weiss, Col	1140.2	494	426	.862	1358	1177	.867
Meares, Min	953.0	403	345	.856	1048	885	.844
Bell J, Pit	1150.0	504	431	.855	1608	1392	.866
Dunston, ChN	1043.2	421	356	.846	699	605	.866
Abbott, Fla	975.0	373	312	.836	699	593	.848
Miller O, Hou	775.1	336	280	.833	365	305	.836
Offerman, LA	988.2	398	328	.824	1223	1039	.850
Cordero, Mon	928.2	382	312	.817	1239	1043	.842

Who Makes Those "Home Run-Saving Catches"? (p. 200)

1993-95 Home Run-Saving Catches

Player	Catches	Player	Catches
Stan Javier	6	Tony Gwynn	2
Kenny Lofton	6	Curtis Goodwin	2
Tim Salmon	6	Mike Humphreys	1
Brady Anderson	5	Kevin McReynolds	1
Rickey Henderson	5	Andre Dawson	1
Otis Nixon	5	Darnell Coles	1
Devon White	5	Carlos Quintana	1
Jim Edmonds	4	Lance Blankenship	1
Lou Frazier	4	Jon Nunnally	1
Lance Johnson	4	Cesar Hernandez	1
Mark McLemore	4	Dan Gladden	1
Glenallen Hill	3	Ken Griffey Jr	1
Raul Mondesi	3	Felix Jose	1
Geronimo Berroa	3	Mike Devereaux	1
Shane Mack	3	Mike Aldrete	1
Brian McRae	3	Danny Tartabull	1
Lee Tinsley	3	Dave Martinez	1
Alex Cole	3	Thomas Howard	1
Chad Curtis	3	John Cangelosi	1
Rusty Greer	3	Brian Jordan	1
Dion James	3	Bip Roberts	1
Luis Polonia	3	David Hulse	1
Mark Whiten	3	Willie McGee	1
Darren Lewis	3	Dave Winfield	1
Paul O'Neill	3	Bernard Gilkey	1
Derek Bell	2	Ernie Young	1
Tim Raines	2	Reggie Sanders	1
Bobby Bonilla	2	Lyle Mouton	1
Darrin Jackson	2	Ryan Klesko	1
Mike Greenwell	2	Wes Chamberlain	1
Daryl Boston	2	Jeromy Burnitz	1
Ellis Burks	2	Tony Tarasco	1
Henry Rodriguez	2	Rob Deer	1
Turner Ward	2	Danny Bautista	1
Ryan Thompson	2	Mike Kingery	1
Wayne Kirby	2	Shawn Green	1
Bernie Williams	2	Darrell Whitmore	1
Steve Finley	2	Jack Voigt	1
Jay Buhner	2	Matt Lawton	1
Chuck Carr	2	Vince Coleman	1
Jeffrey Hammonds	2	Garret Anderson	1
Ruben Sierra	2	Johnny Damon	1
Kirby Puckett	2	Tom Goodwin	1
Dante Bichette	2	Lenny Dykstra	1
Milt Thompson	2	Darryl Strawberry	1
Robin Yount	2	Bob Zupcic	1
Rich Becker	2	Chris Jones	1
Cory Snyder	2	Tom Brunansky	1
Barry Bonds	2	Brett Butler	1
Ray Lankford	2	Dave Henderson	1
Darryl Hamilton	2	Joe Orsulak	1
Troy O'Leary	2	Marty Cordova	1
Sammy Sosa	2		

Who's Best in the Outfield Zone? (p. 202)

Zone Ratings — Outfielders
(minimum 550 defensive innings in 1995)

LEFT FIELD		1995			1993-95		
Player, Team	Innings	In Zone	Outs	Zone Rating	In Zone	Outs	Zone Rating
Cordova, Min	1123.1	368	319	.867	368	319	.867
Belle, Cle	1265.0	340	290	.853	998	811	.813
Anderson G, Cal	814.2	247	208	.842	257	216	.840
Gonzalez L, ChN	1066.0	298	248	.832	953	781	.820
Carter, Tor	943.0	258	213	.826	387	311	.804
Anderson B, Bal	939.1	229	189	.825	701	568	.810
Coleman, Sea	816.2	209	172	.823	603	486	.806
May, Hou	553.1	145	119	.821	580	477	.822
Gilkey, StL	1021.2	236	193	.818	719	563	.783
Gant, Cin	930.1	218	178	.817	532	441	.829
Bonds, SF	1257.0	326	259	.794	898	728	.811
Raines, ChA	878.0	233	183	.785	699	574	.821
Henderson, Oak	741.1	191	149	.780	644	539	.837
Conine, Fla	1010.1	238	183	.769	775	585	.755
Martin A, Pit	657.1	159	121	.761	433	338	.781
Klesko, Atl	754.0	146	109	.747	221	175	.792
Greenwell, Bos	1043.2	267	196	.734	784	587	.749
Bichette, Col	1010.2	231	167	.723	231	167	.723

CENTER FIELD		1995			1993-95		
Player, Team	Innings	In Zone	Outs	Zone Rating	In Zone	Outs	Zone Rating
Edmonds, Cal	1190.1	440	387	.880	459	405	.882
Williams B, NYA	1274.2	482	420	.871	1230	1051	.854
Finley, SD	1202.2	331	287	.867	960	806	.840
Goodwin C, Bal	684.1	236	202	.856	236	202	.856
Grissom, Atl	1158.2	350	296	.846	1207	1022	.847
Javier, Oak	811.1	318	268	.843	649	541	.834
Sanders D, SF	716.1	240	202	.842	630	532	.844
Van Slyke, Phi	617.1	186	155	.833	734	577	.786
McRae, ChN	1213.0	399	331	.830	1151	957	.831
Goodwin T, KC	800.0	245	203	.829	250	207	.828
Lofton, Cle	974.0	296	245	.828	1053	904	.858
Hunter B, Hou	642.2	217	179	.825	232	193	.832
Carr, Fla	735.1	258	212	.822	1073	876	.816
Lewis D, Cin	1023.2	375	308	.821	1067	904	.847
Tinsley, Bos	747.1	273	223	.817	343	282	.822
White R, Mon	967.0	298	243	.815	307	251	.818
Johnson L, ChA	1185.2	403	328	.814	1226	1043	.851
Curtis, Det	1266.0	441	357	.810	1287	1082	.841
Becker, Min	848.0	322	260	.807	424	347	.818
White D, Tor	862.1	314	252	.803	1059	900	.850
Nixon, Tex	1221.0	441	347	.787	1087	885	.814
Hamilton, Mil	841.0	326	256	.785	521	423	.812

Player, Team	Innings	In Zone	Outs	Zone Rating	In Zone	Outs	Zone Rating
Griffey Jr, Sea	596.1	237	186	.785	920	711	.773
Butler, LA	1105.2	360	277	.769	1103	892	.809
Lankford, StL	1116.0	371	281	.757	1064	843	.792
Brumfield, Pit	808.0	311	235	.756	554	431	.778
Kelly R, LA	615.2	184	139	.755	713	565	.792
Kingery, Col	762.0	253	173	.684	478	336	.703

RIGHT FIELD

Player, Team	Innings	1995 In Zone	Outs	Zone Rating	1993-94 In Zone	Outs	Zone Rating
Devereaux, Atl	682.1	188	170	.904	188	170	.904
Sosa, ChN	1274.0	346	307	.887	812	707	.871
Sanders R, Cin	1028.0	259	226	.873	826	714	.864
Mieske, Mil	664.0	198	172	.869	403	337	.836
Nunnally, KC	696.2	191	164	.859	191	164	.859
Gwynn T, SD	1126.2	280	239	.854	761	658	.865
Jordan B, StL	977.2	271	228	.841	360	301	.836
Tarasco, Mon	910.2	244	205	.840	278	234	.842
Justice, Atl	1035.1	269	226	.840	873	724	.829
Whiten, Phi	730.1	181	151	.834	760	637	.838
Greer, Tex	598.2	149	124	.832	257	207	.805
Merced, Pit	855.2	223	185	.830	551	469	.851
Salmon, Cal	1257.1	371	307	.827	989	831	.840
Everett, NYN	586.2	158	130	.823	171	141	.825
Mondesi, LA	981.0	271	221	.815	516	427	.828
Ramirez, Cle	1132.0	257	209	.813	431	352	.817
Hill, SF	1085.0	265	213	.804	344	273	.794
O'Leary, Bos	673.0	190	152	.800	221	176	.796
Bautista, Det	657.0	184	147	.799	228	185	.811
O'Neill, NYA	856.1	239	189	.791	653	535	.819
Green, Tor	867.1	258	204	.791	261	206	.789
Bell D, Hou	725.2	169	131	.775	179	139	.777
Puckett, Min	896.1	236	178	.754	600	470	.783
Walker, Col	1096.2	293	220	.751	738	608	.824
Buhner, Sea	1046.0	217	162	.747	772	587	.760
Sierra, NYA	578.0	152	107	.704	683	537	.786

Who Led the League in Fumbles? (p. 204)

Both Leagues — Listed by Fewest Games per Error (G/E) — 1995
(minimum 550 defensive innings played)

Name	Inn	E	G/E	Name	Inn	E	G/E
Catchers				**Second Basemen**			
Servais, ChN	672.0	12	6.2	Cora, Sea	919.2	22	4.6
Flaherty, Det	916.1	11	9.3	Young E, Col	617.2	11	6.2
Oliver, Mil	730.1	8	10.1	Baerga, Cle	1165.0	19	6.8
Fabregas, Cal	558.1	6	10.3	Frye, Tex	688.2	11	7.0
Lopez, Atl	756.2	8	10.5	Alexander, Bal	564.0	9	7.0
Hundley, NYN	680.1	7	10.8	Durham, ChA	1049.2	15	7.8
Pena T, Cle	703.0	7	11.2	Alicea, Bos	1150.2	16	8.0
Girardi, Col	1044.1	10	11.6	Garcia C, Pit	767.1	9	9.5
Piazza, LA	941.0	9	11.6	DeShields, LA	968.1	11	9.8
Rodriguez I, Tex	1065.0	8	14.8	Vina, Mil	626.2	7	9.9
Ausmus, SD	821.0	6	15.2	Gates, Oak	1129.0	12	10.5
Manwaring, SF	971.2	7	15.4	Easley, Cal	701.0	7	11.1
Johnson C, Fla	844.2	6	15.6	Kelly P, NYA	731.2	7	11.6
Karkovice, ChA	867.0	6	16.1	Kent, NYN	1045.2	10	11.6
Walbeck, Min	932.0	6	17.3	Veras, Fla	1001.0	9	12.4
Parent, ChN	634.0	4	17.6	Knoblauch, Min	1159.2	10	12.9
Eusebio, Hou	821.1	5	18.3	Biggio, Hou	1273.1	10	14.1
Stanley, NYA	893.1	5	19.9	Sanchez, ChN	903.2	7	14.3
MacFarlane, Bos	899.2	5	20.0	Morandini, Phi	1027.1	7	16.3
Steinbach, Oak	916.2	5	20.4	Bates, Col	551.0	3	20.4
Fletcher D, Mon	767.0	4	21.3	Lansing, Mon	1105.1	6	20.5
Wilson D, Sea	1017.0	5	22.6	Lemke, Atl	967.1	5	21.5
Daulton, Phi	814.2	4	22.6	Thompson R, SF	770.2	3	28.5
Mayne, KC	817.1	3	30.3	Reed J, SD	1066.2	4	29.6
Hoiles, Bal	871.2	3	32.3	Alomar R, Tor	1126.2	4	31.3
Santiago, Cin	606.0	2	33.7	Boone, Cin	1214.1	4	33.7
First Basemen				**Third Basemen**			
McGwire, Oak	754.2	12	7.0	Bonilla, Bal	569.0	16	4.0
Williams E, SD	608.2	7	9.7	Phillips T, Cal	734.2	19	4.3
Galarraga, Col	1229.1	13	10.5	Magadan, Hou	736.2	18	4.5
Sorrento, Cle	760.1	7	12.1	Jones C, Atl	1055.0	25	4.7
Thomas, ChA	772.1	7	12.3	Caminiti, SD	1226.0	27	5.0
Vaughn M, Bos	1225.2	11	12.4	Cirillo, Mil	614.1	13	5.3
Fielder, Det	635.2	5	14.1	Cooper, StL	908.0	18	5.6
Carreon, SF	670.1	5	14.9	King, Pit	684.0	13	5.8
Mabry, StL	566.1	4	15.7	Berry, Mon	674.2	12	6.2
Mattingly, NYA	1038.0	7	16.5	Zeile, ChN	641.1	11	6.5
Martinez T, Sea	1195.2	8	16.6	Ventura, ChA	1016.1	17	6.6
Bagwell, Hou	1048.1	7	16.6	Pendleton, Fla	1129.1	18	7.0
Clark W, Tex	1058.1	7	16.8	Williams M, SF	642.1	10	7.1
Morris, Cin	790.2	5	17.6	Leius, Min	911.2	14	7.2
Grace, ChN	1268.0	7	20.1	Naehring, Bos	1077.2	16	7.5
Karros, LA	1271.2	7	20.2	Gaetti, KC	1047.2	15	7.8
Colbrunn, Fla	1163.2	5	25.9	Thome, Cle	1144.2	16	7.9
McGriff, Atl	1240.2	5	27.6	Blowers, Sea	1008.2	14	8.0
Segui, Mon	877.2	3	32.5	Sprague, Tor	1215.0	16	8.4
Olerud, Tor	1173.0	4	32.6	Castilla, Col	1175.2	15	8.7
Palmeiro R, Bal	1238.0	4	34.4	Hayes, Phi	1255.0	14	10.0
Snow, Cal	1249.0	4	34.7	Fryman, Det	1275.0	14	10.1
Jaha, Mil	658.0	2	36.6	Seitzer, Mil	660.0	7	10.5
Joyner, KC	1069.2	3	39.6	Branson, Cin	680.2	7	10.8
Brogna, NYN	1089.2	3	40.4	Wallach, LA	792.0	5	17.6
				Boggs, NYA	935.0	5	20.8

Name	Inn	E	G/E	Name	Inn	E	G/E
Shortstops				Sanders D, SF	716.1	5	15.9
Offerman, LA	988.2	35	3.1	Tinsley, Bos	747.1	5	16.6
Cromer, StL	758.0	16	5.3	Williams B, NYA	1274.2	8	17.7
Gonzalez A, Tor	841.0	17	5.5	Finley, SD	1202.2	7	19.1
Abbott, Fla	975.0	19	5.7	Kingery, Col	762.0	4	21.2
Miller O, Hou	775.1	15	5.7	Kelly R, LA	615.2	3	22.8
Meares, Min	953.0	18	5.9	Van Slyke, Phi	617.1	3	22.9
Cordero, Mon	928.2	17	6.1	Becker, Min	848.0	4	23.6
Gagne, KC	1008.0	18	6.2	White R, Mon	967.0	4	26.9
Clayton, SF	1169.0	20	6.5	Carr, Fla	735.1	3	27.2
Valentin J, Mil	884.1	15	6.6	Goodwin T, KC	800.0	3	29.6
Cedeno A, SD	944.1	16	6.6	Hamilton, Mil	841.0	3	31.1
Dunston, ChN	1043.2	17	6.8	White D, Tor	862.1	3	31.9
Stocker, Phi	1073.1	17	7.0	Griffey Jr, Sea	596.1	2	33.1
Gil, Tex	1100.2	17	7.2	Nixon, Tex	1221.0	4	33.9
Valentin J, Bos	1192.2	18	7.4	Goodwin C, Bal	684.1	2	38.0
Blauser, Atl	997.0	15	7.4	Lankford, StL	1116.0	3	41.3
Gomez C, Det	798.0	12	7.4	Johnson L, ChA	1185.2	3	43.9
Weiss, Col	1140.2	16	7.9	McRae, ChN	1213.0	3	44.9
Guillen, ChA	967.2	12	9.0	Curtis, Det	1266.0	3	46.9
Bell J, Pit	1150.0	14	9.1	Lewis D, Cin	1023.2	2	56.9
Fernandez, NYA	887.2	10	9.9	Butler, LA	1105.2	2	61.4
Larkin, Cin	1090.2	11	11.0	Grissom, Atl	1158.2	2	64.4
Bordick, Oak	1073.1	10	11.9	Edmonds, Cal	1190.1	1	132.3
Vizcaino, NYN	1119.2	10	12.4	Javier, Oak	811.1	0	—
Sojo, Sea	635.2	5	14.1	**Right Fielders**			
Vizquel, Cle	1187.0	9	14.7	Bell D, Hou	725.2	8	10.1
DiSarcina, Cal	864.0	6	16.0	Sosa, ChN	1274.2	13	10.9
Ripken C, Bal	1250.0	7	19.8	Hill, SF	1085.0	10	12.1
Left Fielders				Sierra, NYA	578.0	5	12.8
Klesko, Atl	754.0	7	12.0	Nunnally, KC	696.2	6	12.9
Carter, Tor	943.0	7	15.0	Green, Tor	867.1	6	16.1
May, Hou	553.1	4	15.4	Mieske, Mil	664.0	4	18.4
Anderson G, Cal	814.2	5	18.1	O'Leary, Bos	673.0	4	18.7
Martin A, Pit	657.1	4	18.3	Merced, Pit	855.2	5	19.0
Greenwell, Bos	1043.2	6	19.3	Whiten, Phi	730.1	4	20.3
Gonzalez L, ChN	1066.0	6	19.7	Everett, NYN	586.2	3	21.7
Conine, Fla	1010.1	5	22.5	Greer, Tex	598.2	3	22.2
Bonds, SF	1257.0	6	23.3	Puckett, Min	896.1	4	24.9
Belle, Cle	1265.0	6	23.4	Ramirez, Cle	1132.0	5	25.2
Raines, ChA	878.0	4	24.4	Devereaux, Atl	682.1	3	25.3
Coleman, Sea	816.2	3	30.2	Mondesi, LA	981.0	4	27.3
Cordova, Min	1123.1	4	31.2	Sanders R, Cin	1028.0	4	28.6
Gant, Cin	930.1	3	34.5	Justice, Atl	1035.1	4	28.8
Bichette, Col	1010.2	3	37.4	O'Neill, NYA	856.1	3	31.7
Gilkey, StL	1021.2	3	37.8	Tarasco, Mon	910.2	3	33.7
Henderson, Oak	741.1	2	41.2	Salmon, Cal	1257.1	4	34.9
Anderson B, Bal	939.1	2	52.2	Bautista, Det	657.0	2	36.5
Center Fielders				Walker, Col	1096.2	3	40.6
Hunter B, Hou	642.2	9	7.9	Buhner, Sea	1046.0	2	58.1
Brumfield, Pit	808.0	8	11.2	Gwynn T, SD	1126.2	2	62.6
Lofton, Cle	974.0	8	13.5	Jordan B, StL	977.2	1	108.6

Who Are Baseball's Best "Goalies"? (p. 207)

Both Leagues — Listed Alphabetically
(Minimum 550 Innings Caught)

Catcher	Innings	PB+WP	PB+WP per 100 Inn
Ausmus, SD	821.0	41	4.99
Daulton, Phi	814.2	40	4.91
Eusebio, Hou	821.1	38	4.63
Fabregas, Cal	558.1	26	4.66
Flaherty, Det	916.1	45	4.91
Fletcher, Mon	767.0	22	2.87
Girardi, Col	1044.1	55	5.27
Hoiles, Bal	871.2	22	2.52
Hundley, NYN	680.1	26	3.82
Johnson, Fla	844.2	30	3.55
Karkovice, ChA	867.0	36	4.15
Lopez, Atl	756.2	37	4.89
Macfarlane, Bos	899.2	74	8.23
Manwaring, SF	971.2	38	3.91
Mayne, KC	817.1	25	3.06
Oliver, Mil	730.1	46	6.30
Parent, ChN	634.0	43	6.78
Pena, Cle	703.0	30	4.27
Piazza, LA	941.0	49	5.21
Rodriguez, Tex	1065.0	57	5.35
Santiago, Cin	606.0	36	5.94
Servais, ChN	672.0	23	3.42
Stanley, NYA	893.1	46	5.15
Steinbach, Oak	916.2	46	5.02
Walbeck, Min	932.1	45	4.83
Wilson, Sea	1017.0	44	4.33
MLB Avg			**4.96**

Which Outfielders Have the Cannons? (p. 209)

Both Leagues — 1995 — Listed by Hold Percentage
(minimum 30 baserunner opportunities to advance)

Left Field				Center Field				Right Field			
Player, Team	**Opp**	**XB**	**Pct**	**Player, Team**	**Opp**	**XB**	**Pct**	**Player, Team**	**Opp**	**XB**	**Pct**
Higginson, Det	68	10	14.7	Van Slyke, Phi	87	35	40.2	Merced, Pit	85	30	35.3
Amaral, Sea	32	8	25.0	Goodwin C, Bal	77	32	41.6	Walker, Col	127	47	37.0
Surhoff, Mil	49	13	26.5	Cummings, Pit	38	17	44.7	O'Leary, Bos	91	38	41.8
Plantier, SD	43	12	27.9	Grissom, Atl	137	63	46.0	Puckett, Min	92	39	42.4
Bonds, SF	146	41	28.1	Lofton, Cle	117	54	46.2	Buhner, Sea	100	43	43.0
May, Hou	67	19	28.4	Hunter B, Hou	97	45	46.4	Everett, NYN	55	24	43.6
Williams G, NYA	37	11	29.7	Bell D, Hou	40	20	50.0	Whiten, Phi	68	30	44.1
Greer, Tex	30	9	30.0	Edmonds, Cal	138	71	51.4	Nilsson, Mil	33	15	45.5
Anderson G, Cal	95	29	30.5	Brumfield, Pit	122	63	51.6	Higginson, Det	74	34	45.9
Conine, Fla	122	39	32.0	Lewis D, Cin	139	72	51.8	Bautista, Det	78	37	47.4
Henderson, Oak	78	25	32.1	Anderson B, Bal	25	13	52.0	Sanders R, Cin	69	33	47.8
Phillips T, Cal	37	12	32.4	Butler, LA	123	64	52.0	Tettleton, Tex	56	27	48.2
Belle, Cle	103	34	33.0	Nixon, Tex	181	95	52.5	Sosa, ChN	128	62	48.4
Hulse, Mil	36	12	33.3	Tinsley, Bos	114	60	52.6	Mondesi, LA	73	36	49.3
Gonzalez L, ChN	101	34	33.7	Lankford, StL	137	73	53.3	Nunnally, KC	75	37	49.3
Martin A, Pit	78	27	34.6	Cangelosi, Hou	30	16	53.3	Ramirez, Cle	83	41	49.4
McLemore, Tex	46	16	34.8	Curtis, Det	192	103	53.6	Maldonado, Tex	44	22	50.0
Klesko, Atl	57	20	35.1	Tavarez, Fla	41	22	53.7	Alou, Mon	34	17	50.0
Gilkey, StL	87	31	35.6	Kingery, Col	122	66	54.1	Hiatt, Det	36	18	50.0
Anderson B, Bal	89	32	36.0	Thompson R,NYN	40	22	55.0	Hill, SF	114	58	50.9
Alou, Mon	49	18	36.7	Diaz A, Sea	58	32	55.2	Salmon, Cal	139	72	51.8
Gant, Cin	106	39	36.8	Hulse, Mil	36	20	55.6	Jordan B, StL	83	43	51.8
Goodwin T, KC	57	21	36.8	Johnson L, ChA	174	98	56.3	Tarasco, Mon	77	40	51.9
Raines, ChA	107	40	37.4	Griffey Jr, Sea	71	40	56.3	Justice, Atl	86	45	52.3
Greenwell, Bos	123	46	37.4	McRae, ChN	168	96	57.1	Greer, Tex	55	29	52.7
Frazier, Tex	32	12	37.5	Kelly R, LA	73	42	57.5	Bass, Bal	37	20	54.1
Bichette, Col	116	44	37.9	Finley, SD	123	71	57.7	Dawson, Fla	35	19	54.3
Carter, Tor	118	45	38.1	Carr, Fla	90	52	57.8	Mieske, Mil	81	44	54.3
Ashley, LA	39	15	38.5	Howard T, Cin	38	22	57.9	Berroa, Oak	46	25	54.3
Roberts, SD	31	12	38.7	Burks, Col	81	48	59.3	O'Neill, NYA	71	39	54.9
Newfield, SD	41	16	39.0	Hamilton, Mil	113	67	59.3	Bell D, Hou	65	36	55.4
Tucker M, KC	30	12	40.0	Goodwin T, KC	86	51	59.3	Sierra, NYA	56	32	57.1
Polonia, Atl	47	19	40.4	Becker, Min	131	78	59.5	Gwynn T, SD	117	68	58.1
Nieves, SD	51	21	41.2	Dykstra, Phi	60	36	60.0	Green, Tor	88	52	59.1
Jefferies, Phi	43	18	41.9	Mondesi, LA	35	21	60.0	Devereaux, Atl	75	46	61.3
Orsulak, NYN	45	19	42.2	Walton, Cin	36	22	61.1	Sheffield, Fla	55	36	65.5
Cordova, Min	118	50	42.4	Martin A, Pit	36	22	61.1	Eisenreich, Phi	55	37	67.3
Kelly R, LA	40	18	45.0	Damon, KC	57	35	61.4	Bonilla, Bal	26	18	69.2
Bonilla, Bal	31	14	45.2	Williams B, NYA	170	106	62.4				
Coleman, Sea	88	40	45.5	White D, Tor	137	87	63.5				
Bragg, Sea	32	16	50.0	Sanders D, SF	79	51	64.6				
				Javier, Oak	119	78	65.5				
				White R, Mon	100	68	68.0				
				Amaral, Sea	31	22	71.0				
				Cole, Min	38	28	73.7				

Why Can't Roberto Alomar Zone In? (p. 212)

Plays By Second Basemen, 1993-95

(Minimum 2000 Innings)

Player	Total	In Zone	Out Zone	Out Zone Pct
Gates, Oak	984	736	248	.252
Thompson, SF	692	520	172	.249
Boone, Cin	731	551	180	.246
Biggio, Hou	1152	870	282	.245
Alomar, Bal	1015	780	235	.232
Cora, Sea	835	646	189	.226
Baerga, Cle	1160	900	260	.224
Barberie, Bal	756	590	166	.220
Reed, SD	1051	832	219	.208
Alicea, Bos	797	634	163	.205
Lemke, Atl	967	769	198	.205
Kelly, NYA	820	661	159	.194
Lind, KC	678	548	130	.192
DeShields, LA	952	773	179	.188
Garcia, Pit	829	673	156	.188
Knoblauch, Min	1029	858	171	.166
Kent, NYN	969	810	159	.164
Morandini, Phi	796	675	121	.152

Which Fielders Have the Best "Defensive Batting Average"? (p. 216)

Each chart summarizes, by position, the STATS Defensive Batting Average: a player's zone rating (**ZR**), his fielding percentage (**FP**), his pivot rating (**PR**) if he was a second baseman, and, if he was an outfielder, his outfield arm rating (**OA**). A weighting system (see article on page 224) was used to determine a player's all-around fielding rating (**Rtng**).

Both Leagues — Sorted by Fielding Rating
(Minimum 500 Innings Played in 1995)

First Base	ZR	FP	PR	OA	Rtng	Second Base	ZR	FP	PR	OA	Rtng
Jaha, Mil	.335	.311	—	—	.329	Kelly P, NYA	.289	.279	.257	—	.279
Joyner, KC	.329	.315	—	—	.325	Baerga, Cle	.297	.241	.260	—	.279
Karros, LA	.324	.289	—	—	.315	Kent, NYN	.273	.279	.296	—	.279
Bagwell, Hou	.308	.280	—	—	.301	Gates, Oak	.281	.274	.277	—	.279
Phillips J, SF	.308	.272	—	—	.299	DeShields, LA	.304	.266	.222	—	.278
Hollins, Bos	.321	.222	—	—	.296	Alomar R, Tor	.267	.314	.256	—	.271
Segui, Mon	.290	.308	—	—	.295	Frye, Tex	.284	.248	.249	—	.270
Morris, Cin	.299	.281	—	—	.295	Knoblauch, Min	.257	.284	.258	—	.261
Jefferies, Phi	.291	.284	—	—	.289	Biggio, Hou	.266	.288	.228	—	.260
Olerud, Tor	.282	.306	—	—	.288	Young E, Col	.254	.242	.282	—	.260
Mabry, StL	.286	.280	—	—	.285	Bates, Col	.206	.304	.321	—	.249
Colbrunn, Fla	.280	.297	—	—	.285	Durham, ChA	.250	.243	.244	—	.247
Galarraga, Col	.292	.252	—	—	.282	Garcia C, Pit	.226	.272	.279	—	.246
Fielder, Det	.281	.271	—	—	.279	Alexander, Bal	.216	.236	.313	—	.243
Palmeiro R, Bal	.266	.309	—	—	.277	Cora, Sea	.222	.182	.231	—	.218
Martinez T, Sea	.276	.273	—	—	.275	**Third Base**	**ZR**	**FP**	**PR**	**OA**	**Rtng**
Mattingly, NYA	.270	.277	—	—	.271	Branson, Cin	.353	.316	—	—	.338
Grace, ChN	.257	.288	—	—	.265	Boggs, NYA	.307	.335	—	—	.318
Vaughn M, Bos	.266	.262	—	—	.265	Seitzer, Mil	.307	.311	—	—	.308
McGriff, Atl	.252	.304	—	—	.265	Cirillo, Mil	.337	.258	—	—	.305
Carreon, SF	.259	.275	—	—	.263	Fryman, Det	.297	.313	—	—	.303
Sorrento, Cle	.261	.263	—	—	.262	Hayes, Phi	.301	.302	—	—	.302
Clark W, Tex	.254	.282	—	—	.261	Wallach, LA	.282	.326	—	—	.300
Brogna, NYN	.240	.314	—	—	.259	Williams M, SF	.293	.292	—	—	.293
McGwire, Oak	.260	.205	—	—	.247	Naehring, Bos	.288	.285	—	—	.287
Johnson M, Pit	.256	.205	—	—	.243	Gaetti, KC	.284	.285	—	—	.285
Williams E, SD	.247	.232	—	—	.243	Thome, Cle	.286	.274	—	—	.281
Snow, Cal	.211	.307	—	—	.235	Sprague, Tor	.272	.293	—	—	.281
Thomas, ChA	.218	.253	—	—	.226	Berry, Mon	.282	.274	—	—	.278
Second Base	**ZR**	**FP**	**PR**	**OA**	**Rtng**	Jones C, Atl	.297	.243	—	—	.276
Morandini, Phi	.314	.296	.296	—	.306	Cooper, StL	.276	.268	—	—	.273
Reed J, SD	.316	.315	.269	—	.304	Ventura, ChA	.271	.275	—	—	.273
Lemke, Atl	.304	.302	.305	—	.304	Pendleton, Fla	.268	.281	—	—	.273
Barberie, Bal	.305	.257	.319	—	.302	Manto, Bal	.253	.294	—	—	.269
Easley, Cal	.309	.269	.285	—	.297	Leius, Min	.267	.270	—	—	.268
Veras, Fla	.309	.286	.271	—	.296	Caminiti, SD	.277	.252	—	—	.267
Boone, Cin	.285	.315	.308	—	.295	King, Pit	.268	.263	—	—	.266
Sanchez, ChN	.297	.291	.273	—	.290	Castilla, Col	.247	.292	—	—	.265
McLemore, Tex	.299	.312	.251	—	.289	Paquette, Oak	.241	.251	—	—	.245
Vina, Mil	.264	.278	.349	—	.288	Bonilla, Bal	.274	.200	—	—	.244
Alicea, Bos	.285	.257	.305	—	.286	Blowers, Sea	.219	.272	—	—	.240
Lansing, Mon	.293	.305	.257	—	.286	Zeile, ChN	.224	.257	—	—	.237
Thompson R, SF	.272	.311	.282	—	.281	Phillips T, Cal	.237	.230	—	—	.235

Third Base	ZR	FP	PR	OA	Rtng
Magadan, Hou	.236	.229	—	—	.233

Shortstop	ZR	FP	PR	OA	Rtng
DiSarcina, Cal	.335	.316	—	—	.331
Bordick, Oak	.332	.308	—	—	.327
Ripken C, Bal	.323	.323	—	—	.323
Stocker, Phi	.319	.271	—	—	.309
Gagne, KC	.309	.271	—	—	.301
Fernandez, NYA	.300	.291	—	—	.298
Cromer, StL	.308	.248	—	—	.296
Valentin J, Mil	.301	.275	—	—	.295
Gil, Tex	.298	.284	—	—	.295
Valentin J, Bos	.292	.280	—	—	.290
Blauser, Atl	.279	.274	—	—	.278
Vizquel, Cle	.268	.315	—	—	.277
Vizcaino, NYN	.268	.310	—	—	.276
Gomez C, Det	.270	.282	—	—	.273
Sojo, Sea	.263	.307	—	—	.272
Guillen, ChA	.268	.289	—	—	.272
Larkin, Cin	.265	.299	—	—	.272
Cedeno A, SD	.272	.261	—	—	.270
Gonzalez A, Tor	.274	.238	—	—	.267
Weiss, Col	.259	.285	—	—	.264
Clayton, SF	.261	.272	—	—	.263
Bell J, Pit	.254	.294	—	—	.262
Meares, Min	.254	.261	—	—	.256
Dunston, ChN	.246	.270	—	—	.251
Miller O, Hou	.236	.258	—	—	.240
Abbott, Fla	.239	.243	—	—	.240
Cordero, Mon	.223	.246	—	—	.228
Offerman, LA	.229	.173	—	—	.218

Left Field	ZR	FP	PR	OA	Rtng
Polonia, Atl	.323	.330	—	.247	.309
Cordova, Min	.324	.299	—	.237	.303
Belle, Cle	.314	.279	—	.285	.303
Anderson G, Cal	.305	.271	—	.297	.298
Higginson, Det	.274	.296	—	.378	.298
Gonzalez L, ChN	.298	.270	—	.281	.290
Anderson B, Bal	.292	.303	—	.270	.289
McLemore, Tex	.286	.310	—	.276	.287
May, Hou	.289	.247	—	.308	.286
Gilkey, StL	.286	.293	—	.271	.284
Gant, Cin	.285	.290	—	.265	.282
Carter, Tor	.292	.251	—	.259	.280
Bonds, SF	.268	.276	—	.310	.278
Alou, Mon	.280	.276	—	.266	.276
Coleman, Sea	.290	.288	—	.221	.276
Henderson, Oak	.257	.298	—	.289	.270
Raines, ChA	.261	.278	—	.262	.264
Conine, Fla	.249	.265	—	.290	.259
Martin A, Pit	.242	.249	—	.276	.250
Greenwell, Bos	.222	.256	—	.262	.235
Bichette, Col	.213	.286	—	.260	.233
Klesko, Atl	.231	.174	—	.274	.231

Center Field	ZR	FP	PR	OA	Rtng
Goodwin C, Bal	.309	.293	—	.337	.315
Edmonds, Cal	.326	.316	—	.292	.314
Grissom, Atl	.301	.304	—	.317	.306
Van Slyke, Phi	.292	.267	—	.342	.303
Finley, SD	.317	.251	—	.264	.291
Williams B, NYA	.320	.266	—	.243	.289
Lewis D, Cin	.283	.305	—	.291	.289
Lofton, Cle	.288	.229	—	.316	.288
McRae, ChN	.289	.297	—	.267	.284
Javier, Oak	.299	.324	—	.229	.282
Curtis, Det	.275	.298	—	.282	.281
Hunter B, Hou	.286	.180	—	.315	.279
Tinsley, Bos	.280	.257	—	.287	.279
Johnson L, ChA	.278	.297	—	.270	.278
Goodwin T, KC	.289	.281	—	.257	.278
Carr, Fla	.284	.282	—	.264	.278
Sanders D, SF	.298	.252	—	.233	.272
Nixon, Tex	.258	.289	—	.288	.272
Becker, Min	.273	.278	—	.256	.269
Butler, LA	.245	.302	—	.290	.267
Griffey Jr, Sea	.257	.292	—	.270	.266
White D, Tor	.270	.289	—	.238	.263
Hamilton, Mil	.257	.289	—	.257	.262
White R, Mon	.279	.275	—	.218	.260
Lankford, StL	.236	.293	—	.284	.259
Brumfield, Pit	.235	.225	—	.291	.250
Kelly R, LA	.235	.257	—	.265	.247
Kingery, Col	.182	.256	—	.280	.223

Right Field	ZR	FP	PR	OA	Rtng
Merced, Pit	.285	.273	—	.341	.303
Sanders R, Cin	.314	.294	—	.287	.302
Sosa, ChN	.324	.239	—	.284	.297
Devereaux, Atl	.336	.292	—	.228	.292
Whiten, Phi	.288	.274	—	.303	.291
Jordan B, StL	.293	.324	—	.270	.289
Everett, NYN	.281	.281	—	.305	.289
Mieske, Mil	.312	.280	—	.259	.288
Nunnally, KC	.305	.251	—	.280	.288
Tarasco, Mon	.292	.300	—	.269	.285
Justice, Atl	.292	.293	—	.267	.284
O'Leary, Bos	.265	.273	—	.313	.283
Gwynn T, SD	.301	.314	—	.242	.283
Salmon, Cal	.284	.303	—	.270	.282
Mondesi, LA	.276	.292	—	.281	.280
Bautista, Det	.264	.303	—	.289	.279
Walker, Col	.232	.302	—	.334	.278
Greer, Tex	.287	.275	—	.266	.278
Ramirez, Cle	.274	.278	—	.280	.277
Buhner, Sea	.229	.306	—	.308	.268
Puckett, Min	.234	.282	—	.311	.268
Hill, SF	.268	.231	—	.274	.264
O'Neill, NYA	.259	.295	—	.256	.263
Green, Tor	.259	.266	—	.238	.253
Bell D, Hou	.248	.196	—	.254	.243
Sheffield, Fla	.265	.226	—	.210	.240
Sierra, NYA	.200	.223	—	.247	.220

Glossary

Batting Average

Hits divided by At Bats.

Bequeathed Runners

Any runner(s) on base when a pitcher leaves a game are considered "bequeathed" to the departing hurler; the opposite of "inherited runners" (see below).

Defensive Batting Average

A composite statistic incorporating various defensive statistics to arrive at a number akin to batting average. The formula uses standard deviations to establish a spread from best to worst.

Earned Run Average

(Earned Runs times 9) divided by Innings Pitched.

Favorite Toy

The Favorite Toy is a method that is used to estimate a player's chance of getting to a specific goal—in the following example, we'll say 3,000 hits.

Four things are considered:
1) Need Hits—the number of hits needed to reach the goal. (This, of course, could also be "Need Home Runs" or "Need Doubles"—Whatever.)
2) Years Remaining. The number of years remaining to meet the goal is estimated by the formula 24- .6(age). This formula assigns a 20-year-old player 12.0 remaining seasons, a 25-year-old player 9.0 remaining seasons, a 30-year-old player 6.0 remaining seasons, a 35-year-old player 3.0 remaining seasons. Any player who is still playing regularly is assumed to have at least 1.5 seasons remaining, regardless of his age.
3) Established Hit Level. For 1996, the established hit level would be found by adding 1993 hits, two times 1994 hits, and three times 1995 hits, and dividing by six. However, a player cannot have an established performance level that is less than three-fourths of his most recent performance— that is, a player who had 200 hits in 1995 cannot have an established hit level below 150.
4) Projected Remaining Hits. This is found by multiplying the second number (ears remaining) by the third (established hit level).

Once you get the projected remaining hits, the chance of getting to the goal is figured by (projected remaining hits) divided by (need hits), minus .5. By this method, if your "need hits" and your "projected remaining hits" are the same, your chance of reaching the goal is 50 percent. If your projected remaining hits are 20 percent more than your need hits, the chance of reaching the goal is 70 percent.

Two special rules, and a note:
1) A player's chance of continuing to progress toward a goal cannot exceed .97 per year. (This rule prevents a player from figuring to have a 148 percent chance of reaching a goal.)
2) If a player's offensive winning percentage is below .500, his chance of continuing to progress toward the goal cannot exceed .75 per season. (That is, if a below-average hitter is two years away from reaching a goal, his chance of reaching that goal cannot be shown as better than nine-sixteenths, or three-fourths times three-fourths, regardless of his age.)
3) For 1994 and 1995, we used projected stats based on a full season of play..

Fielding Percentage

(Putouts plus Assists) divided by (Putouts plus Assists plus Errors).

Go-Ahead RBI

Any time a player drives in a run which gives his team the lead, he is credited with a go-ahead RBI.

Ground/Fly Ratio (Grd/Fly)

Simply a hitter's ground balls divided by his fly balls. All batted balls except line drives and bunts are included.

Hold

A Hold is credited any time a relief pitcher enters a game in a Save Situation (see definition below), records at least one out, and leaves the game never having relinquished the lead. Note: a pitcher cannot finish the game and receive credit for a hold, nor can he earn a hold and a save.

Inherited Runner

Any runner(s) on base when a relief pitcher enters a game are considered "inherited" by that pitcher.

Isolated Power

Slugging Percentage minus Batting Average.

K/BB Ratio

Strikeouts divided by Walks.

No Decision (ND)

The result when a starter is credited with neither a win nor a loss.

OBP+SLUG

On-base percentage plus slugging percentage.

Offensive Winning Percentage (OWP)

The Winning Percentage a team of nine Jeff Bagwells (or anybody) would compile against average pitching and defense. The formula: (Runs Created per 27 outs) divided by the League average of runs scored per game. Square the result and divide it by (1+itself).

On-Base Percentage

(Hits plus Walks plus Hit by Pitcher) divided by (At Bats plus Walks plus Hit by Pitcher plus Sacrifice Flies).

Outfielder Hold Percentage

A statistic used to evaluate outfielders' throwing arms. "Hold Percentage" is computed by dividing extra bases taken (by baserunners) by the number of opportunities. For example, if a single is lined to center field with men on first and second, and one man scores while the other stops at second, that is one extra base taken on two opportunities, a 50.0 hold percentage.

Pivot Percentage

The number of double plays turned by a second baseman as the pivot man, divided by the number of opportunities.

Plate Appearances

At Bats plus Total Walks plus Hit By Pitcher plus Sacrifice Hits plus Sacrifice Flies plus Times Reached on Defensive Interference.

Pickoffs (Pk)

The number of times a runner was picked off base by a pitcher.

Quality Start

Any start in which a pitcher works six or more innings while allowing three or fewer earned runs.

Quick Hooks and Slow Hooks

A Quick Hook is the removal of a pitcher who has pitched less than 6 innings and given up 3 runs or less. A Slow Hook goes to a pitcher who pitches more than 9 innings, or allows 7 or more runs, or whose combined innings pitched and runs allowed totals 13 or more.

Relief Points (Pts)

Wins plus saves minus losses

Run Support Per 9 IP

The number of runs scored by a pitcher's team while he was still in the game times nine divided by his Innings Pitched.

Runs Created

A way to combine a batter's total offensive contributions into one number. The formula:
(H + BB + HBP - CS - GIDP) times (Total Bases + .26(TBB - IBB + HBP) + .52(SH + SF + SB)) divided by (AB + TBB + HBP + SH + SF).

Save Percentage

Saves (SV) divided by Save Opportunities (OP).

Save Situation

A Relief Pitcher is in a Save Situation when:

upon entering the game with his club leading, he has the opportunity to be the finishing pitcher (and is not the winning pitcher of record at the time), and meets any one of the three following conditions:

(1) he has a lead of no more than three runs and has the opportunity to pitch for at least one inning, or

(2) he enters the game, regardless of the count, with the potential tying run either on base, at bat, or on deck; or

(3) he pitches three or more innings regardless of the lead and the official scorer credits him with a save.

SBA

Stolen-base attempts against a catcher

Secondary Average

A way to look at a player's extra bases gained, independent of Batting Average. The formula:
(Total Bases - Hits + TBB + SB) divided by At Bats.

Slugging Percentage

Total Bases divided by At Bats.

Zone Rating

Simply the percentage of balls fielded by a player in his typical defensive "zone," as measured by STATS reporters.

About STATS, Inc.

STATS, Inc. is the nation's leading independent sports information and statistical analysis company, providing detailed sports services for a wide array of clients.

One of the fastest-growing sports companies in the country, STATS provides the most up-to-the-minute sports information to professional teams, print and broadcast media, software developers and interactive srevice providers around the country. Some of our major clients are ESPN, Turner Sports, the Associated Press, *The Sporting News*, Electronic Arts and Motorola. Much of the information we provide is available to the public via STATS On-Line.

STATS Publishing, a division of STATS, Inc., produces 11 annual books, including the *STATS Major League Handbook*, the *Pro Football Handbook*, the *Pro Basketball Handbook* and, new for 1996, the first *STATS Hockey Handbook*. These publications deliver STATS expertise to fans, scouts, general managers and media around the country.

In addition, STATS offers the most innovative—and fun—fantasy sports games around, from *Bill James Fantasy Baseball* and *Bill James Classic Baseball* to *STATS Fantasy Football* and *STATS Fantasy Hoops*.

Information technology has grown by leaps and bounds in the last decade, and STATS will continue to be at the forefront as both a vendor and supplier of the most up-to-date, in-depth sports information available. If you haven't already, you will most certainly be seeing us at an infobahn rest stop in the near future.

For more information on our products, or on joining our reporter network, write us at:

STATS, Inc.
8131 Monticello Ave.
Skokie, IL 60076-3300

...or call us at 1-800-63-STATS (1-800-637-8287). Outside the U.S., dial 1-708-676-3383.

Index

Bill James Fantasy Baseball

Bill James Fantasy Baseball enters its eighth season of offering baseball fans the most unique, realistic and exciting game fantasy sports has to offer.

You draft a 25-player roster and can expand to as many as 28. Players aren't ranked like in rotisserie leagues—you'll get credit for everything a player does, like hitting homers, driving in runs, turning double plays, pitching quality outings and more!

Also, the team which scores the most points among all leagues, plus wins the World Series, will receive the John McGraw Award, which includes a one-week trip to the Grapefruit League in spring training, a day at the ballpark with Bill James, and a new fantasy league named in his/her honor!

Unique Features Include:

• **Live fantasy experts** — available seven days a week

• **The best weekly reports in the business** — detailing who is in the lead, win-loss records, MVPs, and team strengths and weaknesses

• **On-Line computer system** — a world of information, including daily updates of fantasy standings and stats

• **Over twice as many statistics as rotisserie**

• **Transactions that are effective the very next day!**

"My goal was to develop a fantasy league based on the simplest yet most realistic principle possible. A league in which the values are as nearly as possible what they ought to be, without being distorted by artificial category values or rankings...."

- Bill James

All this, all summer long...for less than $5 per week!

Order from STATS INC. Today!

Use Order Form in This Book, or Call 1-800-63-STATS or 847-676-3383 or e-mail: info@stats.com!

STATS Fantasy Hoops

Soar into the 1995-96 season with STATS Fantasy Hoops! SFH puts YOU in charge. Don't just sit back and watch Grant Hill, Shawn Kemp, and Alonzo Mourning - get in the game and coach your team to the top!

How to Play SFH:
1. Sign up to coach a team.
2. You'll receive a full set of rules and a draft form with SFH point values for all eligible players - anyone who played in the NBA in 1994-95, plus all 1995 NBA draft picks.
3. Complete the draft form and return it to STATS.
4. You will take part in the draft with nine other owners, and we will send you league rosters.
5. You make unlimited weekly transactions including trades, free agent signings, activations, and benchings.
6. Six of the 10 teams in your league advance to postseason play, with two teams ultimately advancing to the Finals.

SFH points values are tested against actual NBA results, mirroring the real thing. Weekly reports will tell you everything you need to know to lead your team to the SFH Championship!

STATS Fantasy Football

STATS Fantasy Football puts YOU in charge! You draft, trade, cut, bench, activate players and even sign free agents each week. SFF pits you head-to-head against 11 other owners.

STATS' scoring system applies realistic values, tested against actual NFL results. Each week, you'll receive a superb in-depth report telling you all about both team and league performances.

How to Play SFF:
1. Sign up today!
2. STATS sends you a draft form listing all eligible NFL players.
3. Fill out the draft form and return it to STATS, and you will take part in the draft along with 11 other team owners.
4. Go head-to-head against the other owners in your league. You'll make week-by-week roster moves and transactions through STATS' Fantasy Football experts, via phone, fax, or on-line!

Order from *STATS* INC. Today!

STATS On-Line

Now you can have a direct line to a world of sports information just like the pros use with STATS On-Line. If you love to keep up with your favorite teams and players, STATS On-Line is for you. From Shaquille O'Neal's fast-breaking dunks to Ken Griffey's tape-measure blasts — if you want baseball, basketball, football and   hockey stats, we put them at your fingertips!

STATS On-Line

- **Player Profiles and Team Profiles** — The #1 resource for scouting your favorite professional teams and players with information you simply can't find anywhere else! The most detailed info you've ever seen, including real-time stats. Follow baseball pitch-by-pitch, foot ball snap-by-snap, and basketball and hockey shot-by-shot, with scores and player stats updated continually!

- **NO monthly or annual fees**

- **Local access numbers** — avoid costly long-distance charges!

- **Unlimited access** — 24 hours a day, seven days a week

- **Downloadable files** — get year-to-date stats in an ASCII format for baseball, football, basketball, and hockey

- **In-progress box scores** — You'll have access to the most up-to-the-second scoring stats for every team and player. When you log into STATS On-Line, you'll get detailed updates, including player stats and scoring plays while the games are in progress!

- **Other exclusive features** — transactions and injury information, team and player profiles and updates, standings, leader and trailer boards, game-by-game logs, fantasy game features, and much more!

Sign-up fee of $30 (applied towards future use), 24-hour access with usage charges of $.75/min. Mon.-Fri., 8am-6pm CST; $.25/min. all other hours and weekends.

Order from STATS INC. Today!

Use Order Form in This Book, or Call 1-800-63-STATS or 847-676-3383 or e-mail: info@stats.com!

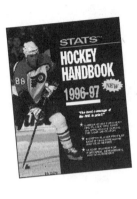
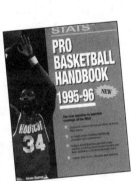

STATS INC Order Form

Name_____ Phone_____

Address_____ Fax_____

City_____ State_____ Zip_____

Method of Payment (U.S. Funds Only):

❏ Check/Money Order   ❏ Visa   ❏ MasterCard

Cardholder Name_____

Credit Card Number_____ Exp. _____

Signature_____

BOOKS

Qty	Product Name	Item #	Price	Total
	STATS 1996 Major League Handbook	HB96	$17.95	
	STATS Hockey Handbook 1996-97	HH97	$17.95	
	STATS Projections Update 1996	PJUP	$9.95	
	The Scouting Notebook: 1996	SN96	$16.95	
	STATS Player Profiles 1996	PP96	$17.95	
	Player Profiles 1996 (Comb-bound)	PC96	$19.95	
	STATS Minor Lg. Scouting Ntbk. 1996	MN96	$16.95	
	STATS Minor League Handbook 1996	MH96	$17.95	
	Minor League Hndbk. 1996 (Comb-bnd)	MC96	$19.95	
	STATS 1996 BVSP Match-Ups!	BP96	$12.95	
	STATS Baseball Scoreboard 1996	SB96	$16.95	
	STATS 1995-96 Pro Basketball Hndbk.	BH96	$17.95	
	Pro Football Revealed (1995 Edition)	PF96	$16.95	
	STATS Pro Football Handbook 1996	FH96	$17.95	
	For previous editions, circle appropriate years:			
	Major League Handbook 91 92 93 94 95		$9.95	
	Scouting Report/Notebook 92 94 95		$9.95	
	Player Profiles 93 94 95		$9.95	
	Minor League Handbook 92 93 94 95		$9.95	
	Baseball Scoreboard 92 93 94 95		$9.95	
	Basketball Scoreboard 94 95		$9.95	
	Pro Football Handbook 95		$9.95	
	Pro Football Revealed 94		$9.95	

FANTASY GAMES & STATSfax

Qty	Product Name	Item #	Price	Total
	Bill James Classic Baseball	BJCG	$129.00	
	How to Win The Classic Game (book)	CGBK	$16.95	
	The Classic Game STATSfax	CGX5	$20.00	
	Bill James Fantasy Baseball	BJFB	$89.00	
	BJFB STATSfax/5-day	SFX5	$20.00	
	BJFB STATSfax/7-day	SFX7	$25.00	
	STATS Fantasy Hoops	SFH	$85.00	
	SFH STATSfax/5-day	SFH5	$20.00	
	SFH STATSfax/7-day	SFH7	$25.00	
	STATS Fantasy Football	SFF	$69.00	
	SFF STATSfax/3-day	SFF3	$15.00	

STATS ON-LINE

Qty	Product Name	Item #	Price	Total
	STATS On-Line	ONLE	$30.00	

For faster service, call
1-800-63-STATS or 847-676-3383, fax
this form to STATS at 847-676-0821, or
send e-mail to *info@stats.com*

1st Fantasy Team Name (ex. Colt 45's):_____   _____

What Fantasy Game is this team for?_____

2nd Fantasy Team Name (ex. Colt 45's):_____   _____

What Fantasy Game is this team for?_____

NOTE: $1.00/player is charged for all roster moves and transactions.

For Bill James Fantasy Baseball

Would you like to play in a league drafted by Bill James?   ❏ Yes   ❏ No

TOTALS

	Price	Total
Product Total (excl. Fantasy Games and On-Line)		
For first class mailing in U.S. add:	+$2.50/book	
Canada—all orders—add:	+$3.50/book	
Order 2 or more books—subtract:	-$1.00/book	
IL residents add 8.5% sales tax		
Subtotal		
Fantasy Games & On-Line Total		
GRAND TOTAL		

FREE Information Kits:

❏ STATS Reporter Networks
❏ Bill James Classic Baseball
❏ Bill James Fantasy Baseball
❏ STATS On-Line
❏ STATS Fantasy Hoops
❏ STATS Fantasy Football
❏ STATS Year-end Reports
❏ STATSfax

BOOK

Mail to: STATS, Inc., 8131 Monticello Ave., Skokie, IL 60076-3300